WHORES IN HISTORY

WHORES IN HISTORY

Prostitution in Western Society

NICKIE ROBERTS

HarperCollinsPublishers

HarperCollins*Publishers*
77–85 Fulham Palace Road
Hammersmith, London W6 8JB

Published by HarperCollins*Publishers* 1992
9 8 7 6 5 4 3 2 1

A catalogue record for this book
is available from the British Library

ISBN 0 246 13234 5

Set in Bembo

Photoset by Deltatype Ltd, Ellesmere Port, Cheshire
Printed in Great Britain by
HarperCollinsManufacturing Glasgow

Contents

Come yourself to me, and in this enclosure we will fall into one another's arms. The gods will not be shocked; they are our own creation.

The Greek courtesan Phryne, 4th century BC

This book is dedicated to the abolition of all prostitution laws everywhere. Also to Miss D—, my fourth-form teacher at Burnley High School for Girls, who told me I was 'irredeemable'. You were right.

Acknowledgments

I would like first to acknowledge the huge amount of work Steve Roberts put into this book – namely, four years' research. I'd also like to thank my parents, Lily and George Greenwood, for their love and support; a special thank you to my in-laws, Helen and Geoff Roberts, for all their help, not least of which was the space in which to work. Thanks also to my friends Helen Hymans, John Cummins and Susanne Kappeler, for their help with research; my editors at HarperCollins, Richard Johnson and Betty Palmer, for their excellent, sympathetic and enthusiastic work on the manuscript; and my long-suffering agent, Barbara Levy, for her patience and confidence in me. I would also like to thank a succession of extremely understanding bank managers at Lloyds Bank, Norwich, and, last but definitely not least, my dear old faithful patron of the arts (erotic and literary), Frank W., a.k.a. 'Henry', without whose financial support I would have well and truly buckled.

A work of broad synthesis like this one inevitably rests on the work of many previous researchers and writers. Among those whose work has been particularly useful are Fernando Henriques, E. J. Burford, and others; but we are especially indebted to recent women researchers in the field, notably Leah Lydia Otis, Jill Harsin, Mary Gibson, Judith Walkowitz, Ruth Rosen and Jess Wells, all of whom have done so much to give whores back their hidden histories. We must also acknowledge Margo St James, who was the first whore to have the courage to come out and openly fight for prostitutes' rights.

Picture Credits

Author's Note

I use the word 'whore' throughout this text interchangeably with 'prostitute'. Like other sex workers, I am in the process of reclaiming this word (as lesbians have in recent years reclaimed 'dyke') so as to defuse it of its pejorative sense.

Also – 'working class'. Occasionally this term is used outside of its usual modern context; this is to underline the historical continuities in the experience of whores, the overwhelming majority of whom came and still come from the classes of people throughout history who had nothing, and who had to work for those who had plenty, in order to survive. Classical slaves, medieval serfs, modern workers – these are all different types of working classes.

A Personal Introduction:
Another Hidden History

I first had the idea of writing a history of prostitution five years ago, just after my first book about
the sex industry, *The Front Line*, was published in
1986. I was a veteran of the Soho sex trade and well
knew what it felt like to be on the receiving end of
the whore-stigma. Having written about this in
the earlier book, I will only say here that it took me
a long time to work out what bearing this burden
means to women. I endured years of bitterness and
frustration before finally realizing that the whore-
stigma was indeed a form of oppression. My main
motivation, therefore, was to explore the origins
of this prejudice, which I strongly suspected were rooted in the
historical development of patriarchy. How right I was!

There was something else. Everything I had read about prostitution
and prostitutes appeared to have been written by men – the client class
– mostly academics who claimed scholarly objectivity. The thought
occurred to me that if prostitution truly is the world's oldest
profession, then men writing about it is certainly the second oldest.
From the time ink was invented, it seems that male writers have been
obsessed with the whore. Well, who could blame them? Whores were
and are interesting women, the first to say 'No' to patriarchal
ownership.

Only fairly recently has the subject of prostitution been tackled by
feminists, often of the radical/revolutionary tendency; women who
have an anti-sex industry axe to grind. To put it bluntly, the feminist
movement has failed the prostitute, and failed her badly, in my view.
The embarrassment and hostility of many middle-class feminist
writers has occasionally given way to references to the earliest forms
of prostitution, the religious practices of earlier civilizations – but we

are assured that there can be no similarity between the high-status whore-priestesses of yore and the latterday streetwalker. I happen to disagree; there is more than a link, as I hope this book will show.

One of the things the women's movement has surely taught us in recent years is that women are the real experts about our own lives – after all, we live them. With this in mind, and with the encouragement of some whore and ex-whore friends, I therefore decided to search out that most hidden history of all: the history of the Bad Girls. What I discovered impressed and amazed me, as I hope it will you.

Writing this book has been a vindication for me, I have to admit – for the years of putting up with the ignorance and prejudices of other people. But above all it has been a learning experience, for the knowledge it contains *does* challenge many orthodox (male?) views not only on prostitution but also on women's sexuality in general – and about time, too.

I have one more thing to say in this personal introduction: I don't profess to be objective (nobody ever is, in practice); I'm even biased, in the sense that I am wholeheartedly on the side of the unrepentant whore, the most maligned woman in history. What has always made working on this book worthwhile has been the voice of the prostitute, often but never totally silenced by the tumult from experts of every variety: priests, professors, doctors, and the rest. In the final chapter, the whore – the real expert – speaks up to denounce and challenge her oppressors, and thereby overcome the centuries of lies, denial and stereotyping that have been her lot. *Only when she is listened to by the rest of our society will women finally and irrevocably be able to end our division into Good Girls and Bad Girls.*

As a woman, and as a former sex worker, I'm proud to have rediscovered my sisters, the whores in history. This book is above all *for* them, as well as about them.

Nickie Roberts, 1992

CHAPTER ONE

Origins:
the Goddess and the Whore

'A Prostitute compassionate am I.'
The Goddess Ishtar, Sumerian clay tablet text

In the beginning was the matriarchy; a fact not widely acknowledged by the patriarchal societies of today. Contemptuously dismissed by generations of male scholars as an aberration from the (patriarchal) 'norm', the long-spanning age of goddess-worship – estimated at over 25,000 years – is usually downgraded to a series of awkwardly explained 'fertility cults', if not ignored altogether. But the evidence is there, incontestable: in the period of time men have labelled 'prehistory' (prepatriarchy, if we are to be accurate), it was woman who was seen as creator of the life force. She was worshipped as the Great Goddess and as such was at the hub of all social activity.

This is hardly surprising when we look at Stone Age culture, since women were far more important participants in it than men. Recent studies in prehistory and anthropology, especially those by feminist scholars, have thrown a flood of light on archaic human societies.[1] The anthropologist Evelyn Reed shows that women raised humanity out of the animal kingdom when they invented our first social organization, the matriarchal clan. Women were also central to the economy of these first societies, since they gathered between 65 and 80 per cent of the community's food. In a remarkable chapter devoted to 'The Productive Record of Primitive Women',[2] Reed lists their early technological accomplishments, including their discovery of food plants, their invention of the first tools – such as digging sticks, containers made of bark or skin, and stone scrapers – their

domestication of fire and of animals, and their use of plants for
healing, and she speculates that language itself evolved out of
women's communal work activities. Perhaps most miraculous of all,
women were capable of producing children from their own bodies:
an act of pure creative magic in the eyes of men, ignorant of their
own part in reproduction. Encompassing as they did all the essential
activities which gave rise to the human world, women were
naturally enough seen as the living embodiment of a universal
generative force, which Stone Age humans conceptualized in the
form of a goddess.

Evidence from Stone Age art confirms this central position of
women. From as far back as the Gravettian-Aurignacian cultures of
the Palaeolithic or Old Stone Age (around 25,000 BC onwards), nearly
all the sculptures and statues surviving in sites stretching across
Europe from Spain to Russia are of women; and in some cultures – the
Aurignacians of the East European steppes, for example – men are not
represented at all. According to Monica Sjöö and Barbara Mor, the
two writers who have probably gone furthest towards reconstructing
prehistoric religion, these statuettes and paintings of women depict
holy figures; and the sacred women of Stone Age art represented a
great deal more than the one-dimensional 'fertility figures' beloved of
male prehistorians. Sjöö and Mor show that the power of the Stone
Age goddess went far beyond the simplistic notion of fertility: like the
creative activity of real women, but expanding from this to symbolize
an overarching ontological principle, she was all-encompassing, and
thus expressed the original power which animated the universe and
the whole of nature. In her three aspects of maiden, mother and crone,
based on the three faces of the moon observed by Stone Age women,
the Great Goddess was creator, preserver and destroyer of all life.

Since women were seen as the goddess's earthly incarnation, it was
natural that some of them should provide the vital link between the
community and its deity, and this they did as shamanic priestesses.
With their sacred rituals and trance-dances, the priestesses channelled
the creative energy of the goddess into the material world: 'The
earliest communicators with [the goddess] were ecstatic women . . .
shamans and seers. In their trance-states they were responsible for
keeping the channels open between the individual, the group and the
cosmic source.'[3]

These trance-states were a form of enhanced awareness, a waking,
controlled dreaming during which everyday consciousness and what

we would call the unconscious mind fused to enable ideas and images to take shape – an ancient creative technique still current in surviving Stone Age societies. The myths and art forms of the culture came about through this sacred channelling, with the female as the main transmitter.

Because women held such a powerful position, it was inevitable that they should control their own sexuality. Evidence from contemporary Stone Age cultures suggests that women were autonomous and uninhibited in their sexual expression; and Palaeolithic counting-sticks, ancient moon calendars, show the earliest women already controlling their fertility by following their menstrual rhythms. Since men were ignorant of the role they played in procreation, there was not the obsession with paternity (definable here as male ownership of offspring) that was to become typical of later, patriarchal cultures. The basic unit of social life was matrifocal, centring on the mothers and their children.

Within these prehistoric societies, Sjöö and Mor tell us, culture, religion and sexuality were intertwined, springing as they did from the same source in the goddess. Sex was sacred by definition, and the shamanic priestesses led group sex rituals in which the whole community participated, sharing in ecstatic union with the life force.

With the establishment of the first settled agricultural communities from around 10,000 BC, the goddess-religion took root in specially built temples. The first 'cities' known to archaeologists, built by matriarchal peoples at places like Çatal Hüyük (c.6500 BC) in what is now Turkey, were organized with the temples at their heart. Here the priestesses lived and worked, owning and administering the land on behalf of the community; here too, they continued to practise their age-old religion, with the sexual rites through which all people had access to goddess-power.

The peace-loving goddess-cultures were not to be allowed to develop undisturbed, however. Tribes of warlike, male-dominated nomads, whose new awareness of the man's role in procreation was an essential part of their cattle-breeding economy, began to invade the matriarchal territories from around 3000 BC, eventually subduing the goddess people and subjecting them to the power of the masculine. The first civilizations of the historical era, at the time when the record of the past began to be written down, evolved in Mesopotamia (mostly in modern Iraq) and Egypt, and were born out of this upheaval. These societies were hybrids of matriarchal and patriarchal forms, with the balance of power continuing to shift towards the male. New forms of marriage were introduced, specifically aimed at controlling women's sexuality in order to establish beyond doubt the paternity of every child. The line of property inheritance from father to son now formed the economic basis of men's power, just as common land ownership had been the basis of women's. The married woman became little more than a go-between from one male generation to the next. Male gods were introduced to compete with the goddess for supremacy; male rulers were established, and these men ensured the systematic subversion of women's status by inventing new and increasingly restrictive legislation. It was at this point in human history, around the turn of the 2nd millennium BC, that the institution of sacred prostitution became visible, and recorded in writing for the first time.

Sacred prostitution was in fact the tradition of sexual ritual which had persisted from the Stone Age to become an integral part of religious worship in the world's earliest civilizations. The tradition did not survive without changes, however. The great cities of Mesopotamia and Egypt were still centred upon the temples, but a struggle was being waged within them. The new male rulers knew that it was essential to counteract the influence of the goddess-religion; to this end they created male priesthoods to promote their alien gods and to control and exploit the temple women. But overthrowing the goddess was no easy task; it was to take many thousands of years to root her out of the hearts of the people. In the temples the people continued to pay allegiance to her through the ancient sexual rites, and this continued even while the priestesses were being undermined and prised from their positions of power. It is here that the true story of prostitution begins; with the temple priestesses who were both sacred women *and* prostitutes, the first whores in history.

The Great Goddess, known first as Inanna, later as Ishtar, held sway over the whole birthplace and cradle of civilization in the ancient Middle East from the beginning of historical times at around 3000 BC; and wherever she was worshipped, sacred prostitution was a focal point of the holy ritual. With Ishtar herself identified as a prostitute, and with prostitute-priestesses staffing the temples that were still at the centre of religious, political and economic power in Mesopotamia, the status of whores was high. One of the world's first recorded poems, the *Epic of Gilgamesh*, written down in Sumer (southern Mesopotamia) around 2000 BC, reputedly from a much older oral source, shows how very far these early whores were from being stigmatized as they are today. In the poem a prostitute plays a crucial role; and she is not only acknowledged as being holy, her work is also seen as civilizing.

The wild man Enkidu, who lives in the forest among the animals, is created by the gods to contend with the arrogant Gilgamesh. A hunter discovers him, and to flush him out of the forest sends a 'harlot from the temple of love, a child of pleasure' to waylay him:

> . . . and [Enkidu] possessed her ripeness.
> She was not bashful as she welcomed his ardour.
> She laid aside her cloth and he rested upon her.
> She treated him, the savage, to a woman's task,
> And his love was drawn unto her.[4]

The poem tells us that Enkidu lay with the harlot for six days and seven nights, during which time she lavished upon him the grace of the goddess: 'a combination of mother-love, tenderness, comfort, mystical enlightenment and sex'.[5] When Enkidu recovered from his idyll, he was no longer a beast-man: 'he now had wisdom, broader understanding'. The whore's arts had so civilized him that he was unable to go back to his previous life among the animals. The 'prostitute compassionate' then led him away 'like a mother' to take up a new, humanized life in the city.

This tale from the Gilgamesh epic recounts in allegorical form how the goddess, through her shamans and priestesses, led the human race out of the wilderness of the animal kingdom by inspiring it with the gifts of culture. The goddess – Inanna, in this early fable – was the benign deity of the civilized arts of music, dance, poetry, human relationships and healing: that legacy of the women-centred societies that was personified by the whore-priestesses. At the heart of this culture of love, pleasure, and knowledge, was the sexual-spiritual communion experienced by Enkidu and practised by the mass of the people well into the historical era.

As the balance of power shifted from women to men, society grew increasingly hierarchical, with a huge and ever-widening gap between 'high-born' and 'low-born'. The distinctions between the two were reflected in the sacred world of the temple priestesses where, through compromise with the new patriarchal regime, an upper-class echelon of whores developed and managed to retain some of their ancient powers and privileges. The various ranks of the whore-priestesses were well-documented by the Old Babylonians (*c*.2400 BC), who recorded that the highest-ranking priestesses of the goddess Ishtar, the *entu*, were to be considered on equal footing with the male high priests.

> The *entu* wore distinctive clothing; a cap with a raised rim, a folded garment, jewellery and a staff – the same insignia and garments worn by the ruler. They lived inside the sacred shrine, had charge of temple management and affairs, and performed ritual and ceremonial functions.[6]

It was the *entu* priestesses who performed the ritual of the 'sacred marriage' with kings and priests. Some historians believe that the ceremony dates back as far as 6500 BC, at a time when men and women still lived in harmony. The sacred marriage ceremony was purported to express this harmony in ritualized form, as annually the goddess and her son/lover celebrated their sexual and spiritual union. By early patriarchal times, however, the original meaning of the ritual had been lost; in the city-states of Sumer the sacred marriage had become a state ceremonial, a dramatization of the king's right to rule over the people. One Sumerian text from around 2800 BC describes a priestess being decorated with clusters of freshly-harvested dates (to signify continuing wealth and prosperity) in preparation for her 'marriage'. She waits for her 'husband' – the king – at the lapis lazuli door of the *giparu* (the temple inner chamber), where other priestesses have prepared the marriage bed. She receives the king at the door, then leads him into the sacred chamber where, at the heart of the temple, the sacred marriage is consummated.

Both male and female historians have labelled the sacred marriage a 'fertility rite', somehow managing to ignore its political dimension altogether. Later feminist writers have on the other hand explained it away as a public demonstration of men's power over women in a culture which already used the latter as breeders and 'sex objects': more a ritual of sexual humiliation than a religious affirmation. But the feminists' line of argument is as flawed as that of the academics – even though the perspective differs – since it too ignores the fact that the king had actively to seek the blessing of the goddess in the eyes of his people, in order to legitimize his rule. This could be achieved only by engaging in ritual sex with one of her venerated priestesses. King

Lipit-Ishtar of Sumer (*c.*2000 BC) even went as far as to adopt the goddess's name as a symbol of that authority; and King Esarhaddon of Assyria was called 'the beloved of Queen Ishtar, the Goddess of Everything'.[7] The high-ranking temple whores, then, were powerful and prestigious agents in their own right; they were not the mere downtrodden victims of men so beloved of latterday feminists.

Second in line to the *entu* of Babylon were the *naditu*, another group of high-born women who reaped special privileges in return for their temple activities. In theory the *naditu* were forbidden to marry or have children; in practice they did both with impunity. Their economic power must have compared in no small way with that of the earlier matriarchal priestesses, since they engaged in commerce 'on equal, perhaps more than equal, terms with men. They bought, sold and hired out; lent money and grain; invested, imported, exported, dealt in slaves, managed land and people, played from their cloisters an essential part in the . . . economy of the country.'[8]

The hierarchy of temple whores in Babylon reflected a wide and varied range of functions and specialities, not all of which are clear from the available evidence. The *entu* and *naditu* were unquestionably the highest-ranking priestesses; beneath them were the *qadishtu* (*lit.* sacred women) and the *ishtaritu*, whose lives and work were specifically dedicated to the service of the goddess Ishtar. Many of these women specialized as singers, musicians and dancers. In addition there was a class of women called the *harimtu*, described by some historians as semi-secular prostitutes; which presumably means they worked both inside the temples and out in the streets. Many of the temple *harimtu* were apparently slaves, probably women who had been captured in warfare; to the ordinary men who worshipped at the shrines they still represented the goddess but, unlike their higher-class sisters, they were subject to the control of temple officials and priests. Like all the sacred whores, however, the *harimtu* enriched the temples through the offerings of food, wine, oil and precious goods that worshippers laid at their feet before participating in the sexual rites.

The *harimtu* who worked outside the temples were history's first streetwalkers, operating independently and on a commercial basis; even so, the connection between sex and religion persisted, for the streetwalkers were still regarded as holy women, protected by Ishtar, and their earnings came in the form of offerings in the name of the goddess. In one text the goddess is quoted as saying: 'When I sit in the entrance of the tavern, I, Ishtar, am a loving *harimtu.*' The streetwalkers operated mainly from the taverns; some tavern-keepers are recorded as having performed special rituals entreating the goddess to bring in plenty of trade.

In ancient Egypt, too, the temple priestesses were demoted from their former high status roles to semi-secular dancers and musicians. As male rulers and priests consolidated their power, many of the temple women were ousted from the temples and formed troupes of professional singer-dancer-prostitutes, travelling the rounds of religious and social festivals in order to provide the entertainment and ritual sex that always formed part of the celebration. Even now there exists in the Upper Nile region of Egypt a nomadic tribe of women who combine the ancient traditional skills of the entertainer-prostitute: known as the *Ghawazee*, they are regarded by Egyptians as the world's finest exponents of Arabic dance. These women are perhaps the direct descendants of the original priestesses who were cast out of the temples of ancient Egypt.

Like the profession of prostitution, the division of women into wives and whores is as old as (patriarchal) history. It was in ancient Sumer at around 2000 BC that the first laws segregating the two put in an appearance. The code of Lipit-Ishtar stated that: 'If a man's wife has borne him no children but a prostitute from the street has borne him children, he shall provide for that prostitute her wine, oil and clothing, and the children which the prostitute has borne him shall be his heirs; but as long as the wife lives the prostitute shall not abide in the house with the wife.'[9]

The whore who provided a man with heirs in the service of patriarchal society thus got her reward – albeit on the understanding that she was to be kept strictly apart from the legitimate wife. However, when whores themselves chose to marry, their independent habits presented a problem for their husbands. In another Sumerian text a father advises his son not to marry a temple prostitute or make one the mistress of his home, for 'besides being accustomed to accepting other men, she would make an unsympathetic and intractable wife.'[10] Already the gap was beginning to widen, between 'good' – docile and obedient – wives and 'bad' – sexually autonomous – whores.

As the power of the male religious and political institutions grew, the patriarchal form of marriage in which the husband literally owned wife and children drove the wedge between wives and whores even deeper. At the same time, the laws surrounding prostitutes and their work became more oppressive. In 1100 BC the Assyrians enforced the first legal prescriptions on dress codes for whores; they were instructed to wear special leather jackets, 'to attract attention', and a cheery little law decreed that they should on no account wear the veil, which was reserved as a mark of the wife's subjection to her husband. Prostitutes who defied this particular law risked being beaten fifty strokes with rods and having pitch poured over their heads.

While the domesticated female was sexually licensed – and therefore controlled – by her exclusive attachment to one man, the reverse did not apply. Men were not prepared to give up old freedoms, and the double standard was born. Not content with owning several wives and/or concubines, men resorted to sexual relations with prostitutes whenever they felt bored with the restrictions of marriage. Whores also managed to retain their sexual and economic autonomy and continued to resist domestication, but they did so in the face of increasingly harsh and punitive laws. Their rebellious sexuality and lack of dependence on one master was an obvious threat to patriarchal authority – as it has been ever since. And yet throughout the history of Mesopotamia and ancient Egypt, sex was still regarded as sacred to a great extent, and in spite of the laws, there was no puritanical morality to stigmatize women who chose to support themselves by selling sex. If the male élites were decisively to overturn the whores' power, they had to invent a system of sex-repressive morality that would be sufficiently negative to make sacred women into social pariahs. It is at this stage that we meet with a more familiar tradition: that of the Old Testament prophets.

> She is loud and stubborn; her feet abide not in her house; now she
> is without, now in the streets, and lieth in wait at every corner.
>   Proverbs 7:11–12 (description of a prostitute)

Thus wrote the Levite warrior-priests, leaders of the Hebrew tribes who, some time after 1300–1250 BC, invaded and settled the fertile, goddess-worshipping land of Canaan. To these military-religious chieftains, worshippers of the vengeful father-god Yahweh, or Jehovah, prostitution – particularly the religious version – was anathema. There were to be no compromises with goddess-worship; there would be no sacred marriage between their rulers and the whore-priestesses, for the warrior-priests were patriarchal fanatics who recognized no woman's authority. The tactics they employed to suppress the goddess-religion were stark and unequivocal: wholesale destruction accompanied by relentless propaganda. Nevertheless their task was by no means an easy one, for their own people had once worshipped the goddess and displayed an embarrassing tendency to backslide into their former, pleasure-oriented ways. The Levite priests had to fight a constant battle to establish the distant, stern and intolerant father-god in the minds and hearts of their people.

The stridency of the Old Testament prophets' denunciation of whores bears witness to the difficulty the priests had in controlling their people's sex lives. Prostitution, both religious and secular, flourished in ancient Canaan; whores 'could be seen almost every-where . . . passing along the city street where they sang and played the harp; sitting at key intersections; in the doorsteps of their houses provocatively calling to passersby, or even parading in their colourful attire throughout the city. Houses of prostitution . . . were a permanent feature of city life, and they attracted a host of onlookers as well as customers.'[11] And the scandalized Victorian historian of prostitution Dr William Sanger reported that whores 'multiplied so fast that the prophets speak of them wandering on all the hills, and prostituting themselves under every tree . . . they even invaded the Temple and established their hideous rites in its courts.'[12]

The Hebrew priests always referred to the 'hideous rites' of goddess-worship as 'whoredom', in that word's newly-devised pejorative sense; as in for example the infamous 'Whore of Babylon'. The prophet Ezekiel (Ezekiel 23) admonished the two Hebrew nations and likened them to two sisters who had learned their 'harlotry' – freedom – in Egypt, where women were still relatively strong. The priest-leaders could not reconcile this tradition of female indepen-dence with their own plans to confine all women in exclusive marriages, where the male would indisputably be the master. According to the feminist historian Merlin Stone, 'The Hebrew prophets and priests wrote with an open and scornful contempt of any woman who was neither virgin nor married. They insisted that all women must be publicly designated as the private property of some man – father or husband. Thus they developed and instituted the concept of sexual *morality* – for women.'[13] In other words, in order to make submission to a husband look like an attractive proposition, the priests invented the notion that women's sexual autonomy was the root of all evil – and they identified whores as the living embodiment of this evil. The ecstatic sexual rites of the goddess-religion became the gravest 'sin'; her priestesses the most abhorrent 'sinners'. This new doctrine, which was made an article of faith in Hebraic religion, came to encompass female 'bad' behaviour in general, all of which the priests now labelled 'whoredom'. Any woman could find herself vilified, a victim of the reign of moral terror, if she dared to take a lover, dress as she pleased, worship the goddess, or earn her own living without reference to men or their notion of 'morality'.

As far as the whores themselves were concerned, though, there was never any question of a stigma being attached to their profession. They continued to cling to their goddess-worshipping traditions and fiercely asserted their desire to live independently of 'the man' by *choosing* prostitution as their career. And there was no shortage of clients, for men – as ever – had no intention of confining themselves to their own marriages, in spite of the priests' exhortations. Whores were indeed the stubborn and rebellious women denounced by the Old Testament prophets – the opposite of the submissive and housebound Hebrew wives.

All such women were the prime targets of the priests' hate-campaigns, and this was where patriarchy's greatest victory lay: in the Hebrew leaders' successful institutionalization of the doctrine that insisted that women's unfettered and uncontrolled (by men) sexuality, as personified by the whore, was evil. To this day, the whore-stigma affects *all* women, whether or not we subscribe to the mythical Good Girl/Bad Girl dichotomy which can be traced to the very dawn of patriarchal thought. Any woman can be branded a 'whore' if she steps out of line. The major patriarchal religions that were to follow – Christianity and Islam – recognized the devastating impact of the whore-stigma in dividing and ruling women, and took it up enthusiastically, slotting it into their own preferred versions of anti-woman mythology. From the ashes of the compassionate whore-goddess, the priests had created a sinful temptress Eve, whose carnal curiosity, we are still taught today, led to disaster for all 'mankind'.

CHAPTER TWO

Classical Attitudes:
Wives, Slaves and Whores

Man has the courtesan for erotic enjoyment;
concubines for daily use, and wives of his own rank
to bring up [his] children and be faithful housewives.

Demosthenes[1]

Hermione, that sweet enchantress,
I played with once, O Paphian Goddess!
Her harlequin step-ins were scrolled
with her philosophy in gold,
'Love me, but don't get angry when
I'm just as kind to other men.'

Asclepiades[2]

Like its historical predecessors, ancient Greece was a patriarchal,
class-based society. A male-dominated, slave-owning class
governed the city-states of the Greek classical era in the 5th century
BC, just as slave-owning men had ruled over Sumeria in 3000 BC.
And yet it is to classical Greece that the West looks back with such
admiration, claiming it as our direct ancestor – not Sumeria, or the
empires of Akkad and Assyria. Classical Athens in particular has
been presented by generations of male scholars as all that is excellent
in the Western tradition; and if we take a look at the period from
their point of view, it is easy to see why otherwise dry academics can
become as eager as schoolboys when writing about it. For Athens
not only developed two institutions beloved of Western thought –
democracy and rationalistic philosophy – it was also apparently a
sensual paradise, scene of what one historian describes as a
'tremendous, uninhibited flowering of human sexuality which has

never been seen since in Europe, nor indeed elsewhere'.[3]

Small wonder, then, that male historians can identify with a culture which combines their masculine intellectual heroes, the statesmen and thinkers of old Athens, with the relaxed sexual lifestyle of the ancient Greek capital, by all (their) accounts a playground of leisure and pleasure. There was plenty going on. The wealthy Greek male had access to a phenomenal range of sexual services, quite openly and without fear of shame or social stigma. There were temple whores, high-class courtesans, dancer-prostitutes, streetwalkers, brothel-slaves . . . and, should the selection prove too limiting, he could always avail himself of the services of adolescent boys, concubines, household slaves, even, at a pinch, his own wife. It was indeed a sexual golden era – for the men with the gold. But for the women of ancient Athens it was, of course, another story; they were the servicers, providers and workers in this great 'flowering of human sexuality'.

History has, as usual, overlooked or at best played down the role of women in Greek society, seeing that role as of limited importance in the grand scheme. But if we look at ancient Greece from a female perspective, a different – though no less fascinating – picture emerges; starting with the continuing suppression of women's rights that had begun in earlier societies.

Greek mythology records this struggle in its tales and legends, reflecting the fact that, as with all the ancestor societies, the first inhabitants of Greece were goddess-worshipping peoples. From around 2000 BC, successive waves of Indo-European invaders swept into the country, bringing with them their male gods; what ensued was a repetition of earlier cultural patterns: the two cultures fused for a time, eventually producing the hybrid that comes down to us today as Greek mythology and religion. The Indo-Europeans' supreme deity, the father-god Zeus, married Hera, a powerful goddess-survivor of the earlier cult, and within the combined mythology, the two were constantly battling with each other. But in spite of this marital disharmony between gods, Zeus was unable to rule alone, in his own right; like the Mesopotamian kings and deities before him, his authority derived from a sacred marriage to the goddess.

Nevertheless, by the time of the flowering of classical Athens, real life no longer reflected divinity, and Greek men had already advanced far beyond the uneasy power-sharing of their gods and goddesses. Women were firmly under male control – at least in the private sphere

of the home. The much-lauded concept of democracy did not apply to
them, since only property owners had the right to vote – and only men
were allowed to own property. This outright denial of women's
power in society had come about through the efforts of a line of male
dictators, but it was one man in particular who was responsible for
establishing and institutionalizing the roles of women in Greek
society. This was 'wise' Solon, who ruled Athens at the turn of the 6th
century BC, just before the height of its glory.

Solon had ridden to power on the back of a middle class of farmers
and merchants who were jockeying for a share of power with the old
aristocracy; and so it was inevitable that he should consolidate his
position by ensuring the continuing success of the newly-formed
class. A crucial part of his strategy was the regulation of its family
structures. Divided as they were into small nuclear family units, the
men of the middle class were all in fierce competition with each other,
hell-bent on accumulating property and wealth to hand on to their
male offspring. Whereas in the old aristocratic order heirs were bred
from an extended family unit that had included several wives and
concubines, in the new middle-class families only one woman – the
wife – could provide a legitimate heir. Bearing all this in mind, Solon
introduced a comprehensive programme of laws that were designed
to regulate the place of all women in Athenian society, while at the
same time continuing in the patriarchal tradition of dividing them into
'good' women – and the rest. Inevitably, the lives of the former group
became increasingly restricted as a result of these divide-and-rule
tactics. Plutarch summed up the attitudes of classical Greeks to their
'respectable' women when he observed that: 'Unmarried girls in
particular need to be guarded, and housekeeping and silence befit
married women.'

In effect, the 'respectable' wives and wives-to-be of free Athenian
citizens spent almost their entire lives under conditions that can only
be described as house-arrest. Permitted out only for funerals or the
occasional religious festival or theatrical event (at which they were
expected to behave with due 'moderation'), they were forbidden even
to visit the marketplace in many cases; shopping was done by men or
household slaves. Life within the household was grim enough; the
interior of an Athenian home was dark, dismal and insanitary, and
women were restricted to their own quarters, deep within the recesses
of the house – so that no stranger should accidentally catch sight of
them. If a man brought guests home, his wife should on no account

meet them: she was to be neither seen nor heard; but even if she had been permitted to socialize with the highly-educated men of her class, she would have been incapable of conversing with them on anything like equal terms. The education of an Athenian wife was restricted to the domestic skills of cookery, sewing and 'housekeeping'; intellectual knowledge on the part of a wife was forbidden, for it was the sign of a harlot.

This physical and mental confinement was reflected by women's lack of economic and legal power. Throughout her life a 'respectable' woman was placed under the 'guardianship' of men: first her father had control, then her husband; finally, should he die before her, the eldest son took charge of her life. Apart from her dowry, which was delivered from father to husband on marriage, to be used for her maintenance, the Athenian wife possessed nothing – neither property nor inheritance rights. Hers was a stunted life; an existence of unremitting frustration, obedience and silence. The story of the 'good' Athenian wife – her only role being to provide her husband with male heirs – is a true Greek tragedy.

Solon's views on women were unequivocal: they were either wives or whores. Any woman attempting to live independently of men, all poor women, foreigners and slaves who worked outside the home, fell into the latter category. And in many cases it was true, for women who were not model wives had little choice other than to prostitute themselves in order to survive. Secular prostitution began to flourish in Athens on a scale previously unimagined. Solon, quick to assess the enormous profits made by both commercial and religious whores, began to organize the business himself, with the result that official, state-run brothels sprang up all over Athens. This enterprise proved so successful that Solon made more than enough to finance his huge military machine: it was said that the Athenian port of Piraeus was virtually built on the proceeds of its massive sex trade. In 'gratitude', Solon built a magnificent temple in honour of Aphrodite, the Greek goddess of love; and other Greek cities, such as Corinth, which became famous for the fabulous wealth generated in its brothels, were not slow in following his example.

For the free men of Athens, too, their ruler's pioneering state enterprise was a brilliant success, for it provided them with access to a vast pool of sex workers. Greek writers were swift to congratulate Solon for his initiative. The poet Philemon praised him for having the 'justice of a public-spirited measure'[4] while the sycophantic writer

Athenaeus warmly thanked his ruler in what can best be described as an early example of tabloid-style writing:

> You, Solon . . . seeing that the state was full of randy young men whose natural appetites were leading them where they had no right to be, bought some women and put them in certain places where they were to be public and available to everyone. They stand there uncovered. Take a good look at them, boy. Don't be deceived. Are you satisfied? Ready? So are they. The door is open, the price one *obol*. In with you. There is no nonsense, no chitchat, no trickery here. You do just what you like and the way you like. You're off: wish her goodbye. She has no further claim on you.[5]

In another passage, Athenaeus drooled over the brothel girls, whose 'breasts [are] bare beneath thin dresses of gauze, they flaunt themselves in the sunlight. You pick whichever takes your fancy . . . slim or well-covered . . . the girls themselves drag you into the house by force, calling you "Daddy" if you are getting on in years, "Little Brother", or 'Little Boy", if you're still young . . .'[6]

But this kind of admiration for Solon's sexual civil service was not restricted to men of his own era; among his latterday admirers is the historian of prostitution Fernando Henriques, who comments wistfully that Athenaeus 'conjures up a wonderful picture of sundrenched naked girls, offering paradise for an *obol* . . .'[7]

Paradise indeed . . . for the clients. But for the slave-women who staffed these state brothels, the *deikteriades* as they were known, life was hardly idyllic. Most of them were Asian war captives, although they later included women who were bought by specially appointed state repesentatives on the open market. The women lived in appalling conditions, in cramped and unhealthy cell-like dwellings; and, like the 'good' wives of Athens, they had no control over their lives whatsoever. Solon's laws decreed that they prostitute themselves on demand, contrary to Athenaeus' description of girls 'forcing' clients into the brothels. The whores' state-registered fees were paid not to them but directly to the *pronobosceion*, a male official who managed the brothel as part-private, part-state enterprise. The *deikteriades* were then obliged to coax 'presents' from their clients – and even these were then taxed by the shrewd and greedy Solon. In the interests of accuracy, to describe the brothel-workers as whores is misleading: they were sex-*slaves*. In a sense they represented the other side of the marriage coin, for both sets of women were entirely subject to the roles and conditions that Solon had laid down for them. The wives had one owner – their husbands – whereas the *deikteriades* were, in Athenaeus' words, 'public and available to everyone'. Who is to say which of them had the more miserable existence? Probably the brothel girls could hope to buy their freedom eventually and work independently, but with the set-up so clearly in favour of the state, getting out of the brothels would have been extremely difficult to achieve. For the first time in history, women were being pimped – officially. Men were making vast fortunes out of the forced selling of their sexual services: first the brothel managers, then the tax farmers, finally – at the top of the heap – the state, with 'wise' Solon at its head. State and private pimp were thus born, hand-in-hand.

Alongside the state brothels, many independent streetwalkers plied their trade, in spite of Solon's legislation. Bribery and corruption among the legal enforcers were rife, and arrests seldom made; consequently the working women were confident enough to be a highly visible presence in many sectors of the cities. Henriques describes the main square of the Athenian port Piraeus by night as '. . . given over to the prostitutes. The city centre of any modern European city would be a cathedral close compared to Piraeus at the height of its fame.'[8]

These red-light districts were lucrative female enterprise zones, for the whores who traded in them engaged in a business in which men had no financial stake other than that of paying client – or bribed official. Many of the women organized themselves into groups, working communally with one older woman, a 'mistress', who looked after their interests – nowadays we would of course recognize these female managers as madams. Some streetwalkers were completely independent, operating their trade from private rooms or from inns and taverns. Henriques paints a lurid picture of the spread of street prostitution in ancient Athens: 'If necessary,' he reports, 'quiet streets, a temple wall, a hundred-and-one corners any city offers, could be put to use.'[9]

According to some sources, a plentiful supply of male prostitutes could be found working the streets; they were usually young boys who paraded like their female counterparts in brightly coloured robes and garish make-up. An Athenian proverb of the time suggested that you could sooner slip five elephants under your armpit than hide one of these boy whores.

While Solon, then, coveted the profits of the whole Athenian sex trade, the city's vibrant street scene easily rivalled his enterprises at the bottom end of the market.

A form of religious prostitution continued to survive well into the classical Greek era; it was, however, a shadow of its former self. Temples were to be found all over the Greek mainland, notably at Corinth, the 'luxury city of the Greek world', where the temple to Aphrodite (reputed to be one of the richest temples in the ancient world) was staffed by over a thousand 'sacred' whores. These women, the *hieroduli*, were a curious class of prostitute; no longer priestesses, they were technically slaves, but because they were seen as hand-maidens of the goddess they retained the aura of sacredness and were to some extent honoured by their customers. A slave bought for the temple represented an intermediary between buyer and goddess; rich citizens would consequently buy large numbers of women from the market and dedicate them to Aphrodite in return for a favour. The athlete Xenophon promised a hundred slave women if he won the crown at the Olympic Games; and when he triumphed, the poet Pindar wrote effusively in celebration of his gift to the temple:

> Young girls, hospitable to many guests, servants of Persuasion in wealthy Corinth, you who burn the golden tears of fresh frankincense, many times soaring upward in your thought to Aphrodite, heavenly mother of loves:
> To you, girls, she has granted blamelessly on lovely beds to harvest the fruits of delicate spring, for under love's necessity all things are fair.[10]

More often than not, however, the ancient Greeks were rather more down to earth in their references to the beloved goddess: she was worshipped in Athens as Aphrodite the Courtesan, at Syracuse as Aphrodite of the Beautiful Buttocks. Elsewhere she was at various times referred to as Aphrodite of the Hole or of Copulation; Aphrodite Who Rides Astride, Who Opens Herself Up; and further variations included Aphrodite Who Writhes and Aphrodite of the Night. At Abydos, after that city had been saved from its enemies through the efforts of its prostitutes (no details are available; perhaps the ladies offered themselves as peace negotiators . . .), a temple was dedicated unequivocally to Aphrodite the Whore.

The Greek island of Cyprus was particularly noted for its association with Aphrodite. (*Chambers 20th Century Dictionary* still defines Cyprian as: *lewd, licentious – a lewd woman.*) Where once the erotic rites of the ancient goddesses Ishtar and Astarte had been celebrated through sexual ritual, the followers of the Greek goddess now worshipped, maintaining the old traditions. Aphrodite's links to the island became so strong that she was often referred to in tales and legends as 'the Cyprian', as the following story illustrates.

> A girl disenchanted with spinning and weaving and all the chores which withered and wasted the flower of a girl's life, made a bonfire of her gear, outside the door of her house, and chose garlands and music and the sweet life instead: she became a courtesan and in her new career she naturally called on Aphrodite:

> > Cyprian, she said, you shall have ten per cent of all I earn,
> > Just find me work, and you shall have your cut.[11]

This tale is an interesting early account of one woman's rejection of a life of drudgery in favour of sexual and economic independence. Many others apparently made a similar choice – an act of direct rebellion against Solon and his anti-woman laws.

For women to step out from under the shadow of their husbands meant being identified publicly as whores. Even 'respectable' women who traded in the marketplace were branded; the writer Julia O'Faolain quotes the case of an Athenian freewoman who, on being widowed, attempted to support herself by selling ribbons. She was accused of being a prostitute, the evidence against her consisting solely of the fact that she had the audacity to attempt to trade in the marketplace, where no 'good' woman would dream of setting foot. This was considered sufficient to prove the case.

And yet there is no escaping the fact that many women actively chose prostitution as a career, seeing it as a road to freedom; a means of controlling their own lives and a positive alternative to the tyranny of the domestic regime. Indeed, some women went so far as to encourage their own daughters into the life. A dramatic dialogue by the classical writer Lucian shows the widow Crobyle trying to talk her nubile daughter Corinna into working as a whore:

CROBYLE: All you've got to do is go around with young
            men, drink with them, and sleep with them for
            money.

CORINNA: The way Daphnis' daughter, Lyra, does!

CROBYLE: Exactly!

CORINNA: But she's a prostitute!

CROBYLE: Well, is that such a terrible thing? It means
            you'll get to be as rich as she is, and have lots of
            lovers. What are you crying for, Corinna?
            Don't you see how many men chase after
            prostitutes, even though there are so many of
            them? And how rich they get! Look, I can
            remember myself when Daphnis was in rags.
            That was before Lyra grew up. Now look at
            the style of her! She has heaps of gold, marvel-
            lous clothes, and four servants.[12]

The life of the higher-class independent whore had obvious
advantages over that of a Greek citizen's wife; so despite Solon's
efforts to regulate and control all prostitution, many thousands of
women worked independently – though under constant attack from
the legislators – and continued to enjoy full sexual and economic
autonomy. They were the only women in ancient Greece who were
able to do so; and in this sense they could accurately be described as
history's first feminists.

Probably the most famous and respected of these women were the
hetairae (lit. 'companions of men'), élite whores of ancient Greece who
were renowned as much for their intellect as their beauty and love-
making skills. These courtesans have fascinated historians for
centuries, and no wonder: their free and cultivated lifestyle could not
have provided a greater contrast to the seclusion and obscurity of
married women. Even historians as diametrically opposed in their
views and beliefs as the prudish and disapproving Victorian Dr Sanger
and radical feminist Jess Wells are forced to acknowledge that the
hetairae were 'intelligent, witty, articulate and educated: the only
women in Athenian society allowed to manage their own affairs, stroll
through the streets anywhere, at any time. They were free to attend
plays, ceremonies and speeches; to speak with whomever, whenever
they pleased, to share the intellectual activities of Greece.'[13]

Many of these courtesans possessed fabulous wealth in their own right: Rhodopis, who although Greek-born spent much of her working life in Egypt, earned such a fortune in her profession that she was able to have her own personal pyramid built. Thais was mistress to the Emperor Alexander, and upon his death she became the queen-consort of Ptolemy, King of Egypt. The *hetairae* were mistresses and 'muses' to the greatest of the Greek poets, artists and statesmen; Theoris and Archippe were lovers of the dramatist Sophocles; Lais the Elder was sought after by the philosophers Diogenes and Aristippus, while the clients of her daughter, Lais the Younger, included a bevy of established artists and orators. The courtesan Peitho married Hieronymous, ruler of Syracuse; Pythionike rose to become Queen of Babylon, and upon her death had a great monument built in her memory by another doting king, Harpalos of Tharsos.

The *hetairae* went about their business quite openly in Athens, working independently of both state brothels and the temples. They often used a beautiful cemetery garden, Ceramicus, as an ancient equivalent of a modern-day contact magazine. Each courtesan had a stone she used to record messages on, and every morning a client would write compliments to her, along with the more practical details, such as a suggested time and price. The whore's personal slave then relayed the message to her mistress and, if the terms were agreeable to her, the courtesan would arrange to meet her client at the cemetery later in the day. In the evenings, the garden would be crowded with beautiful women and their customers, flirting, joking, bargaining.

Occasionally the courtesans had problems with clients who tried to treat them as their own property – as wives. Athenaeus relates the story of Mania, a *hetaira* who was renowned for her wit and whose lover the athlete Leontiscus was jealous of any rival for her services. When Mania took another athlete, Antenor, to her bed, Leontiscus was angry – he wanted her all to himself – but Mania remained unruffled and told him good-naturedly: 'Don't let it bother you, sweetheart; I just wanted to find out what two wrestlers, Olympic champions, could do, stroke for stroke, in a single night.'

The *hetairae* were reputed to be excellent businesswomen – another failing in the eyes of many historians, who consistently portray them as mercilessly grasping, ruthless and greedy (all 'faults' to be admired, of course, in business*men*). In a story taken from Alciphron's *Letters of Courtesans*, the prostitute Petale writes to her stingy patron about her own economic needs: 'I wish that a courtesan could keep house with tears. I should be well off then, for I have had plenty of them from you. But as things stand, it is money that I need, and clothes and furniture and servants. On that the whole business of life depends. Unfortunately I didn't inherit an estate at Myrrhinus, nor do I possess any shares in silver mines. I have only the money I earn and such miserable tear-stained presents as my lovers make me.'[14]

Finding herself in a similar predicament, the courtesan Philumena addresses her own client, Criton, bluntly: 'Why do you trouble yourself with long letters? I want fifty gold pieces, but no letters. If therefore you love me, pay up; but if you love your money more, then you needn't bother me anymore. Goodbye!'[15]

Men's reluctance to shell out money for their lovers' sexual services seems to have preoccupied them as much in ancient Greece as it does today. One anonymous client who obviously resented the power his mistress held over both his financial and sexual affairs eventually retreated into the fantasy realm of the wet dream, declaring that:

> She who sets the town on fire, Athenlais, the high-priced whore, whose breath smells of gold for those that desire her, lay beside me naked in my dream all night long until the sweet dawn, giving herself to me for nothing. No longer shall I implore the cruel beauty, nor mourn for myself, now that I have Sleep to grant me what he granted.[16]

One of the best-known *hetaira* courtesans was Phryne, mistress of the sculptor Praxiteles and considered in her lifetime the most beautiful woman in Athens. She inspired many artists, often modelling for portraits and statues of the goddess Aphrodite. The most famous of these works of art is her lover's statue of the goddess, which is still regarded today as perhaps the most perfect sculpture of classical times. In its day, the statue caused a sensation throughout the Greek world, because, instead of veiled, as was the custom, Praxiteles portrayed the goddess entirely naked. The citizens of Cos, who had originally commissioned the statue, promptly rejected it in favour of a more conservative, draped figure; it was, however, enthusiastically received by the city of Knidos, where it was displayed in a lovely garden setting, eventually to become a source of great revenue. The stone Aphrodite possessed 'a sensual tremor which . . . led poets, emperors and boatloads of tourists to linger in the sanctuary of Knidos.'[17]

The whore Phryne also impersonated Aphrodite in religious ritual, and was immensely popular with the people of Athens in this role – a 'prodigious favourite', according to Sanger. He goes on to describe her performance in the festival of Poseidon and Aphrodite: 'At a certain point . . . she appeared on the steps of the temple at the seaside in her usual dress, and slowly disrobed herself in the presence of the crowd. She next advanced to the waterside, plunged into the waves, and offered sacrifice . . . returning like a sea-nymph, drying her hair from which the water dripped over her exquisite limbs, she paused for a moment before the crowd, which shouted in a phrensy of enthusiasm as the fair priestess vanished into a cell in the temple.'[18]

In this passage Sanger (apparently in the throes of his own personal 'phrensy of enthusiasm') was describing the ritual enactment of the goddess Aphrodite emerging from the waters. To the people of Athens, Phryne's ceremonial striptease made her the living embodiment of their goddess, and as such she would have been regarded with great respect. Even so, the beautiful courtesan was unable to avoid coming up against Solon's legislation against independent whores, and was brought to trial on the charge that her performance as Aphrodite had profaned the sacred mysteries – a trumped-up but none the less capital offence. The subsequent court hearing provides a classic example of the ambivalent attitudes of Greek upper-class men to the *hetairae*.

Phryne's case went badly from the outset. She was a whore, living in sumptuous splendour; she was educated and independent – in brief, she was the opposite of the model Athenian woman, who was supposed to be downtrodden and invisible. Her accusers railed against her. Finally, when the case looked a lost cause, her defence counsel Hyperides made a last desperate attempt to save her: dramatically, he tore off part of her clothing to reveal her naked breasts to the court. It was a winner. Hyperides argued that such obviously goddess-given beauty could not possibly profane any religious occasion. The judges, to a man, agreed; for them to condemn Phryne would be tantamount to condemning Aphrodite, and this they dared not do for fear of divine retribution. All charges against Phryne were dropped, and the lady was acquitted.

Another *hetaira* who fell foul of Solon's laws was Aspasia, 'a shameless whore', according to the playwright Cratinus[19] and perhaps the most famous prostitute of classical Athens. Mistress to the Athenian ruler Pericles, Aspasia had the reputation of being highly educated and a brilliant philosopher – equal to any male intellectual. The historian Plutarch praised her as 'a wise woman (with) a great understanding in matters of state and government' and the philosopher Socrates often took his friends and pupils to listen to Aspasia's lectures. She was particularly renowned for her public speaking, at a time when this was unthinkable for a 'respectable' Athenian woman.

When her lover Pericles died, Aspasia composed and recited a funeral oration which has since become famous for its erudition; during his lifetime, however, she was often envied and hated for her power, especially by the 'virtuous' wives of Athens, who wanted her brought down a peg or two. Inevitably, this culminated in Aspasia being dragged before the courts, the charges being 'impiety' and brothel-keeping; but she too won her case and was eventually acquitted – the educated men could not, after all, be denied access to their 'companions'.

The charges that were levelled against Aspasia were similar to those that had brought Phryne to court, but it is interesting to note that 'brothel-keeping' was mentioned in Aspasia's case. In fact, Aspasia did not preside over a working brothel but a *gynaceum* – a school where aspiring *hetairae* were educated and learned their trade. As well as perfecting the art of love-making, the young women and girls who lived at Aspasia's *gynaceum* studied the arts and sciences of literature, philosophy and rhetoric. These students went on to become the wisest and most learned women in Greece; even the radical feminist historian Jess Wells describes Aspasia's home as an early women's refuge 'in a society where women were totally sequestered and deprived of all intellectual and cultural activities, taught not to speak or be seen when discussions took place.'[20]

The *gynaceum* links Aspasia – and other *hetairae* – with the famous women-centred colleges that were known to have existed in Greece several centuries before the 'golden' age of 5th-century Athens. The poet Sappho, Aphrodite's greatest champion in poetry and one of the best loved of all the Greek poets, ran such a school on the island of Lesbos in the 6th century BC. Young girls would leave their homes and families on the mainland and move to Lesbos, where they would be educated to a high level by the foremost women intellectuals of their day. There was another, equally famous, institution in Corinth, where the temple of Aphrodite possessed a college for the education of young would-be *hetairae*, in both academic subjects and the arts of love sacred to the goddess.

According to the anthropologist Paul Friedrich, these skills included 'the varied positions and movements of lovemaking . . . styles of singing and dancing, the arts of coiffure, the use of oils and cosmetics . . . lore about aphrodisiac drinks and foods . . . [and] skill in reciting and composing certain kinds of poetry, especially the genres related to song, empathy, sensitivity, and weddings.'[21]

To this impressive list other sources add the skills of the midwife, herbalist and aromatherapist. The courtesans of Greece made it their business to keep alive the sensual arts of pleasure, healing and relating – human contact on every level. Often, they handed down their learning to their own daughters; Aspasia and other courtesans were also known to have rescued abandoned Greek baby girls and raised them to become *hetairae*.

The spirit of the whores' culture can be found in the fragments of Sappho's poetry that remain to this day, for she wrote many beautiful works on the themes listed by Friedrich. She wrote especially powerfully about love in all its aspects – from the erotic passions of heterosexual and lesbian love to the fierce, protective and tender maternal love she felt for her own daughter, Cleis. Sappho's writing celebrated the full spectrum of the senses, in which no hard-and-fast distinctions were drawn between the different states of love and desire, whether hetero- or homosexual, or indeed maternal. This was the tradition inherited by the *hetairae* of the classical period; consequently, it is interesting to note that historians from Sappho's own time right down to the present day have consistently branded her a 'whore' (in the stigmatized sense). Yet there is no evidence whatsoever to suggest that Sappho was a practising prostitute of any kind. It seems that to be at all identifiable with the ancient female cultural tradition was, and is, enough to condemn a woman, in the eyes of many educated men.

The hostility that was directed at the *hetairae* prostitutes eventually made it necessary for them to organize themselves into corporations; in this way they were able to defend themselves against Solon's laws. The women employed clients such as Hyperides, Phryne's successful counsel, to defend them: victory for one whore was regarded as a victory for all, as is demonstrated by a letter written to Hyperides by the courtesan Bacchis, soon after the successful outcome of Phryne's court case:

We courtesans are grateful to you, and each one of us is just as grateful as Phryne. The suit, to be sure . . . involved Phryne alone, but it meant danger for us all: for if we ask our lovers for money and don't get it, or if we find paying customers and then face prosecution for impiety, it's better for us to have done with this way of living and no longer have trouble ourselves or cause trouble for those who frequent our company . . . You have not merely saved a good mistress for yourself, but you have put the rest of us in a mood to reward you on her account. And furthermore, if you would write out the speech that you composed in Phryne's defence, then we courtesans would really and truly set up your statue in gold wherever in Greece you wish.[22]

Solon's laws were in no small way aided and abetted by the ponderings of a newly-emerging group of intellectuals: the philosophers, who were keen to introduce a new 'rational' mode of thinking and looking at the world. This latest science, philosophy, reduced the universe to abstractions. Where there had previously been a world seen through the imagination and poetry, a world peopled by spirits and marvellous beings, from the sixth century onwards the outlook had begun to change, and the change was rapid. It was epitomized by the work of men like Pythagoras, who divided everything into opposing pairs of abstract qualities: light/dark, odd/even, mind/matter, left/right, good/bad and, inevitably, male/female. A convenient result of this dualistic thinking was the fact that it completely justified Solon's measures against all women on 'moral' grounds. In the distorting mirror of masculine philosophy, women were identified – of course – with darkness and chaos; seen as intrinsically evil and inferior to men – to whom were attributed the 'masculine' principles of light, order and intellect. The spirit (male) was superior to the flesh (female), so the theory went; correspondingly, the desires of the body became tainted from their supposed origin in the 'feminine' half of the cosmic scheme. A rationalized terror of the body, sexuality, women and the natural world, became the basis of Greek thought, with Pythagoras and his disciples teaching that men should improve themselves by 'escaping from the domination of the flesh'.[23] Greek scholars began to extol the virtues of 'overcoming pleasure'; some went so far as to condemn outright all sexual intercourse unless it took place within the confines of marriage and for the purpose of procreation, which was interestingly pre-Christian of them.

But the lofty ideals of the great thinkers of Athens were seldom borne out in real life; typically, many of the 'rationalists' had mistresses of their own, and these were chosen from the ranks of their intellectual equals – the *hetairae*. Although they loudly deplored prostitution in their orations and writings, it seems that these paragons were willing enough to abandon their superior masculine principles when it came to the realm of their own sexual pleasure.

Athenaeus tells the story of a philosopher who pretended to be unmoved by the dancing-women at a party; he spent the entire night drinking. Later, however, when the whores began to auction off their sexual services to the guests, the philosopher came to physical blows with the auctioneer, who had 'sold' a particular girl to another client. And while there was no place for whores in the imaginary utopia described in Plato's *Republic*, the great man nevertheless found them less dispensable in real life: his mistress was the courtesan Archeanessa.

A story taken from Alciphron's *Letters of Courtesans* satirizes the double standards held by many philosophers on the subject of prostitutes. The courtesan Thais complains to her lover Euthydemus, who has abandoned her for the study of philosophy. In her letter, she makes a persuasive case for the arts of pleasure, as opposed to the science of philosophy:

Ever since you took it into your head to study philosophy you have put on airs and raised your eyebrows above your temples. Then, in a pompous fashion and with a book in your hands, you stalk along to the Academy and walk past my house as if you had never so much as set eyes upon it before. You've gone mad, Euthydemus; don't you know what sort of a person the sophist is, the man with the solemn countenance who delivers those wonderful lectures to you? But how about me? How long do you think it is that he's been pestering me for an appointment? And he's crazy over Megara's maid Herpyllis. Well in the old days, I wouldn't take him on, preferring rather to sleep with you in my arms than with the gold of the sophists. But since he's apparently turning you away from your intimacy with me, I'll let him come; and if you like, I'll show you that your woman-hating schoolmaster is not content with the usual pleasures of a night. It's stuff and nonsense and money-making off boys, that's what it is, you ninny. Do you think a sophist is better than a courtesan? . . . No one, when he's with a courtesan, dreams of a tyrant's power or raises sedition in the state; on the contrary, he drains his early-morning beaker and then prolongs his rest until the third or fourth hour. We teach young men as well as they do . . . Abandon this foolish, odious pose, Euthydemus . . . eyes such as yours ought not to be solemn . . . and come to your sweetheart as you are when you have come back, for instance, from the Lyceum [i.e. the gymnasium], wiping off the sweat, that we may carouse a bit and give each other a demonstration of that noble end, pleasure. The deity gives us no long time to live; do not wake up to find you have wasted yours on riddles and on nonsense. Farewell.[24]

Greek writers and poets also joined in the fray, vying with each other to downgrade and denounce the courtesans, who in turn fought a constant battle to assert themselves. One anecdote tells of the Corinthian courtesan Lais coming up against the moral indignation of the dramatist Euripides. Lais encountered the playwright in a garden one day, as he was busy concocting his plots. The whore challenged him:

'Tell me, poet, what you meant when in your play you made Jason say to Medea, "To hell, you perpetrator of foul deeds"?'

Euripides, taken aback by the courtesan's impudence in daring to question him, replied, 'Why, what are you yourself, woman? Are you not a perpetrator of foul deeds?' To which Lais responded with a laugh: 'What is foul, if it seems not so to those who indulge in it?'[25]

The whore apparently had no trouble bettering the great dramatist in the wit stakes, at least.

Eventually, the state declared a truce and became less severe in its dealings with independent prostitutes, even though the great men of Greece continued to insult and condemn them in their writings and speeches to the public. But at some point it must have become obvious that the major stumbling-block faced by Solon's legislators was not so much the existence of the hetairae as the overwhelming demand for their services; a demand that came exclusively from the very class of males who vilified them. It is also feasible that the whores themselves banded together and agreed to boycott their statesman and judge clientele until these worthies guaranteed that there would be no further prosecutions of working ladies. Whatever the case, we know that the hetairae continued to follow illustrious careers, amassing fabulous wealth and a enjoying degree of power over their own 'sweet lives' that their 'virtuous' married sisters of Athens could never have dreamed of.

Male-only banquets were a popular and frequent occurrence in classical Athens, for with their dear wives safely ensconced within the home, Greek men were free to indulge themselves elsewhere. At these parties they were entertained by groups of dancer-musician-prostitutes – the *auletrides* – who played their flutes, drums and finger cymbals, and performed the sensuous dances of the Middle East (many of the women had originally been captured slaves from the cities of Asia Minor). After the entertainment, the men vied with each other for the sexual services of the performers. The historian Henriques reflects longingly: 'One can imagine the scene – rich and exotic foods, and continuous flowing of wine, the strangely exciting music, and above all, the lascivious movements of the almost naked girls as they danced.'[26] Truly a punter's paradise.

Breakfast parties were also highly fashionable as a pastime. Athenaeus relates the following 'disgraceful' scene that took place at one of these: 'When the drinking was going on apace and there entered, among other entertaining shows, those Thessalian dancing-girls who danced, as is their custom, in loin-cloths without other covering, the old men could no longer restrain themselves, but started up from their couches and shouted aloud at the wonderful sight they were seeing . . . and then they proceeded to commit many other vulgarities' – which Athenaeus, prudishly, on this occasion, declines to elaborate upon.

Theoretically, the *auletrides* were slaves, but such was their popularity and earning power that many were able to buy their freedom and go on to earn great fortunes for themselves. Their homes often rivalled those of the *hetairae*, for their sumptuous beauty. The *auletrides* could live wherever they chose and were also free to indulge in long-term liaisons with individual clients, *hetaira*-style. Several of them are recorded as having attained a status equal to that of any of the famous courtesans, notably the prostitute Lamia, who began her working life as an *auletrides* dancer and was so successful in her career that she became the favourite of King Ptolemy of Egypt and King Demetrius, ruler of Macedonia. Her power over the latter was apparently so great that he was rumoured to have levied a special tax on Athens, just to keep his mistress in soap.

Alciphron describes a light-hearted and erotic contest between two *auletrides*, giving us an idea of the talents these ladies possessed:

Myrrhina unfastened her girdle (her shift was silk) and began to shake her loins (visible through her shift), which quivered like junkets, the while she cocked her eye back at the wagglings of her buttocks. And so gently – as if she were in the act – she sighed a bit, that, by Aphrodite, I was thunderstruck. Thryallis, nevertheless, did not give up; on the contrary, she outdid Myrrhina in wantonness. 'I certainly am not going to compete behind a curtain,' said she, 'nor with any affectation of coyness, but as if I were in a wrestling match, for the competition brooks no subterfuge.' So she put off her shift and, puckering her croup a little, she said, 'There, see these rosy hips, how they merge into the thighs, how there's neither too much plumpness nor any thinness, and the dimples at the tips. But, by Zeus, they don't quiver,' said she with a slight smile, 'like Myrrhina's.' And then she made her buttocks vibrate so fast, swaying their whole bulk above her loins this way and that with such a rippling motion, that we all applauded and declared that the victory was Thryallis's.[27]

Sometimes the *auletrides* and *hetairae* indulged in their own single-sex gatherings: all-female banquets and festivals at which the participants both honoured their goddess, Aphrodite, and celebrated their calling. On these occasions it seems that the whores were able to amuse themselves at least as well as the men at their own junkets: 'What a party we had! . . . songs, jests, drinking till cockcrow, perfumes, garlands, sweetmeats . . . We've had lots of drunken frolics, but rarely such a pleasant one as this.'[28]

Lesbian activities were rife, much to the horror of historians such as the priceless Sanger, who informs us that: 'modern tastes will not allow us to transcribe the details.' He goes on: 'It has been suggested that these festivals were originated by or gave rise to those enormous aberrations of the Greek feminine mind known to the ancients as lesbian love. There is grave reason to believe something of the kind. Indeed, Lucius affirms that, while avarice prompted common pleasures, taste and feeling inclined the flute players towards their own sex. On such a repulsive theme it is unnecessary to enlarge.'[29]

The men of the Greek upper classes also indulged in homosexuality;

another facet of Greek sexual life that Solon attempted to legislate against (despite the fact that he was himself gay). Male homosexuality was widespread in Athens, although it had rather more to do with a form of male prostitution than with the kind of reciprocal sexual relations enjoyed by the *auletrides*. Adolescent boys were the favoured prey of the older Greek male, who would spend many hours at the gymnasium, watching them exercise. Paedophilia was more accurately the name of the game. Although outright prostitution for money was forbidden, boys gave sexual favours in return for 'presents'. The older partner was ostensibly acting from altruistic motives, interested only in furthering the education of his young paramour.

The line between this kind of activity and actual mercenary prostitution was a thin one; many boys managed to capitalize on their popularity and earn regular incomes from several 'admirers', thus blurring the distinction even further. But if their behaviour became too overt, they risked being punished by law. In his study of Greek homosexuality, K. J. Dover refers to the trial of a man named Timarkhos, whose political rivals accused him of having prostituted himself in his youth. Even though the case against Timarkhos was concocted mainly from gossip and hearsay – he had been a 'youth of "easy virtue", ready to live off men', rather than a working prostitute, according to Dover – the verdict went against him and he was stripped of all civil liberties and political rights. The unfortunate Timarkhos paid the price for crossing the invisible boundary between legitimate and non-legitimate trading in sex.

After Solon's death, the Athenian laws that surrounded prostitution in all its guises were relaxed considerably; later rulers recognized the literal value to the state that all whores represented – even the lowly *dikteriades* slaves were eventually given the freedom to roam the city. Legislation went through periodic waves of tightening and relaxation, but never regained the severity that Solon had envisaged; so in one sense the great ruler failed dismally – the independent and educated whores of Athens flourished.

But Solon was all too successful in his attempts to segregate women and institutionalize the Good Woman/Bad Woman split. While the 'virtuous' wives of the free citizens of Athens lived as prisoners and dependents of their husbands, enabling the middle class to survive and establish itself, the poor women and slaves who staffed the vast, state-regulated sex industry continued to ensure that the Athenian state made huge profits through its pimping on a grand scale. Meanwhile, the philosophers and writers of Athens found time to invent the 'moral' sexual dualism that associated everything good with man, and everything bad with woman, thus carving misogyny deep into the Western tradition.

CHAPTER THREE

The Roman Circus:
the Imperial Sex Trade

A prostitute is like a prosperous city . . .
she can't get on without a lot of men.

.Plautus

The second great classical civilization beloved of
Western scholars is ancient Rome: 'the most
elegant and logical structure yet created by mankind', according to the writer Reay Tannahill.
From the tiny city-state of the 8th century BC to the
gargantuan empire of the first five centuries AD,
Roman society and culture have enthralled the
writers and academics who have recorded its history. Yet alongside
the 'elegant and logical structure' they admire so much, a fantastic and
chaotic profusion of sexual practices flourished, for the Romans were
self-indulgent to the extreme. To label them perverse is an understate-
ment, since they flouted any notion of moral or sexual convention and
deviated from every norm that had been invented to date. The
outright ownership of huge numbers of human beings encouraged the
ruling classes to put their wildest fantasies into practice, and they did
so with great gusto. Also, the massive urban sprawl of the city itself –
reaching 2½ million inhabitants at its height – encouraged the growth
of prostitution on a vast scale. Life was cheap, sex was cheaper still,
and the Roman aristocracy were determined to enjoy both commodities, unreservedly.

To understand Roman attitudes to sexuality, and the place of
prostitution within that society, it is helpful to recall the development
of Roman culture from its beginnings.

Like other early civilizations, the first Romans were an agricultural
people, divided into clans. The name of the entire people – the Latins –

was derived from the legendary first queen of the race, Latia, indicating that the clans were matriarchalists. According to legend, it was the clan-mother Acca Larentia who left her land to the Roman people; interestingly, Larentia is described as 'the noble whore', which gives a clue to the existence of the old goddess-religion in Roman prehistory. It seems likely that Larentia, the clan-mother and land-owner, was also a high priestess of that religion.

In prehistoric Rome, as in all the other Mediterranean civilizations, property and power were handed down through the female line and the ancient kings were entitled to rule only by right of marriage to whichever woman inherited land and throne. Here too, men managed to subordinate women by taking control of and institutionalizing patriarchal forms of marriage. In the case of Rome, however, the revolution was particularly violent and sudden, with the result that the male rulers were able to introduce some of the most draconian patriarchal laws of the ancient world. Like the men of ancient Greece, Roman men now monopolized power through land ownership and their own newly forged political structures; but in Rome the *paterfamilias*, literally father of the family, held absolute power over his wife, children and slaves, to the extent that he was entitled by law to condemn them to death and kill them without fear of retribution or interference from the state. In the earliest times of ancient Rome, there are many examples of this happening, but as the empire developed and expanded, so the ruling aristocracy grew complacent. The reins of discipline were consequently relaxed and the older, severe laws quashed.

Unlike their Greek counterparts, the wives of the Roman ruling class were not cloistered in their homes or banished from the public sphere. They went out and about frequently (though nominally with their husband's consent); attending plays and visiting the temples and law courts. They were allowed to be educated, usually by private tutors in their family homes. Certainly, Roman women were much more liberated than their less fortunate Greek sisters and – somewhat ironically – it was the structure of Roman patriarchal society that worked in their favour. Whereas in Greece the merchant class had succeeded in ousting the old aristocracy from power, in Rome the upper class was never challenged. Assured of its safe succession, the aristocracy set the standards of behaviour in the city for all to follow, and this continued as late as the 4th century AD, until the rise of Christianity.

Roman women were therefore proud and spirited, valuing their independence to such an extent that, when the first emperor, Augustus, introduced laws specifically aimed at forcing women of the ruling class to marry and bear children, many of them preferred to register voluntarily as prostitutes, thus exempting themselves from the regulations. The lower classes of Rome, meanwhile, continued to ignore all patriarchal forms of marriage, preferring to retain the sexual customs of their predecessors. In his *Sexual Life in Ancient Rome*, Otto Kiefer points out that: 'Marriage as a binding union was certainly unknown to the [common people]; accordingly, their children belonged to the mother's family. This . . . marriageless relationship still existed at Rome in later times, and was the basis of a widely developed system of free love, which soon changed into different kinds of prostitution.'[1]

In fact there was rather more to it than that. Rome's expansionist policies ensured a vast and constant supply of sex workers, for not only did the conquest of foreign colonies result in successive waves of thousands of captured slaves being swept into the city, the peasantry, too, ruined by the wars that had accompanied the period of expansion at the beginning of the first millennium AD, were wrenched from their land and had no alternative but to flock to the city in a desperate search for waged labour. In some respects these 'free poor' were even worse off than slaves, who were at least housed and fed, since their masters regarded them as investments.

For the former peasants, survival in the city was difficult. Unemployment was rife and many were forced to subsist on state handouts of grain. Under these circumstances, it was inevitable that many of them turned to prostitution in order to survive. Even so, the majority of sex workers in ancient Rome were not freeborn peasants but slaves (as indeed were most of the city's workforce). It was this exploitation of slave labour on a scale undreamed-of by earlier cultures that enabled Rome to become the greatest and richest empire the ancient world had ever seen; and it was slavery that enabled the city to retain that power for many centuries. Roman lawyers were the first to devise the concept of outright ownership, which, when applied to slaves, meant that they were legally defined as *objects*, possessing no more rights than animals – or even tools. The power of the slave-owner paralleled that of the earlier paterfamilias, and if the subordination of slaves proved more effective than that of wives, it was only because the very existence of the Roman empire depended on it.

Unlike classical Greece, Rome never developed a democracy, so the city's political power was never allowed to spread across a numerous middle class. A tiny aristocracy remained in power over the whole empire. The emperors who decreed themselves gods are the perfect example of this combined expansion and concentration of power: they considered themselves lords of all creation, whose will was, naturally, divine law – and they wielded it ruthlessly, over a massive underclass of slaves. The infamous brutality of the Roman world was largely due to the complete freedom of the aristocracy to exercise its whims on the slave population. The horrors of the circuses, where human lives were thrown away daily as a form of mass entertainment, are rightly notorious, but it should be recognized that the example was set by those at the top. The codes of social and moral behaviour were laid down by the 'divine' emperors and their families, for after the establishment of the empire as a single unchallenged power (c. AD· 100), there was literally no power on earth that could restrain the emperor-gods from acting out their most outrageous fantasies. Needless to say, the realm of the senses proved no exception to this rule.

Latterday historians have, somewhat hilariously, provided us with a roll-call of the divine emperors, accompanied by a catalogue of their sexual antics; and 'it requires no small research,' as Sanger remarks, 'to discover a single character in the long list . . . who was not stained by the grossest habits.'[2]

Julius Caesar, 'the bald adulterer', was 'commonly said to be "husband of all men's wives".'[3] Augustus, the self-same emperor who instituted laws to enforce marriage and fidelity among the ruling class, led a 'dissolute' youth, was himself a notorious adulterer, and in his old age had young women sought out for him by his friends, 'who stripped and inspected married women and maidens, as if the whoremonger Torianus had been selling them'.[4] As for Tiberius: '[his] amours cannot be described . . . it will suffice to say that there was no invention of infamy which he did not patronize; that no young person of any charms was safe from his lust.'[5]

Tiberius' successor Caligula gained notoriety for committing incest with all his sisters and ritually disembowelling one of them. He also amused himself by displaying his wife Caesonia to his friends naked, had a well-publicized affair with the actor-prostitute Mnester, and set up a brothel in the imperial palace. The emperor Nero was a frequent visitor to the city's brothels, and 'dined in public at the great circus among a crowd of prostitutes. He founded, on the shore of the Gulf of Naples, houses of prostitution and filled them with females, whose dissolute habits were their recommendation to his notice,' Sanger primly informs us.[6] Nero also set a precedent by 'marrying' his male favourite, Sporus.

The emperor Domitian 'bathed habitually in company with a band of prostitutes, and set an example of hideous vice while enacting severe laws against debauchery'.[7] Commodus, who converted his palace into a brothel, retained the services of 300 of Rome's most beautiful girls – and an equal number of boys; as he grew older, he 'revived his dull senses by the sight of pleasures he could no longer share'.[8] In common with Nero, Commodus violated his sisters; he also cross-dressed and on one occasion 'gratified the court with the spectacle of his marriage to one of his freedmen'.[9]

Finally, Elagabalus, 'whom the historian could only compare to a wild beast', according to Sanger, brought the imperial sexual circus to its climax:

> [he] surpassed even the most audacious infamies of his predeces-
> sors . . . It was his pride to have been able to teach even the most
> expert courtesans of Rome something more than they knew; his
> pleasure to wallow among them naked, and to pull down into the
> sink of bestiality in which he lived the first officers of the
> empire.[10]

Without a doubt the emperor Elagabalus emerges as the star of the show; he appears to have dedicated his life to exploring his sexuality. This most outrageous of the transvestite emperors frequently bathed among women, sharing their perfumed oils and joining them in removing unwanted facial and body hair; he also built a bath in the imperial palace and threw it open to the populace, so that he might have a plentiful supply of male lovers to choose from. Elagabalus liked to have little scenarios from mythology enacted in his house, delighting in playing the role of Venus (Roman counterpart to the Greek Aphrodite). He showed a penchant for masochism; one of his many little diversions was to have his own foreskin sewn up, or closed with a clasp. And, in the tradition of his predecessors Nero and Commodus, the emperor married one of his male favourites, the actor-whore Zoticus.

Not surprisingly, in view of his activities, Elagabalus was extremely popular with the sex workers of the city. Henriques describes him as 'the greatest friend that the whores of both sexes ever had in Rome'.[11] He opened brothels in the palace for his friends, clients and slaves; on one occasion he gathered together all the whores from the circus, stadium, theatres, baths and other places of amusement in order to deliver a long oration to them. He called them his 'comrades' and elaborated at great length on the various different ways in which the sexual act could be performed. On another occasion he held a similar convention for procurers, male prostitutes and 'lascivious boys and young men'. Where he had appeared before the female whores in women's attire – complete with false bust – for the male whores the emperor chose to parade himself in the costume of a boy prostitute. But Elagabalus was not totally devoid of human compassion, unlike many of his predecessors: he at least showed some concern for the well-being of his prostitute subjects, and was known to have personally distributed his own kind of state welfare in the form of both grain and money handouts to whores throughout the city.

Sexual excess was not confined to the males of the Imperial Roman family: some of the women were at least as depraved, if not more so. According to the writer and orator Seneca, Julia, daughter of the emperor Augustus, had scores of lovers: 'At night she revelled through the city streets; she chose for the scene of her embraces the very Forum and the platform from which her father had promulgated his laws against adultery' – a neat revenge – '[and] made rendezvous at the statue of Marsyas, for she had now turned from adulteress to whore, and permitted herself any licence with unknown lovers.'[12]

Messalina, wife of Claudius, was probably the most notorious of the women of the imperial family. Like Julia she went out into the streets and stews of the Roman night to sell herself, in imitation of the professional whores. Legend has it that Messalina was still sexually unsatisfied after the brothels had closed for the night, and had to be physically thrown out on occasions. Her most famous exploit was to hire a prostitute who was well known for her sexual stamina and challenge her to a contest to see who could accommodate the greatest number of men in a single night. The empress won.

With the supposedly god-like first families of ancient Rome setting this kind of example, it comes as no surprise to find that sexual restraint or inhibition was the exception rather than the rule, throughout the empire. Once Rome had been established as the mightiest power in the world, there was little incentive for the ruling class to curtail their desires and endure monogamous marriages; they wanted to relax and abandon themselves sexually. Men of all ages preferred to indulge in sexual activities and relationships with prostitutes, concubines and slaves. There was always somebody around who could satisfy their desires, for, as the poet Horace wrote:

> And when your lust runs hot you surely
> won't choose to grin and bear it
> if a maid or slave-boy's handy to leap on there and then?
> *I* won't! I like a cheap and easy love!

Once again, it was the slave and servant class who bore the brunt of their masters' sexual excesses. For these unfortunate women and boys, rape and sexual abuse were an everyday fact of life; perhaps their only hope of escape lay in running away to work on the streets or in brothels as anonymous, full-time whores. In this way they would at least have been paid for their sexual labour.

Generally speaking, prostitution in ancient Rome was a natural, accepted profession with no shame attached to the working women. One illustration of this lack of stigma can be found in the story of the emperor Augustus' marriage legislation, alluded to earlier in this chapter.

Augustus, worried that the aristocracy's reluctance to marry and reproduce would lead to the ruling class dwindling away for want of heirs, introduced a system of penalties which he applied to single people of marriageable age. He then supplemented these measures with a series of rewards for married women who produced more than three children (a kind of procreative 'piece-work' system). But the emperor's plan backfired in some instances, for rebellious aristocratic women took the option of registering themselves as whores rather than succumb to forced marriages. It was Augustus' successor Tiberius – himself famed for his debaucheries – who struck the decisive blow, by banning women of the ruling class from working as whores.

Roman attitudes towards prostitution were in some respects similar to those of the ancient Greeks; men were inclined to justify it in terms of it protecting their own marriages by diverting randy youths from adultery, or, as Cato more pithily put it: 'Blessed be they as virtuous, who when they feel their virile members swollen with lust, visit a brothel rather than grind at some husband's private mill.'[13]

Cicero argued against the perennial moralists who compared the degeneracy of their day with the supposed righteous self-denial of the past: 'If there is anyone who thinks that young men should be forbidden to make love, even to prostitutes, he is certainly a man of stern righteousness . . . but he is out of touch not only with the free life of today, but even with the code and concessions which our fathers accepted. For when was that not customary? When was it blamed? When was it not allowed? When was it not lawful to do what is a lawful privilege?'[14] And the poet Horace eulogizes the virtues of prostitution as opposed to adultery:

Nor has [this married woman], amidst her pearls and emeralds, a softer thigh, or limbs more delicate than yours, Cerinthus [a prostitute]; nay, the prostitutes are frequently preferable. Add to this that [she] bears about her merchandise without any varnish, and openly shows what she has to dispose of: nor, if she has aught more comely than ordinary, does she boast and make a show of it, while she is careful to conceal that which is offensive . . . But if you will seek after forbidden charms (which make you mad after them), surrounded as they are with a fortification, many obstacles will then be in your way: such as guardians . . . dressers, parasites . . . a multiplicity of circumstances, which will hinder you from having a fair view. The [prostitute] throws no obstacles in your way; through the silken vest you may discern her, almost as well as if she was naked . . . Nor am I apprehensive, while I am in her company, lest her husband should return from the country; the door should be broken open; the dog should bark; the house, shaken, should resound on all sides with a great noise; the woman, pale with fear, should bound away from me; lest the maid should cry out, she is undone . . . lest I must run away with clothes all loose, and bare-footed, for fear my money, or my person, or finally my character, should be ruined.[15]

Truly an adulterer's nightmare scenario, and one that demonstrates the attitude of ruling-class Roman men towards their sexuality. Once again in classical history, prostitution was seen to be both companion to and antidote to 'exclusive' marriage, with all that that entailed. Plautus spells out the philosophy for us, in his usual blunt way: 'Don't touch a wife, a widow, a virgin, a youth, or a freeborn child . . . take all the rest!'

Although the Romans did not own and operate state brothels, as the Greeks did, they did manage to introduce the first system of state registration of lower-class prostitutes into Europe. This resulted in the dividing of whores into two categories: the registered *meretrices*, and the unregistered *prostibulae* (source of our word prostitute). In theory, all whores were required by law to register with an official known as the *aedile*; in practice, the vast majority did not; for once a woman's name was put on the list there was no question of it being revoked. Her name, age and birthplace were recorded on a scroll; she then stated her price and was given a licence. High-class prostitutes were not legally bound to register; nor were the many actresses, dancers and musicians, who sold sexual services 'on the side'. In spite of the regular sweeps of the houses and streets made by the *aediles*, most lower-class whores, both streetwalkers and brothel-workers, did not bother to register; after all, the city was vast and the Roman police system small and inefficient – not to mention corrupt. More often than not, the women's gambling on not being netted paid off.

Among these lower-class whores there was a profuse variety of talents and specialist services, each group of workers operating from a particular patch or business. The *dorides* advertised themselves naked in their doorways; the *lupae* (she-wolves) attracted clients with their high-pitched imitation wolf-cries; while the *aelicariae*, or bakers' girls, sold small cakes made in the shape of male and female genitals for sacrifice to Venus, the love goddess, and Priapus, the phallic god. Perhaps the strangest category of lower-class prostitute (at least, from a modern point of view) were the *bustuariae*. These ladies plied for hire in the city's graveyards, used tombstones as beds and alternated the profession of whore with that of funeral mourner. The *scorta erratica* were Roman streetwalkers; the *blitidae* solicited in taverns, taking their name from the cheap wine, *blitum*, that was sold on those premises; the *copae* were serving-girls who doubled as whores. The *gallinae* (hens) combined prostitution with robbery, while the *forariae* were country girls who picked up clients on rural roads outside the city. Finally, at the bottom of Rome's lower-class prostitute hierarchy were the *diobolares*, who charged only two obols for their services and the *quadrantariae*, who were the lowliest whores of all, charging so little that their fee is not quantifiable in modern currency.

Again, laws dictated that all lower-class prostitutes had to wear a particular costume so as to distinguish them from 'respectable' women; again, many whores refused to be restricted in their choice of clothing and openly flouted the regulations. Legally, they were bound to wear the male *toga* instead of the female *stola* – an interesting ordinance in itself. They were also supposedly forbidden to wear purple robes, shoes, jewellery or the fillets with which Roman matrons bound their hair; the whores were instructed instead to wear sandals and their dress was to be of a floral pattern. Many prostitutes chose to be blatant about the whole business of dress and presentation, deliberately distinguishing themselves from their married sisters by ostentatiously dyeing their hair yellow or red, painting their faces and choosing diaphanous silk and gauze dresses – filmy, exotic costumes that 'seemed invented to exhibit more conspicuously what they were intended to hide'.[16]

Although latterday feminist writers tend to assert that the whores were forced to dye their hair, paint their faces, etc., it is more likely that the women chose to do so as a gesture of mutual solidarity. Nevertheless, it is apparent that the state was trying to control and inhibit the women by its use of petty legislation – no matter how futile that legislation turned out to be in the long run. Another by-law stated that whores were forbidden to ride in litters – but many women disobeyed the injunction; indeed some of them rode the streets in litters whose curtains were drawn, for obvious reasons.

Elsewhere, prostitutes operated wherever their ingenuity and enterprise suggested; the streets of the city were thronged with them, at all times of the day and night. The *fornices* (from which our word fornication is derived) were the arches underneath the theatres, circuses and private houses; many prostitutes entertained clients within their shadowy recesses. The fornices of the circuses and stadia were particularly popular, for the crop was plentiful among men whose blood had been stirred up by a good afternoon's 'sport' – a Roman equivalent to Cup Final night in Soho. Other favoured locations outside the brothels and inns were balconies overhanging the streets (*pergulae*); houses known as the *stabulae* ('where no cells were used, and promiscuous intercourse took place openly'[17] Sanger worries); and the *turturillae*, or 'pigeon-houses'. Shady gardens were popular haunts for the whores and their customers, too; they could often be seen frolicking around the statues and temples. Prostitutes could also be found attracting custom for other businesses, notably butchers, bakers and barbers. Bakers' premises often had prostitutes' 'cells' built into the cellars of their flour mills and these were hired out to street whores. They were, however, subject to frequent raids by *aediles* on the look-out for unregistered women.

Another source of rich pickings for prostitutes was of course the public baths, where upper-class Romans came to relax and socialize. Although these were originally intended to be sexually segregated areas, it did not take the Romans long to intermingle in the relaxed and sensual atmosphere. Whores and their clients eventually infiltrated the baths to such an extent that specific areas were incorporated into their design to cater for the demand. Private cubicles were built for the specific use of men who opted for massage with aromatic essences – plus a variety of 'extra' services: birth of the massage parlour. Skilled *fellatrices* and young boys trained in the arts of oral stimulation were a popular speciality. But the bath cubicles were not restricted to male clients – Roman matrons were frequent visitors, too, there to relieve the boredom and stress of their empty, luxurious lives.

For the lower-class prostitute, the open street was a far better working environment than the city's registered brothels. The *lupanar* – house of prostitution – was usually a small building; in the more up-market areas the whores' rooms were arranged round a shady courtyard, but lower down the scale amenities were, to say the least, very basic: a simple hall led to the prostitutes' cells. And cells is precisely what they were: small, ill-lit and badly-ventilated, with minimal furnishings; sometimes as little as a lamp and some cushions and coverlets on the floor. Hanging on each cell door was a sign; one side stipulated the woman's fee while the other bore the inscription *occupata*, not unlike a public toilet. The brothel was decorated on the outside by a flamboyant – and explicit – sign that advertised its business; within the building there were erotic statues and murals. Little was left to the client's imagination – even the lamps were shaped like winged phalluses or vaginas.

Apart from harassing prostitutes who were unwilling to register with him, the *aedile*'s duties included keeping 'order' in the brothels and making sure that they observed the legal opening times – from three in the afternoon until dawn the next day. They were also responsible for seeing that the women who worked wore the dress specified by law and guaranteeing their right to be paid the correct fee. This was the only regulation that operated in the whores' interest: the rest were prohibitions and injunctions against them. Small wonder, then, that the majority of working prostitutes preferred to defy the lawmakers and look out for themselves.

There were two kinds of brothel operating in ancient Rome; in the first, the brothel-owner or *leno* (*lena* if a woman) made his profit from a staff of slaves or hired freedwomen, each of whom was paid a small fee for her work. The second type was less common: here, the proprietor was little more than a landlord, letting out rooms to whores who operated independently. Whereas at the lower end of the market facilities were basic, the more expensive houses were luxuriously fitted out and the whores earned higher incomes. The proprietors employed touts to solicit for custom throughout the city and once a customer was enticed into the brothel, his every whim was catered to by an army of servants. A cashier, the *villicus*, talked business and took the client's money before admitting him to the prostitute; while young boy-servants, *aquarii*, provided wine and other refreshments, as well as bringing fresh supplies of water for washing. And for the whores themselves there were special maid-servants, *ancillae ornatrices*, who, as their name indicates, had the task of keeping the women looking fresh and beautiful between prospective clients.

As in later ages of European corruption, notably the Victorian era, ruling-class men developed an obsessive lust for the virgin whore. Whenever a brothel-owner acquired a fresh virgin (usually a slave-girl) he left a wreath of laurel on his door along with a lamp burning above a notice which described the attributes of the girl in graphic detail. The 'lucky man', as Henriques puts it,[18] who bid a high enough price was fêted and crowned with the laurel leaves after deflowering the virgin. Rupturing the hymen of an adolescent slave-girl was considered a mighty achievement by the upper-class men of ancient Rome.

According to many historians, prostitution in ancient Rome differs from that of other early civilizations in that there was no religious version. However, some feminist writers have more recently begun to speculate that there may well have been a link between religion and the practice of some sexual rites. In her *Woman's Encyclopedia of Myths and Secrets*, Barbara Walker writes that the Vestal Virgins, keepers of the sacred flame which symbolized the spirit of Rome, may originally have participated in some form of sacred marriage ceremony with the *pontifex maximus*, or High Priest. As in earlier cultures, the ceremony would have legitimized the ruler's power in the eyes of the Roman people (Julius Caesar, for example, was both political leader of Rome and its High Priest). The mythology of early Rome certainly indicates that matriarchal sexual rites were part of the culture, as previously noted in the figure of Acca Larentia, 'most noble whore' – and mother of Rome. Latin sources such as the historian Livy indicate that prostitution existed in Rome as far back as the 6th century BC; and given the rapid emergence of Rome from matriarchy, it seems inconceivable that some forms of the old worship should not have survived.

In later, more clearly-documented times, however, prostitution was linked to worship of the goddess Venus, who was regarded as the whores' protector. According to Barbara Walker, the temples of Venus were 'schools of instruction in sexual techniques, under the tutelage of the *venerii* or harlot-priestesses',[19] who taught a sexual-spiritual path apparently similar to that of Indian Tantrism. And while authorities such as Henriques claim that 'there was no major development of forms of religious prostitution',[20] there is clear evidence that whores played a prominent part in a variety of religious festivals. *Venus Volgivava* (Venus the Streetwalker) was one name given to the goddess in her whore aspect; and prostitutes of both sexes celebrated her festival on 23 April every year. A goddess known as *Fortuna Virilis* was adored by lower-class Roman women, who worshipped her while bathing in the men's baths, which were notorious houses of prostitution. Another festival that was celebrated by prostitutes, with enthusiastic support and participation on the part of the public, involved a series of games, beginning every year on 28 April. They were held in honour of the goddess Flora, a legendary whore who had bequeathed the proceeds of her staggeringly success-ful career to a grateful and delighted Rome. At the climactic final ceremony of the games, held in the Circus on 3 May: 'The gathered prostitutes of Rome stripped and performed dances of growing lasciviousness until a crowd of naked young men came whooping into the arena and performed as you might expect while the crowd applauded their efforts.'[21]

Although the misogyny of many male writers makes it difficult sometimes to separate fact from fantasy in their accounts of prostitutes in every age, the claims of generations of outraged historians that Roman women worshipped their gods and goddesses with orgiastic rites appear to be based in reality. The worshippers of the goddess

Bona Dea were all-female, and while Plutarch's description of her rites is fairly restrained and neutral, a hysterically overblown passage by Juvenal (quoted with relish by latterday scholars) depicts the women as a frenzied crowd of drunken nymphomaniacs who were ready to rape any passing male or even – in the absence of men – to drag donkeys from stables in order to sate their lusts. Juvenal's account in fact reads like lurid fantasy. Nevertheless, whores were known to take part in the Bona Dea festivities, so sexual activities would certainly have been on the menu. These were known to include 'more than a suggestion of Lesbian practices',[22] which may explain in some part the antipathy of observers such as Juvenal.

One of the most popular goddesses of the Roman empire was Isis, who had been imported wholesale from Egypt. Isis was seen as a supreme deity, encompassing all aspects of divinity; there was a strong emphasis on her merciful, 'motherly' qualities but, like her predecessor Ishtar, she was also a whore-goddess. It was perhaps because Isis represented so forcefully and creatively the image of assertive womanhood that the Roman state found her popularity so threatening, for a long and ultimately futile official campaign of persecution was waged against her devotees and priests. Eventually the authorities had to concede defeat and tolerate her temples, both within the city itself and throughout the empire. Isis was venerated all over the Roman world, even in far-flung Britain.

Probably the major reason for its popularity was the fact that the Isis religion was open to all. Women and slaves in particular loved this goddess, and although she did become fashionable among the aristocracy after the persecution against her followers ceased, she was largely worshipped by the common people of Rome, many of whom had originated in lands far away from the empire and thus had no stake in Roman power. But as the empire grew in size and wealth and the women of the upper classes became relatively emancipated, the Isis religion spread rapidly among them, to the extent that: 'Women were her most constant and fervent devotees, from empresses down to the lowest slave-prostitute.'[23]

As always, it is difficult to sift the truth from the distortions in men's accounts of Isis-worship; some are certainly more balanced, or at least less paranoid, than others. Ovid, for instance, suggests that Isis helped make women sexually free, which may well have been the case; but Juvenal condemned the women who worshipped her, saying that the priestesses were 'no better than bawds'. And yet it was well known (the poet Propertius complained about it) that women had to remain celibate for up to ten days before participating in certain of the rituals of Isis; indeed some women dedicated themselves to a life of celibacy in the service of the goddess. The classical scholar Sarah B. Pomeroy simply states that 'Eroticism and asceticism were mingled in the cult.'[24] It does seem likely that the Isis religion involved some element of sacred prostitution – whores were certainly known to revere and worship her – but the evidence is not conclusive. Whatever the truth about ritualized or sacred prostitution in Roman society, it is clear that the link was not entirely lost, at least as far as the common people were concerned, for the temples of Isis, Ganymede (a homosexual god) and Ceres (earth goddess) were favourite meeting-places for lower-class whores and their clients. The step from religious to sexual ecstasy was but a short one.

The Roman theatre held a special attraction for prostitutes. In his celebrated erotic poem *The Arts of Love*, Ovid advises aspiring punters that:

> – above all the playhouse is the place . . .
> there's choice of quarry in that narrow chase.
> There take thy stand, and sharply looking out
> soon mayest thou find a mistress in the rout,
> for length of time, or for a single bout.[25]

But whores did not restrict themselves to working in the auditorium or under the arches upon which the theatres were built; many were to be found working as actors and actresses, for the theatre was the one place in which they could flaunt themselves and their talents to wide public acclaim. There was even the possibility of a rise in station, from lower-class prostitute to 'lady', which must have acted as an added incentive. Prostitutes were often professional actors, and vice versa.

This seems a logical progression in view of the fact that the Roman theatre itself had developed out of a tradition of peasant festivals, many of which celebrated all aspects of sexuality. Theatre therefore never lost its close association with the bawdy – and audiences loved it. Whores and whore-mongers were favourite characters in comedy, while adultery, homosexuality and incest were popular themes. One much-adhered-to convention was that the female comedians should appear almost naked by the end of the play; another was the enacting of erotic scenes from mythology, both in mime and dance. The empress Theodora, wife of Justinian (a 6th-century AD Byzantine emperor), was a former actress-prostitute. Hers is an interesting, though rather exceptional, story.

Born into a very poor family, Theodora was to become the most powerful woman of her time; historians acknowledge her as 'one of the most influential women of any past era'.[26] In her youth she was one of the most famous actresses of the day – a gifted mimic and a 'virtuoso in the modern burlesque routine',[27] that is, a talented stripper. At the height of her theatrical career, Theodora became the mistress of a provincial governor, but at some point they split up and she paid her way back to Constantinople by selling sex. Once there she reached the peak of the profession and caught the eye of Justinian, who was at that time a senator. Although Roman law forbade senators from marrying whores, Justinian was so smitten by Theodora that he managed to persuade his uncle, the emperor Justin, to revoke the law; he then married his beloved, who became empress when Justin died and Justinian succeeded him.

Male dancers and actors fared well out of the theatre, too, often becoming famous in their own right – a Roman equivalent of 20th-century film-stars. They were fêted and courted by the nobility, especially by the divine emperors and their wives. Caligula had an affair with the actor Mnester, Nero with Paris, and the emperor Domitian went so far as to separate from his wife because of her much-publicized affair with an actor. All the theatre-whores had started life on the streets, but certainly did not stay there. And if the law – or their sex – prevented them from marrying and founding noble houses with their aristocratic lovers, then at least they could achieve some degree of wealth and status in their lives, which was certainly more than the majority of street-whores could expect.

Another group of entertainer-prostitutes were the dancing girls of Rome; usually professional dancers or talented slaves who had been imported from Syria (like the *auletrides* of ancient Greece) and Spain, particularly from Gades (Cadiz). Dancing was an activity beloved by all echelons of Roman society, from slaves to senators; many of the upper classes sent their children to dancing schools. It was at one of these that the writer Scipio saw a boy of twelve perform a dance 'with castanets . . . which not even a brazen slave could have performed with decency'. Some wealthy Romans employed tutors to teach their

children the popular dances of the time – but the usual double standard
applied even here: while it was frowned on for 'respectable' women to
love dancing or to perform in public, Roman men enjoyed watching
their hired performers or dancing slaves. Ovid describes a dancer of
ancient Rome:

> Graceful her arms, moving in subtle measures;
> insinuatingly she sways her waist,

and Martial another:

> She trembles, quivers, sways her loins, and wriggles . . .
> She'd make Hippolytus forget himself.[28]
> [Hippolytus, in the myth of Phaedra, was fabled for his chastity.]

Although the dancers were not primarily prostitutes, many of them
supplemented their earnings through the sale of sexual services and
were able to attain some degree of luxury in their lives, living in
comparative grandeur. Occasionally, too, some of these dancer-
prostitutes managed to reach the top of the whores' hierarchy,
achieving the status of the envied *delicata* and *famosa* courtesans, who
were the Roman equivalent of the Greek *hetairae*. But the majority of
these élite whores were in fact women from 'respectable' families,
educated, beautiful and accomplished; consequently, many historians
are at a loss to explain why they chose prostitution as their profession.
Sanger condemns the women's 'lust and avarice' whilst Henriques
vaguely alludes to 'a desire for money' or 'inclination' as motivations.
But the most compelling reason for a high-born woman to become a
courtesan was of course to be financially autonomous, and under no
obligation to any one man.

The *delicatae* and *famosae* lived independently, receiving visits from
several wealthy clients; occasionally a subservient husband lurked in
the background, acting as a discreet pander. The courtesan Cytheris,
formerly an actress, was mistress to Brutus, Mark Antony and the
poet Gallus; like their Greek sisters, the *delicatae* and *famosae* numbered
among their clients the greatest of Roman society, from senators to
writers. Many of Rome's finest poets frequented the courtesans –
among them Catullus, Ovid, Horace, Tibullus and Propertius – and
were fond of celebrating the women in verse. Propertius, whom the
historian Otto Kiefer refers to as 'the greatest of Roman elegiac poets',

used his affair with the courtesan Cynthia as inspiration for some of his best work. Interestingly, although Kiefer refers slightingly to Cynthia as 'a common prostitute', his own descriptions of her make it clear that she was educated, witty, refined, elegant – easily the intellectual equal of the poet himself: 'She had . . . the many-sided education which distinguished women of her type from respectable matrons. Not only could she dance, sing and play the lyre, like others of her class, but she was able to criticize poetry . . . indeed, she composed it herself.'[29]

Alas, Cynthia's love was not romantic: 'Cynthia loves not power nor follows honour,' wrote the dejected Propertius: 'She judges every lover by his purse.'[30] His was a classic client's lament: Cynthia's freedom to sleep with whomever she wanted made the relationship a battlefield of jealousies, for the poet wanted her attention all to himself. In the end, Cynthia held the reins of power: the whore's eternal power over the sexually dependent client. This gave the poet's passion a masochistic quality, since he was always destined to be the 'loser' in love, or, rather more accurately, in his romantic fantasy; indeed Propertius was blatant in his celebration of the pain – physical as well as emotional – he 'suffered' in his relationship with Cynthia:

> I relished fighting with you in the lamplight
> last night, and hearing all your furious oaths.
> Why throw the table down when mad with liquor
> and wildly hurl the wineglasses at me?
> Come, come, attack my hair in your savage temper,
> and scar my features with your pretty nails!
> Dearest, threaten to burn my eyes to ashes,
> split my robe wide open, and bare my breast!
> Surely all these are signs of a true passion . . .
> Love is uncertain, if it never rages . . .
> may my worst enemy have a placid girl!
> May those who know me see the marks of biting
> and bruises which betray a happy love![31]

From this account of her behaviour it is clear that Cynthia was indulging in the sadistic habits of her own slave-owning class; the catch here is that she was applying them to a male member of the ruling class. On another occasion, Propertius describes an incident when, calling unannounced on the poet one evening, Cynthia discovered him frolicking in the garden with two girls 'of easy virtue'. She flew into an unholy rage:

> She wounds my face with angry random blows,
> she bruises all my neck, her teeth leave bloodstains,
> and most she strikes my eyes, the criminals.
> Then, when her arms were tired with my chastisement,
> she caught the pageboy hiding behind the bed . . .
> he prayed me on my soul for mercy, grovelling . . .
> but what could I do, I, a prisoner too?
> At last my pleading hands procured her mercy
> and grudgingly she let me touch her feet.[32]

Here Propertius is describing the sexual predilection of the masochistic client who takes pleasure in grovelling to his mistress and relishes the violence he receives from her. His submission and humiliation are the vital components of this erotic game. Cynthia, meanwhile, has a choice of targets for her aggression – first, her paying lover and then his unfortunate slave, whom she victimizes. Not so the 'respectable' Roman matron who, as Juvenal records, had only the second alternative:

> But you should know what Everywoman does
> at home all day. Suppose her husband turns
> his back to her in bed. God help the housemaid!
> The lady's maids are stripped, the coachman's thrashed
> for being late (punished because another
> slept), rods are broken, bleeding backs are scourged
> and lashed: some women keep a private flogger.
> She scourges while her face is made up, talks
> to her friends, examines a gold-braided frock
> and thrashes, reads the daily paper through
> and thrashes, till the thrasher tires, and she
> screams GO NOW, and the inquisition's over.
> She rules her home more savagely than a tyrant.
> Has she an assignation, wants to look
> more beautiful than usual, quick, he's waiting
> under the tree, or in Queen Isis' brothel . . .
> poor Pescas combs the mistress's hair, her own
> tattered, with naked shoulders and bare breasts.

> 'This curl's too high.' At once the oxhide thong
> lashes the wretch: her crime was a coiffure.[33]

True to form, Juvenal denounces his 'Everywoman' with all the viciousness and loathing he can muster, and in doing so manages to complete the cycle of sadistic pleasures, by verbally lashing the 'respectable' lady. Yet at the same time Juvenal does provide evidence that women have never been immune to the corrupting influence of absolute power, whether high-class whores or high-born 'ladies'. There is also evidence to suggest that antagonism between the two groups of women was as much a feature of Roman life as it was in Greece, with the wives openly envious of their whore-sisters' financial and sexual freedom.

The dramatist Plautus gives us an idea of this mutual hostility in the following dialogue between two *delicatae*:

Right it is and proper
that women in our walk of life
should be good friends and allies.
Look at the blue-blooded ladies, wives in lofty families,
see how close they keep their friendship, how they back each other up.
If we copy them and do the same, we have a hard life still.
They detest us! and they wish we needed all their help:
never to stand on our own feet,
always to need *their* backing,
humble suppliants.
Go to them! You'll soon prefer to leave them, for they flatter us
openly at least; in private, if they get the chance,
they pour cold water on us,
say we catch their husbands,
rival themselves in love.
They try to keep us down . . . we're freedwomen![34]

Like the *hetairae* of ancient Greece, the Roman *delicatae* depended upon their professional solidarity in order to protect themselves from the acrimony of jealous or neglected wives. Also like the Greek courtesans, they forged their own unique and diverse culture, scorning the subordinate position of the 'respectable' Roman matron and preferring to retain the ancient whores' tradition of complete sexual autonomy, of not 'belonging' to any one man. The Roman courtesans prided themselves on their education, wit, beauty and independence; and they knew themselves to be Rome's true 'freed-women'. Perhaps this was why the wives of the Roman ruling class envied and resented them so much. This antagonism between two groups of women was set to recur throughout history, and at its core lay the greatest irony of all: the fact that the wife needed the whore in order to boost her own status. After all, if the 'Bad' woman did not exist, with whom could the 'Good' woman compare herself favour-ably?

There remains one group of sex workers specific – and vital – to the Roman empire who are never mentioned in the history books: the so-called 'camp followers', captured female slaves who provided the 'rest and recreation' facilities required by soldiers on lengthy foreign campaigns or in remote postings on the outer reaches of the empire. Rome in fact owed a great debt to these unfortunate women, since its economy for a long period relied entirely on continual military expansion; and even after the final boundaries of the empire were drawn, the empire's security depended on the frontier garrisons.

Unlike the Greeks, who had not discovered this basic fact of warfare (it was said of the soldiers who besieged Troy for ten years that they hadn't seen a whore for so long that their arses were as wide as the gates of the city), the soldiers of ancient Rome were efficiently catered for: wherever they were stationed a row of brothels was constructed, alongside the rest of the garrison. These brothels were crude indeed, consisting of a cell for each woman, as in the cheapest houses in Rome. The slaves who staffed them were exploited with military ruthlessness and efficiency: their role was to fuck day and night for the 'relief' of the soldiers, as well as patching up wounds, cooking and performing all the other domestic duties the men took for granted. Their only hope of escape from this miserable existence was to be bought by some officer who was rich enough to possess a woman for his own private pleasures; this to some extent would have lessened the sex-slave's workload. But for the majority of 'camp followers' life was an endless round of degradation, disease and exhaustion, with no hope of reprieve. This exploitation of soldiers' sex-slaves epitomizes the organization of the lower-class sex industry in ancient Rome. In a society in which slavery was the norm, where a huge mass of slaves existed for the sole purpose of creating wealth for the benefit of a tiny élite, it was inevitable that sex work should develop along parallel lines, with masses of women (and children) devoting their working lives to the pleasure of those who had money.

Historians have invariably blamed unbridled sexuality for the decadence and decline of ancient Rome; but the true corruption always lay rooted in the institution of slavery – human misery on an immense scale. All work performed by women and men of the slave and impoverished proletarian classes was degraded in its conditions; it is therefore disingenuous to insist – as many have – that prostitution was a uniquely degrading occupation. On the contrary, for many women, becoming independent whores was a positive choice on their part.

Sexuality and prostitution were accepted facts of life in ancient Rome; openly displayed, exploited, discussed and celebrated. The Roman state was not ashamed to profit publicly from the trade; after the emperor Caligula imposed a tax on whores, it enjoyed immense profits. This continued even when the first Christian emperor, Constantine, came to power and saw fit to trawl in a tax of such abundant return that he labelled it the *Chrysargyrum* – gold and silver. Senators and high state dignitaries directly profited from the sex industry by renting properties to brothel-keepers, and they flouted no law in doing so. Prostitution at all levels was deeply entrenched in the Roman economy, with no shame or stigma attached either to the buyers or the sellers of sexual services; from the 'divine' emperor to the lowliest slave, it was simply another activity of the society. Tenuous links with sacred prostitution still existed, and there was no notion of 'sin' involved in the institution. It was not until after the downfall of Roman civilization that the new religion of Christianity completed its stranglehold on official dogma; and the men in power began to pay lip service to the idea that prostitution was morally reprehensible, and that whores themselves were an evil and corrupting menace to the rest of society. The prelude to a new era of woman-hating was set to begin.

CHAPTER FOUR

The Dark Ages:
the Martyrdom of Sexuality

Woman is a temple over a sewer.

Tertullian

Suppress prostitution, and capricious lusts will overthrow society.

Saint Augustine

With the disintegration of the Roman world, Western history enters the period we call the Dark Ages, an era that roughly spans the five centuries that followed the collapse of the Roman empire. The historical thread almost – but not quite – disappears from view. If we look closely, and with particular reference to the early Christian Church, it becomes possible to shed some light on the events of this turbulent time, and we can then begin to speculate about the lives of the women who worked as prostitutes throughout the period.

During the 5th century AD the Roman empire, weakened by internecine strife, economic crises, and slave and peasant rebellions, began to give way to the pressure of the Germanic tribes on its borders. As these invaders swept across Western Europe and into France, Britain, Spain, Italy itself, and even as far as North Africa, the empire was shattered. Naturally enough, the effect of these defeats on the empire's city-based culture was devastating. The invader tribes brought with them their own forms of social organization, which were agricultural and village-centred, although they did not represent any kind of return to the ancient matriarchal-style farming communities. Barbarian warlords grabbed huge estates for themselves, with a view to establishing their own kingdoms, while free peasants and former slaves settled wherever they could, forming their own village-style communities.

There followed centuries of social chaos, with the Germanic tribes at constant war among themselves. Monetary currency and written language disappeared, along with the authoritarian 'peace', or law and order, that the Romans had imposed on the ancient world. Inevitably, the focus of life shifted from the urban centres, now decayed and empty, to the rural regions: this, for whores, must have been the single most catastrophic change in their lives during the entire period.

For the cities of the Roman world had been the sex trade's major centres; with their disintegration, and the subsequent introduction of a less complex society with fewer needs, no money and, above all, no demanding leisure classes, the urban whores saw their way of life vanish virtually overnight. But although many must have perished in the collapse of the society of which they had been so central a part, many must have adapted to the new conditions in which they found themselves. Whores had already built a strong tradition of surviving in the face of seemingly impossible odds.

It seems likely that many women would have taken to the road, plying their trade from village to village, in the form of bartering; while others would have followed the various armies which swept back and forth across Europe. A not inconsiderable number were destined to become 'hearth-girls' – a euphemism for the concubines kept by Christian priests.

But if the whores themselves were not obliterated with the decline of ancient Rome, their cultural tradition certainly was. The civilizing arts of love, pleasure and knowledge, erotic and otherwise, were eclipsed during the Dark Ages. Traces of the lost arts were to re-emerge later, in the cult of courtly love, but the ancient tradition of a proud and celebratory female sensuality was gone for ever. Ironically, the one tradition to survive intact from the Roman world throughout the Dark Ages and into all the societies that followed was that of the destroyer of the female arts: the Christian Church.

When the emperor Constantine embraced Christianity on his deathbed in 337, the new religion became the official creed of the whole imperial structure; and a whole new race of beings came into existence – the clergy. These men spread like wildfire, swiftly becoming a vast bureaucracy that outweighed the Roman state itself.

They saw as their chief task the conversion of the lowly masses of the empire, and throughout the 4th and 5th centuries, at a time when the empire had already begun its decline, priests in their thousands ranged through the territories in an orgy of conversion. They were highly successful, so much so that the culture of the peasants in the provinces of the Western empire – France, Spain and Portugal – was changed irrevocably; even their languages changed within this relatively short timespan, from the old Celtic to the simplified versions of Latin that were later to develop into their modern-day counterparts of French, Spanish and Portuguese.

After the fall of Rome, the Church alone survived intact, and emerged as a power within its own right. This was to have dismal consequences for Western sexuality in general, and women in particular; as the writer Elizabeth Fisher notes in her *Women's Creation*: 'Christianity took the Jewish mistrust for women and added its own repressions, in a much stricter interpretation of Hebrew mores. Significant was the fact that the idealisation of chastity was transformed into a loathing for the body and a severe condemnation of sexual acts.'[1]

Already, the men of the Christian Church were inventing dogma that went far beyond anything Christ himself was supposed to have said or written; for although Jesus condemned 'lust' in either thought or deed, he seems to have considered whores mere small-fry sinners, who would reach the Kingdom of Heaven well ahead of such major-league transgressors as the Pharisees. And it should be remembered that it was the whore Mary Magdalene who played such a central role in the drama of Christ's life. This former Galilean prostitute became one of the master's most devoted followers; it was she who first discovered his empty tomb and first witnessed his resurrection. Most notably – and unfortunately – however, it was Mary Magdalene who provided the Christians with the prototype for one of their favourite role-models: the Repentant Whore (a stereotype which remains popular in Western society to this day; ironically it is the latterday feminist movement that has taken over its promotion where the Church left off).

The Magdalene also served as an effective counterpart to Christianity's other Mary – history's first, pre-technological virgin mother. But in spite of the relative importance of these two women in the life of Jesus, the early Church was swift to reject the female principle and it went on to become increasingly misogynistic, its doctrines and ideology shaped by the likes of Saint Paul, Saint Augustine, and other patriarchal relics of the Roman empire. Sexual paranoia became a basic Church tenet, largely as a result of the new religion's reaction to the moral and sensual life of the declining Roman empire. Yet although the Christians deplored the riotous amorality of the Romans, they enthusiastically adopted and enlarged upon the theory of duality that had originated with the thinkers of ancient Greece and passed into Roman thought: that of a world divided into opposing pairs, with women, the flesh and the senses identified as evil, and men, with their disembodied 'spirituality', identified as godlike – and never the twain should meet. The philosopher Musonius Rufus (1st century AD) first began to propagate the notion that was later to become Christian doctrine: sex in marriage was just about permissible for the purposes of procreation; sex for pleasure, and especially extramarital sex, were anathema.

One of the greatest influences on later Christianity was the Alexandrian Jew Philo (c.30 BC–c. AD 45) who combined Jewish and Graeco-Roman teachings. Philo was apparently under the impression that the 'original sin' of Adam and Eve was none other than sexual desire. According to this theory, all the ills of civilization stemmed from the indulgence of sensual pleasure, and had nothing whatsoever to do with greed, slavery, tyranny, or war.

Another important figure who helped shape the official credo of the early Christians was Plotinus, a mystic of the 3rd century AD, who taught that the soul could only be united with God-the-father if it threw off all earthly influences and, above all, transcended sexual feelings. While Plotinus argued that it was necessary for the wise man to discipline his body to become indifferent to sex, his eager and attentive follower Porphyrios went even further, and condemned *all* forms of pleasure as sinful.

It was against this intellectual backdrop that the new religion of Christianity evolved. Although such asceticism was never a prominent feature in the teachings of Christ, later propagandists for the religion drew heavily from the anti-sexual traditions of earlier patriarchal thought. Most notable among these men was Saint Paul, whose teachings helped shape the ideology of the Christian Church. Predictably, Paul exalted celibacy as the ideal state for 'mankind'; equally predictably, his philosophy involved an inhuman attitude towards women in general, and whores in particular. The message was clear enough: 'Let a woman learn in silence with full submissiveness. I do not allow any woman to teach or exercise authority over a man; she is to remain silent.'[2]

It is important to remember that in the early, pioneering days of Christianity, the Church had been a loose collection of democratic congregations, in which women often held equal rank with men. Following Christ's apparently tolerant attitude towards them, women enjoyed some measure of freedom and authority within the new religion; they could teach, and even administer sacraments. Thanks to Paul, however, a process began which turned Christianity into a male-dominated, hierarchical power structure that could be and was used as a religious and ideological tool for the Roman state. Paul's distortions of early texts became the basis for later Christian doctrine; and his misogyny was equally institutionalized by the Church.

Paul saw women as 'naturally' inferior beings; they were a kind of afterthought on the part of God, when the serious business of creating men was done with. Although early texts of Genesis had described man and woman as being created in the image of God, Paul saw man alone as 'the image and glory of God'. Woman got the booby prize; she was but 'the glory of the man'. According to Paul, 'the man is not of the woman' (contrary to biological evidence) 'but the woman is of the man.'

Inevitably, whores drew the fiercest of Paul's attacks; to him they epitomized the 'basely sexual' nature of womankind. Conveniently forgetting his Saviour's affection for the Magdalene, Paul wrote a despairing diatribe against prostitutes and their clients:

Do you not know that your bodies are members of Christ? Shall I therefore take the members of Christ and make them members of a prostitute? Never! Do you not know that he who joins himself to a prostitute becomes one body with her? For, as it is written, 'The two shall become one flesh'.[3]

Paul has a lot to answer for, as far as the Church's condemnatory attitude towards women is concerned. But he was far from exceptional in his fear and hatred of the female sex. Anti-woman tirades were the order of the day among the early Church Fathers. In his 'Apparel of Women', Tertullian of Carthage (150–230) recommended that women should wear perpetual mourning clothes in order to atone for the 'ignominy and odium of having been the cause of the fall of the human race'. He elsewhere dismissed women as 'dripping breasts, stinking wombs, and crying babies'. (Women of his time could be forgiven for thinking they were damned if they didn't procreate and damned if they did.)

'Every woman ought to be filled with shame at the thought that she is a woman,' wrote the charitable Clement of Alexandria. Not to be outdone, Saint John Chrysostom (he who reputedly pushed a woman off a cliff to demonstrate his immunity to temptation) disclosed that 'among all the savage beasts, none is found so harmful as woman.'

These and other similarly grim outpourings demonstrated the Church's attitude towards female sexuality; the other side of the coin was reflected in its official policy towards men's own sensuality. This can be summed up by the words of Saint Jerome, who instructed men to 'regard everything as poison which bears within it the seeds of sensual pleasure.'

The early Church's main authority on sexuality and marriage, however, was Saint Augustine, who was also vehemently anti-pleasure. 'I know nothing,' he wrote 'which brings the manly mind down from the heights more than a woman's caresses and that joining of bodies without which one cannot have a wife.'[4]

Before his conversion to Christianity, Augustine had been a follower of the 3rd-century prophet Mani, which goes some way to explaining his foibles. For Mani was extreme even by the misogynist standards of the day; according to him, the two kingdoms of Light and Dark (no prizes for guessing which sex lined up in which corner) were locked in a perpetual struggle. The earthly body and its desires were creatures of the Dark, and the sole purpose of life was to 'liberate' man's spirit into the Light. Sexual intercourse – what else? – chained the soul to Satan, thus blocking its progress into the realm of Light. Mani went so far as to denounce legitimate marriage as a sin, and procreation as a defiler of the 'divine substance'.

If nothing else, this kind of anti-sexual ranting shows us the tenor of the Church Fathers' twisted logic. To these deeply disturbed men, *life itself* was a monumental error, to be rectified only through denial, alienation and above all through the fear and loathing of the female body. According to the new religion, celibacy was the desired state for the whole of mankind. This was what they preached, at least. What they practised was, as usual, another matter.

The Church's pursuit of power and the negation of sexuality went hand-in-hand, for the men of God were strongly patriarchal. They rightly realized that the patriarchy could not ultimately secure itself until women were abjectly under the control of men; the old battle was reaffirming itself, with vigour. By the closing years of the Roman empire, the Church's hysterically anti-female campaigns were gaining force. However, its attitude towards prostitution was curiously pragmatic.

Augustine put it in a nutshell: 'Suppress prostitution', he said, 'and capricious lusts will overthrow society.'

His statement shows to what extent the frantic advocacy of total abstinence was a sham. The Church Fathers had to address the real world of men who would always persist in flouting the rules of monogamy; and they knew this. In the end a compromise was reached: a marriage of Augustine's pragmatism and Paul's outright woman-hating. From now on, whores were to be specifically identified with the evil lusts of the flesh; the prostitute was regarded as a kind of drain, existing to siphon off the sexual effluent which prevented men from rising to the level of their God. In this way the Church could have its cake and eat it: on the one hand they condemned all sexual intercourse, on the other they accepted the existence of prostitution as a necessary evil. Needless to say, the Church's attitude to prostitutes themselves was unambiguous:

> Do not hearken to a wicked woman; for though the lips of a harlot are like drops from a honeycomb, which for a while is smooth in thy throat, yet afterwards thou wilt find her more bitter than gall, and sharper than a two-edged sword.[5]

Whores were officially excommunicated from the Church so long as they practised their profession – and good Christian men were constantly urged to keep their distance from the 'strange and wicked women' – not that they took any notice of their spiritual mentors' advice.

In the meantime, the dreary revulsion and prejudice that so many of the Greek and Roman élite had felt towards women became firmly rooted into the religious establishment. After the collapse of the empire, the Christians had *carte blanche* to denigrate the female principle. Reading and writing became the preserve of the monasteries; anything that was not sanctioned by the Catholic Church was destroyed. It is estimated that this destruction of the arts, libraries and other cultural records of previous societies 'set the intellectual development of the human race back . . . thousands of years.'[6]

What the Church did not or could not destroy, it assimilated; thus we meet many of the old pagan deities – including several former whore-goddesses – reconstituted as Christian saints. A surprising number of prostitutes who had seen the error of their ways were also admitted into the ranks of sainthood; the result was a bizarre genre of pious legend, often with a dollop of religiose sadism thrown in for good measure. The story of Saint Mary the Egyptian is one of the better known.

Mary entered a brothel in Alexandria at the age of twelve, and worked there for seventeen years, until one of her clients brought her the message of Jesus Christ. The spirit moved her to make a pilgrimage to Jerusalem (paying her way in kind by servicing the ship's men), and, after she had taken in the city's holy places, she retired as a hermit to the desert, where her new-found saintliness enabled her to survive for 47 years on three loaves of bread.

Other legends surround the sainted ex-whores Afra, Pelagia, Thais and Theodota; and in keeping with the genre, severe mortification of the flesh is a recurring theme in the women's stories. This was how they made the transition from Wicked Harlot to Christian Saint. Saint Afra was martyred during a period of persecutions at the time of the emperor Diocletian (3rd century), along with three of her former colleagues, Digna, Eunomia and Eutropia. Saint Pelagia had been an actress and grand courtesan in the city of Antioch; she was converted by the Bishop Nonnus, travelled to Jerusalem disguised as a male, and lived there for the rest of her life as the holy 'eunuch monk' Pelagius. Saint Theodota meanwhile became a martyr when she died under torture, after refusing to recant her beliefs.

All of these women had to renounce their female sexuality, by becoming a hermit, a transvestite, or a corpse. But it is surely in the story of Saint Thais that the ultimate in Christian sado-masochistic climaxes is reached. The historian Bullough gives us the gory details, in which, as a penitence for her past sins, Thais was 'walled up in a cell in a convent in which there was but one small opening through which she received a little bread and water. Her cell became filled with excrement, until at the end of three years she was thoroughly cleansed of her sins.'[7]

The irony of being 'cleansed' by being walled up in a shit-filled cubicle seems to have escaped Bullough; none the less, this grisly little tale provides us with a supreme example of the Christians' obsession with flesh, sin, and filth.

There were other more direct associations between prostitution and early Christianity, however. It seems that some of the earlier sects displayed an intriguing tendency to revert to the pagan practices of former times. Curiously enough, it is William Sanger, that most Christian of writers, who alone provides a glimpse of these practices: 'Prostitution,' he writes, 'may have again become a religious rite in certain deluded or knavish sects. Nor was it unnatural, unjust though it certainly was, for the heathen to charge Christianity at large with the vices of those of its followers who worshipped in a state of nudity, and accompanied prayer with promiscuous intercourse.'[8]

The line between these very early manifestations of Christian worship and those of their pagan predecessors was indeed thin; and must have worried those austere Church Fathers a great deal. Clearly, if the new religion did not distinguish itself from the older ones, it would have no future, and this realization must have been a decisive factor in the Christian insistence on purity and celibacy. The asceticism of its lower clergy became a preoccupation with the higher echelons.

In order to promote its anti-sex policies, the Church had to keep its own house in order; the hierarchy therefore demanded that its clergy stay celibate. As usual, the (clergyman's) flesh proved weak on this issue. Priests throughout the period of the Dark Ages, and indeed well into the Middle Ages, openly married or kept concubines known as *focarii* (hearth-girls). Popes, bishops, councils and other senior churchmen repeatedly debated and condemned the practice and hopped from one side of the fence to the other on the issue of clerics' wives. In about 304 the Council of Elvira declared that priests should live in celibacy with their wives or be drummed out of holy orders, and this was followed in 386 by a decree of Pope Siricius to the same effect. They might as well have saved their breath; the married clergy formed powerful lobbies and staunchly, often violently, defended their non-celibate lifestyles: 'Monks repeatedly murdered their abbots for preaching better behaviour to them.'[9]

To further complicate the issue, some elements within the Church establishment hit on the bright idea of charging the recalcitrant priests a special licence-fee, the *couillage*, for keeping hearth-girls. Attempts to ban the concubines continually ran foul of the money interests involved, for corruption was rife. As late as 1129 the English king Henry I manipulated this situation to his own advantage.

A papal decree banning (once again) the hearth-girls had been issued, and Henry met with the country's leading churchmen ostensibly to confirm and enforce the holy ban. Having secured their co-operation, Henry promptly double-crossed them by allowing the priests to keep their concubines – with the proviso that the *couillage* was paid directly to him. This solution must have kept all the parties involved reasonably happy: the Church leaders were to all intents and purposes doing their duty; the king was getting his cut; the priests retained their sexual partners – and the whores were still in business.

But the new religion was as intolerant in its attitudes towards 'wicked women' as the Hebrews had been. Although it would be many centuries before the Christians could achieve the kind of power that would enable them to persecute, torture and punish prostitutes, the Church was already institutionalizing the hatred of female sexuality to a degree previously unseen. From this period onwards the religious establishment chose the Female Sinner as dumping-ground for the whole of society's projected sexual guilt and hypocrisy. Once again, women were divided into Good and Bad; with an added bonus for the former, especially mothers, who were now permitted to bask a little in the glow of the Virgin Mary's halo. Unless she repented, the whore had no such luck. To the Men of God, she was to bear the entire burden of their vilification of the body and its senses, and of life itself. This denial was to take its toll in the centuries to come, up to and including our own times. The proliferation of guilt, trapping human beings in an endless cycle of sin-and-repentance was the cultural legacy of the Dark Age of early Christianity. Western society is only now beginning to crawl out of its shadow.

CHAPTER FIVE

The Roaring Trade: Prostitution in Medieval Europe

Youre faces tricked and paynted bee
Youre breastes al open bare
So far, that a man may almoste see
Untoe youre lady ware.

15th-century verse[1]

Out of the confusion and turmoil of the Dark Ages a new order began to emerge that was later to be known as feudalism. Originating in northern France early in the 10th century, it rapidly spread throughout the rest of Western Europe, reaching Britain with the Norman conquest of 1066. From the collision between the disintegrating Roman aristocracy and the invading barbarian warlords a new ruling class had arisen, an élite of nobles whose wealth was based on the land they conquered and the produce of the peasants who farmed it. This new nobility was a class of professional warriors; their principal form of wealth was land ownership and they continually sought to expand their fortunes by seizing more, either from their own neighbours or from foreign powers.

Warfare was therefore endemic; it could break out at any time, totally disrupting the lives of the ordinary people who worked the land. The feudal lords began to realize that the only way in which they could offset the resulting chaos and in some way stabilize their system was by outright control of the peasants. This they achieved through the institution of serfdom, which was a medieval form of slavery (although technically not defined as such).

The serf was a peasant farmer who lived and worked on land

belonging to his lord; he was the property, body and soul, of his master and was legally bound to the land he farmed. In return for the 'protection' of the lord and his fighting men (against the other lords in the area and their fighting men), the serf was duty bound to provide certain services and pay taxes: for example, as well as farming his own subsistence plot, he would give a fixed number of days' labour to the land attached to the lord's manor. Male serfs were also called upon to serve their masters at times of war, which were frequent enough to ensure that the life of these peasants was by no means a settled one. At any time the serf's farming work could be disrupted by fighting, at home or abroad; a situation which in turn created a constant stream of displaced working people who would roam the countryside looking for work. Women numbered highly among them: widows, daughters, and wives of these itinerant serfs. For them, prostitution would have been a means of survival.

The sale of commodities obviously gravitates towards the market, and commercial sex was never an exception to this rule. When at the end of the Dark Ages the Western economy began to revive, country markets and travelling fairs began to appear throughout Europe. The historian James Cleugh paints a vivid picture of these caravans of commerce – and pleasure:

> [They] attracted thousands of men and women of all types. Knights and men-at-arms acted as protective escorts. The clergy came to look after their flocks. Pedlars and artisans swarmed, almost overwhelming the merchants and their staff who formed the nucleus of these roving crowds. They had to be entertained on their long journeys. The gipsy-like musicians and singers, tragedians and comedians, tumblers and conjurors, charlatans and bear-leaders . . . together with their families, the younger women and girls being practically all ready to sell their favours, plus a great host of professional harlots and a few runaway nuns, swelled the multitudes of wayfarers.[2]

Some prostitutes specialized in servicing pilgrims; men who were journeying to pay their respects to the sites of holy martyrdom apparently felt the need to be 'entertained' en route. Their female counterparts, meanwhile, often supported themselves by selling sex in the towns they passed through; indeed some women pilgrims actually changed career in mid-journey. Throughout the period various popes castigated the women who had fallen by the wayside on the road to Rome and taken up the oldest profession in the towns of France and northern Italy. This practice was especially prevalent amongst English nuns.

Whores were also in great demand, as ever, with the armies which roamed the countryside of medieval Europe; not only in the capacity of sexual servants but also as cooks, cleaners, and above all, nurses. In 1476, for example, 2000 of these fellow-travellers accompanied the army of Charles the Bold, Duke of Burgundy. The writer Hilary Evans comments that these 'camp followers': 'lived off the soldiers, providing them with food, drink and sex'.[3] Which rather begs the question, who did the living, off whom?

In fact the prostitutes who serviced the armies of medieval Europe were regarded as essential, to the extent that, by the end of the period, most armies had special officers whose duty was to regulate the women and make sure they were performing their numerous duties adequately. But who precisely were these women? Certainly, they did not represent an independent, autonomous class of prostitutes. Most historians do not bother to speculate about them at all, beyond the flippant assumption that the women were parasitic, sex-starved vagrants who insisted on attaching themselves to the roaming armies of the day. But it is much more likely that the vast majority were displaced peasant women who had no other means of survival. As 'camp followers' they could take their chances alongside the men. Living conditions must have varied, according to the success and fortunes of the soldiers they were following, from the hellish to the tolerable.

During the crusades of the early Middle Ages thousands of whores made the journey to the Holy Land with the Christian armies. On one notable occasion in 1189, French soldiers recruited a shipload of women and refused point-blank to set sail without them. It is said that on one of the French forays, in the mid-13th century, the saintly King Louis IX was so distressed by the prevalence of prostitution on his campaign that he ordered the removal of a brothel tent that had been erected within sight of his royal pavilion. Louis was also reputed to have made an example of one unfortunate knight who had been plucked from a brothel tent. The man was given a choice of punishments: he could either give up his horse and armour and leave the army in disgrace, or be led around the camp at the end of a rope –

by the whore with whom he had been found dallying. Rather than suffer the latter indignity, the knight errant chose to make his own way home.

It is from the time of the crusades that we come across one of history's most haunting and fascinating documents about prostitution. Written by the 12th-century Arab chronicler Imad ad-Din, it is a breathtakingly ornate description of the whores who accompanied the European armies to the Holy Land:

> There arrived by ship three hundred lovely Frankish women, full of youth and beauty, assembled from beyond the sea and offering themselves for sin. They were expatriates come to help expatriates, ready to cheer the fallen and sustained in turn to give support and assistance, and they glowed with ardour for carnal intercourse. They were all licentious harlots, proud and scornful, who took and gave, foul-fleshed and sinful, singers and coquettes, appearing proudly in public, ardent and inflamed, tinted and painted, desirable and appetising, exquisite and graceful, who ripped open and patched up, lacerated and mended, erred and ogled, urged and seduced, seductive and languid, desired and desiring, amused and amusing, versatile and cunning, like tipsy adolescents, making love and selling themselves for gold; bold and ardent, loving and passionate, pink-faced and unblushing, black-eyed and bullying, callipygian and graceful, with nasal voices and fleshy thighs, blue-eyed and grey-eyed, broken-down little fools. Each one trailed the train of her robe behind her and bewitched the beholder with her effulgence. She swayed like a sapling, revealed herself like a strong castle, quivered like a small branch, walked proudly with a cross on her breast, sold her graces for gratitude, and longed to lose her robe and her honour. They arrived after consecrating their persons as if to works of piety, and . . . maintained that they could make themselves acceptable to God by no better sacrifice than this. So they set themselves up each in a pavilion or tent erected for her use, and opened the gates of pleasure. They dedicated as a holy offering what they kept between their thighs; they were openly licentious and devoted themselves to relaxation . . . They plied a brisk trade in dissoluteness, adorned the patched-up fissures, poured themselves into the springs of libertinage, offered their wares for enjoyment, invited the

shameless into their embrace, mounted breasts on backs, bestowed their wares on the poor, brought their silver anklets up to
touch their golden earrings, and were willingly spread out on the
carpet of amorous sport. They put up the tent and loosed the
girdle after agreement had been reached . . . They took the
parched man's sinews to the well, fitted arrows to the bow's
handle, cut off sword-belts, engraved coins, welcomed birds
into the nest of their thighs, caught in their nets the horns of
butting rams, removed the interdict from what is protected,
withdrew the veil from what is hidden. They interwove leg with
leg, slaked their lovers' thirsts, caught lizard after lizard in their
holes, disregarded the wickedness of their intimacies, guided
pens to inkwells, torrents to the valley bottom, streams to pools,
swords to scabbards, gold ingots to crucibles, infidel girdles to
low dungeons, money-changers to *dinar*, necks to bellies, motes
to eyes. They . . . maintained that this was an act of piety
without equal, especially to those who were far away from home
and wives. They mixed wine, and with the eye of sin begged for
its hire.[4]

This remarkable passage is a masterpiece of ambivalence: Imad
manages to both celebrate and condemn the women and their
activities in a literary orgasm that almost – but not quite – obliterates
his pious disapproval. His words remain to this day an unparalleled
testament to the paradox of male attitudes towards female sexuality.

With the revival of the agrarian economy came the rise and development of urban centres of commerce. The towns and cities of medieval
Europe expanded rapidly from the 11th century onwards, and urban
life came to be dominated by a small class of rich and powerful
burghers: the bourgeoisie. These merchants, bankers and lawyers
amassed their fortunes through trading privileges laid down in law;
they then went on to use their wealth to monopolize power within
their urban communities. Meanwhile, as the bourgeoisie sought to
establish itself, the urban populace beneath them continued to grow,
consisting mainly of craftsmen and their families, small traders and
shopkeepers, apprentices, and an ever-swelling mass of the very poor.

For these lower classes, the towns presented an alternative to a
lifetime's bondage to the lands of the rich lords: in the towns and cities
there were no nobles to tie them down or force labour and military

service from them. Thus all over Europe, bands of men, women and
children made for the towns, seeing in them a sanctuary from the
depredations of the lords. But town life was not without its dangers:
the urban economy revolved, by necessity, around the market, so that
those without something to sell – whether agricultural or craft
produce and skills – were forced to find work as servants of the
bourgeoisie, or live on the margins of society, scratching a living from
begging – or crime.

Women, however, always had a commodity they could trade on;
they could support themselves and their families by selling sex. At
first the authorities tried to discourage prostitution by refusing to let
whores work within the town; the women simply set up their houses
and brothels directly outside the town gates – close enough for urban
clients who wished to 'slake their thirst' without having to go too far
out of their way. Eventually the authorities capitulated and permitted
the prostitutes to operate inside the townships, although there were
often restrictions. In some places, whores were only allowed to work
after dark; at Nuremberg, for example, they were restricted to the
first two hours after sunset in summer, the first three in winter. The
women carried lanterns, in order to be easily located.

The revived trade began to flourish once again, with whores openly
soliciting wherever the fancy took them. We meet our first historically
attested prostitute since the fall of Rome on the streets of London in
1058: 'Seated on a jade mule, her locks falling over her shoulders,
holding a little gilt rod in her hand . . . by means of indiscreet clothing
she attracted the travellers' attention in the highways.'[5]

As in the times of Rome and Athens, whores once again solicited in
the streets, or worked from inns and taverns, as well as their own
rooms or homes. Some reports also cite the churches as favoured
haunts. Bath houses, or 'stews', regained their former popularity; for
although the custom of public bathing had virtually disappeared
during the Dark Ages, returning crusaders brought with them a taste
for the Arab custom of the *hammam*, and public bathing once again
became fashionable. Records of 12th-century Paris show that the city
had a public bath in nearly every street by that time; and if anything the
practice was even more widespread in Germany, where every village
kept its own stew. Bathing was communal, a social ritual, with large
tubs capable of seating half a dozen people at a time. Two-seaters were
discreetly made available for those desiring greater intimacy.

The bath-keeper would announce opening-time every day by

blowing a horn, whereupon people of all classes would promptly strip at home and walk to the stews, often completely naked (this presumably took place during the summer months only). The medieval German writer Guarinonius complained about the practice:

> How often indeed does the father run naked from the house through the streets to the bath with his naked wife and naked children? How often do I see . . . young girls of 10, 12, 14 and 16 years quite naked and with only a short linen bath robe, often torn . . . as sole covering in front and round the shoulders! With this and bare feet, and one hand held behind for propriety, out of the house they go, through the long streets in broad daylight, running to the bath![6]

Inevitably, facilities for eating, drinking, gambling and sex became optional extras at the local bath-houses, until eventually the word 'stew' became synonymous with brothel.

During these early years of the medieval revival of the sex trade, prostitution remained a small-scale and largely freelance profession that conformed to the general conditions of market trading at the time. Whores worked independently at all levels, mostly on a small-scale, cottage industry basis. Some women were successful and enterprising enough to own and operate brothels, inns or taverns, where they effectively set themselves up as the 'madams' of medieval urban culture. Most important of all, though, is the fact that the whores of this period were an accepted feature of society. In spite of the Church's fulminations against them, the women maintained a high profile and were free from exploitation either by the state or by individual men. For prostitute women of medieval Europe, this was one of the least oppressive eras they had known. It was not, of course, destined to last.

By the 12th century, European civilization and culture were beginning to flourish once again, and men of the educated classes began to pit their wits against the 'abhorrence' of prostitution. In this they were greatly encouraged by their spiritual advisers, who continued in the woman-hating tradition of their predecessors. Thus the Bishop Huguccio of Pisa (d. 1210) advised his flock that 'sex (could) never be without sin', while his pupil Pope Innocent III went on to add that 'conjugal intercourse is never committed without itching of the flesh, and heat and foul concupiscence, whence the conceived seeds are befouled and corrupted.'[7]

These two jovial statements summarized the Church's official attitude towards sexuality; it was the same old song. For women, who were to bear the brunt of the Church's abhorrence, it was a case of heads I win, tails you lose. The myth of the Virgin Birth gave the men of God all the ammunition they needed; for it was against this impossible ideal – the asexual mother – that women were measured. In fact there was absolutely no way in which a woman could win in the rigged game of medieval Christianity. While she was required to be perfect, theologians pronounced her naturally sinful, lustful, and lacking in the intellectual and spiritual faculties which raised men to semi-divine status.

But the churchmen were faced with an uphill struggle, for women's position in early medieval society was a relatively strong one, a legacy of the Dark Ages, when centralized patriarchal authority had collapsed with the Roman state. Women maintained their active participation in public life well into the Middle Ages; noblewomen managed the family estates for years at a time while their husbands were away waging war, and women of the merchant classes were often full partners with their husbands, running the whole business when their husbands went abroad trading. The peasant women of medieval Europe shared in the hard labour of the fields and often worked independently as brewers, bakers and butchers; whilst the women of the towns and cities engaged in a seemingly endless variety of occupations: they were silk-spinners, embroiderers, clothes-dealers, pedlars, wax-mongers, pancake-makers, bath-managers, weavers, brewers, book-sellers, illuminators, fish-sellers, 'women who shampooed heads' – and whores.

Nor were medieval women noted for their submissiveness. Women's historian Margaret Wade Labarge remarks that they 'had quick sharp tongues which they delighted in using to deflate male pomposity.'[8] Labarge quotes one Robert Holcot, a Dominican friar, who complained that it was 'the whole apparatus of womanhood, that it should be garrulous and wandering, impatient of quiet, not wishing to stay at home'. The good friar then went on to muse: 'It is a matter of astonishment that women, who have fewer teeth than men (and teeth are needed for talk) should yet have not less to say than men, but a good deal more.'[9]

From their position of relative strength, women were not likely to feel much sense of shame if they chose to trade in sex. Such defiance must have greatly exacerbated the wrath of the men of God. From their point of view, a crusade of sorts was called for. In opposition to the sexually assertive and financially independent whore the Church promoted the saintly nun as an ideal of womanhood, with her vows of poverty, chastity and, above all, obedience. Out of this tradition came the impetus for the conversion movement, with preachers vying with each other to convert as many repentant whores as they could. Early in the 12th century the French cleric Henry the Monk urged his many followers to convert harlots – and then marry them. But it was somewhat later that the movement really took off. In the last decade of the century, Fulk of Neuilly founded the convent of St Antoine near Paris, as a shelter for former prostitutes. For those women who were not inclined to spend the rest of their lives in otherworldly seclusion he provided dowries; having collected 1000 livres from the 'honest bourgeoisie' of Paris, and 250 livres from the city's students. In 1198 conversion fervour reached Pope Innocent III, who exhorted all good Christians to reclaim whores. As a result, a full-scale movement spread across France, Germany and Italy; it was officially sanctioned by Pope Gregory IX in 1227. Great numbers of the lower clergy found themselves caught up in the enthusiasm – notwithstanding their own penchant for entertaining whores – and campaigned noisily to 'save' wicked prostitute women. From their point of view, each penitent whore was a potential Saint Mary of Egypt.

Monastic communities of converted former whores, imaginatively designated 'Magdalene Homes', sprang up all over Europe, mostly but not exclusively founded by the clergy (other patrons included the nobility, some rich burghers and the occasional member of royalty: Queen Esclarmonda of Majorca was reported to have endowed a home at Perpignan).

The regime in these Magdalene Homes varied widely, from the liberal to the punitive. One example of the more enlightened type was to be found at Montpellier, in southern France. Here, prostitutes of all ages were welcomed; older women could retire in guaranteed security, while their younger colleagues were permitted to make use of a one-year trial period if they wished to leave prostitution and re-enter respectable society. Other institutions took a harsher line: needless to say, these were in the majority. At the home in Avignon, records show that the authorities were choosy about the women they accepted: only those under the age of 25 were allowed to stay there, and even then there was a catch – after eight to ten days of lodging, the inmates were obliged to take holy vows. Infringements of minor house rules were dealt with severely; women were placed on a diet of bread and water, and even imprisoned.

Many institutions saw to it that the ex-whores did good honest (and unpaid) work as spinners or embroiderers; some offered the good life in the form of market gardening. One of the most famous of the Magdalene Homes was founded in Vienna in the 14th century, and known locally as the 'Soul House'. Although it resembled a convent, this particular home was of the more liberal variety, and its inmates were never required to take the vows. The house had an excellent reputation, since many of the women who passed through it went on to marry respectable citizens; it was regarded as a great success, and attracted plenty of public funds. In 1480 the German Emperor Frederick III granted its occupants the right to sell wines from their vineyards, and the house rapidly grew into a centre of local trade. Encouraged by this, the women diversified and began selling sex; but the revival of their former trade proved to be the downfall of the Soul House. Outraged by its transformation into a brothel, and perhaps more than a little piqued at the disruption of their school for wives, the good burghers of the district promptly evicted the whores, and the building was donated to an order of Franciscan monks.

Throughout the entire period of the conversion movement it must be remembered that the numbers of penitent prostitutes were minuscule in proportion to the total number of women who ignored the churchmen's clamour, preferring to continue with their legitimate trade. The movement itself peaked in the early years of the 14th century, then went into a dramatic decline as the Black Death raged through Europe in the 1340s and 1360s, decimating the inmates of the Magdalene Homes.

In the meantime, and with consummate hypocrisy, the Church developed its other line on prostitution, based on the 'necessary evil' argument of the early Fathers. Thus they were obliged to both accept and condemn the practice, and this they did with typical patriarchal doublethink. The 13th-century theologian Saint Thomas Aquinas put it in a Christian nutshell, arguing that 'fornication' was *always* sinful – but sometimes necessary: 'Prostitution in the towns is like the cesspool in the palace: take away the cesspool and the palace will become an unclean and evil-smelling place.'[10] Aquinas also endorsed prostitution on the grounds that it was necessary in order to prevent the world from being engulfed in 'sodomy', the medieval term for illicit sex.

The Church set out its policy towards the sex industry on the basis of this forked-tongue attitude, so that even as the conversion movement was sweeping through Europe, the men of God were complacently setting out to define and regulate the 'illicit' trade. Clerical lawyers provided each other with plenty of work in the attempt to establish the whore's position in society. Setting themselves up as the bureaucrats of immorality, these men spent their lives labouring over the fine print of canon law and debating among themselves on the various issues that surrounded prostitution. One of the more challenging questions to keep the quills busy was that of the profits earned through the trade. In an early 13th-century manual for confessors, Thomas of Chobham devoted four chapters to the issue of whores and their rights. He argued that the women were no different from other traders and workers in that they provided a form of labour in hiring out their bodies. This was a legitimate trade, and by the standards of secular justice there was nothing wrong if the whores received the correct fee.

His seems an enlightened attitude, on the face of it, but Thomas was a Christian and, like the rest of his brethren, he frowned on sexual pleasure; an outlook which in turn led him to pronounce that if a prostitute derived pleasure from any sexual transaction, she should forfeit her fee, for it no longer constituted an act of labour.

> Prostitutes should be counted amongst the wage-earners. In effect, they hire out their bodies and provide labour . . . If they repent, they may keep the profits from prostitution for charitable purposes. But if they prostitute themselves for pleasure and hire out their bodies so that they may gain enjoyment, then this is not work, and the wage is as shameful as the act.[11]

Thomas considered that any make-up or artifice designed to make a woman more attractive to the client was a form of deception, for the client would then be paying more than the real value of the 'goods'. In such circumstances, wrote Thomas, the whore was entitled to keep but a fraction of her money; the remainder should be given back to the poor deceived client – or donated to the Church.

During the 12th century the first laws specifically aimed at controlling prostitutes were concocted by French jurists; but since there were virtually no forces of 'law and order' to carry them out on the scale they demanded, these laws were largely ineffective. Nevertheless, their very appearance on the statute books meant a turning-point for the women concerned. For by now, secular lawyers from the urban bourgeoisie were muscling in on the act, and even though these men accepted the existence of prostitution, they also took the Church line that marginalization and victimization of women who practised the trade were desirable.

The lawyers' strategy was to deprive whores of their basic legal rights: thus they were prohibited from testifying in court, and from accusing others of committing crimes against them. This was tantamount to inviting men to abuse prostitutes. The *Très ancien coutume* of Normandy (1200) spelled it out even more graphically: the rape of prostitutes was sanctioned by law.

Encouraged by the Church, several European rulers and emperors of the early medieval period made it their business to issue edicts on the subject of prostitution. The famed and ferocious crusading Emperor Frederick Barbarossa was one of the first to do so when in 1158 on the road to Italy he tried to prevent his soldiers from consorting with whores. The men were threatened with 'severe punishment' (the historians neglect to specify what this entailed); the whores had their noses cut off. Some historians interpret this as an attempt to rid the imperial army of its camp followers, which seems unlikely, in the light of the services these women provided. Whatever the case, Barbarossa's action against the whores was a uniquely sadistic one; it also seems to have been a speciality of his, for in Naples, a city which came directly under his rule, the emperor ordered that procuresses and adulterous women were to have their noses slit.

Other royal decrees made specific attempts to outlaw prostitution, although none succeeded in doing so; notably the 12th-century Code of Alfonso IX of Castile. Although prostitution *per se* was not made illegal, it was sufficiently ringed with prohibitions to make it almost impossible for a whore to work without running foul of the law. The Code specifically focused on third-party 'profiteers' of prostitution, naming five categories who could be punished: wandering procurers, or 'traffickers in debauch' (to borrow one of Sanger's arch phrases) – these were to be banished; landlords who let their houses to prostitutes (these men could be fined and have their houses impounded); procurers who kept brothels and hired out women (if the women were slaves, they were to be freed; if not, they were to be married off with a suitable dowry; failure to comply was punishable by death for the procurer); husbands who prostituted their wives (again, punishable by death); and 'ruffiani', or pimps and ponces (penalties included flogging for a first offence, banishment for a second, and being sent to the galleys for a third).

Whilst ostensibly a piece of legislation designed to protect women from exploitation by third parties, Alfonso's Code effectively prevented whores from going about their business in peace. A prostitute could not work from a brothel or house unless she owned the property; she could not have a husband or lovers for fear of the punishments they might incur as pimps or procurers. And if a woman was found to be supporting a pimp, she herself would be stripped of her clothes and publicly flogged.

The net result of this kind of official harassment was the isolation of women who worked as prostitutes in Alfonso's realm. For in order to work at all, whores must have been obliged to reach 'arrangements' with the authorities whereby in return for immunity from the full weight of the law the women handed over a portion of their earnings – not to mention free sex on demand.

Only one medieval ruler went so far as to try to ban prostitution outright: France's Saint Louis IX; he who took umbrage at the presence of whores during the crusades. Before he left for Palestine in 1269, Louis pursued another kind of crusade in his native land. His aim was to eradicate all prostitution from the country.

At that time, the whores of Paris were enjoying a particularly high status. They had organized themselves into a professional guild, with none other than Mary Magdalene as their patron saint; they had even succeeded in building themselves a chapel, featuring a stained-glass window which showed a prostitute-saint embarking on a boat to Jerusalem. In the picture, the whore had her skirts hitched up around her thighs, and beneath the panel an inscription informed worshippers 'how the saint offered her body to the boatmen to pay for her passage'[12] – recalling the tale of Saint Mary the Egyptian.

Louis was so incensed by this sacrilege that in 1254 he issued an ordinance declaring that: 'Public prostitutes are to be expelled from the fields as well as the towns, and once these warnings or prohibitions made, their goods are to be seized by the judges of the localities, or taken, by their authority, by anyone else, unto the tunic and the robe.'[13]

Had the ordinance been successful, it would have not only outlawed prostitutes throughout the land, but also confiscated their homes and possessions, to the benefit of the local lords. Needless to say, it proved impossible to implement such a sweeping edict. Feeble attempts were made, with some local authorities providing patchy support and banishing the whores they managed to round up, but as fast as they could move against the women, others moved in to take their place. Nevertheless, for a short time the whores of France kept a somewhat lower profile than they had previously – until the bourgeoisie started to complain that their wives and daughters were being besieged by sex-starved young men. A mere two years after initiating the ordinance, King Louis was forced to admit defeat and repeal it, and France returned to its former laissez-faire policy on prostitution. Louis made a final, almost pathetic, attempt to proscribe the sex trade, decreeing as he left for the crusades in 1269 that all brothels throughout the land were to be destroyed, but with the king away nobody took any notice. The historian Fernando Henriques, commenting on Louis' ill-fated laws, makes the pertinent point that: '[his] edicts were about as effective as the Volstead Act in the USA in preventing the consumption of alcohol. All attempts to eradicate prostitution by legislation and force have met with the same result.'[14]

With the rise of 'respectable' bourgeois society, 'public order' became an issue. When honest citizens began to complain about the commotion made by some whores and their clients and hangers-on, the city councils stepped in and ordered the rabble outside the city walls. The first recorded instances of this public banishment were at Carcassonne and Toulouse, in the 13th century, when prostitutes were accused of causing 'great evil and damage' by some of the local burghers. The city consuls of Toulouse decreed that 'no public prostitute shall stay nor live in any way or for any time within the walls of Toulouse or its suburbs.'[15]

However, issuing decrees was one thing; having them carried out was another. Given the lack of effective law enforcement at the time, not to mention the general corruption of officialdom, it seems unlikely that the decrees had any lasting effect. City authorities throughout the Europe of the early Middle Ages made continuous attempts, at the behest of 'respectable' society, to control the movements of lower-class whores (streetwalkers in particular) and confine them to certain quarters of the cities, but contemporary accounts reveal that the women swarmed through the streets wherever and whenever they chose.

Coupled with the attempts at regulating the movement of lower-class prostitutes was the old ploy of imposing dress-codes. As in earlier times, the concerned bourgeoisie wanted desperately to 'mark' prostitutes, thus setting them apart from 'respectable' women. What seems to have incensed them most of all was the prestige these lower-class whores enjoyed, and their ability to flaunt clothes that other women of their class could only dream about. A prostitute's earnings often enabled her to adopt the trappings of a comfortable, middle-class lifestyle; this was a social sin as much as a sexual one, in the eyes of the scandalized burghers. These good men did not merely have whores in mind when, in the London of 1351 they dictated that 'lewd' or 'common' women were to go 'openly with a hood of cloth or ray single [i.e. striped and unlined] and with vestments neither trimmed with fur nor lined . . . *so that all folks shall know of what rank they are*' (my italics).[16] In fact this ordinance was aimed at *all* lower-class women, lest they entertain ideas above their station – it just so happened that whores were the only ones with the economic power to put such ideas into practice.

Authorities throughout Europe turned their attention to the whore's sartorial niceties. In Leipzig it was decided that she should wear a yellow coat, trimmed with blue; whereas in Vienna the whore should tie a yellow kerchief across her shoulder; in Augsburg she should wear a green sash. Berne and Zurich, meanwhile, decreed red caps; Bergamo, yellow cloaks; Parma, white cloaks; and Milan, black cloaks. In Bristol, as in London, striped hoods were to be worn, while officials in Avignon banned furred cloaks, especially of squirrel or lined with fine cloth. Also outlawed were silk and cloth-of-gold bonnets, gold and silver rings, and chaplets of coral, amber, silver or precious stones. The penalty for sporting any of these luxury items was confiscation and a huge fine. Finally, the whores of Avignon were ordered to distinguish themselves by wearing a red shoulder-knot, as were those of Paris.

Legal records of the period show that the women habitually disregarded these petty rules, with the result that many municipal authorities made a tidy profit from the legalized theft – 'confiscation' – of the wages of sin. One well-documented case brought against a Parisian whore in 1459 details the forfeit she paid for wearing 'immodest' dress: the woman was stripped of her shoulder-cape of satin 'furred with minniver', a silver-gilt belt, and her coral rosary. Also confiscated was the woman's book of hours 'with a silver clasp';[17] books, too, were expensive items, and therefore considered the preserve of the pious, educated and 'honest' wives of the bourgeoisie.

It is not known to what extent – if any – the women who worked as prostitutes in medieval Europe chose to follow the dress-codes that were laid down for them, but it is certainly the case that throughout the period, whores were often the fashion leaders of their time. In 15th-century England they created the look that was popular with many wealthy women – deeply-cut cleavages that exposed most of the breasts. Many whores took this style to its extreme limit, baring their rouged nipples. A contemporary verse berates the women:

> Youre faces tricked and paynted bee
> Youre breastes al open bare
> So far, that a man may almoste see
> Untoe youre lady ware.

In his poem *The Tunnyng of Elynour Rummyng*, John Skelton (1460–1529) ruminates, somewhat obsessively, on the sartorial habits of the 'harlots of this time':

> Some wenches come unlaced
> some huswyves come unbraced
> with theyre naked pappes
> that flyppes and flappes
> it wigges and wagges
> like tawny saffron bagges.

Given the fact that, in its wider economic significance, prostitution in the medieval towns sustained much of the trade in luxury items – 'wine, spices, jewellery and high-quality cloth'[18] – it seems reasonable to assume that the whores of the period continued to flaunt their stylish, flamboyant and often sumptuous clothing in the face of a disgruntled bourgeoisie. Interestingly, not all of the latter were men. The 15th-century French writer Christine de Pisan was one of the few female commentators of the period, and as such is often cited by modern feminists as a pioneer of women's liberation. In fact de Pisan was a kind of medieval Tory lady, who advised the whore to repent and seek her salvation in self-help. She should 'leave her old haunts and fancy clothes, live simply and soberly in a small chamber on a good street. There she should have honest neighbours and take licit employment'[19] – as a lowly-paid scullion in a wealthy (but honest!) household, for example.

This type of 'modest proposal' was to surface again and again throughout history, usually uttered by privileged and educated feminists who would never question their assumption to know what was best for their less fortunate sisters. Then, as now, they refused to see that the dearth of work options for lower-class women was the problem, and that favouring straight work over sex work was no solution. Then, as now, whores solved this problem by opting for the better living they could make through selling sex.

CHAPTER SIX

An Unholy Trinity:
Organized Prostitution, the Crown and the Church

Methinks it must be a bad Divinitie
That with the stews hath such affinitie.

14th-century ballad

Throughout the first part of the Middle Ages royalty, the clergy and secular authorities had neither the will nor the power to suppress prostitution. In spite of the Church's fulminations against all sexuality, medieval Europeans were in practice tolerant and uninhibited about sexual behaviour.

As for the royal families and their noble followers: with a very few exceptions, such as the saintly and eccentric Louis IX, the majority were as dissolute as ever. The practice of keeping *gynacea* – households of young and beautiful concubines – was widespread; these were the Western equivalent to the harem. Some European princes amused themselves by turning their *gynacea* into exclusive brothels for the use of their close friends: William IX of Poitou was one such royal pander. In 1324 the English King Edward II built himself a 'retreat' on the south bank of the Thames; the house was staffed with whores, for the king's relaxation and recreation.

The élite did not restrict themselves to their own private sexual facilities, however; they availed themselves of the services of public prostitutes when the occason called for it. When the Holy Roman Emperor Sigismund visited Berne in 1414, the council ordered all the local brothels to open their doors to the royal entourage – free of charge. Municipal councils often arranged for visiting dignitaries to be met and fêted at the gates of the city by parties of whores; when, for instance, Henry VI of England visited Paris in 1431, he was confronted at the Porte de Saint Denis by a fountain in which three naked *filles de joie* frolicked. His Majesty was ten years old at the time. In 1461, Louis XI was greeted at the gates of Paris by a similar *tableau vivant* (precursor of the modern-day striptease); the contemporary writer Jean de Roye paints a vivid picture of the scene: 'And there were also three very handsome girls, representing quite naked sirens, and one saw their beautiful, turgid, separate, round and hard breasts, which was a very pleasant sight, and they recited little motets and bergerettes.'[1]

Apparently, however, not all the whores who greeted royalty were quite so charming, or obliging; at Nuremberg in 1471 their 'welcoming party' is reported to have held the Emperor Frederick III to ransom.

As for the Church, its hypocrisy and corruption knew no bounds. Throughout the entire period the men of God, even while they spouted an endless stream of anti-pleasure propaganda, were unable to control their own sexual habits, let alone those of the populace. Moralist observers of the Middle Ages constantly bemoaned the clergy's behaviour. The French writer Jean Gerson exhorted people to: 'Open your eyes again, and see whether nowadays the cloisters of nuns have become as it were brothels of harlots, and whether the consecrated monasteries of canons become as it were market places and inns'; while the Dutch humanist Erasmus complained that:

> There are monasteries where there is no discipline, and which are worse than brothels . . . A monk may be drunk every day. He may go with loose women secretly and openly. He may waste the Church's money on vicious pleasures. He may be a quack and a charlatan, and all the while an excellent brother and fit to be made an abbot.[2]

In Britain, Chaucer and Langland satirized monks and nuns who took vows of chastity and then proceeded to flout them openly. Clearly, the Church did not set a good example to its flock. But the rot set in at an early stage. Some of the best-documented evidence of the clergy's profligacy emerges from 13th-century Paris, when the student-clerics mingled with prostitutes in the same quarters of the city, often sharing the same lodging-houses. Writing around the year

1230, Jacques de Vitry describes 'buildings which house a college upstairs and a brothel downstairs; on the ground floor professors are lecturing while below them the prostitutes exercise their shameful trade.'[3] With regard to the apprentice divines themselves, de Vitry comments that 'they count fornication no sin. Prostitutes drag passing clerics to brothels almost by force, and openly through the streets; if the clerics refuse to enter, the whores call them sodomites.'[4]

Other contemporary accounts show the students to have been rather more willing clients. The great French writer François Villon was a student in Paris at this time; he was later to join many of his fellows in a vagabond-like life that took him all over the country, consorting with whores and criminals. But the special affection Villon retained for his formative years in underworld Paris is expressed in his poem 'The Ballad of Fat Margot', in which the writer celebrates his life as a student cleric – and pimp.

> I love and serve my lady with a will,
> but that's no reason you should call me mad.
> For her, I'd hitch on sword and shield to kill.
> She is the goods to please my every fad.
> When customers arrive, I lightly pad
> to bring in pots and wine. I serve them cheese
> and fruit, and bread and water as they please
> and say (depending on the tip I'm paid)
> 'Do call again and come here at your ease
> in this whorehouse where we do a roaring trade.'
>
> But then fine feelings end and turn to ill.
> When she comes home without the cash, I'm had.
> I cannot stand her, she has blood to spill.
> I hate her, grab her belt, gown shift and plaid
> and swear I'll flog the lot and her to add
> up for the loss of all the nightly fees.
> But hands on hips she hollers if you please
> how I am anti-Christ and won't get paid.
> I grab a club and sign her, nose to knees,
> in this whorehouse where we do a roaring trade.
>
> We make peace then in bed. She takes my fill,
> gorged like a dung-beetle, blows me a bad

and mighty poisonous fart. I fit her bill
she says, and laughing bangs my nob quite glad.
She thwacks my thigh and, after what we've had,
dead drunk we sleep like logs – and let the fleas.
Though when we stir her quim begins to tease.
She mounts; I groan beneath the weight – I'm splayed!
Her screwing soon will bring me to my knees
in this whorehouse where we do a roaring trade.'[5]

This, then, was the attitude of the God-fearing student cleric – and it was shared by many of the fully-fledged clergy, whose standing as moral exemplars within their communities was seized upon by the craftsmen of the day. Sculptures lampooning the sexual antics of the clergy were carved in many of the great cathedrals of the period and, according to Sanger: 'In one place a monk was represented in carnal connection with a female devotee. In others were seen an abbot engaged with nuns, a naked nun worried by monkeys, youthful penitents undergoing flagellation at the hands of their confessor, lady abbesses offering hospitality to well-proportioned strangers, etc., etc.'[6]

In fact the clergy's sexual excesses extended to the very top of the Church hierarchy, where carnal indulgence could be seen at its most blatant and outrageous. When for example Pope Innocent IV left Lyons after an eight-year visit, Cardinal Hugo, who accompanied His Holiness, made some interesting remarks in his farewell address: 'Since we came, we found but three or four brothels. We leave behind us but one. We must add, however, that it extends without interruption from the eastern to the western gate.'[7]

Many individual high-ranking churchmen gained reputations for their licentiousness – among them Archbishop Christian of 12th-century Mainz, who was notorious for spending more time and money on whoring than on official Church business – but they were hardly exceptions to the rule. Any great Church gathering of the high-and-mighty could be guaranteed to provide prostitutes with a veritable bonanza. It was reported that more than 1500 *filles de joie* made their way from all over Europe to ply their trade at the Council of Constance in 1414; further, that each of these ladies could expect to earn up to 800 gold ducats in a single night, servicing the ecclesiastical élite. And during the four years that the Council met, a certain 'Poggio of Florence' was said to have made his fortune by laying on sexual leisure pursuits for the assembled clergy at his 'thermal baths' in neighbouring Baden.

Prostitution also thrived within the Holy City of Rome – even inside the Vatican itself, where many whores lived in properties owned by the Church. The women went about their business openly, parading the city streets in the company of the clergy, most of whom appear to have devoted their lives to the quest for sexual pleasure. The example was, as is often the case, set from the top: the lower orders of the clergy took their cue from the Holy Fathers themselves. Dr Sanger, reduced to near-apoplexy by the carryings-on of the popes and their high-ranking colleagues, gives us few of the spicy details; he simply lists Popes John XXII and Alexander VI, as 'monsters'; describes Julius II and his successor Leo X as 'syphilitic through excessive carnal indulgence', and reports that Sixtus IV was 'rotten from his middle to the soles of his feet'.[8]

Pope Alexander VI (a Borgia, incidentally, and father to the infamous Cesare) is reputed to have enjoyed holding little family soirées in the papal palace. At one such entertainment, 50 whores were hired to dance with servants and guests alike:

> At first they wore their dresses, then they stripped themselves completely naked. The meal over, the lighted candles, which were on the table, were set on the floor, and chestnuts were scattered for the naked courtesans to pick up . . . crawling about on their hands and knees between the candlesticks. The Pope, the Duke [Cesare Borgia] and his sister Lucrezia all watched. Finally, a collection of silk cloaks, hoses, brooches and other things were displayed, and were promised to those who had connection with the greatest number of prostitutes. This was done in public. The onlookers, who were the judges, awarded prizes to those who were reckoned to be the winners.[9]

From this and other accounts it can safely be deduced that the ancient Roman tradition of sexual excess was alive and kicking within the medieval Vatican.

Leaving aside its own outright depravity, the medieval Church had an excellent – and much more pragmatic – reason for wanting the sex industry to continue: quite simply, it was making a good income from the proceeds of prostitution. Like the kings and the nobles, the clergy fully realized that to outlaw prostitution would lose them a source of both pleasure and profit, for with the growth of the urban centres, and the consequent development of a centralized power-base, the church/court rulers of medieval society had become major landlords and property owners in the towns and cities. As such, they were directly involved in the sex industry, collecting inflated rents from the brothels they owned.

At the head of the aristocratic families, the kings set a fine example. William the Conqueror (or William the Bastard, as his grateful subjects dubbed him) owned brothels in Rouen; and the Plantagenet Kings of England, including Richard the Lionheart, were the owners of extensive property in the Parisian red-light districts. In early 13th-century Paris, a *roi des ribauds* (king of bawds) was officially attached to the court, his duty being to extract 'fees' from the city's whores and camp followers – a royal pimp, in other words.

But it was the Church which held the major economic interest in the medieval sex industry, both as landlords and through more direct exploitation. According to some historians, there were brothels where the inmates doubled as nuns and whores (an intriguing combination and, as it happens, a popular theme in present-day strip-club acts); but while such blatant promotion was probably rare, the Church ownership of whorehouses was undeniably rife. Many bishoprics, abbeys and monasteries – even the papacy itself – included brothels amongst their properties. The Pope's 'marshals' zealously collected fees from His Holiness's Roman brothels; and even this was not enough for some Popes: Clement II passed legislation that required all prostitutes in his houses to bequeath half of their belongings to a convent when they died (this law apparently proved unenforceable; no further details of it appear). More effective was the system of licensing and direct taxation of whores introduced by the syphilitic Pope Sixtus IV in 1471, the revenues from which partly financed the building of St Peter's in Rome.

There are a few reports of even more enterprising men of God, notably one Bishop Johann of Strasbourg who, in 1309, went so far as to pay for the construction of a magnificent new brothel in that city. The revenues generated by these Church-run brothels must have been immense – but they were still not enough. To augment the Church coffers still further, the prelates made a policy of collecting a small 'fine' from their lower clergy, whenever the latter visited a brothel.

The medieval Church's involvement in the English sex industry is well documented. One London nunnery, the Priory of St Mary Overie, let out its properties in Chancery Lane and Fetter Lane to whores in the city; and in 1337 the nuns of Stratford acquired the whorehouse known as 'The Barge', in London's Southwark district. The Dean and Chapter of St Paul's Cathedral owned brothels in the aptly named Cock's Lane, and in 1321 the Pope's envoy to Britain, Cardinal William de Testa, bought a brothel in the city for the Church's 'investment', naming it (in Latin of course) 'The Social Club'.

Probably the best-documented account of the Church's racketeering activities is the case of Southwark, the red-light quarter on the south bank of the Thames opposite the City of London. Here, too, the story of more overt state intervention begins.

The line of Church ownership of the site had been unbroken since the days of Saint Swithin, Bishop of Winchester, who built a monastery there in the 9th century. Whorehouses in the area date at least as far back as his time, and probably before, since this was near the site of the Roman military garrisons. William the Conqueror bestowed the manor on the Abbot of the Priory of Bermondsey, who in turn rented it to another Bishop of Winchester. The whores who worked in Southwark were so closely identified with their illustrious landlord that they became known locally as the 'Winchester geese' and the money they brought in helped finance the Bishop's lavish lifestyle. Indeed, so successful were the brothels that their income was to continue financing the Church's building programme throughout the entire Middle Ages. In 1161, in a unique 'ordinance for the governance of the stews', King Henry II guaranteed the bishopric's right to exploit the Southwark brothels for the next 400 years, and many of London's churches were subsequently built on the proceeds of prostitution.

Henry's ordinance also marked an important turning-point in the working lives of medieval prostitutes in another respect, although the effects were not immediately apparent. At a time when many other European authorities were resorting to attempts at mass banishment in order to control the growth of the sex trade, Henry's act could be seen as a harbinger of the movement to confine and regulate prostitution that was to sweep through the urban centres of mainland Europe in the following century. In effect, Henry's solution to the problem of the ubiquity of prostitution was to create a ghetto for the sex trade. He designated as an official red-light area the district that had been associated with the stews 'according to the old customs that had there been used time out of mind': Southwark. Henceforth the sex trade was banned from all other areas of the city. At once prohibitive and protective, the act also laid down in law the rights of whores to practise their profession – but it restricted their freedom of movement. The chronicler John Stow lists some of the rules pertaining to the ordinance:

No stew-holder or his wife should let or stay any single woman to go and come freely at all times when they listed [i.e. wanted].

No stew-holder to keep any woman to board but she to board abroad at her leisure. To take no more for the woman's chamber in the week but fourteen pence.

Not to keep open his doors upon the holydays. Not to keep any single woman in his house on the holydays, but the bailiff to see them voided out of the lordship.

No single woman to be kept against her will that would leave her sin.

No stew-holder to receive any woman of religion, or any man's wife . . .

No man to be drawn or enticed into any stew-house.

No stew-holder to keep any woman that hath the perilous infirmity of burning.[10]

Amongst the plethora of rules and regulations can be seen both rights and restrictions for the whores who worked at Southwark; also, interestingly, the clause mentioning 'the perilous infirmity of burning' demonstrates the authority's awareness of and concern about the existence of sexually transmitted diseases (although it was not until the 16th century that these illnesses acquired medical terms and social stigma).

On the prohibitive side, whores were not permitted to advertise their services by calling or gesturing – or by 'seizing men by the gown or harness'. They were also forbidden to 'swear, grimace' or throw stones at passing men, on pain of three days and nights in jail plus a fine of six-and-eightpence. But the huge volume of court cases for infringements of these rules show that whores frequently disobeyed the ordinance; nor did they confine their professional activities to

Southwark. Although by 1240, the City of London's Cock's Lane had also been designated an official red-light district, the whole of London was still regarded by many whores as legitimate territory; and they continued to roam wherever the fancy – and the demand – took them.

During the 13th century the movement to confine and regulate prostitution in the main urban centres spread throughout Europe, with varying degrees of success. The municipal authorities often used the bourgeoisie's terror that 'its' women would become 'corrupted' by the whores who wandered openly throughout the cities and towns as a pretext for their attempts to ghettoize the sex industry. Another worry for the authorities was the burgeoning criminal underworld. Although prostitutes were not outlaws as such, they were suspected of having a foot in both criminal and straight communities. By focusing on prostitutes, whose visibility made them an easy target, the lawmakers could claim to be dealing with at least one aspect of the lawless underworld. Moreover, the confinement of the sex trade to officially designated districts enabled the municipal councils to take a cut of the profits.

According to the historian E. J. Burford, the southern French town of Avignon was running a municipal red-light district as early as 1234; if so, the home of many a pope and prelate was one of the pioneers of the regulation movement. Other southern French towns and cities followed suit later that century; Montpellier was known to have designated a street as its municipal brothel quarter in 1285, and by the end of the century, both Nîmes and Toulouse (where profits from the city's officially sanctioned brothel helped finance the building of its university) were operating similar schemes. In all cases the laws that prohibited the women from working in other areas of the town were partly balanced by protective legislation that guaranteed a prostitute's right to work and live in peace: municipal whores were declared to be 'under the King's protection'. Some southern French authorities meted out public floggings to whores who persisted in working outside the municipal brothels, although the records show that, as often as not, these punishments were commuted to fines. (Records also show that some women, arrested on the charge of *pailhardize* – debauchery – were simply let free, on account of their being too poor to pay the fines.)

In Paris, meanwhile, the city authorities repeatedly banished women who attempted to work in 'respectable' streets; to no avail, for the independent sector continued to thrive. Records of 15th-century

Paris show that the trade was actively encouraged by at least one city provost: Ambroise de Lore. During his term of office whores had the freedom of the city, and according to one contemporary chronicle, the *Journal of a Citizen of Paris*, '[de Lore] always protected loose women, of whom through his laxity Paris had far too many, and got himself a bad reputation with everyone, because it was almost impossible for the law to correct the prostitutes in Paris, since he always protected them and their bawds.' The wealthier and more successful of their number often bought houses in 'respectable' areas outside the brothel quarter, and there they would entertain clients (often in the garden, to the chagrin of their honest neighbours). Some of these larger private houses operated in time-honoured tradition as private, women-owned, women-operated brothels. Lower-class whores meanwhile continued to use the city inns and taverns as meeting-places. A late medieval poem describes the services on offer there:

> *Avez vous faim? Vous y mangerez;*
> *avez vous soif? Vous y buvez;*
> *a-t-on froit? On s'i chauffera;*
> *ou chault? On s'i rafreschira.*

('Are you hungry? You can eat there; are you thirsty? You can drink there; are you cold? You can get warmed up there; or hot? You can get cooled down there.')

The great medieval cathedrals were also popular haunts for whores and their clients, since they were public spaces where the whole of society, from kings and their courts down to the lowliest beggar, might pass through in a single day. The records of Notre Dame de Paris show that *filles de vie* were regularly arrested within its precincts. The rewards must have been considerable, for prostitutes who were caught soliciting on Church property were sentenced by special ecclesiastical courts; punishments included being put in the pillory and, in some cases, being branded – not to mention the 'confiscation' of the woman's belongings.

Independent streetwalkers also worked on the banks of the Seine, underneath the arches of the bridges, and, weather permitting, in and around the city's public gardens. There was even the medieval equivalent of our latterday callgirl: the Parisian whore who specialized in visiting her clients at their home, hotel – or monastery.

Apart from the plethora of full-time prostitutes, Paris thronged with part-timers; these were women who sold sex on the side, to supplement their meagre incomes as spinners, serving-maids, and so on. The outraged men of the bourgeoisie constantly railed against the 'immorality' of these working-class girls. Indeed, 'every unmarried woman, and every girl who lived separately from her parents and outside the context of family, if she belonged to the popular and plebeian classes, was suspected of immorality.'[11]

At Strasbourg, too, the great meeting-place of France, Germany and the Low Countries, the sex trade's independent sector thrived, despite council attempts to regulate it. Whores from all over Europe flocked to the city, so great was the demand for their services. Trade was excellent – and quite blatant; Henriques notes that 'six streets alone accounted for fifty-seven brothels.'[12]

The authorities in Spain and Portugal also instituted the state brothel, although rather later than the rest of Europe; details are scarce. Early in the 15th century the magistrates of Lisbon voted through the money to construct a municipal whorehouse, after a 30-year campaign by local entrepreneurs; they then proposed to recoup their expenditure by taxing the women who worked there (in addition to the official cut). Valencia constructed an entire ghetto of brothels that was bounded by a wall with just one door. Virtually imprisoned within it, the whores who worked there were reduced to the lowest fees and had no control over their working conditions whatsoever. An official was posted at the entrance to this state-run brothel; he advised customers to leave their valuables outside the ghetto, in case of theft. Perhaps the councillors would have been better advised to have permitted the women to make a living wage.

In Italy, the laws that attempted to regulate prostitution fared no better than those in France and England. Licensed brothels were established in many urban centres, but the independent sector continued to thrive; for as elsewhere, the authorities were notoriously corrupt. In Venice (described by Sanger as 'a very sink of prostitution') there were attempts to regulate the trade along the lines of the French municipal brothel from 1360, but the sheer number of prostitutes made this an impossible task. The city was, incidentally, a celebrated centre for male prostitution; with one bridge in particular a favourite stamping-ground for whores of both sexes. A spirit of competition prevailed, the women parading with breasts unveiled, in order to upstage their transvestite brothers. The famous Ponte delle Tette exists to this day.

Meanwhile, the whores of Naples continued to ensconce themselves in the most beautiful palaces of the city centre, 'and there,' fulminates Sanger, 'with incessant clamour, congregated a horde of thieves, profligates, and vagabonds of every kind, until the chief quarter became uninhabitable.'[13] Naples provides us with an interesting example of the lawmakers' corruption; for here, extortion, not regulation, was the name of the game. It was even official: the whores of Naples were controlled by a special 'Court of Prostitutes', which consisted of many of the city fathers. Its system was simple and effective: a woman could be arrested at any time, and thrown into jail arbitrarily until an agreed sum of money was paid to the authorities; the woman was then released – until the next time. The court's reign of absolute power over the city's sex trade proved to be much more effective than mere regulation; it lasted until the end of the 18th century.

One of the legacies of the medieval attempts to regulate and confine the sex industry was the plethora of colourful and explicit street-names that spread throughout Europe; some of which still exist today.

Many German towns have streets whose names betray their original purpose: Frauengasse, Frauenpforte and Frauenfleck are among the more obvious ones. Popular, too, is the name Rosenstrasse, which springs from the old slang phrase for having sex with a prostitute: plucking roses. In Britain, most towns and cities still have their Love Lane or Maiden Lane, although some of the more explicit names have either vanished or undergone subtle variations in the intervening centuries. Thus the City of London's Codpiece Alley and Gropecunt Street are more innocuously known to us today as respectively Coppice Alley and Grape Street. Slut's Hole, Cuckold Court and Whore's Nest are no longer, alas.

In the beautiful, conservative and extremely wealthy Loire Valley town of Blois, in northern France, there were two well-known streets: the rues Rebrousse-Pénil (Hairycock Street) and Pousse-Pénil (Thrustcock Street); neither exists today. The medieval Parisians showed a particularly inventive flair when it came to pornographic street-names; thus we read of the rues Trousse-Puteyne (Whore's Slit); de la Con Réerie (Gaping Cunt); Grattecon (Scratchcunt); Puits d'amour (Loveholes). The rue Poil au Con (Hairy Cunt Street) is the only one to have survived, having retained a Chinese-whisper trace of its origins in the name by which it is known today: rue Pélican.

★ ★ ★

From the mid-14th to mid-15th centuries feudalism found itself in deep crisis – a crisis that broke on several fronts at once. Firstly, there was an ecological catastrophe, which came about as a direct result of the nobility's policy of land expansion through such means as forest clearance: a policy that had profited a few at the expense of the many. More land had consequently been put to the plough, but the drawbacks soon became apparent – hasty expansion and intensive farming wore out the new fields and, as the older land also began to erode rapidly, the amount available for farming shrank. The outcome was a series of massive famines in the early part of the 14th century, which devastated large numbers of the working population.

Meanwhile, an economic calamity loomed. Shortages of silver resulted in the debasement of coinages across Europe, which in turn led to a disastrous spiral of inflation. While the price of grain slumped – the rural population had declined and the demand for cereals was low – the luxury items the nobility bought with their agricultural wealth rocketed in price. The nobles, squeezed by this economic vice, promptly fell back on their age-old habit of scrapping among themselves for more land, thus inaugurating a series of devastating wars. The Hundred Years War, which swept across France from 1337 to 1453, and the 15th-century English Wars of the Roses were products of this 'Baronial gangsterism'.

As if all this were not enough, the people had another scourge to face: the Black Death, which ravaged Europe in the second half of the 14th century. It arrived in England in 1348 and by the year 1400 had claimed two-fifths of Europe's population. It now seems likely that the Black Death, thought to have originated in Asia, was the result of massive forest clearance. Rats which normally lived in the woods invaded the cities, infecting urban mice and rats with plague bacteria which were transferred to humans by fleas.

The ruling class was thus faced with an acute shortage of the labour it needed to produce its material wealth, and this in turn led to a rise in the price of labour itself. The nobility's subsequent attempt to force wages down by launching an offensive on the peasant population met with an unexpectedly violent resistance. Peasants' revolts spread throughout Europe in the late 14th and early 15th centuries: the Grande Jacquerie in France (1358) was one of the more famous rebellions, as was the Peasants' Revolt of 1381, in England. Although these risings were nearly all bloodily suppressed, it is clear that a shift of some kind in the class balance had occurred. Working people were fewer in number; hence their value was enhanced, so that through-out the 15th century, both wage levels and living standards rose steadily.

The situation of prostitutes at this time reflected the struggles that were going on throughout society. Brothels began to be associated –as far as the authorities were concerned – with dissent and public disorder, as was any place where working people might gather and air their grievances. The municipal councillors began to tighten up the laws that surrounded the sex trade. In 1417, the Mayor and Aldermen of the City of London issued an ordinance for the abolition of 'Illegal Stews' within the city. The new law lamented the many 'grievous abominations, damages, disturbances, murders, homicides, larcenies and other common nuisances' the independent whorehouses sup-posedly encouraged.

In many French towns and cities, the second half of the 14th century saw red-light districts reduced to a single street, these 'hot streets' being stringently owned and operated by the municipality. At the same time the practice of 'brothel farming' took off, whereby ownership and management of the state-run brothels increasingly passed into the hands of the high bourgeoisie. Burghers distributed among themselves the right to 'farm' brothels, in return for a flat fee paid to the town council. The net result of this semi-privatization of the sex trade was, inevitably, a loss of autonomy for the whores – and more control and profit for the new male bosses. This was accom-panied by an intensification of the burghers' struggle to monopolize the sex industry, by attempting to outlaw the streetwalker and thereby 'dissuade' women from working independently. Measures used to counter this effrontery were punitive, often brutal. In Avignon, whores were kept cloistered in the state brothel; they were not allowed to walk the streets at any time, in case they took it into their heads to do a little moonlighting. The brothel regulations stated that:

> If any girl has thus offended, and persists in her offence . . . then the Claviger, or Chief of the Beadles, shall lead her through the city by Beat of Drum, a red knot hanging at her Shoulder, back to the Brothel, and shall prohibit her from walking about any more, under the Penalty of being lash'd privately for the first offence, and of being whipp'd publicly and turned out of the House for the Second.[14]

By the late 14th century, any London whore found working outside Southwark or Cocks Lane faced the prospect of having her head shaved and being driven to the nearest prison in a cart especially designed for the purpose. Decked out with a red and white awning, to match the unfortunate woman's striped hat, it was accompanied by hired minstrels who would stir up the crowds of respectable citizens to gather at the gates of the prison and enjoy the spectacle of a prostitute being pilloried, whipped, and thrown out of the city gates.

Although this treatment was in theory aimed at any disobedient whore, in practice the sadistic pantomime was more likely to be waived in favour of a fine. The unlucky ones who suffered such a brutal public humiliation at the hands of the authorities were, as ever, the poorest and therefore the most vulnerable class of prostitute.

Historians of the medieval period are very divided on the issue of prostitution within that society. Some writers claim or imply that whores were in no way discriminated against, whereas others give the impression that prostitution was at all times illegal throughout the entire Middle Ages. In fact neither of these claims is true. In spite of the Church's condemnation and 'fuck then repent' policy, in spite of the authorities' attempts to regulate and control them, whores were never totally segregated from the rest of the community. Records show that these women were not the mere victims of confinement, regulation and barbaric punishment that some feminist writers like to depict; they had their own dignity and solidarity which they often brought into play in resisting both Church and state campaigns to exploit and control them. Likewise, any gains made by the legal pimps were offset by their total inability to stamp out independent prostitution. By the end of the 14th century, the women's confidence and economic power had increased, alongside that of the working population in general. Expediency triumphed: instead of paying good money to have whores flogged for working independently, or for dressing too well, the authorities preferred to fill their coffers with the hefty fines they could trawl from the women. These laissez-faire policies were the result of men's greed and pragmatism.

The invention of the municipal brothel also gave the trade a kind of official respectability, which in turn came to be reflected in law. In France at the end of the 14th century, whores had their legal rights restored to them: they could testify in court, freely enter into contracts, and bequeath their worldly goods to whomever they chose.

No longer was it a common practice to assume that a whore's profession legally excused her rape.

While whores were being treated leniently, however, the authorities operated a crack-down policy on anyone, male or female, who threatened their monopoly on pimping. Council measures against these third parties were severe, and were never waived in favour of a fine. Ordinances forbade whores to entertain 'beloved men', and one Parisian decree of 1416 threatened pimps and other male procurers with the pillory, branding and banishment. Females who 'procured' were to have their hair burnt off. But despite the harshness of their rulings, the authorities could not contain this aspect of the burgeoning independent sector any more than they could prevent the vast majority of women from working outside their municipal brothels. Freelancing *ruffiens* were men of the poor, for whom the stakes were high, and worth any amount of risk.

In common with other working people of the late 14th and 15th centuries, prostitutes were increasingly militant against would-be oppressors, and often engaged in open conflict with the men in power. Historical records give us tantalizing glimpses of the women's resistance during this period. At Châteauneuf-Calcernier in 1387 the local prostitutes staged an occupation of the town's royal officer's church pew, in a dispute whose reasons are not recorded. Respectable citizens were so outraged that they broke up the pew; the commune then had to pay for a new one. A better documented case concerns the whores of the Grande Abbaye, official brothel of the city of Toulouse. When King Charles VI visited them in 1389 the women petitioned him against city rules that now required them to wear white hoods and ribbons. The king granted them the right to dress as they pleased, so long as they wore 'a thin contrasting edging on one sleeve' – but this was not satisfactory to some of the good burghers of Toulouse, who took to assaulting the prostitutes whenever they went out. The women retaliated by going on strike; they retreated into their brothel and locked the doors. The recorded outcome of this dispute was that the whores moved to another quarter of the city, and both sides called a truce.

The whores of Toulouse were at the centre of another rebellion, in 1462; this time it was because the municipality had replaced their madam with a male 'abbot', whose instructions were to milk maximum profits out of their labour. The ensuing plea that the whores brought before the Parlement de Toulouse was 'essentially an indictment of the system of brothel farming as it was practised . . . in the mid-15th century.'[15] In other words, the whores were waging a conscious, organized resistance against the city fathers' attempts to turn their brothel into a sex factory. The women craftily incorporated bourgeois sentiments into their argument, and accused the municipality of encouraging vice. The brothel farmer, whom the whores called 'in derision . . . the abbot of the brothel', was in effect no better than a common pimp, since he wanted to extort as much profit as possible from them, by increasing the turnover of 'sinful sex'.

The women denounced brothel farming as 'a foolish custom' and put forward their own alternative plan of 'government', suggesting that one of their number should manage the brothel. The outcome of this particular dispute is not recorded, but we do know that the practice of municipal pimping continued unabated in the city of Toulouse, eventually becoming as unpopular with the citizenry as it was with the prostitutes themselves. By early in the next century, the citizens were protesting about town councillors who bought themselves plush robes with their ill-gotten gains from the exploitation of the brothels.

From the women's point of view, prostitution represented the only path of upward mobility and, as often as not, survival; particularly for those whose livelihoods had been ruined by war, famine, plague – or taxes. The historian Nicholas Orme tells us of one low-class independent whore who was paid 12d., twice the daily wage of a skilled craftsman, 'for her wicked . . . behaviour';[16] and whores rightly saw that their relatively high earnings could not only better their standard of living but also provide them with the means of setting themselves up in some other 'respectable' business later in life.

By the end of the Middle Ages, whores enjoyed a period of freedom and relatively high status; some were confident enough to establish their own trade guilds, along the lines of other crafts and businesses. The 4000 prostitutes of 15th-century Paris formed a federation, for which they received royal gifts of a flag, drum and fife band of their own. The whores of Avignon were also given guild statutes by the owner of the town's brothel, Queen Joanna of Naples. In this case the requirement to wear a red braid on the shoulder was conceived of more as a badge of office than a stigma.

It is perhaps the historian Leah Lydia Otis who comes closest to defining the general status of whores in medieval society, and she does so by comparing their position with that of Jews of the period. In an age when lending money with interest was prohibited by the Church, Jewish moneylenders were essential to the urban economy; similarly, while sexual abstention was preached as the Christian ideal, and 'fornication', 'adultery' and so on were among the blackest sins, the average good Christian male found the notion of life without extramarital sex untenable. Thus both prostitutes and Jews occupied an ambiguous position in the community; and pogroms and attacks on the sex trade of later centuries were to show just how vulnerable the position of both groups was.

There were also similarities in the way they were treated by the authorities. In 13th-century Avignon, for example, petty rules and regulations prohibited both prostitutes and Jews from touching bread or fruit in the market unless they then bought the produce. And in Marseilles local bathkeepers were instructed to admit Jews on Fridays only – and whores on Mondays. But the most striking similarity was the dress code requirement, in which the authorities attempted to compel both groups to wear distinguishing signs on their clothing. This distinction was to find a vile and sinister echo in our own century when, in Nazi Germany, Jewish people were deported to the concentration camps with yellow stars sewn to their clothing. Alongside them went the prostitutes, wearing black stars.

The overall picture of prostitution in medieval Western Europe confirms that the last vestiges of a religious connection had been wiped out with the advent of the Christian Church. Now the profession was entirely secularized; nevertheless it thrived under the new conditions of the market. But this situation was not to continue for much longer: an epoch of savage repression lay just around the corner, with the arrival of the religious reformers of the 16th century. Ironically, it was to be these Protestant fanatics who would succeed in popularizing the Catholic Church's notion that female sexuality was the root of all evil. And who better to blame than the whore?

CHAPTER SEVEN

Splendours and Miseries: Prostitution in the Renaissance and Reformation

Lassa andar le cortesane
se non voi disfarte del tutto
Come l'altre son puttane
na più caro vendon lor frutto.

(Leave the courtesans alone,
if you don't want to lose all you've got
They're prostitutes like the rest,
but they cost more, for you know what.)

contemporary rhyme, or pasquinade[1]

The end of the Middle Ages came with the rediscovery in the 14th century of ancient Greek and Roman learning: the Renaissance. The rational, restlessly enquiring cast of mind of the classical writers encouraged a rebirth of the spirit of 'free thought' that had hitherto been crushed by the Catholic Church; the subsequent liberation of educated (male) minds from the straitjacket of religious dogma proved unstoppable in its momentum.

It was not by chance that northern Italy was the cradle of this rebirth of classicism and reason, for not only was the region technically and economically far in advance of the rest of Europe during the 14th and 15th centuries but – as in ancient Greece – its centres of power and wealth were city-states, ruled by bourgeois and aristocratic élites. These powerful men, whose riches came from trading, agriculture, finance and manufacture, used the writings of the pre-Christian thinkers of classical antiquity to loosen the Church's stranglehold on society and culture. Thus they paved the way for the breakthroughs in economy, science and technology – breakthroughs that were to signify the end of the Middle Ages.

The society that began to emerge was inevitably a masculinist one, and from our point of view the most significant aspect of classical thought to be given a new lease of life by Renaissance men was the Greek approach to relations between the sexes. Women were promptly demoted from partners to subordinates, with the resurrection of the classical doctrine that the public domain of business and politics should be reserved for men, while the private – and inferior – sphere of domestic life was to be the woman's realm. The ancient double standard that demanded chastity for women, but not for men, was doubly reinforced, and the housebound Athenian wife was reincarnated in the refined matron of Renaissance Italy. Wives were kept in strict seclusion, imprisoned within their homes except for public holidays; on these occasions they were permitted to trot to and from church accompanied by their husbands. Possessive men were known to keep their wives under these conditions of house-arrest for years at a time. Gone was the medieval tradition of strong and relatively independent women who participated fully in their family's affairs. According to the Renaissance ideal, married women were to be self-effacing and obedient, confined to the shadowy sidelines of their men's lives.

The inevitable counterpart to the confinement of Renaissance wives was the rebirth of that other classical institution: the high-class courtesan. Like the earlier Greek *hetairae*, the *cortegiane* of Venice, Florence and Milan were educated, influential and talented beauties who specialized in catering to the sexual and social needs of men who had excluded their wives from fully participating in their lives. The Italian high-class whores were rich and independent; they held court in their own sumptuous homes, where they received the leading artists, philosophers and statesmen of the day. The artists Titian, Raphael and Cellini and the writer Aretino figured in the ranks of the many famous men who frequented the *cortegiane*. By way of a change, 'even princes of the Church were no strangers to their company.'[2]

But the talents of these ladies were by no means limited to the art of love-making; many were artists in their own right: Tullia d'Aragona (a cardinal's daughter) was a renowned poet who won the patronage of one of the most powerful political figures of the period, the great Cosimo de'Medici. Veronica Franco was another prominent intellectual and courtesan, fluent in several languages and a talented musician.

She was a close friend of the painter Tintoretto, and numbered King Henri III of France among her more illustrious clients. The lovely courtesan despised ignorance and apparently gained most of her own pleasure in the pursuit of knowledge. To one eager young suitor she wrote, almost wistfully: 'You know well that all those who claim to be able to gain my love, are strenuous in studious discipline . . . If my fortune allowed it I would spend all my time quietly in the academies of virtuous men.'[3]

Because she was a woman, Veronica was unable to pursue the full-time education she would have liked to have had; but her profession at least provided her with the financial and social ability to participate in the masculine world of education and culture. In a society where personal wealth equalled power, the *cortegiane* were extremely successful, commanding high prices for their services. The historian Reay Tannahill quotes a sum of four to five crowns for a kiss from Veronica Franco (this was the figure a servant could earn in six months), and fifty crowns for 'the complete transaction'. Another lady, Imperia Cognata (who modelled for Raphael), was reputed to have charged a German client 100 crowns for a whole night in her company. (An anecdote concerning the extremely wealthy Cognata relates how on one occasion a Spanish client, looking round her exquisite apartments for somewhere to spit, chose the face of a manservant as the only ugly thing in the room.) Cognata died at a romantically early age, variously given between 26 and 31; there is speculation amongst historians that she committed suicide. Whatever the circumstances of her death, Cognata was known to have left a generous contribution to the paving of the Strada del Populo in Rome, a street to which her less fortunate country sisters flocked in order to follow their mutual profession.

Like the whores of ancient Rome, many Renaissance beauties dyed their hair blond; they were no doubt influenced by the success of their fair-haired prostitute sisters from Germany and England, who continued to pour into the wealthy Italian cities throughout the period. The Italian whores used marigold petals, camomile flowers, henna and lemon juice, pounded and blended into a paste which they left on their dark hair until they had achieved the desired shade of *capelli file d'oro* (golden-thread hair). The painter Titian's cousin, Cesare Vicallio, writes that the women spent 'hours under the *solana*, a special crownless hat with a huge brim which was used to spread their long hair on as they sat on the roofs of their *palazzi* to dry their hair after it had been dipped in liquid dyes.'[4]

In his gloating book *Great Bordellos of the World*, Emmett Murphy pinpoints the Western male obsession with blondes as originating in the Renaissance period; it is certainly the case that the neurotic maunderings of a few privileged men were in part responsible for the Renaissance 'cult of the blonde'. The 14th-century writer Boccaccio set the ball rolling with his assertion that the 'ideal beauty' should have fair hair; half a century later this notion was taken to lunatic extremes by the Abbot of San Salvatore in his *Dialogo delle bellezze donne*:

> [He] lectured ladies of the city . . . [and] pieced together an ideal beauty from a number of beautiful parts. Not the smallest part of the female anatomy escaped his observation or dictum. The eyes, preferably goddess blue, although lustrous brown was admired, would be large and full. The ears, neither too large nor too small, would be firmly and neatly joined. The chin would be round, a dimple its glory. The leg would be long and not too hard in the lower parts. When speaking or laughing or smiling the beautiful woman would show no more than six of her upper teeth.[5]

And on and on . . .

As usual we are forced to rely on the accounts of male observers of the time for information about the courtesans, but it has to be said that these can be as entertaining as they are informative. Thomas Coryat, an English traveller who visited Venice at the end of the 16th century, provides a detailed contemporary close-up of the lives of the high-class courtesans, as well as frequently hilarious insights into his own attitudes. After estimating the number of prostitutes in Venice at that time at around *twenty thousand* ('whereof many are esteemed so loose, that they are said to open up their quivers to every arrow'), Coryat gives us his account, prefacing it with the traditional disclaimers of the incorruptible Christian gentleman: 'A most ungodly thing without doubt,' he clucks, 'that there should be a tolleration of such licentious wantons in so glorious, so potent, so renowned a city. Methinks the Venetians should be daily afraid lest their winking at such uncleanliness should be an occasion to draw down upon them God's curses and vengeance from Heaven and to consume their city with fire and brimstone.'

Coryat was none the less astute enough to acknowledge the male rationale that excused this 'licentious' trade; he wheeled out the usual justifications: 'For they thinke that the chastity of their wives would be

the sooner assaulted, and so consequently they should be capricorni-
fied [i.e. cuckolded] . . . were it not for these places of evacuation.'
And of course, 'The revenues which [the courtesans] pay unto the
Senate for their tolleration, doe maintain a dozen of their galleys . . .
and so save them a great charge' – a line of thought that was also
directly inherited from classical antiquity.

Coryat's own personal response to the courtesans is a revealing, if
familiar, amalgam of male inconsistencies: sensual attraction liberally
doused in 'moral' (that is, patriarchal religious) opprobrium, with an
added dash of jealous indignation at the amount of wealth the ladies
had independently managed to amass. Indeed many of them had
'scraped together so much pelfe by their sordid faculties as doth
maintaine them well in their old age: for many of them are as rich as
ever was Rhodope in Egypt, Flora in Rome, or Lais in Corinth. One
example . . . is Margarita Aemiliana, that built a faire monastery of
Augustine Monkes.'

Coryat becomes increasingly overwrought in his descriptions of the
physical allure of the *cortegiane*:

So infinite are the allurements of these amorous Calypsoes, that
the fame of them hath drawn many to Venice from some of the
remotest parts of Christendom. When you come into one of their
Palaces, . . . you seem to enter into the Paradise of Venus . . . As
for herselfe shee comes to thee decked like the Queene and
Goddess of Love, in so much that thou wilt thinke she made a late
transmigration from Paphos, Cnidos, or Cythera, the auncient
habitations of Dame Venus. For her face is adorned with the
quintessence of beauty . . . Also the ornaments of her body are
so rich, that except thou dost even geld thy affections (a thing
hardly to be done) . . . shee will very neare benumme and
captivate thy senses . . . For thou shalt see her decked with many
chaines of gold and orient pearle like a second Cleopatra, divers
gold rings beautified with diamonds and other costly stones,
jewels in both her eares of great worth. A gowne of damaske . . .
either decked with a deep gold fringe . . . or laced with five or six
gold laces each two inches broade. Her petticoats of red chamlet
edged with rich gold fringe, stockings of carnasion silke, her
breath and her whole body, the more to enamour thee, most
fragrantly perfumed.

It is at this point that Coryat regains his Christian self-righteousness, albeit rather unconvincingly: 'Though these things will at the first sight seeme unto thee most delectable allurement,' he tells us sternly, 'thou wilt say with the wise man, that they are like a golden ring in a swines snowt.' Sound advice, perhaps: however, Coryat neglected to follow it himself – instead, he got closer still:

> Moreover shee will endeavour to enchaunt thee partly with her melodious notes that shee warbles out upon her lute . . . and partly with that heart-tempting of her voice. Also thou wilt find the Venetian Cortezan . . . a good Rhetorician and a most elegant discourser, so that if she cannot move thee with all these foresaid delights, shee will assay thy constancy with a Rhetorical tongue. And to the end shee may minister unto thee the stronger temptations to come to her lure, shee will shew thee her chamber of recreation, where thou shalt see all manner of pleasing objects . . .

Now comes the warning – perhaps drawn from bitter experience:

> But beware . . . that thou enter not into termes of private conversations with her. For then thou shalt finde her . . . the crafty and hot daughter of the Sunne. Moreover . . . if thou shouldest wantonly converse with her, and not give her that *salarium iniquitatis* [wages of sin], which thou hast promised her, but perhaps cunningly escape from her company, shee will either cause thy throate to be cut by her Ruffiano, if he can catch thee in the City, or procure thee to be arrested . . . and clapped up in the prison, where thou shalt remain till thou hast paid her all thou didst promise her.

Coryat caps his pious little morality play with a final malicious insult: 'If thou dost linger with them thou wilt finde their poyson to be more pernicious than that of the scorpion, aspe, or cocatrice.'[6]

Alas, few men were deterred by Coryat's dire warnings; in fact so determined were they to continue hunting the 'poyson' of the Venetian *cortegiane* that, in order to cater to the demand, the authorities were obliged to import large numbers of women from abroad. These foreign whores were housed in special buildings under the direction of an official madam, who distributed their earnings monthly – after the government had had its rake-off.

Among the natives of the Venetian courtesan class, it seems that the trade was handed down from mother to daughter, in time-honoured tradition. When the young girls were considered ready to practise their profession, the mothers paraded them at the May Fair, and in the markets. Another male observer of the time rhapsodizes over the dress and allure of these 'charming little creatures', then adds doubtfully, 'but it is an expensive merchandise; one cannot have a virgin girl for less than 150 gold écus, as well as a year's keep. For 200 one can choose throughout the town.'[7]

The openness and celebratory aspect of the trade in virgins – May Fairs, flowers, proud mamas – demonstrates that in early modern Venice prostitution was not regarded as a degrading means of making a living; at least, not for those whose beauty and education qualified them to join the élite class of whores. As in neighbouring France at the court of Francis I, the *cortegiana* was the object of a romantic cult. According to the Abbé Brantôme, the 16th-century 'chronicler of the lives of fair and gallant ladies', it was *de rigueur* for the men of the French court to pursue at least one courtesan. The Cardinal of Lorraine gains a place in the history books as one who took a special interest in initiating attractive female newcomers into the sexual customs and practices of the court.

Nevertheless there was one crucial difference between the Renaissance beauty and her *hetaira* predecessor: in ancient Greece the high-class whore had retained vestiges of religious charisma in the hearts and minds of the people; this was definitely not the case in Renaissance Italy. Leaving aside the hyperbole of the few contemporary writers, the Italian courtesan was in no way seen to incorporate a goddess-aspect; her profession was entirely secularized. As a mere mortal, non-sacred woman, she was no longer regarded with awe, or even with particular respect, by her male lovers. This inevitably led to the problem of male violence. Every courtesan had at least one body-guard, but this was no guarantee of safety. Emmett Murphy describes the chillingly Mafia-type practice of *sfregia* – face slashing – that was carried out on some prostitutes, at the behest of men – 'jealous lovers or disgruntled customers'.[8] Murphy also mentions in passing the vile practice of gang-rape as another form of punishment: 'the *trentuno*, an occasion when the offending woman [*sic*] was raped by upwards of thirty hired men, or the *trentuno reale*, an attack by seventy-five hired thugs.' Murphy thoughtfully adds that: 'Such gross indignities caused both clients and revenue to fall off sharply.'[9]

The life of a *cortegiana*, then, was not entirely without its dangers – but her lot was certainly better than that of her lower-class sister, the street *puttana*. For the latter, life was totally circumscribed by regulations and prohibitions: the usual mish-mash of rights and (mostly) restrictions. Although she had certain rights (for example, insulting a whore was punishable by a fine of 100 ducats and imprisonment for a month), the lower-class whore was forbidden to frequent inns, taverns or churches; she was also not allowed to sell sex to Turks, Moors and Jews. Any transgressions could be punishable with the lash and the pillory. The lowly street whore could rarely hope to attain the status and wealth of her high-born sister, despite the fact that class barriers within the ranks of prostitution were less rigid and divisive than those of 'respectable' society.

The background to the shift in attitudes which was further to marginalize prostitutes was the sequence of massive economic, social, political and religious changes which remoulded Western society during the Reformation period of the 16th century. These upheavals were to reach far into the lives of working people in general and women in particular. On the political front, the feudal crisis of the 14th and 15th centuries had left rural workers powerful enough to succeed in throwing off the bondage of serfdom; in response to this outrage, the ruling classes were obliged to go on the offensive, reorganizing their political dominion in the form of the 'absolutist' states which were to have their heyday in the 16th to 18th centuries. The absolutist state, so-called because it rested on the divinely ordained *absolute* power of the monarchy, was a tightly organized repressive machine which enabled secular power to shift from the decentralized rural/feudal model to the centralized city/court. Crucial to this shift was the Church's support for the court, which it gave unreservedly. The intention was obvious: to clamp the lower classes firmly back in their 'rightful' place in the social hierarchy.

A ferocious offensive against the labouring classes swiftly and inevitably followed. One feature of this offensive, particularly in England, was the enclosure movement, which began in the 16th century and radically altered the pattern of the countryside in the 17th and 18th centuries. The English nobility and gentry were realizing the profits to be made from modern agriculture, using 'free' instead of serf labour; part of the attraction of this kind of farming was that the hired, landless labour force it required had much less power than a peasantry attached to its own land. The aristocratic response to the liberation of the serfs was thus to destroy the peasantry's power base by stripping it of its land. Unscrupulous landlords used every means at their disposal: peasants suddenly found their rents vastly increased, heavy fines imposed on them and, perhaps most devastating of all, their common lands seized from them and enclosed, to become the private property of the local noble or country squire. One 17th-century writer describes 'lords devising new means to cut [their tenants] shorter, doubling, trebling, and now and then seven times increasing their fines, driving them for every trifle to lose and forfeit their tenures.'[10]

This policy was also very convenient for the bourgeoisie. The middle classes had emerged from the feudal crisis decisively strengthened; they were now in command of the urban economies which had forged ahead while the rural world had stagnated. Finance – that largely masculine pursuit of shuffling money to and fro – became a major source of middle-class power, with kings and nobles borrowing copiously from the burghers' coffers. The power of the state also depended to no small extent on the products manufactured by the middle classes, notably the armaments that were beginning to be produced on an increasing scale. More and more, the bourgeoisie was in need of workers to exploit in these flourishing new industries: people who were 'free' of their attachment to the land which had supported them from time immemorial; people who would 'freely' choose to come and labour in the towns and cities. Thus enclosures played into the hands of the middle class, 'liberating' ever-larger masses of country people to flock to urban centres in search of work.

These political and economic pressures combined with inflation and a demographic boom to undermine the price of all working-class labour, which in turn created increasing hardship for the poor. Many became vagabonds, only to be further harassed by the brutal punishments devised by the new absolute monarchies. It was an offence to be unemployed; whippings were doled out to the workless with increasing regularity, until by Elizabethan times begging was punishable by the sadistic measure of burning through the gristle of the right ear – a second offence met with the death penalty. On the Continent things were no better for the lower classes. In France, Germany and Flanders the governments intervened to maintain artificially low wage-levels; at the same time the price of basic foodstuffs doubled. Workers were bound in military style servitude to their employers; the formation of anything so much as resembling a union was punishable by flogging, imprisonment and banishment. Striking was outlawed. In the Low Countries and France, too, the unemployed were condemned to the dreadful slavery of the galleys, with frequent 'vagabond-hunts' to augment the galley-crews. All over Europe, workhouses and 'houses of correction' were being established, in which the poor and destitute were forced to toil under the most inhumane conditions.

While working people were being stripped of their livelihoods and dragooned into forced labour, the so-called 'free' labour market moved towards male domination. Women began to be excluded from the crafts and trades they had participated in equally with men during the Middle Ages. In the new wage economy, men's pay – low though it was – and opportunities far outstripped those of women, who were also faced with the growing tendency of men to organize trades in a way that excluded them. Women were thus far more likely to be left landless and jobless than their working-class brothers. Given the Hobson's choice of life as a working wife – 'subjected to a crushing burden of toil . . . while . . . kept in a thoroughly subservient position'[11] – or the illegality and persecution of unemployment, it comes as no surprise to learn that a steadily rising number of them chose instead to work as prostitutes.

The conditions whores had to endure, however, were no longer the toleration and relative security they had enjoyed throughout most of the Middle Ages. Apart from the economic factors that increasingly undermined their position, there were new laws to restrict them. At first these were aimed at the female sex in general; the French jurist Tiraqueau made a start in 1522 by defining the legal 'incapacity' of women, which effectively prohibited any woman from making contracts or acting in any capacity within the court system. In French criminal law women came to be considered irresponsible because of the 'imbecility' of their sex; soon, as a corollary to this, the rape of a prostitute ceased to be a crime.

Prostitutes could no longer look to the newly centralized state authorities for protection. The spirit of the time was characterized by an extreme misogyny which was demonstrated by the mass terror and murder of tens of thousands of women throughout Europe during the so-called 'witch-craze'. History's first religious holocaust, the 'witch-craze' spanned over three centuries following a Papal Bull of 1484. Although sources disagree on the actual number of women tortured and murdered throughout the period (mainly in Germany and

France), one figure is certain: of those who died, 80 per cent were females. And the massacres were directed by Christians.

The explosion of Protestantism in the 16th century, a process known to history as the Reformation, broke the religious monopoly of the Catholic Church and thoroughly remoulded the moral order of Western Europe, at a time when society and the economy were shifting decisively towards a more modern form. As the historian Christopher Hill puts it: 'The Protestant revolt melted down the iron ideological framework which held society in its ancient mould . . . In a society already becoming capitalist, Protestantism facilitated the triumph of the new values. There was no inherent theological reason for the Protestant emphasis on frugality, hard work, accumulation; but that emphasis was the natural consequence of the religion of the heart in a society where capitalist industry was developing.'[12]

The immediate pretext of the Reformation was the urgent need to reform the blatant corruption of the Catholic Church, and by the end of the Middle Ages a strong movement with this aim had grown up within the Church itself. Summing up the level of corruption, Pico della Mirandola, 'one of the great men of the Italian Renaissance', complained to the Pope and the Lateran Council in 1513:

> Holy Father . . . the consecrated houses and temples [have been] given over to panders and catamites . . . in many cities the precincts formerly dedicated to virgins [have been] changed into brothels and dens of obscenity. Yet these, I fear, are but the beginnings of evil, and a mere foretaste . . . unless we avert it by our amended manners.[13]

Round about the same time, the churchman Johann Geiler fulminated from the pulpit of Strasbourg Cathedral that 'he would rather his sister should become a prostitute than that she should be thrust into a nunnery of lax life or should be made abbess of a community of wanton canonesses.'[14] And Geiler must have had plenty of opportunities to observe the whores' operations, since the cathedral was a main rendezvous for them and their clients. They conducted business in the aisles and even the belltower, and were known colloquially as 'swallows'.

Matters came to a head in 1517, with the publication of the first manifesto of Protestantism: 95 theses, or statements, written by

Martin Luther, a German theologian with plenty of time on his hands. Luther's manifesto was to signal the definitive break with the Catholic Church. Protestant leaders emerged, men who saw not only the clergy but the whole of society as being in need of urgent moral reform. In fact their proposals were mostly aimed at giving themselves and their new Protestant credo the moral authority to remake the social world: the construction of a 'purified', obedient, God-fearing and work-orientated society was what they had in mind. It was this dangerously idealistic scheme which led Luther's French contemporary John Calvin to set up the first Protestant state in Geneva; a theocracy with powers as sweeping as any absolute monarchy, through which Calvin attempted to legislate the new moral order into the public and private lives of its citizens.

Lutheranism spread like wildfire across Germany, while its Calvinist counterpart conquered Switzerland and was taken into France by Huguenot zealots, where it triggered off the 16th-century Wars of Religion. John Knox took Calvin's 'model state' to Scotland, and in England Henry VIII – largely for dynastic reasons, but with an astute sense of political timing – split from Rome to set up the Anglican Church. As northern Europe began to slip from their grasp, the Catholics were obliged to react, and did so by instigating their own reform movement, the Counter-Reformation, which aimed to preserve the essential spirit of traditional Catholicism in a new-look, 'reformed' body. From about the year 1530, Catholics and Protestants competed in reforming zeal; the Catholic Council of Trent (1545–63) gave its official stamp to reformist policies by entrusting the newly formed Jesuits with the awesome task of purging the old Church of its corruption and thus regaining the moral high ground.

At the heart of the new Protestant image of man and society was a new sexual morality – one that was both more pragmatic and more repressive than that of the early Church. Luther and his compeers recognized that the extreme anti-sexual attitudes of the Church Fathers were damaging in theory and unworkable in practice. Priestly celibacy was an impossible ideal and in itself the source of much of the old Church's corruption, so the argument went. In its place, Luther and Calvin proposed the upgrading of the patriarchal institution of marriage: a man had only to get married and *voilà!* – he could have all the sex he wanted, just so long as it was for the divine purpose of creating future God-fearing congregationalists. Procreative sex,

within the confines of holy matrimony, was thus sanctified openly by
the Protestant reformers; conversely, there was no room for the
tolerance of extramarital sex that had been shown by medieval Catholics.
Luther was of the opinion that sex itself was 'unclean', and Calvin was
quick to emphasize the evil nature of sexual pleasure. Their goal was total
chastity outside the married state; they argued bitterly against the notion
that young men's promiscuity was natural and inevitable, and that
prostitution was therefore permissible. While medieval Catholicism's
despair about the sexually weak nature of man bred, in practice, a
laissez-faire attitude to 'wicked fornication', Protestant zeal insisted that
man could – and therefore should – attain moral perfection on this earth,
an ambitious programme, which was to be taken up by both Protestant
and Catholic churchmen alike. It also spelled disaster for all who – like
the whore – stood on the margins of sexual life, and outside the accepted
institutions of marriage or the nunnery.

Like the Renaissance before it, the Reformation was a male-dominated movement, and as such it continued to define any independent
female sexuality as threatening-therefore-evil. Once again, marriage
was used to erode the position of independent women; for in Luther's
view the sole purpose of woman was as child-bearer. In fact his
attitude even to the women he himself defined as 'good' was
remarkably callous: 'And if a woman grows weary and at last dies
from child-bearing, it matters not. Let her die from bearing, she is
there to do it.'

Reformation leaders in general 'limited women's activities strictly
to the home and emphasized the subordination of women to their
husband's will',[15] while at the same time extolling the virtues of
wifehood and motherhood (death in childbirth notwithstanding).
Any manifestation of woman's independent spirit was to be stifled,
and that of the whore was particularly vilified. In some ways
Reformation ideas took the Renaissance revival of the Greek prisoner-
wife a stage further, throwing in a sizeable helping of fanatical Hebrew
misogyny for good measure. The resulting concoction ensured that
the good-wife/bad-whore split would become even more deeply
rooted within Western civilization.

Luther was resolutely anti-prostitution, particularly the legalized
state-run variety. In 1520 he wrote in an *Address to the German Nobility*:

Is it not a terrible thing that we Christians should maintain public
brothels, though we all vow chastity in our baptism? I know well

all that can be said on this matter, that it is not peculiar to one nation, that it would be difficult to alter, and that it is better thus than that virgins or married women or honourable women should be dishonoured. But should not the spiritual and temporal powers combine to find some means of meeting these difficulties without any such heathen practice? If the people of Israel existed without this scandal, why should not a Christian nation be able to do so?[16]

(Luther's reading of the Old Testament was highly selective.)

In accordance with these views, and often under Luther's own personal direction, public brothels were shut down throughout Germany, as Reformation fever spread from city to city. Whorehouses were forcibly closed in Augsburg (1532), Ulm (1537), Regensburg (1553) and Nuremberg (1562), and their inmates evicted. Occasionally a brothel might attempt to reopen, if the heat was off, as was the case with the Freiburg municipal brothel, which was closed in 1537. When it tentatively reopened three years later, Luther wrote an immediate letter of protest, in which the Protestant position was made perfectly clear: 'Those who wish to establish such houses,' he stormed, 'should first deny Christ's name, and recognize that, rather than Christians, they are heathens, who know nothing of God's name.'[17]

Fine words, for the pious Christian burghers, but for the working women who were on the receiving end of Luther's campaign it was another matter. When evicted from the brothels of Strasbourg, the women got up a petition in which they pointed out that they pursued their profession not because they enjoyed it but because they needed to make a living. If, therefore, the authorities were determined to deprive them of their means, they should at least be prepared to provide the women with an alternative 'honest' way of surviving. This reasonable request met with much municipal head-shaking, although it appears that, under pressure, the city's burghers made some attempts to find the whores work. (They even tried to marry the women off to husbands who would then presumably keep them on the straight and narrow.) But the usual problem reared its head: independent work for lower-class women was difficult to come by, and in the end the authorities offered no real response to the poor women who had suddenly found themselves jobless and penniless after the wave of reforming zeal had swept through their city.

Calvin was if anything even more implacably opposed to the sex trade than his German contemporary. He maintained that all forms of 'lechery' were detested by God and must be stamped out altogether. On the eve of Calvin's arrival in Geneva, therefore, the city council hurriedly decreed that all its prostitutes must repent and give up their trade immediately, or be exiled. Calvin ensured that this law was rigorously enforced, along with similar draconian measures that punished 'fornication and adultery' with fines, imprisonments and banishment. In 1556, he went so far as to demand the death penalty for adultery, taking his cue from a passage in Deuteronomy 22: 'If a man be found lying with a woman married to a husband, they shall both of them die.' Although Calvin's proposal did not actually manage to reach the statute books, the city council did execute two 'adulterers' in 1560.

Elsewhere in Switzerland the moral terror was somewhat lessened by the fact of its being outside Calvin's immediate range: in Zurich, for example, the municipal brothels were permitted to stay open, albeit under the supervision of an official whose duty supposedly included the barring of married men from the premises.

The Catholic reformers entered the fray with an equally oppressive zeal. In 1563 the Council of Trent, in a decree on marriage, pledged to stamp out extramarital sexual activity of any kind. With this in mind, Pope Sixtus V introduced the death penalty for adultery and all 'unnatural vices' in 1586. During the interim period Pius V had made a concerted effort to eradicate prostitution in the city of Rome – by no means an easy task. Pius must have had a taste for the sensational, for he chose 22 July – the feast-day of Mary Magdalene – 1566 upon which to publish his edict expelling all whores from the city. The entire Roman populace was scandalized, from the street whores to the social élite:

> The city council sent a deputation of forty citizens to remonstrate with the Pope. The edict would cause a grave economic recession. It would lead to the depopulation of the city, to a slump in the import of luxury goods, to the bankruptcy of respectable tradesmen. The diplomatic corps was troubled, and the ambassadors of Spain, Portugal and Florence added their protests.[18]

In the streets of Rome there was mass panic as 25,000 people – the

In the beginning was the matriarchy: a cast of the 'Venus of Willendorf' from the Gravettian–Aurignacian site (Upper Paleolithic or Old Stone Age).

Goddess seated on an animal throne: Çatal Hüyük in Anatolia, c. 6000 BC. To the ancients, the Goddess was seen as an all-encompassing deity – contrary to male mythologizing about mere 'fertility cults'.

LEFT: 'The lady at the window', possibly Ishtar, the 'compassionate whore', enticing clients: an Assyrian ivory, c. 8th century BC.

'The little goddess of the serpents': Knossos, Crete, 2000–1800 BC. Crete was one of the most important centres of matriarchal civilization.

A Greek *hetaira* or courtesan plays her flute to Aphrodite: side panel of the Ludovisi Throne, c. 470–460 BC. The *hetairae* were renowned for their artistic and intellectual accomplishments.

BELOW: A *hetaira* entertains her client. 'Man has the *hetairae* for erotic enjoyment, concubines for daily use, and wives of his own rank to bring up children and to be faithful housewives': Demosthenes.

ADSORORES·IIII

LEFT: 'To the sisters': a Roman brothel signboard. The three-sisters motif recalls the threefold Goddess.

BELOW: High-class Roman courtesans: from a wall-painting in Pompeii. These were the ladies who entertained the likes of the poet Propertius.

RIGHT: A public bath-house in 15th-century France: the affluent classes at their communal *toilette*.

BELOW: Wealthy clients amuse themselves at 'the Naked Banquet': from a medieval illustrated manuscript.

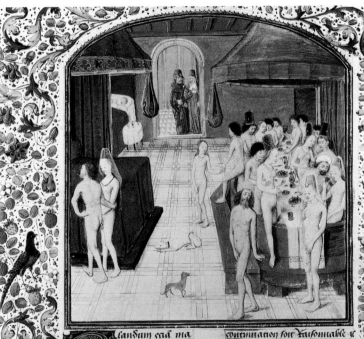

BELOW: A 15th-century
German *frauenhaus*.

High-class *cortegiane* (the *hetairae* of Renaissance Italy) on a balcony: from a painting by Carpaccio, c. 1500.

prostitutes and their dependents – prepared to leave the city. By 17 August, less than a month after he had first pronounced his edict, the Pope was forced to rescind it, and the whores stayed put. Pius none the less managed to keep up the pressure on Rome's lower-class prostitutes, although he spared the luxury trade. As usual it was the all-too-visible streetwalker who was on the receiving end of the Holy Father's ire; she faced banishment or, alternatively, being forced into a ghetto and forbidden to leave it, on pain of whipping and/or exile.

In France, meanwhile, the influence of the Reformation and Counter-Reformation grew from the mid-16th century onwards. Protestant troops set the tone for the new moral era when they beat up the whores of the town of Gaillac and cut their ears off. All the French local authorities began to crack down on their prostitutes, handing out barbaric punishments for offences which would previously have merited only small fines. Records tell of a woman from the public brothel at Toulouse who was arrested while walking in the town; she was sentenced to run naked through the streets before being cere-moniously banished from the city. When the woman protested that she 'only went to the town to buy victuals', the magistrates annulled the banishment order and decreed that she would 'be delivered to the executioner of high justice, who will make her run, beating her until the blood flows, and then sent back to the public house, forbidden to wander about the town on pain of hanging.'[19]

Another popular form of punishment for the whores of Toulouse at this time (as indeed it was in many other 16th-century towns and cities throughout Europe) was ducking. This barbaric practice, applicable to females only, is often recounted uncritically – if not fondly recalled – by male historians. In Toulouse the ritualized ordeal was known as the *accabussade*, and it served two purposes: as well as being an individual punishment for the unfortunate woman, it was a piece of grim theatre that would remind the lower classes of the price paid by those who flouted the new morality. A contemporary account described the procedure:

A woman condemned (of prostitution) is taken to the town hall; the executioner ties her hands, puts on her a sugar-loaf bonnet trimmed with feathers, with a label on the back on which could be read full details of her guilt . . . Then she is taken near the bridge to a rock in the middle of the river. There she is put into an iron cage made for the purpose and dipped three separate times and then she is left for some time in such a way, however, that she cannot suffocate, a spectacle which attracts the curiosity of nearly all the inhabitants of the town. That done, the woman or girl is taken to the prison where she is condemned to spend the rest of her life in the hard labour section.[20]

Throughout the mid-16th century the southern French authorities closed down their municipal brothels. In 1555 the council of Castelnaudry in Languedoc voted to pull down their whorehouse and sell the land on which it stood; two years later Montpellier sold its house to the highest 'respectable' bidder; finally, the house at Toulouse was not farmed out in 1557–8, after which it too was converted to 'respectable' use. By the following decade this repressive climate had reached the rest of France; in 1561 the government of King Charles IX abolished the remaining municipal brothels throughout the country. Although many independent whorehouses kept going – their owners had friends in high places – Charles' decrees spelled the official end of the medieval policy of open toleration of the French sex industry.

Charles was not alone in his policy of riding the wave of religious reform by introducing his own laws concerning prostitution; other monarchs had the same idea, and for the same reason: they were not slow to realize that any tightening of the controls over public morality could only lead to the strengthening and extension of their own secular powers. Henry VIII of England and the Emperor Charles V of Germany tightened up their countries' criminal laws – including those specifically aimed at curbing prostitution – and saw to it that they were rigorously enforced. Ferdinand I of Austria went a stage further; in 1560 he created a 'Chastity Committee' (*keuschheitskommission*) whose sole motive was to police the private lives of his subjects. All over Europe prostitution and brothel-keeping were targeted by special morals laws that were specifically intended to discipline the working population and, as a corollary, reduce their opportunity for subversive activity.

In England during the reign of Elizabeth I (herself reputed to have clandestinely visited a London stew or two, *à la* Messalina), the persecuted whore could be punished by having her head shaved, after which she would be carted through the streets wearing a paper hat that announced her 'crime'. She would be accompanied throughout her degradation by a jeering band of barbers, whose duty it was to rattle their basins in derision. If she was unlucky enough to be arrested more than once, the whore would be tied to the 'cart's arse' and dragged through the streets, often being flogged on arrival at the Bridewell, or 'house of correction'. The prison beating soon became a pompous ritual, supervised by a board of governors, voyeurs whose hypocrisy Shakespeare castigated in the words of King Lear:

> Thou rascal beadle, hold thy bloody hand!
> Why dost thou lash that whore? Strip thine own back:
> Thou hotly lust'st to use her in that kind
> For which thou whip'st her.

English law had actually begun to target prostitution from the beginning of the 16th century. A contemporary chronicle records that 'in the year 1506, the 21st of Henry VII, the . . . stew-houses in Southwarke were for a season inhibited, and the doors closed up, but it was not long . . . ere the houses there were set open again.' The writer goes on to specify 'the Boars Head, the Cross Keys, the Gun, the Castle, the Crane, the Cardinal's Hat, the Bell, the Swan, etc.'[21]

In 1535, Henry VIII tried to close down the Southwark stews, but met with the same lack of success as his father. But there was one crucial difference: Henry's seizure of Church lands at the time of his break with Rome had irrevocably changed the ancient order of things at Southwark. Their passing into the hands of the Anglican Bishop of Winchester, Stephen Gardiner, rendered the brothels much more vulnerable to the whims of the monarch, upon whose patronage the Bishop of course depended. No doubt this was one reason why Gardiner operated a special service to His Majesty, offering him the pick of Bankside's 'Winchester Geese' (and even on some occasions joining the king at his recreation).

Henry was a notoriously fickle monarch, whose repression of the London sex trade obviously stimulated his appetite for power. With a display of compassion rarely seen in a cleric, the Reverend Symon Fysshe appealed to the king to effect reforms, because the poor of the realm were lamenting their miserable state – and the clergy were, true to form, exploiting them terribly. The people, wrote Fysshe, were 'oppressed with muche greater rentes than hath of ancient tyme been payd for the same groundes . . . Who is shee that will set her handes to worke to get three pence a daye, and may have at least twenty pence a daye to slepe an hour with a frere (friar) or a moncke or a preste? What is hee that wolde laboure for a grote a daye and may have at least twelve pence a day to bee a Baude to a prest or a moncke or a frere?'[22]

Henry's response to this earnest plea was to introduce yet another sadistic form of punishment for prostitution: branding on the face with hot irons for any whore caught trading sex with his soldiers. He followed this up with a royal proclamation, issued on 13 April 1546, which put down the stews again and denounced: 'toleration of such dissolute and miserable persons as, putting away the fear of almighty God and the shame of the world, have been suffered to dwell beside London and elsewhere, in common open places called the stews, and there without punishment or correction to exercise their abominable and detestable sin.'[23] (This came, it should be remembered, from a man who was already three-quarters dead from syphilis.) A herald at arms, preceded by a trumpet fanfare, read the proclamation on the Bankside, where it was decreed that brothel-keepers and whores alike should leave forthwith, 'bag and baggage', and return to their homes. According to the new law, the house-owners were forbidden to lease them to anyone who could not 'keep good and honest rule' in them. A new phenomenon sprang up in 16th-century London as an immediate upshot of these changes on Bankside: the property developers got their hands on the prime sites and soon the spacious gardens running down to the Thames were buried beneath rows of jerry-built tenements.

Henry's policies show how neatly the political requirements of absolute monarchy dovetailed with the moralism of the religious reformers; for both, the intention was total secular control. The Reformers' ambition to regulate the thoughts and behaviour of the people – reaching into both their minds and their bedrooms – was a timely ally for a political system that had pretensions to absolute power. And as with all systems of social control, sexuality was a major target of the Church-State, control of the people's bodies being the key to control of their minds and actions. The proclamations – all swathed in pious language – that put down the brothels and other working-class places of recreation were (primarily) intended to prevent potentially subversive assemblies of the common people; the cynical new moralism thus proved an effective camouflage for the increasingly heavy hand of the state. But the new sexual repressiveness did not of course apply to the nobility; for at this time the houses of the great and powerful all contained special chambers that were set aside for 'embroideresses' and other 'needlewomen' – in fact whores, for the sexual use of the nobility and their illustrious guests. The notorious royal thug Wolsey (whom Anne Boleyn once derisively referred to as 'that old Church pander') had such a chamber in his sumptuous palace at Hampton Court. Over the entrance leading to the room was a sign inscribed in the most impeccable Church Latin: 'The house of the whores of my Lord the Cardinal'. Henry, it goes without saying, had a similar 'house'.

One of the most common fallacies about the 16th-century wave of repression is that it was brought about by the arrival in Europe of the venereal disease syphilis. This assumption obscures the real social and political roots of the clampdown.

Syphilis was first identified in 1495 among French soldiers garrisoned in Naples; from there it appears to have spread rapidly across the rest of Europe. But whether the disease was in fact new is largely a matter of conjecture; it may well have been officially recognized in the 16th century thanks to advances in the medical classification of disease at that time. Whatever the case may be, the link between the syphilis 'epidemic' and the brothel closures is extremely dubious, for by the time the closures were in full swing (around the 1550s) the scare was well on the wane.

It is also important to note that the fact of the sexual transmission of syphilis was not understood at the time; it was in no way differentiated from other infectious diseases such as the plague. People believed that syphilis could be transmitted through the air, in food, through breast-feeding, in clothes and utensils; there were even some who believed that a look could communicate it. There was no medical reason for connecting the disease with prostitution: and lately, even the historians have begun to debunk the theory that such a connection was ever made:

> The fear of syphilis does not appear to have been primarily responsible for changing the medieval attitude of tolerance towards licensed prostitution. The general closure of licensed brothels . . . seems to have had no direct relationship with the spread of the disease or views about it. Sanitary motives were not uppermost in the official pronouncements which ordered the brothels to close.[24]

In fact the authorities were more concerned with moral than sanitary conditions. Plagues and epidemics of all kinds were to be seen by the populace as the scourge of an angry deity on a corrupt world; a point of view that had been summed up by the Emperor Maximilian who, in a proclamation on syphilis (1495), declared that it had been unleashed as a punishment for men's immorality. Inevitably, in the sexually paranoid minds of the Reformers, prostitution was pinpointed as the source of men's corruption; and it was in this context that whores were scapegoated and persecuted by what was in effect a 16th-century 'Moral Majority'. Syphilis was merely the pretext: a convenient symbol that pointed to the need for a purge.

CHAPTER EIGHT

Feign'd Tears and Forg'd Smiles:
Prostitutes' Lives in the 16th
and 17th Centuries

If all the bysshopps of England were hanged whiche
kepe harlots and whorys, we shuld have fewer
pompeos bysshops.

Anonymous Puritan, 1542

Luckily for whores, the permanent repression of
the sex trade was in practice a legal fiction. Thanks
to the continued expansion of the cities and towns,
the rise in population, the impoverishment of the
people (especially women), and the spread of free market conditions,
prostitution continued to prove unstoppable: too many people had a
stake in it. A year after he had put down the stews at Southwark,
Henry VIII was dead, and it was business as usual for the whores and
their hangers-on. Although the brothels were still technically illegal,
the accession to the throne of Henry's sickly heir Edward emboldened
the operators to try their luck. In a sermon before the young king,
Bishop Latimer thundered despairingly: 'I say that there is now more
whoredom in London than ever there was on the Bancke . . . You
have put down the stewes, but I pray you, how is the matter amended?
What avayleth it that you have but changed the place and not taken the
whoredom away?'[1]

What indeed? And yet while this particular bishop was bemoaning
London's 'whoredom' a great many of his holy brothers were
continuing in their grand old traditions, or, as one contemporary
writer bitterly observed: 'bischopps . . . may fuck their fill and be
vnmarit.'[2]

In the meantime, other unscrupulous men of God were agitating for the ban against the brothels to be lifted entirely; interestingly, this movement gathered pace during the brief Catholic restoration of Queen Mary's reign. A witness writes, in 1572:

> The Stewes and publicke bordell howses are abolished and so continue untill the tyme of Quene Marie, in whose daies some of the Clergie made laboure to have them restored agine; and were very likely to have gained their sute if shee had lived a while longer. Suche trees. Suche frute. For the Stewes, saith one of them in a Sermon at Pauls Cross, are so necessary in a common welthe as a jaxe [toilet] in a mannes howse.[3]

Here the Catholic argument of Thomas Aquinas was being resurrected, but to no avail: the brothels remained illegal – although the authorities could now be encouraged, through bribes and free sex, to turn a blind eye. Thus the landlords and bawds could continue to reap their profits; the clients could have their fun; the whores could make their living – and the state could crack down whenever it felt like it, since the legislation was already in place. A situation not unfamiliar to the sex workers of contemporary England.

In France the situation was developing along similar lines: in theory, all brothels – whether public or private – were to be closed down and prostitution thus expunged from society: in practice, it was business – nearly – as usual. Brothels owned by the rich, who had influential friends and clients, kept open through private deals with the authorities; the remainder had to rely on the traditional corruption of those officials who were charged with carrying out the new regulations. Hence the majority of the brothels succeeded in keeping up their trade – but now they had no legal rights whatsoever. They were allowed to stay open on sufferance only, a precarious state of affairs. Thus, in an *ad hoc* response to the clampdown, the French system of *maisons de tolérance* came into being: selected houses that were to be 'tolerated', but always kept under close scrutiny by the newly developing forces of law and order; a system which characterized the French prostitution scene well into the 20th century.

By the end of the 16th century the ruinous inflation and continuing enclosures and evictions ensured that thousands of dispossessed women and girls continued to flock into the capital to find work. The streets of Elizabethan London thronged with prostitutes, especially in

Southwark, around the area where the brothels, the bear-gardens and the newly-opened theatres (including Shakespeare's Globe) were to be found. The whores were outnumbered only by their clientele, who constantly roved the area in the pursuit of pleasure. For by now there were considerable numbers of wealthy country gentlemen who came to the city in the wake of the centralization of power and the creation of government bureaucracies; when not hanging around at Court, gambling and whoring were the main preoccupations of these worthies. The boom in demand for the whores' services far outstripped that of the supply. The writer Robert Greene vividly describes the scene in 1592:

> Oh, might the justices send out spy-alls in the night! They should see how these streetwalkers will jet in rich-guarded gowns, quaint periwigs, ruffs of the largest size, quarter-and-a-half deep, glorified richly with blue starch, their cheeks dyed with surfling-water . . . thus are they tricked up, and either walk like stales [snares] up and down the streets, or stand like the devil's *si quis* [advertisement] at a tavern or alehouse.[4]

As the trade mushroomed, so did the specializations. Some whores kept up old traditions and became priests' girls or the kept women of nobles and bourgeois citizens, while others gravitated to the theatres and taverns. Many whores managed to avoid the gaze of the law by joining forces with London's criminal underworld, by this time far better organized and more numerous than any forces of law and order. Women known colloquially as 'bawdy baskets' went from house to house, ostensibly hawking pins and other trifles as a cover for selling sex; at the same time they reconnoitred for their criminal associates. There were 'punks' (prostitutes) known as 'crossbiters' who, along with their 'apple-squires' (male accomplices), practised deception and theft on their wealthy 'simplers' (victims). It is also during this period that first mention is made of child brothels in England, which supplied rich clients with girls aged between seven and fourteen years. The children of the poor were sometimes either sold into prostitution by their parents or kidnapped for that purpose.

In addition to the women who through necessity or choice (or a combination of the two) worked as whores, there were some middle-class wives in the profession. In Ben Jonson's play *Bartholomew Fair*, the prostitute Punk Alice berates the wife of a judge for encroaching on her trade: 'A mischief on you, they are such as you that undo us and take our trade from us, with your tuft-taffeta haunches! . . . The poor common whores can ha' no traffic for the privy rich ones; your caps and hoods of velvet call away our customers, and lick the fat from us.'[5]

Alice's pique, though understandable, is badly-targeted, for many bourgeois wives had also suffered from the decline of female employment and the loss of the equality in trades and crafts that they had enjoyed during the Middle Ages. Many middle-class wives had little, if any, money of their own, and the more independently-minded of them would not have relished the idea of being totally dependent on their husbands. According to the poet John Taylor, these middle-class whores first seized their opportunity during Henry VIII's short-lived suppression of the stews:

> The stews in England bore a beastly sway
> Till the eighth Henry banished them away.
> And since the common whores were quite put down
> A damned crew of private whores are grown.[6]

There were cases on record of bourgeois husbands acting as panders and pimps; in 1550 a haberdasher named Middleton was prosecuted for arranging for his wife, their daughter and a ten-year-old serving maid to have sex in return for money with one Nicholas Ballard, 'gentleman'. Clearly, the new morality of the Reformation had made little headway in some 'respectable' circles – at least where there was money to be made.

Nor did bourgeois men restrict themselves to individual pimping, in their involvement with the business side of the sex trade. With the decline in state regulation, private enterprise began to cast a covetous eye on the trade. At the turn of the 17th century a group of businessmen – dye-manufacturers – bought premises in Southwark and turned to the sex trade when they realized the potentially vast profits to be made. These men contrived an ingenious system of exploitation, which they then applied to the whores who worked in their tiny tenement rooms. The women, no longer protected by the statutes of 1161, were charged extortionate rents; they consequently fell into debt quickly. Crippled by repayments, the women were then obliged to buy food and other provisions on credit from their landlord's shop and, if need be, to pawn their clothes at the landlord's pawnshop in order to meet their rent and other bills by the end of each week. These lower-class whores were the *de facto* sexual servants of bourgeois London.

At the other end of the scale were the establishments such as the Holland's Leaguer, a luxury brothel in Southwark which was frequented by the 'lecherous' King James I (and which was, incidentally, rented from Lord Hunsdon, himself a cousin of the old Queen). The contrast between the Leaguer, a grand mansion that stood in its own grounds by the river, and the squalid tenements rented by lower-class whores, could not have been greater.

Houses that catered to the rich were, of necessity, opulent. Built like great inns, they were entered via an archway wide enough to permit a coach to pass discreetly through; this in turn led to a large courtyard, surrounded by reception rooms, a restaurant, and bars which catered to clients of differing status and means. Upstairs was a gallery which enclosed the courtyard on three sides; leading from this were the prostitutes' rooms, and several two- or three-roomed suites in which the wealthier regulars could combine business with pleasure by entertaining their own business clients. A satire of 1614 describes life in the more upmarket brothel, introducing first the bawds:

> . . . now ceaz'd [seized] with age and both of them turn'd Bawds,
> old Hackney-women, they hire out their jades –
> a crew of whores far worse than Crocodiles,
> killing with feign'd Tears and forg'd Smiles.

The writer then launches into a lavish description of the kind of luxuries the wealthier client could indulge in:

> But if some Gallant, whose outside doth holde
> greate expectation of goode store of Golde
> . . . to see their choysest beauties him they bring
> . . . into a private room, which round aboute
> is hung with pictures: all which goodlie Rout
> is framed with Venus's fashyon, female all . . .
> and then good Bacchus' grape
> flowes in abundance . . . provocative to stirr up appetite
> to brutish luste & sensuall delightes . . .

The aperitif is followed by an epic aphrodisiac feast:

> . . . Lobsters' buttered thighs,
> Hartichoke, Marrowbone, Potato Pies,
> Anchoves, Lambes artificiallie drest stones,
> fine Gellies of decocted Sparrows' bones:
> or, if these faile, th'apothecaries' trade
> must furnishe them with rarest Marmelade,
> candid Cringoes & rich Marchpane [marzipan] stuffe
> . . . but then these daynties must be wash'd down well
> with Wine, with Sacke, with Sugar Eggs and Muskadine
> with Allegante [Alicante wine], the blood of Venerie.[7]

The women who worked in these establishments were almost, but not quite, of the courtesan class: well-educated, well-spoken; capable of playing musical instruments and singing to entertain their 'guests' in the palatial waiting-rooms; or of conversing with foreign clients in their native tongues. They were also well schooled in the rites of the gaming-table, since there were usually several gambling rooms on the premises. Above all, the whores were beautifully clean and presentable, for the madam, aided by a resident 'physitian', ensured that all her employees were adequately perfumed, pomandered and powdered, and that no 'vitious smells' should offend the nostrils of the upper-class clientele. Finally, a private garden provided an agreeable backdrop for the client who preferred at least to act out the romantic fantasy of courtship.

The lower-class brothels, meanwhile, were somewhat more utilitarian in decor, although good food and plenty of wine were nearly always available, and even the poorest houses provided drink. In general, the better the house, the fewer men per night a whore was expected to service; estimates vary, but here we should bear in mind that we are once again entering favourite male-obsession territory. A great many professorial brains have taxed themselves over this issue of *how many a night did they take?* – or cock-counts – with most writers assuming that in the top-notch houses such as the Holland's Leaguer, ten to twelve clients may have been the norm. This sounds highly unlikely, given that many of the clients who frequented these luxury establishments would have expected to spend some time – often a whole night – with one girl. Lower down the social scale, the estimates start to rocket, until we are finally presented with the absurd 'average' of 57 clients per night in the poorest whorehouses.

Whatever the actual score, the crucial fact remains that the sex trade was alive and kicking; the Reformation failed to repress it, for the usual reasons – supply and demand never faltered. The great wave of moralism that had opened the 16th century had been unable to 'wash cleaner' after all, although it had to some extent succeeded in terrorizing and punishing the lower classes in general and particularly women. By the early 17th century, prostitution was so widespread that the contemporary writer Thomas Heywood, in his *History Concerning Women*, did not trouble his readers with an account of it, but coyly claimed that every schoolboy of fifteen or sixteen had already had enough experience with prostitutes to write a book of his own.

Fortunes continued to be made, largely by third parties such as landlords and bawds. But many whores became rich in their own right, especially those whose clients came from the nobility, the gentry, and the upper bourgeoisie – precisely those classes who hotly denounced the 'abomination' of prostitution in public. Everyone knew that the men of the Court flocked to follow King James I to the Holland's Leaguer; and that the hypocritical cant of the rich and powerful was, as ever, mere window-dressing.

In spite of the *de facto* toleration of prostitution in the late 16th and early 17th centuries, the misogynistic attitudes of the Reformers had succeeded in tapping a vein of deep hostility towards women, particularly the 'immodest' variety. The Anglican Bishop Aylmer reiterated the clergyman's unquenchable hatred of the female sex during a sermon preached before Queen Elizabeth I. Wary perhaps of placing his own head on the block, the Bishop prefaced his diatribe with a rather obvious sop to Her Majesty:

> Women are of two sorts: some of them are wiser, better learned, discreeter and more constant than a number of men; but another and worse sort of them are fond, foolish, wanton, flibbergibs, tattlers, triflers, wavering, witless, without council, feeble, careless, rash, proud, dainty, tale-bearers, eavesdroppers, rumour-raisers, evil-tongued, worse-minded, and in everyway doltified with the dregs of the devil's dunghill.[8]

No prizes for guessing which sort the Bishop believed to be in the majority! In fact Aylmer elsewhere denounced even that rarest of creatures, the 'good' woman, as 'an eel put in a bag amongst five hundred snakes . . . if a man should have the luck to grope out the one

eel from all the snakes, yet he hath at best but a wet eel by the tail.'[9]
(Such fascinatingly *phallic* imagery might lead one to surmise that the
good bishop was really thinking of men when he wrote this passage.)

Bishop Aylmer was not alone in his low estimation of the entire
female sex. Another post-Reformation male (a member of that very
sex whose demands for commercial sex could never fully be met)
writes in a text dated 1616 that women are full of 'insatiable lust' and
'more desirous of carnall lust than man'; 'more hot than goats'; and
that woman's role in the world was to 'enterteine and nourish
voluptuousness and Idleness'.[10]

But it is Shakespeare's Lear who best articulates the horror with
which educated men of the period regarded the phantom female of
their own imagination:

> Down from the waist they are centaurs,
> Though women all above:
> But to the girdle do the gods inherit,
> Beneath is all the fiend's;
> There's hell, there's darkness, there's the
>   sulphurous pit,
> Burning, scalding, stench, consumption; fie, fie, fie!

(Centaurs were legendary for their sexual appetites.)

Given the wide currency of such hysterical and irrational attitudes,
it is hardly surprising that some of the choicest venom was reserved
for prostitutes. The Elizabethan and Jacobean playwrights, many of
whom were themselves solid burghers with financial stakes in the
Bankside whorehouses, routinely paraded their disgust for the whore.
In his play *The Honest Whore*, Dekker has Hippolito deliver a lengthy
tirade against a prostitute: 'Your body,' he tells her,

> Is like the common shore, that still receives
> All the town's filth. The sin of many men
> Is within you; and thus much I suppose,
> That if all your commiters stood in a rank,
> They'd make a lane in which your shame might dwell
> And with their spaces reach from hence to hell.[11]

Here it all is: *filth, sin, shame, hell . . . ad nauseam*, and beyond. The
anti-sex, patriarchal burden of guilt had at last succeeded in entering

the cultural imagination, where it was to fester for centuries to come. It was from this reservoir of sexual hatred that the Puritan movement drew its support throughout its prolonged struggle for control of British moral and political life in the 17th century.

The Puritans emerged in reaction to the renewed moral laxity (as they saw it) of the English establishment; and they took to extremes the Protestant work ethic, denouncing all forms of pleasure as sinful. The typical Puritan was a small proprietor or tradesman, dependent on hard work – his own, his family's, his employees' – for enrichment and the social climbing he aspired to and which was now possible in post-feudal society. Hence the Puritan attack on all forms of recreation – no matter how innocuous. Nothing was to be permitted that could distract 'Man' from the moral economy, and the iron laws of labour discipline.

The 17th-century Puritan author William Stubbes was a supreme example of the species; he saw multiple opportunities for sin in the working-class tradition of wake days (holidays): 'Why,' he wanted to know, 'should there be more excess of meat and drinks at that day, than at another? Why should they abstain from bodily labour two or three days after, peradventure, the whole week, spending it in drunkenness, whoredom, gluttony, and other filthy sodomitical exercises?'

Stubbes' anxiety over the loss of potential workdays is palpable. He concluded that the wakes were 'to no end, except it be to draw a great frequency of whores, drabbes, thieves and varlets together to maintain whoredom, bawdrie, gluttony, drunkenness – theft, murder, swearing, and all kind of mischief and abomination.' So much for holidays. But another working-class recreation – the heinous practice of dancing – drew out even more bile:

Dancing, as it is used (or rather abused) in these days, is an introduction to whoredom, a preparative to wantonness, a provocative to uncleanness, and an introite to all kinds of lewdness . . . For what clipping, what culling, what kissing and bussing, what smouching and slabbering one of another, what filthy groping and unclean handling is not practised everywhere in these dancings . . . and shewed forth in their bawdy gestures of one to another.[12]

Stubbes' prurient, paranoid imagination, charged with the sexuality he was desperately attempting to repress in everyone (not least himself), saw the hydra 'whoredom' everywhere. Inevitably, prostitution drew his greatest wrath; it also triggered off a kind of literary hurricane in the preacher's tormented brain. To Stubbes, there was 'no greater sin before the face of God than whoredom' – and he listed its dread consequences thus:

> For besides that it bring everlasting damnation . . . it also bringeth these inconveniences, with many more: . . . it dimmeth the sight, it impaireth the hearing, it infirmeth the sinews, it weakeneth the joints, it exhausteth the marrow, consumeth the moisture and supplement of the body, it rivelleth the face, appalleth the countenance, it dulleth the spirits, it hurteth the memory, it weakeneth the whole body, it bringeth it into a consumption, it bringeth ulcerations, scab, scurf, blain, botch, pocks, and biles; it maketh hoar hairs and bald pates; it induceth old age, and, *in fine*, bringeth death before nature urge it, malady enforce it, or old age require it.

If, according to Stubbes, the wages of sin were grim, his recommendations for the perpetrators of this 'crime' were grimmer still; he urged that whores should be 'cauterized and seared with a hot iron on the cheek, forehead or some other part of their body that might be seen, to the end [that] the honest and chaste Christians might be discerned from the adulterous children of Satan.'[13] Precious little in the way of Christian charity here; but when it came to whores, there never seemed to be enough of it to go round.

The Puritans were a cheerless sect, who preached that hard work, woe and the class system were God's will and that any remnants of the people's former pagan habits, such as enjoying themselves, were anathema to the Lord. Perhaps the best summary of Puritan attitudes towards the human race can be found in the text of a 17th-century sermon given by one Reverend Shepherd, in the New World town of Cambridge, Massachusetts: 'Thy heart is a foul sink of all atheism, sodomy, blasphemy, murder, whoredom, adultery, witchcraft, buggery; so that if thou hast any good in thee, it is but as a drop of rose water in a bowl of poison.'[14]

To the Puritans, Catholicism was mere wicked superstition, one step removed from the abomination of the Old Religion of the pagans;

none the less when it came to the subject of women, the Puritan patriarchs were more than happy to concur with the early Church Fathers. 'Who can be ignorant,' crowed John Milton, 'that woman was created for man, and not man for woman?' And: 'He for God only, she for God in him.' *Plus ça change . . .*

Guidelines for appropriate female behaviour were set down in one W. Whately's *The Bride Bush* (1617): 'If ever thou purpose to be a good wife, and to live comfortably, set down this with thyself: mine husband is my superior, my better; he hath authority and rule over me; nature hath given it to him . . . God hath given it to him.'[15]

Meekness was once more dredged up as the ideal attribute for the female sex: the 'good' woman, as far as the Puritan male was concerned, should be a silent, submissive, husband-obeying, child-breeding, modest, de-sexualized, non-answering-back, married un-paid drudge. *Amen.*

The Puritan campaigns to correct the morals of the English people held sway in the towns and cities; they made less headway in backward country regions, however, where to some extent the old ways still counted. Nevertheless, the Puritans tried to promulgate their anti-pleasure ideas wherever they could, even in the tiniest hamlet. The country Puritan tended to be an upwardly mobile small farmer, rising out of the peasantry and aiming for the middle classes. As his poorer neighbours fell victim to the era's economic storms, the Puritan would benefit by buying up their lands at a knock-down price and setting them to work as wage-labourers: thus he feathered his nest at the expense of others, contrary to the ancient social code of co-operation and mutual self-help. In order to justify this exploitation, the Puritan enlisted Protestant ideology, with its much-vaunted individualism and cult of hard work. Meanwhile, those peasants who were less 'morally' motivated held fast to their semi-pagan traditions of work – and play. The result was frequent conflict between the two classes of rural working people.

The Puritans were keen to prosecute and punish their neighbours for moral offences through the court systems (both secular and religious); the sheer volume of their records provides us with a mass of evidence of – in particular – the sexual practices of early 17th-century rural England. As far as the Puritans were concerned, there was always a great deal of scope for their snooping and denunciations, since 'sex was not a moral issue in most peasant communities.'[16] Quite apart from the 'promiscuous' sexuality of many women – both single and married – there was a thriving rural sex trade, which comprised several distinct categories of country prostitute.

At the low end of the scale were the 'vagrant', or wandering, prostitutes; poor women who travelled from parish to parish soliciting wherever they could find trade: at inns, markets, fairs, crossroads, etc. – much as women had done since the Dark Ages. There were also the 'public' whores, who worked from specific inns or bawdy-houses, always with an eye out for Puritan spies. 'Private' whores were still more discreet; these were women who would hire themselves out to a single man, or perhaps two or three, for a few weeks or months, before moving on to find new territory. Finally, there was the traditional 'village' whore, who worked from her own home and was often seen by the local authorities as something of a safeguard, or 'the almost respectable protector of the chastity and fidelity of other village women.'[17] Nor was the village whore necessarily a single woman: wives of local craftsmen and workers were known to work in this way – an indication of how well-integrated into the community was prostitution at this time.

During the 17th century the Puritans subjected all four categories of whores to legal harassment and intimidation, but as usual it was the poorest and most visible actively soliciting whore – the 'vagrant' – who was especially vulnerable to being charged and punished by the self-appointed guardians of morality.

A woman named Lucy Francis was prosecuted after arriving in the village of Dulverton, where she worked the inns and alehouses, and also called on the weavers in their cottages and workshops: 'Putting her back towards the side of the looms [she] said these words . . . Here is a good place to go at trading: [when asked why] she answered, because there was a good footing for that she could not slide.' Later Lucy came into a man's house and thrust herself on his lap, saying, 'I must needs kiss you.'[18]

In the case of the 'public' whores of the inns and taverns, the Puritans often had to compile their accusations by spying on their intended victims. Two such voyeurs witnessed the following scene between a man called Spark and the resident prostitute, Margaret Barber, at a tavern in Bridgewater:

This deponent and his fellow witness went to the door and looked in where they saw . . . Spark throw her down upon the bed, and laid himself upon her, and with his right hand he pulled up all her clothes, and unloosed his hose before, and pulled forth his privy member, and put him in her secret part, and when he had done what he would he rose from her and fastened up his hose again.[19]

The moralists kept a sharp look-out where all-female families were concerned, for many of these plied the old profession together. At Pitminster it was reported that 'Mary Harbord and her sister being young women unmarried doth sell ale and often keepeth much disorder in their house', while at Wells the team of Mary Chaddock, a widow, and her daughters Margery and Mary were prosecuted for keeping a disorderly house and 'suspicion of incontinent living with soldiers'.[20] Ann Morgan of Wells was reported by the nightwatchman, who duly regurgitated the following negotiation: the client enquiring, 'Shall I lie with thee and give thee a shilling?' Ann replied, 'No, I will have eighteen pence for thou hast torn my coat and has hindered me the knitting of half a hose.' This enterprising woman was known to operate a sliding scale, charging soldiers double the usual fee of 1s 3d. Ann was also known to employ neighbouring women occasionally, sending out for three or four of them to help out if demand was high. The Puritan justices of the town punished her in the usual manner: she was clapped in the stocks on market day. One of her unfortunate clients was made to 'ride the wooden horse' and then 'washed in the palace moat'.

Nor were men of the cloth exempt from the Puritans' vigilance. There is evidence to suggest that a number of 'private' whores were part of a circuit involving the clergy: an enterprising ring of prostitution. One west-county cleric, Robert Wolfall, was accused of 'incontinent living' with three such women in succession, one of whom he installed in his house openly as his mistress – 'to the great grief of Mrs Wolfall his wife'. The curate of Locking in Somerset was charged by his Puritan parishioners with frequenting 'the company of . . . a common strumpet, and more hath her abroad at fairs'; while yet another 'notorious clerical lecher' (this one hailed from Glastonbury) 'used the company of three whored women'.[21]

'Private' whores were a particular thorn in the flesh of the moralists. Widows, unmarried women and wives who had left their husbands often transacted with men to maintain them in return for sexual services. The Church courts waged a constant and virulent battle against this amicable practice, denouncing the 'abomination' of

women who preferred to be kept by several men at once, and resisted
Puritan exhortations to be the permanent chattel of one man alone.

By contrast the village whore was rarely prosecuted; she tended to
keep a lower profile and often her transactions were in kind: she would
trade sex for the gathering of her corn or the milking of her cows. Isott
Wall of Tolland in Somerset was a private village whore who would,
she announced, 'open her door at any time of the night either to a
married man or a young man'. Isott was reputedly knowledgeable in
matters of contraception and abortion: in her opinion, 'those are fools
that would be with child.'[22]

The local whore of the village of Pensfield was a married woman;
the parish priest was one of her most regular clients, much to the
disgust of the churchwarden – a Puritan.

Traditionally, a simplistic distinction has been made between the attitudes of the Royalist 'cavaliers' and those of their 'roundhead' enemies
during the period of the English Revolution and Civil War. The former
are depicted as dashing and permissive – in favour of all forms of pleasure
and enjoyment – while the latter are characterized by their dourness.
Although these popular images are in the main correct, they by no means
tell the whole story; the governments of the Stuart kings were in fact
alternately lenient and repressive, according to what suited their political
motives. Equally, the Puritans had their own advocates of a legalized
sex trade – properly regulated and supervised by themselves, of course.

The Royalists played a cat-and-mouse game with the sex trade.
While James I had been the most illustrious client of Mother Holland's
Leaguer, his successor Charles I ordered the authorities to close the
brothel down. A troop of soldiers was duly sent to enforce the closure,
but the unfortunate men were dumped into the moat when Mother
Holland herself let down the drawbridge. The girls of the house then
proceeded to empty their 'pissing-pots' over the squad, who retreated
in some disarray. The whores' victory was short-lived, however; by
the following year the Leaguer was successfully closed down and the
property sold to some 'respectable' traders. Charles also decreed the
suppression of the sex trade in Cowcross, Turmil Street, Charter-
house Lane, Saffronhill, Bloomsbury, Petticoat Lane, Wapping,
Ratcliffe and all the other London districts where passers-by were
'pestered with many immodest, lascivious and shameless women
generally reputed for notorious common and professed whores . . .
exposing and offering themselves'[23] in their doorways.

As usual, a crackdown in one area invariably resulted in the business shifting to another; it was never completely stifled. From 1632 Bow Street was, along with Drury Lane, reputed as 'troblinge the adjacent areas . . . by lewdest *Blades* and female *Naughty-Packs*',[24] and from 1640 onwards Covent Garden was a notorious haunt for whores and their clients; they were 'active' beneath the arches of the Piazza at the centre of the district. In 1641 an Act of the Long Parliament under Charles I proclaimed that prostitution was no longer a criminal offence; henceforth it was to be seen in law as a 'public nuisance' – or a 'gross indecency' if committed in public. Apparently the general trend of the Stuart administration was moving towards liberalizing the laws surrounding prostitution – but this thaw was to be short-lived, and was swiftly overtaken by the events of the Civil War and the ensuing Puritan Commonwealth.

As with any war, the battle between the Royalists and the Puritans was disastrous to civilian life and trade. For many professional whores – and for the 'respectable' women whose livelihoods were ruined in the turmoil – their only chance of survival lay in the time-honoured tradition of becoming camp followers: 'ammunition whores', in the contemporary slang. This so upset the upper ranks of the army that in 1643 King Charles I was forced to issue a proclamation castigating the 'general licentiousness, profanity, drunkenness, and whoremongering of the army'.[25] (It appears that a great number of soldiers preferred to dally with the whores than to go and fight for their king.) Equally outrageous to the senior ranks was the practice of cross-dressing by many of the women, who took to wearing uniform as a way of avoiding the drudgery that was routinely expected from a female camp follower. Another royal proclamation was hurriedly posted at the head of every regiment:

. . . because the confounding of Habits appertaining to both Sexes and the promiscuous use of them is a thing which Nature and Religion forbid and our Soul abhors, and yet the prostitute Impudency of some women . . . have (which we cannot think on but with Just Indignation) thus conversed in our Army; therefore let no Woman presume to Counterfeit her Sex by wearing mans apparell under pain of the Severest punishment which Law and our displeasure shall inflict.[26]

Prostitutes were made to understand that they were permitted to follow the army on sufferance only; and that while they were often tolerated, even quartered with the troops, they could be and were severely punished for any supposed misdemeanour. One whore who had accompanied the Royalist army from London to Coventry was, according to the records, 'taken by the soldiers, and first led about the city then set in the pillory, after in a cage, then ducked in the river, and at last banished the city.'[27]

After the Puritan victory it was assumed that prostitution would be eradicated; although there were those who, even in the Puritan ranks, still saw a place for it in the new moral society. A Doctor Chamberlen proposed to Parliament in 1649, the first year of the Commonwealth, that state-regulated bathhouses with registered whores should be opened throughout the country. This Solonic scheme was turned down, however, and the Puritans busied themselves instead with concocting legislation that would obliterate not only the country's remaining brothels but its theatres, gambling dens, race-courses – and maypoles. All forms of entertainment were anathema to the new Commonwealth; thus actors found themselves lined up in the docks alongside whores and their bawds; all were summarily tried and punished, by fines, beatings and imprisonments. The Puritans went to absurd lengths to enforce their policies: maypoles were pulled down in towns and villages throughout the land, and nude statues were either smashed to pieces or had their insolent genitals 'decently' clothed.

Alehouses and taverns, always a favourite haunt of whores and their clients, were strictly limited in number, and their owners had to be continually on the look-out for army raids. This was undoubtedly one of the bleakest periods in history for the prostitutes of England. A contemporary text commiserates with the whores of London:

> If you step aside into Covent Garden, Long Acre and Drury Lane, where these *Doves of Venus*, those Birds of Youth and Beauty – the Wanton Ladies – doe builde their *Nestes*, you shall find them in suche a *Dump* of Amazement to see the Hopes of their tradeinge frustrate . . . [Before Puritan times] Ten or Twentie Pound Suppers were but Trifles to them . . . they are nowe forc'd to make doe on a diet of Cheese and Onions . . . the ruination of Whoreinge was why the London Bawds hated 1641 like an old Cavalier.[28]

Nevertheless, some high-class London establishments, such as

'Oxford Kate's' in Bow Street, continued to trade, albeit discreetly; presumably this was due to the fact that their owners had powerful and influential clientele. From 1652 the new coffee-houses quickly established themselves as meeting-places for whores and their clients – and if a popular couplet of 1656 is to be believed, the clergy kept up its traditional association with the sex trade:

> lousy cowls come smoking from the stewes,
> to raise the lewd rent their Lord accrues.[29]

In spite of all the crushing propaganda, in spite of the brutal physical punishments, and in spite of the whole dogma of misery and guilt preached by the Puritans, the poor – both peasantry and working people of the towns and cities – attempted to live their lives in the old ways, as best they could. Life was hard, and when they were not working, enjoyment was a priority, even at the risk of punishment. The people did not permit their masters to rob them entirely of their own culture, which was tolerant of and open about pleasure and sexuality; a culture in which the whore had always had an assured and important role. The new bourgeois ideals of chastity and sobriety made little headway against the ingrained traditions of the poor.

By the time Cromwell was dead the steam had gone out of the Puritans' campaigns of moral repression. Instead of creating a nation of God-fearing fundamentalists they had stoked up the fires of an irrepressible popular resentment against state intervention in private pleasures. There were few mourners, and a great many revellers, in the bawdy-houses and lower-class streets of the capital on Tuesday 29 May 1660, when Charles II came home to claim his throne and thereby inaugurate the unprecedented licentiousness of the Restoration period.

CHAPTER NINE

Almighty Curtezan: the Triumph of the Aristocracy

. . . that glorious insolent Thing, that makes Mankind such Slaves, almighty Curtezan.

Aphra Behn (1640–89)

The English revolution in the first half of the 17th century, when the forces of Parliament challenged and defeated those of the Stuart monarchy, was the first great trial of absolutism. Charles I lost his head, and the Puritan Commonwealth was installed. However, thanks to the support of his French cousin Louis XIV, the young Charles II managed to survive the years of turmoil and exile to return in triumph to the throne of England in late spring 1660. With him came a flood of cavalier aristocrats, who were more than eager to resume the leisured lifestyle which they had enjoyed formerly, and which Cromwell had so rudely interrupted. The Restoration was an apparent triumph for the aristocracy – although there were strings attached. For while the monarchy had succeeded in being reinstated, it depended more than ever on the financial and political support of the City of London – the powerhouse of a youthful, hungry capitalism. Now, even the nobility were obliged to dirty their hands in the acquisition of money.

Thus the outward forms of absolutism were maintained while the society it ruled over was transformed; a process that was to continue unabated throughout the coming century, during which time the money economy pursued its implacable erosion of the old feudal ways, until the field was clear for the Industrial Revolution of the late eighteenth century. It is interesting to compare the situation in

England with that of France, the political kingpin of absolutist
Europe, where the apparently unassailable ascendancy of the Bourbon
kings masked social tensions that were perhaps less visible but
certainly no less intense. Here, the centralized absolute power of the
royal state was destined to come under increasing challenge from
reform-minded intellectuals on the one hand and rebellious peasants
on the other; a situation that was to culminate in the French
Revolution of 1789. Arguably, the English aristocracy avoided a
similar bloodbath by engaging in an uneasy compromise with the
Puritan middle classes who held the purse-strings. Not that they were
discouraged from indulging in their old habits of debauchery; quite
the contrary. The English aristocracy were to set the tone for an age of
sensual indulgence that would last for well over a century – they might
have lost control of their finances, but they never lost their enthusiasm
for sexual indulgence.

The English Restoration period was an exemplary one in so far as
matters of morality were concerned: to the rest of society – which
secretly or openly wished to ape its fashionable 'betters' – the example
of public licentiousness given by the aristocracy was certainly
unprecedented. Demoralized by the decay of their old world, they had
begun to gallop after their pleasures with increasing desperation,
cynicism, and violence: drinking, whoring and gambling were the
order of the day. And social conditions could not have been more ideal
for this kind of excessive self-indulgence; for with English society a
melting pot of radical transition, constantly – and dangerously –
approaching chaos, there was always plenty of scope for outrageous
behaviour.

Being in essence a leisured class, one of the main functions of the
aristocracy was to enjoy itself ostentatiously, and this they set about
doing with a vengeance. It has to be said that there was never a king
more congenial to such display than Charles II. The Earl of Rochester
– wit, rake, poet, and great crony of His Majesty – wrote of him:

> Peace is his aim, his gentleness is such,
> And love he loves, for he loves fucking much.
> Nor are his high desires above his strength;
> His sceptre and his prick are of a length . . .
> Restless he rolls about from whore to whore,
> A merry monarch, scandalous and poor.[1]

In fact the court of Charles II was a notorious sexual hive that buzzed with intrigue and scandal; here, affairs with courtesans and mistresses took up at least as much time and energy as affairs of state. Apart from his noble regular mistresses, the king was supplied by the royal pander William Chiffinch with a constant stream of casual partners who were hand-picked from the whores and actresses of the capital. The chief royal mistresses were a motley crew; they included the nymphomaniac aristocratic troublemaker Barbara Villiers, Duchess of Cleveland; silly, simpering Frances Stewart, who alternately exasperated and enthralled the King with her coyness; the pious and arrogant Louise de Kéroualle, a gift from the King's beloved sister at the French court; and Kéroualle's arch-rival, the incomparable gutter-brat 'Mistress Nelly' Gwyn. Between them these constantly bickering, scheming lovelies managed to drive deep furrows into the royal brow. Indeed they so monopolized the king's time that, according to Samuel Pepys, the famous diarist of the period: 'He usually came from his mistress's lodgings to church, even on sacrament days; [he] held as it were a court in them: and all his ministers made applications to them.'[2] The way to His Majesty's heart was, it appears, through his whores.

Needless to say the rest of the court were disposed to follow the royal example – to the extent that aspiring courtiers made sure they took at least one mistress as a matter of course; without a whore as accessory, a gentleman looked ridiculous. The custom became so widespread among the fashionable and wealthy set that it was easy for a woman of independent mind, wit, and passable good looks to make a fine living as the mistress of a nobleman, City gentleman, or government bureaucrat. There were plenty of women who had need of such an outlet for their talents: daughters of nobles impoverished by the Civil War, or of impecunious country clergymen (like the father of Rochester's mistress, 'the exquisite Jane Roberts'), or of bankrupted businessmen; even – occasionally – low-born girls up from the country to escape the drudgery and poverty of provincial peasant life.

But not all the women who took this course did so out of financial need – which is what makes the story of Catherine Sedley so interesting. Daughter of Sir Charles Sedley, renowned wit and a familiar figure at court, and his wife the former Lady Catherine Savage, heiress to Earl Rivers, the young Catherine was the sole legitimate heir to the family fortune, and therefore a rich catch for any nobleman with an eye to marrying into money. But Catherine had other ideas. Born in 1657, and raised amidst the promiscuous Restoration nobility, she knew that as a courtesan she could expect to enjoy a great deal more independence than her pliant married contemporaries, and at the same time increase her own fortune.

Catherine was not particularly beautiful; her talents lay elsewhere – by all accounts she was a great wit and excellent company. When she was placed at court as maid of honour to the wife of James, Duke of York – the king's brother – it was merely a question of time before she became the Duke's mistress. In due course Charles died and the Duke became King James II; Catherine retained her position as his mistress and was promptly installed in a mansion in St James's Square, with a yearly pension of £4000 from the royal purse. By the time the militantly Catholic James had been ousted from the throne in 1688, Catherine had been created Countess of Dorchester and Baroness Darlington; she survived with aplomb into the next reign, receiving a pension of £1500 a year from King William of Orange, who, it was said, 'feared the lash of her tongue'.[3] When in 1696, at the age of 38, she married a veteran Scottish soldier, Sir David Colyear (later Earl of Potmore), Catherine brought with her not only her own inherited wealth but also the riches and titles she had amassed during her courtesan years: all of which gave her autonomy within the marriage. In spite of the jibes and bitchiness of the wits and satirists, this marriage was successful, and Catherine lived to the relatively ripe old age of 60. She died in 1717, having enjoyed a lifetime of both independence and security, not to mention sexual adventure: no mean feat for a woman of any era – including our own.

Although there was a continuous and plentiful supply of potential mistresses from within their own ranks, this did not prevent the upper classes from choosing their sexual playmates from the *hoi polloi* from time to time. The Earl of Rochester captures the Restoration aristocrat's attitude perfectly, in the following description of his daily labours:

> I rise at eleven, I dine at two,
> I get drunk before seven, and the next thing I do
> I send for my whore when, for fear of the clap,
> I come in her hand and I spew in her lap.
> Then we quarrel and scold till I fall fast asleep,
> When the bitch, growing bold, to my pocket doth creep.

> She slyly then leaves me, and to revenge my affront
> At once she bereaves me of money and cunt.
> I storm and I roar, and I fall in a rage,
> And, missing my whore, I bugger my page.[4]

This type of street whore mentioned in Rochester's charming ditty was a regular feature not only in the households of the nobility but also at court. Samuel Pepys tells us of a court club of 'young blades' who called themselves the 'Ballers', at whose meetings a well-known procuress, 'my Lady Bennet', would present her 'ladies'. The company present would proceed to indulge in 'dancing naked, and all the roguish things in the world'.[5] Not that the aristocracy restrained themselves when it came to public behaviour either; on the contrary, they were fond of taking their pleasures at such public houses as Oxford Kate's, or trawling the brothels of the common people. Once again Pepys recounts an edifying anecdote involving Sir Charles Sedley, intimate of the king's circle (and father of the courtesan Catherine):

> Mr Batten [told] us of a late triall of Sir Charles Sydly the other day, before my Lord Chief Justice Foster and the whole Bench, for his debauchery a little while since at Oxford Kate's; coming in open day into the balcone and [showing] his nakedness – acting all the postures of lust and buggery that could be imagined, and abusing of scripture and, as it were, from thence preaching a mountebanke sermon from that pulpitt, saying that there he hath to sell such a powder as should make all the cunts in town run after him – a thousand people standing underneath to see and hear him. And that being done, he took a glass of wine and washed his prick in it and then drank it off; and then took another and drank the King's health.[6]

Sedley, of course, had little to fear by way of retribution from his peers on the Bench; at worst, a prank such as the above would gain its perpetrator a few weeks' banishment from court – the better to sober up at his country seat in preparation for the next bender.

King Charles himself was known greatly to enjoy the carryings-on of the court wits when they graced the nation's common whores with their presence – although on one recorded occasion, this was to backfire on him. The contemporary writer Theophilus Cibber provides an account of an escapade in which his great friend the manic Rochester persuaded His Majesty to visit a whorehouse in Newmarket, in disguise. Unknown to him, the wily Earl had previously instructed the king's whore to relieve him of his money and watch. When the time came to pay up, the King – still disguised – found that he was penniless, and that Rochester had vanished. He was reduced to asking the madam for credit. 'The consequence,' Cibber recalls, 'was [that] he was abused and laughed at; and the old woman told him that she had often been served such dirty tricks, and would not permit him to stir till the reckoning was paid, and then called one of her bullies to take care of him.' Finally, 'after many altercations', the King prevailed on the madam to call out a jeweller to value a ring he had offered as security. The jeweller was duly summoned from his bed and shown the ring, 'which as soon as he had inspected, he stood amazed, and enquired with eyes fixed upon the fellow, who had he got in his house? To which she replied, a black-looking ugly son of a whore, who had no money in his pocket, and was obliged to pawn his ring. The ring, says the jeweller, is so immensely rich, that but one man in the nation could afford to wear it; and that one is the King . . . The old Jezebel and the bully, finding the extraordinary quality of their guest, were now confounded, and asked pardon most submissively on their knees. The King in the best-natured manner forgave them, and laughing asked whether the ring would not bear another bottle.'[7]

Rochester got his come-uppance shortly after this incident. Pepys reports hearing at Whitehall 'the silly discourse of the King, with his people about him, telling a story of my Lord Rochester's having of his clothes stole, while he was with a wench, and his gold all gone, but his clothes found afterwards stuffed into a feather bed by the wench that stole them.'[8]

Given their penchant for disguise and play-acting among themselves, it is hardly surprising that the theatre was one of the favourite haunts of the court nobility. Brutally suppressed by the Puritans, the theatres were swiftly reinstated by Charles, with the innovation that women were now permitted to take over the female roles (where before these had been played by boys). This theatrical revolution was to have important consequences for the women who worked in Restoration theatres – on both sides of the curtain.

As in the days before Puritan rule, the city's whores began to flock to the theatre, where there were rich pickings to be made among the courtiers, gentlemen and burghers in the audience. Two specialist types of theatre prostitute sprang up almost immediately. Firstly, there were the orange-girls, who paraded through the auditorium selling fruit, playbills and themselves, or acting as go-betweens in the intrigues of fellow-whores and their clients. Diverse talents were required in order to be successful at this trade, not the least of which was a ready wit. 'Orange Betty' Mackerell was an almost legendary example of the orange-seller whore: she was much admired for her physical strength and lightning tongue, as well as for her promiscuity. In one contemporary satire the wits of the pit are described as being 'hot at repartee with Orange Betty'.[9]

The second type of theatre prostitute was the true professional; the whore who specialized in working within the auditorium itself. These ladies were known as 'vizards', after the face-masks they wore. Pepys remarks in his diary, after sitting next to one of them at a performance: 'She is a whore, I believe, for she is acquainted with every fine fellow and called them by their name, Jack and Tom, and before the end of the play frisked to another place.'[10] And a somewhat peevish play prologue, written in 1691 by John Dryden, depicts these denizens of the theatrical sex trade in action:

> Permit me now, *Dear Strephon*, to relate,
> The Tricks and Wiles of Whores of *Second Rate*,
> The *Play-house Punks*, who in loose Undress,
> Each Night receive some *Cullies*★ soft Address;
> Reduc'd perhaps to the last poor *half Crown*,
> A tawdry *Gown* and *Petticoat* put on,
> Go to the House, where they demurely sit
> Angling for *Bubbles* in the noisy *Pit*:
> Not *Turks* by *Turbans*, *Spaniards* by their *Hats*,
> Not *Quakers* by Diminutive *Cravats*
> Are better known, than is the *Tawdry Crack*†
> By Vizor-Mask, and Rigging on her Back.
> The Play-house is their place of Traffick, where
> Nightly they sit, to sell their *Rotten Ware*:
> Tho' done in silence and without a Cryer
> Yet he that bids the most, is still the Buyer;

★ Dupe's.
† Whore.

> For while he nibbles at her *Am'rous Trap*,
> She gets the *Mony*, but he gets the *Clap*.
> Intrencht in *Vizor Mask*, they Giggling sit,
> And throw designing Looks about the Pit,
> Neglecting wholly what the Actors say,
> 'Tis their least business there to see the Play.[11]

(Note that, as usual, it is the unfortunate male customer who gets the 'clap' from the whore; *never* vice versa.)

The three tiers of the auditorium provided a stamping-ground for at least three classes of prostitute. The most expensive women prowled the pit and the boxes, where the fashionable courtiers and nobles were to be found. The middle gallery, a bourgeois enclave, was frequented by women whose prices were more moderate; it also appears to have been regularly invaded by drunken pimps and ponces. Finally, the upper gallery was the territory of the common people and their cheap 'bulkers', or poor street whores. Between them the whores and their pimps made such an uproar that playwrights frequently complained of the distraction:

> . . . some there are, who take their first Degrees
> Of Lewdness, in our Middle Galleries:
> The Doughty BULLIES enter Bloody Drunk,
> Invade and grubble one another's PUNK:
> They Caterwaul and make a dismal Rout,
> Call SONS of WHORES, and strike, but ne'er lugg-out:
> Thus, while for *Paultry Punk* they roar and stickle,
> They make it Bawdier than a CONVENTICLE.[12]

One whore of the theatre who was extremely popular was 'Black Bess', a woman of peasant origins whose prodigious attractions ensnared the Earl of Dorset. He addressed the following verse eulogy to her:

> The ploughman and the squire, the arranter clown,
> At home she subdued in her paragon gown;
> But now she adorns both the boxes and pit,
> And the proudest town gallants are forc'd to submit;
> All hearts fall a-leaping, wherever she comes,
> And beat day and night, like my Lord Craven's drums.[13]

Bess was unabashed by the contempt of her female 'superiors'. When one noblewoman called her Dorset's whore, Bess retorted that she was proud that she had at least pleased 'one man of wit' – and let 'all the coxcombs dance to bed with you!'[14]

Prostitution also thrived within the ranks of the acting profession. The Restoration stage was the launchpad of many a brilliant second career for a woman of low birth, so long as she had the necessary talent and drive to raise herself out of poverty. But this could not be achieved through acting alone, for it was a poorly paid profession. Actresses were thus obliged either to marry well, or to take up prostitution as a lucrative sideline. It became a common practice for an actress to use the stage as a means of attracting wealthy clients, and, in many cases, a good match. Soon the word 'actress' became synonymous with 'whore'; for after all, as the satirist Tom Browne wryly observed: "Tis as hard a matter for a pretty Woman to keep herself honest in a Theatre, as 'tis for an Apothecary to keep his Treacle from the Flies in Hot Weather; for every Libertine in the Audience will be buzzing about her Honey-Pot.'[15]

Elizabeth Barry was the possessor of one such honey-pot. Born in poverty and obscurity, she made her stage debut in 1674, at the age of sixteen. It was a disaster. However, the canny Rochester – an unlikely talent-spotter, on the face of it – obviously saw some untapped potential in the girl, for he took her under his wing, wagering with a friend that he could transform her into a successful actress. For the next six months Rochester coached Elizabeth intensively; according to the actor-manager Thomas Betterton, he taught her 'to enter into the meaning of every sentiment; he taught her not only the proper cadence or sounding of the voice, but to seize also the passions, and adapt her whole behaviour to the situations of the characters.'[16]

Rochester, it seems, was the original teacher of 'Method' acting. He was immensely successful, for when Barry returned to the stage Betterton judged her to be 'incomparable'; she could, he observed, transform the dullest production into something of rare quality.

Another result of the collaboration was that Rochester became infatuated by his protégée; it was, however, a case of unrequited love. Her new success ensured Elizabeth a rich harvest in generous beaux, and Rochester, after the initial heat of their affair had died down, was often left in the cold. "Tis impossible for me to curse you,' the disappointed Pygmalion wrote to Elizabeth, 'but give me leave to pity myself, which is more than you will ever do for me.'[17]

Barry had a reputation for haughtiness and a businesslike attitude towards her lovers; Tom Browne bemoaned the fact that 'should you lie with her all night, she would not know you next morning, unless you had another five pounds at your service.'[18]

All told, Elizabeth received little by way of finance from Rochester; he nevertheless provided her with a sound training – and a daughter. However, the famous playwright George Etherege gave her a generous settlement after his liaison with her; and at the end of a long and illustrious career as an actress-whore Elizabeth retired to the country at Acton. Upon her death her theatrical contemporary Colly Cibber wrote in his obituary to her:

> Mrs Barry, in Characters of Greatness, had a Presence of elevated Dignity, her Mien and Motion superb and gracefully Majestick; her Voice full, clear, and strong, so that no Violence of Passion could be too much for her: and when Distress or Tenderness possess'd her, she subsided into the most affecting Melody and Softness. In the Art of exciting Pity she had a Power beyond all the Actresses I have yet seen, or what your Imagination can conceive.[19]

The best-known and most beloved actress-courtesan of the Restoration period was without a doubt the legendary 'pretty, witty' Nell Gwyn, who rose from the gutter to become King Charles II's favourite and most long-standing mistress. In a sense Nell's birth in a backstreet bawdy-house in the slums of Covent Garden was an auspicious one; for although poor, she came of age at a time when the regenerated English theatre was wide open to female talent. Also, Nell was close enough to it – the King's Theatre was in Drury Lane, just around the corner from her mother's bawdy-house – to have daily access to its colourful world of actors, actresses, and whores. As a child Nell served 'strong waters' (Nantes brandy) to the customers in her mother's house; a fitting apprenticeship for a girl with ambition; for here she would have needed a fast and ready wit.

By the time she was thirteen Nell had graduated to working at the theatre, as an orange-girl. There, her beauty, charm and wit were soon noticed by the actors, and she quickly made the transition to the stage. At fifteen she was appearing in minor roles, and had scored her first major success – as the mistress of the actor-manager Charles Hart. Samuel Pepys, an indefatigable theatre-goer, first encountered Nelly on 23 January 1667, when a friend took him back-stage: 'and Knipp took us all in, and brought us to Nelly, a most pretty woman, who acted the part of Celia today very fine . . . I kissed her, and so did my wife; and a mighty pretty soul she is.'[20]

Nell, who was by nature 'impudent, brazen, and devastating in her mimicry',[21] had an unsurpassed comic talent; her performance as the 'mad girl' Florimell, in Dryden's *The Maiden Queene*, made her a star of the Restoration theatre. Pepys went into raptures when he first saw the play, in March 1667:

> There is a comical part done by Nell, which is Florimell, that I never can hope ever to see the like done again by man or woman. The King and Duke of York was at the play; but so great performance of a comical part was never, I believe, in the world before as Nell doth this, both as a mad girle and then, most and best of all, when she comes in like a young gallant; and hath the motions and carriage of a spark the most that ever I saw any man have. It makes me, I confess, admire her.[22]

Having the heroine of a play disguise herself as a 'spark', or fashionable youth, was a common device which allowed actresses to show off their bodies in tight breeches: and it was generally acknowledged at the time that little Mrs Nelly was the possessor of a particularly fine, shapely pair of legs. The King was so pleased with *The Maiden Queen* – and with its leading actress – that he ordered it to be performed at the palace. From this time onwards, Nell's star was firmly in the ascendant.

The first courtier to come buzzing at her honey-pot was Lord Buckhurst, a well-known wit and *bon viveur*, who gave her £100 a year to quit the stage and, for a brief time, kept a 'merry house' with her at Epsom. The liaison did not last, however, and soon Nell was back treading the boards; this time winning the favours of Buckhurst's brother Charles, Earl of Dorset. Before long Nell rose even higher in her secondary career; first she became an occasional night visitor to the king, then eventually she was established as principal royal mistress. Bishop Burnet, cleric to the rich and powerful at court, wrote of her:

> . . . the indiscreetest and wildest creature that ever was in court, continued to the end of the king's life in great favour, and was maintained at vast expense. The Duke of Buckingham told me,

that . . . she had got of the king above sixty thousand pounds. She acted all persons in so lively a manner, and was such a constant diversion to the king, that even a new mistress could not drive her away . . . [She] called the king her Charles the third. Since she had been formerly kept by two of that name [i.e. Hart and Dorset].[23]

As the rather churlish Burnet noted, the rise and fall of subsequent mistresses never eclipsed 'Mrs Nelly', who always retained a down-to-earth awareness of the role played by the women of the king's harem. She had no time for the posturings and hypocrisy of her arch-rival the French noblewoman, Louise de Kéroualle, who continually put on airs and graces in order to distract attention (so she thought) from her status as royal whore. Nell said of her, bluntly: '[she] pretends to be a person of quality. She claims that everyone in France is her relation; the moment some great one dies she puts on mourning. Well! If she be a lady of such quality, why then does she demean herself to be a courtezan? She ought to die with shame . . . as for me, 'tis my profession; I do not pretend to aught better.'[24]

And it was a profession which paid her handsomely, notwithstanding a brief period of insecurity when Charles died and was succeeded by his dour brother James II. The latter had often been the butt of Nell's lethal wit at court – she had memorably dubbed him 'dismal Jimmy'. Charles's last words, however, had been 'Let not poor Nelly starve'; and James eventually honoured his brother's dying wish. Although Nell's annual pension from Charles of £4000 was also deceased, the new king granted her a generous £1500 a year for life, as well as paying off all Nell's creditors. In addition, the former royal mistress retained the houses, estates and incomes which Charles had granted her during the long years of their liaison; thus the one-time gutter-brat possessed an estate valued at around £100,000. Her will mentions 'houses, lands, tenements, offices, places, pensions, annuities, and hereditaments';[25] her house in Pall Mall was worth at least £10,000; while the one at Windsor, Burford House, was valued at twice that figure. Because of her low origins Charles had hesitated to reward Nell with titles (his death had inconveniently forestalled his creating her Duchess of Greenwich), but he had made their son Charles Duke of St Albans; thus from Nell Gwyn and Charles II there descends a ducal dynasty which flourishes to this day.

As a rags-to-riches story, Nell's is unique; although she was by no means the only poorly-born girl who succeeded in carving out a place for herself among the wealthy and privileged in Restoration society. Prostitution – and, to a lesser extent, the stage – were the only careers open to talent and ambition for women in a society in which there were rigid boundaries between the classes. No actor, it must be stressed, could ever have earned as much as Nell did; and no male could dream of rising from the gutter to the court. But this is not to undermine Nell's triumph, far from it. Her success was never compromised by her conforming to alien standards of ersatz 'respectability' – which was perhaps her secret. In whatever circles she moved, Nell was always free to be her own subversive, scandalous self: 'the darling strumpet of the crowd,' as Rochester called her. 'By nature humorous, pleasure-loving, and frankly carnal, she chose prostitution as an honourable and lucrative profession in an age when the successful courtesan was socially approved.'[26]

And by that same route Nell Gwyn succeeded in raising herself as far above the common lot of her working-class sisters as it was possible to go; this was her supreme achievement.

The moral decadence of the aristocracy continues to be one of the major themes that animated history during the eighteenth century. In France, Louis XIV finally managed to die in 1715; his lengthy reign gave way to 'one of the most flamboyantly licentious and corrupt moments of French history', during which fashionable society, headed by the Regent, the Duke of Orleans, 'gave itself up to an orgy of extravagance and frivolity'.[27] As the century progressed, the nobility became ever more cynical and corrupt: in England, gangs of aristocratic youths such as the Mohocks roamed the streets of London by night, mugging, raping and murdering innocent citizens – for kicks. Their titled elders, meanwhile, formed themselves into exclusive sects such as the infamous Hell-Fire Club, at whose meetings the lords and ladies amused themselves by indulging in orgies and partner-swapping in the ruins of an ancient abbey. Both the upper-class taste for the defloration of virgins, and the 'English Vice' – the penchant for flagellation amongst the rulers of British society – spread like wildfire. The French historian Taine wrote a brief but accurate description of an English 'Don Juan'; his sketch could equally have applied to any noble rake of the period: 'Unyielding pride, the desire to subjugate others, the provocative love of battle, the need for ascendancy, these are his predominant features. Sensuality is but of secondary importance compared with these.'[28]

Such prepossessing characteristics hardly made for amicable relations between the sexes, which swiftly degenerated into more or less undeclared war. 'Men sought to use women as instruments for their convenience. Women accepted men as filthy creatures, whom one could unfortunately not do without.'[29]

Against such a backdrop of contempt and aggression, the sexual violence of the Marquis de Sade appears quite unremarkable. This late 18th-century flower of the French nobility (who is still, depressingly, proclaimed a sexual liberator of women by some 'libertarians') took great delight in imprisoning, torturing, and poisoning prostitutes and other working-class women. He wrote exhaustively – and tediously – about his pleasures, and capped the period by giving his own name to the sensibility of his class: 'sadism'.

In the context of aristocratic excess, the court of Catherine the Great, Empress of Russia (1762–96), makes an interesting digression. Here, it was a woman rather than a man whose carnal habits set the example for the rest of high society to follow. Catherine was a woman with an immense appetite for both power and sex, both of which she indulged in with her male favourites in an intimate club of handpicked courtiers: the 'Little Hermitage' was a kind of Russian counterpart to the Hell-Fire Club. The great majority of Catherine's whores were 'men of the people' – like Korsakov, who had started his career as a sergeant in the palace guards. At least a dozen of Catherine's temporary bedmates were eventually pensioned off with positions at court, complete with salaries and honours, when their services were no longer required. The most famous of the empress's male courtesans was Potemkin, who became her cherished companion, friend, adviser, and husband in all but name. He rose to command not only her affections but her armies, eventually becoming the most powerful man in Russia: 'The fact that he would receive princes and grand dukes as he would footmen, and that he would burst into Catherine's apartments bare-legged and tousled in a dressing-gown, is some indication of his omnipotence.'[30]

The ladies of Catherine's court followed her example enthusiastically, keeping male favourites and joining the Club of Natural Philosophers, an association which emulated the debauches of the Little Hermitage. Although the case of the Empress of Russia is an anomaly, it nevertheless shows that power and wealth have always been an irresistible stimulant to sexual excess – which in itself is not necessarily a prerogative of the male.

At the French court it was of course men who held the reins of power, and here the keeping of a mistress was *de rigueur*. Louis the Sun King had been as fond of his mistresses as had his cousin Charles II of England; but the last of them, the sober Madame de Maintenon, had imposed a regime of dour religiosity on the French court similar to that espoused by James II across the Channel. Consequently, after Louis' death the French nobility, freed once again from moralistic constraints, held to its 'flamboyantly licentious' habits right up until the Revolution: at first with the Duke of Orleans at the helm, and then under King Louis XV. Here, as in England and Russia, the profession of whore to the nobility and especially to royalty, was open to talent and initiative.

One outstanding product of the age was Claudine du Tencin – courtesan, intellectual, and patron of the arts. Born in Grenoble, in 1685, she first evaded the conventional fate of women when she fled to a nunnery to avoid an arranged marriage. Here, the young Claudine carried on a number of *affaires* with apparent impunity (one of these, incidentally, was with the poet Louis Camus, by whom she had a son who grew up to become the philosopher d'Alembert). After Claudine left the nunnery, her brother – an 'unprincipled abbé' – introduced her to the Regent of France, whose chief mistress she became. Theirs was by all accounts a stormy relationship, and after a final set-to, du Tencin abandoned the dissolute Orleans in favour of his Prime Minister, Cardinal Dubois, who gratefully awarded her brother a bishopric. Claudine's next lover was the powerful Duc de Richelieu; but in the end she left him in order to pursue an intellectual and literary career. The rewards of a life of prostitution enabled her to set up her own *salon*, which became a favourite haunt of the brightest lights in French cultural life and where the former whore nurtured such talents as the philosopher Montesquieu. Claudine du Tencin should be remembered not only for the books her 'wages of sin' allowed her to write towards the end of her life but, more importantly perhaps, for the unquenchable spirit of independence she showed throughout it.

Before the accession of Louis XV, the chief mistresses of the French king had without exception been daughters of the nobility; the new king, however, broke with this tradition, first with Madame de Pompadour and then with Jeanne, Comtesse du Barry. Pompadour was originally a humble, untitled bourgeoise, born Jeanne-Antoinette Poisson, whose beauty and intelligence were to make her one of the most desirable women in France. Her silver-blond colouring and, in particular, the 'incomparable' texture and sheen of her skin – described by contemporaries as 'sans ombre', a 'déjeuner de soleil' – helped ensnare the noble Charles Guillaume la Normant d'Etoiles in a marriage of convenience and thus gained her access to the court. Here, at a masked ball, the lovely Jeanne-Antoinette met the king. She was twenty-four years old and in the prime of her beauty; the king, enchanted, desired her; but she sued for a high price, demanding the position of chief mistress before she would sleep with him. That His Majesty submitted to these conditions was 'an unheard-of breach in royal etiquette', which established the principle that the royal bedchamber was no longer the preserve of the high-born whore. The new chief mistress was created Marquise de Pompadour, the title under which Jeanne-Antoinette reigned in the royal household for twenty years – 'presque reine de France' – until her death in 1764. Like du Tencin, Pompadour was both talented and beautiful; as well as being the king's trusted adviser throughout her life, she made a lasting contribution to French culture as a patron and supporter of the arts.

Pompadour was succeeded by a woman whose background had much in common with that of Nell Gwyn. Jeanne, Comtesse du Barry, was the daughter of a woman innkeeper; her father was unknown. Born Jeanne Bécu, she had been taken to Paris as a child, when her mother became housekeeper to one of the capital's leading courtesans. Eventually, her mother married a clerk and Jeanne was packed off to be educated in a convent where, like Claudine du Tencin, she learned the tricks of the sex trade. After her apprenticeship she left the nunnery to work under the guidance of Madame Gourdan, a celebrated procuress and madam of the period; and it was probably through this connection that the young woman met, then became mistress to, the Comte Jean du Barry, who was himself a kind of high-society sex trader. Du Barry had made it his business to select promising mistresses from among the city's whores, groom them for life with the leisured classes and, finally, auction them off to the highest bidder. It was while Jeanne was his mistress that du Barry heard that the post of royal whore was vacant, and so he began to prepare his young protégée for the role.

Jeanne was introduced at court as the wife of the Comte's younger brother; and, it was said, the king was captivated not only by the young woman's beauty, but also by her intelligence, her good taste, her 'gaiety and generosity'. By the time the embarrassing details of her origin had leaked out, the royal fish was hooked, and the lowly

Jeanne's ascent to the throne of chief mistress was assured. To make
her acceptable to the court nobility, the king furnished her with a
paper marriage to du Barry's brother, a fortune in diamonds and a
forged certificate of noble birth. Thus armed with all the trappings of
aristocracy, Madame du Barry ruled the royal roost as Louis' mistress
until his death in 1774. In spite of the snobbishness and hypocrisy of
the French court, the former Jeanne Bécu had achieved the same
dazzling rise from gutter to peerage as had Nell Gwyn at the English
court a hundred years earlier.

Unfortunately, she paid the ultimate price for her class transition;
she was brought to trial and executed during the bloody Terror of the
French Revolution. At her trial, much was made of the 'shameful and
infamous prostitution' of this 'celebrated Lais'. 'La Citoyenne
Dubarry' pleaded for her life right up until the end; even from the
tumbril she begged the crowds to save her, crying that she had 'never
done harm to any person'. It was to no avail, for the wretched
50-year-old former royal mistress was guillotined on 8 December
1793, after making a final poignant plea to her executioner for 'encore
un moment, monsieur le Bourreau . . . encore un petit instant . . .'[31]

Like Charles II of England, Louis XV did not confine himself to his
royal mistresses; he had to be provided with plenty of casual sexual
partners as well. The system that was devised in order to cater to the
royal libido was elaborate and formal – typical of the French
aristocracy at that time, in fact. The king bought a discreet house in the
Deer Park area of his Versailles estate; hence its name, the Parc-aux-
Cerfs. Into this house poured a constant stream of nubile young
lovelies, each handpicked by the royal procuress, Mère Bompart,
herself a formidable woman and the subject of this extract from
Madame du Barry's *Mémoires secrètes*:

In every truth Mère Bompart was a wonderful animal. Picture to
yourself a woman rather small than large, rather fat than lean,
rather old than young, with a good foot, a good eye, as robust as
a trooper, with a decided 'call' for intrigue, drinking nothing but
wine, telling nothing but lies, swearing by, or denying God, as
suited her purpose. Fancy such a one, and you will have before
you Mère Bompart, procuress-in-chief to the cells of the Parc-
aux-Cerfs. She was in correspondence with all sorts of persons

. . . Everybody at court received her graciously; everybody but the king and myself, who held her in equal horror.[32]

Parents of pretty young girls, whether noble or common, were not reluctant to deliver their daughters into this royal harem. The girls entered the house at the age of nine, and from this time on they were kept under the rigorous discipline and propriety of 'madame' – 'an elderly canoness', who was, according to du Barry, 'of a noble order, belonging to one of the best families in Burgundy'. The girls were educated in polite behaviour, music, painting, dancing, history and literature; until at the age of fifteen they were deemed sufficiently mature and refined to receive the royal embraces, and accordingly presented to the king, who, they were told, was a Polish nobleman with a high position at court. At eighteen they 'graduated' from this august institution. Any children the young women had had by the king were quietly farmed out to foster-mothers, and they themselves were given dowries and husbands, or failing that, a 'respectable' retirement to a nunnery.

For lower-class parents, the Parc-aux-Cerfs undoubtedly offered a good income, as well as a unique opportunity to raise their daughters' social status; while parents of the nobility regarded it as a mark of royal favour (not to mention the dowry it incurred) if their daughter were chosen. In any event, none of them showed any scruple in selling their daughters into concubinage; on the contrary, they were by all accounts very pleased with their deal. History fails to record, however, what the young girls themselves thought of their fate. As for the cost to the French nation: the Parc-aux-Cerfs soaked up a staggering £200,000 per year – an immense sum in those days.

CHAPTER TEN

The Age of Debauchery: 18th-Century Europe

Of all the Crimes condemn'd to Woman-kind
WHORE, in the Catalogue, first you'll find.
This vulgar Word is in the mouths of all
An *Epithet* on ev'ry Female's fall.
The *Pulpit-thumpers* rail against the WHORE
And damn the Prostitute: What can they more?
Justice pursues her to the very Cart,
Where for her Folly she is doom'd to smart.
Whips, Gaols, Disease – all the WHORE assail
And yet, I fancy, WHORES will never fail . . .
Yet Everyone of Feeling must deplore
That MAN, vile MAN first made the Wretch a Whore.

Lady Dorothy Worseley, 18th century aristocratic
feminist, poet, gambler, *bonne viveuse*[1]

Although there had been bawdy-houses of various types at all levels of society throughout history, the fondness of the 18th-century upper classes for sexual experiment promoted the growth of new-style brothels that could cater to all kinds of specialist tastes. A model of the genre was Mme Gourdan's establishment in the rue des Deux Ports, Paris. One of this lady's innovations was to centre her house around the 'seraglio', a great salon where the whores advertised their services to clients by striking provocative poses. Madame also provided an extremely comprehensive range of sexual services, a menu that would in effect satisfy the most varied – and bizarre – tastes. Pornography and 'stimulating slaves' were available for those who required a little assistance; for voyeurs there was a peep-room from which they could watch the sexual activities of others; and for clients with a sado-masochistic bent there were the delights of the 'chamber of horrors'.

The whores who worked *chez* Mme Gourdan needed to be both professional and adaptable; with this in mind they were given a complete and thorough training. This would begin in the so-called *piscine*, where girls newly arrived from the provinces or the city's slums were cleaned up and made presentable; they would then move on to the '*Cabinet de Toilette*', to be further instructed in the arts of whoring. These lessons would certainly have resembled the instructions given a century earlier by the English bawd Mother Cresswell, as described in a satire known as *The Whore's Rhetorick*:

> You must not forget to use the natural accents of dying persons . . . You must add to these ejaculations, aspirations, sighs, intermissions of words, and such like gallantries, whereby you may give your Mate to believe, that you are melted, dissolved and wholly consumed in pleasure, though Ladies of large business are generally no more moved by an embrace, than if they were made of Wood or stone.[2]

The clients who flocked to Mme Gourdan's establishment were the wealthy and powerful, many of whom were outwardly respectable – men of the church, for instance. Taking this into account, Madame la Patronne thoughtfully provided a discreet means of entrance to the brothel: a secret doorway in an innocent-looking house in a side street. Madame also maintained another property; a country house which was cynically referred to by local peasants as 'the convent'. Here, the more favoured rich customers could retire for extended periods of debauchery.

Mme Gourdan's ideas were widely copied, particularly the innovation of the central seraglio. Two other outstandingly successful Parisian brothel-keepers of the mid-century, Mesdames Paris and Dupuis, operated similar establishments; the former ran several houses during the 1740s and 1750s. At one of them, the Hôtel du Roule, there was a central salon where the women sat around in light *déshabille*, waiting to be chosen by wealthy clients. Mme Paris was put out of business in 1752 by a prosecution for corrupting a twelve-year-old girl; her place as leader of the field was immediately taken over by Mme Dupuis. She had started her career as a professional mistress, being kept in turn by a doctor, a banker, a musketeer, and an abbé, before ploughing her savings into her first brothel. Hers was an efficient if somewhat bizarre establishment, a kind of luxury cattle-market in which the central seraglio was filled with fifty whores at a time, separated into groups with ribbons and accessories in different colours, and with the price of each woman clearly displayed.

Other brothels slotted themselves into the specialist corners of the sex-market; one catered exclusively to clergymen, another was staffed entirely by black women, yet another specialized in (mostly ersatz) virgins, and at least one house boasted inmates who were all supposedly of noble birth. Such was the diversity and competitiveness of the Parisian sex industry at this time that the secondary trade of advertising was created as a by-product. Brothel-owners posted men in busy parts of the city to distribute cards extolling the virtues – and vices – of their whores, and listing the myriad specialities they offered. Individual whores also handed out their own cards, and mainstream publishers cashed in with detailed brothel-creepers' guides. The sex business was truly booming, as never before.

The high-class commercial sex scene was revolutionized in Britain along Parisian lines when one Mrs Goadsby, a frequent visitor to the French capital, opened her house in Berwick Street, Soho, around the year 1750. Taking her cue from the wildly successful Parisian high-class enterprises, she catered to all tastes, at the most exclusive prices. Other madams watched with interest; it did not take them long to realize the profits to be made in this way and soon the French-style *maison* became a widespread phenomenon in London.

Another London madam, 'Miss Fawkland', took a leaf out of Gourdan's book and put her whores through a rigorous training before permitting them to qualify as full-time professionals at one of her three adjoining houses in St James's Street, Westminster. La Fawkland's establishments were decked out as temples; the first was the 'Temple of Aurora', which specialized in neophyte whores – girls aged between eleven and sixteen. In this 'first novitiate of pleasure' elderly clients were permitted to fondle and slobber over the under-aged lovelies – but no more than that was allowed. After their 'schooling', the mature girls graduated to the so-called 'Temple of Flora', which was run along the lines of a regular luxury brothel. The third house, or 'Temple of Mysteries', catered to a whole gamut of outlandish tastes, notably the sado-masochistic practices so beloved of the upper classes.

Miss Fawkland's trio of brothels were a runaway success, with the highest in the land among her regular customers. Included in their number were the Lords Cornwallis, Buckingham, Hamilton and Bolingbroke, and the writers Sheridan and Smollett.

Amongst the high-class brothels to be found clustered at the fashionable end of town, in close proximity to the royal palaces, Houses of Parliament, and mansions of the nobility, was the celebrated Mrs Hayes's 'cloister' – an establishment with a novel line in theatrical orgies. At one of these, during the 1770s (the height of the brothel's success) several MPs participated in a little soirée which took its theme from Captain Cook's account of his voyage of discovery in the Pacific: 'This evening at 7 o'clock precisely, 12 beautiful nymphs will carry out the famous Feast of Venus, as it is celebrated in Tahiti, under the instruction and leadership of Queen Oberea (which role will be taken by Mrs Hayes herself).' During the ceremony,

They stretched a large and beautiful carpet on the floor, and decorated the scene with furniture suitable for the different attitudes in which the actors and actresses devoted to Venus should appear . . . Afterwards the men gave each of their mistresses a nail at least two inches long, in imitation of presents received on similar occasions by the ladies of Otaheite, who preferred a long nail above anything else. They started their devotions and passed with the greatest dexterity over all the different evolutions of the rites more or less under the directions of Santa Carlotta [i.e. Mrs Hayes].[3]

Clients paid highly for their excursions to Mrs Hayes's 'cloister'. A price list, which fictionalizes (and to some extent satirizes) the clientele, nevertheless provides an accurate guide to the prices charged for specific services:

Sunday the 9th January

A young girl for Alderman Drybones. Nelly Blossom, about 19 years old, who has had no one for four days, and who is a virgin .... 20 guineas
A girl of 19 years, not older, for Baron Harry Flagellum. Nell Hardy from Bow Street, Bat Flourish from Berners Street or Miss Birch from Chapel Street .... 10 guineas
A beautiful girl for Lord Spaan. Black Moll from Hedge Lane, who is very strong .... 5 guineas
For Colonel Tearall, a gentle woman. Mrs Mitchell's servant,

who has just come from the country and has not yet been out in the world .... 10 guineas
For Dr Frettext, after consultation hours, a young agreeable person, sociable, with a white skin and a soft hand. Polly Nimblewrist from Oxford, or Jenny Speedyhand from Mayfair .... 2 guineas.
Lady Loveit, who has come from the baths at Bath, and who is disappointed in her affair with Lord Alto, wants to have something better, and to be well served this evening. Capt. O'Thunder or Sawney Rawbone .... 50 guineas.
For His Excellency Count Alto, a fashionable woman for an hour only. Mrs Smirk who came from Dunkirk, or Miss Graceful from Paddington .... 10 guineas
For Lord Pyebald, to play a game of piquet, for *titillatione mammarum* and so on, with no other object. Mrs Tredrille from Chelsea .... 5 guineas.[4]

Here we have virtually the entire range of specialities catered for by the up-market brothels: masturbation, fondling without intercourse, defloration, flagellation – and male prostitutes for the wealthy female client. It is interesting to note the discrepancy in the prices charged male and female clients; this presumably reflects the greater social risks run by women who wanted to buy sexual services. The demand was there, however, and Mrs Hayes was by no means the only madam to offer commercial sex to ladies of the upper classes: a Mrs Banks in Curzon Street provided male and female whores for her mixed clientele, and Mrs Redson of Bolton Street made her rooms available for ladies to make 'romantic' assignations of their choice.

Then of course there was the lesbian trade to cater for: 'Mother Courage' of Suffolk Street and one Miss Frances Bradshaw in Bow Street obliged in this department. Sisters Anne and Elanor Redshawe ran 'an extremely secretive . . . discreet *House of Intrigue*' in Tavistock Street, for 'the Highest *Bon Ton* . . . catering for Ladies in the Highest Keeping';[5] and Mrs Elisabeth Wiseborne of Drury Lane was famous not only for her 'finest curtezans' but also her stable of 'stallions', as this contemporary satire attests:

My name is WISEBOURN: from all parts repair
to my fam'd Roof the discontented Fair.

> Rich City Wives, and some not far from Court
> Who loath their Husbands and who love the Sport:
> Brides match'd with Impotence that wants an Heir:
> Numbers of these I succour ev'ry Day
> Who keep their Stallions well in Pay . . .
>
> To gratify the *Nymph*, if tales say true
> The famous WISEBOURN often lay *perdu*
> And rang'd all the corners of the Town
> To find sound handsome Youths,
> Well-limb'd and strongly chinn'd . . .[6]

Mrs Wisebourne also ran a roaring trade in virgins. Clutching her Bible (she made much of being deeply religious) she toured the inns and taverns every morning to pick up girls fresh from the country; she scoured the prisons of London and bribed jailers to release their prettier captives; she examined the children who were offered for sale every day outside the church of St Martin in the Fields 'as a Butcher might chuse a Mare at Smithfield'. Those the madam bought were cleaned up, 'drest with Paint and Patches . . . and let out at extravagant Prices . . . she always calling them young milliners or Parson's daughters'.[7]

Once their real maidenheads had been offered to the highest bidder, 'their virginities were restored as often as necessary' – for the demand for virgins always outstripped the supply. The use of techniques for 'rearranging the crumpled blossoms of the rose' as the contemporary euphemism had it, was so widespread that the price of a virgin dropped from £50 to £5 during the century.

The eponymous heroine of John Cleland's novel *Fanny Hill*, published in 1748, follows a similar course to that of Mrs Wisebourne's girls: a green youngster arriving in London to seek work, she is picked up by a madam and put to work in a brothel. During her varied career she experiences most of the different aspects of the 18th-century sex trade, with which the author was intimately familiar. Although the book is ostensibly written from the woman's perspective, it is indisputably a punters' classic; everything is geared towards arousing the upper-class male reader. In one exclusive brothel, Fanny takes part in a sex game typical of the age: a club of young aristocrats frequents the house; she is assigned to one of them as a regular mistress, and at one of the club's meetings each couple takes turns to strip and have sex in front of the others. Bearing in mind the antics of the Hell-Fire Club, this anecdote has more than the ring of truth about it.

Fanny is involved in an episode of flagellation; the book would not have been complete without one, given the rage for the 'sport'. Flogging had begun to seep into the public consciousness back in the Restoration period – in *The Virtuoso* (1678), Thomas Shadwell portrays an elderly gentleman who 'loves castigation mightily' – but it became a passion after the publication in 1718 of the pornographic *Treatise on the Use of Flogging*. Mother Burgess's Covent Garden house, which specialized in flagellation, appears in a satire of 1738, *The Paphian Grove*:

> With Breeches down, there let some lusty Ladd
> (To desp'rate *Sickness* desperate *Cures* are had!)
> With honest Birch excoriate your Hide
> And flog the *Cupid* from your scourged *Backside*![8]

Flogging brothels mushroomed throughout the fashionable streets of London. In 1777 Mary Wilson, one of the city's best-known madams, published the two-volume *Exhibition of Female Flagellants*, which celebrated the whipping of upper-class men by lower-class women. Another madam, Mrs Berkley, was reputed to have made a fortune of £10,000 in eight years as mistress of a flagellatory house. But the most famous – or infamous – of these establishments was probably the Covent Garden house of Mrs Colet, which was established in 1766 and frequented by King George IV himself. Such was the fever for scourging during this period that 'Chace Pine [a roué of the period] devised a machine which could whip forty persons at a time.'[9] Chastisement has held a special appeal for the upper-class male ever since.

The *bagnios*, or bathhouses, which again flourished in the Covent Garden area in the 18th-century were also well-equipped to supply a flogging to 'old people and degenerates', as the contemporary German writer Johann von Archenholz put it.[10] These establishments were no Parisian fad, but a revival of the medieval tradition. The first *bagnio* – a genuine bathhouse – had opened in the Covent Garden Piazza in 1681, and was an immediate success; within ten years there were several others in the vicinity. By the turn of the century, they had evolved into 'houses of assignation' – again, in the old tradition; and soon the name *bagnio* became a synonym for brothel. Casanova tried one out during his *séjour* in London; he mentions it briefly in passing: 'I also visited the bagnios, where a rich man can sup, bathe and sleep with a fashionable courtesan, of which species there are many in London. It makes a magnificent debauch and only costs six guineas.'[11]

As with the Parisian sex trade, the proliferation of high-class organized prostitution in 18th-century London resulted in a great deal of competition among operators; although this was not so much for custom (there was always more than enough of that), but for the *best* custom. Like their Parisian counterparts, the London brothel-owners and some independent high-class whores took to advertising; with the result that a variety of guides to the city's whores and brothels appeared on the scene. *The Ranger's Magazine* published a 'Monthly list of the Covent Garden Cyprians; or the Man of Pleasure's *Vade Mecum*'; while a mock-epic poem devoted to the subject – *The Meretriciad* (1770) – gave a particularly warm recommendation to 'Mrs Susannah Birch's' establishment in Exeter Street:

> Birch for the Bum; ye floggers here resort . . .
> All kinds of Instruments, all kinds of Ware
> To raise your Passions . . .[12]

The Bible of sex-guides was the best-selling *Harris's List of Covent Garden Ladies*, 'an annual directory of call-girls, with prices, specialities, and descriptions which combined lyrical enthusiasm with extreme anatomical precision'.[13] Harris extolled the courtesan Betty Davis thus:

> . . . a second *Circe* in her wiles
> Who, Syren-like, enchants ye and beguiles;
> Sings, swears and riots o'er the sparkling Wine
> Until she makes ye, like Ulysses – a Swine.[14]

And the 1786 issue wrote memorably of one whore (amongst 105 listed) that, in spite of her seven-year career:

> the coral-tipped clitoris still forms the powerful erection . . . nor has the sphincter vaginae been robbed of any of its contractive powers; the propelling labia still make the close fissure.[15]

From the beginning of the Middle Ages the aristocracy had been society's undisputed rulers, the model to which the lower social orders looked for an example. If the bourgeoisie wished to compete as a potential ruling class it had to define itself as a viable alternative, and do so, furthermore, in terms which would clearly contrast with the values held by the nobility. One of the most important means by which the middle class set out to accomplish this was by defining itself as the 'moral' class – not a difficult task, in view of the aristocracy's penchant for debauchery. Once again, the ideal of the nuclear family, and its attendant female chastity, were promoted, as the middle-class male looked fondly back to classical Athens for his inspiration.

The family became a central tenet of the programme put forward by the leading thinkers of the Enlightenment; that new (but not so new in some respects) wave of ideology which dominated Europe and America through much of the 18th-century. The Enlightenment had its origins in France, where progressive thinkers had to struggle to assert their world-view against the rigid triumvirate of Catholic Church, absolutist state, and complacent aristocracy. Having bene-fited from the scientific advances of Newton, Descartes and others in the previous century, the new *philosophes* – Voltaire, Diderot, Montesquieu among them – applied rational analysis to every aspect of life, denying God and all arbitrary power. For political inspiration they looked to the Athenian democracy, following the trend begun in the Italian Renaissance of basing their attitudes towards women on those of the ancient Greek thinkers. Once again, women were to be separate from and unequal to men, confined to the home and to lives of housework and mothering. Regular as clockwork, this idealization of woman's role in the family brought with it the double standard; for men were able to build careers, make money – *and* sow their wild oats.

The writer Jean-Jacques Rousseau, a leading figure of the En-lightenment, epitomized this double standard. The most systematic and influential of Enlightenment thinkers on the family, Rousseau provided a direct link with the Reformation: he was a citizen of the Calvinist republic of Geneva, which he idealized as a modern incarnation of classical Athens. Predictably, he also modelled his sexual philosophy on that of the Athenian rationalists: 'Women,' he wrote, 'are made for the delight of men, and the bearing of children is their proper business . . . motherhood is a total career and commitment in itself.'[16]

According to Rousseau, women had no contribution whatsoever to make to civilization; the Greeks had been right, he believed, to cloister their wives and daughters in the home and separate the spheres of the sexes, even to the point of refusing to dine with their womenfolk. For while women were created to 'submit to men', he wrote, it was 'indecent' for them to seek men's company, whether they were married or single. As far as women were concerned, the much-heralded new 'Age of Light' was as murky – and *un*reasonable – as ever.

Where Rousseau's sexual ideology went further than that of the ancient Greeks was in the insistence on the concept of motherhood as a *career* (although he never did get round to mentioning the concept of wages for this 'career'). And throughout the 18th century, the close-knit, nuclear family he idealized was in the process of coming into being, particularly amongst the middle classes of north-western Europe. In England the Puritans had already realized the potential use – and power – of the role of motherhood, particularly as a means of inculcating religious and moral beliefs into the minds and hearts of children; they had therefore built a tradition of emphasizing the value of the *work* of mothers. Previously, most parents had taken little notice of their children; now, the middle classes began to understand that mothers who occupied themselves with the earliest education of their offspring could instil in them the values of the class. This proved an effective and necessary weapon on three counts: against a society which still enshrined the alien manners of the aristocracy; against the sexual promiscuity of the lower classes (especially as embodied in prostitution); and against the tendency of the market economy, hub of its own middle-class world, to reduce all morality to a question of hard cash.

'The family', then, was the institution through which the bourgeoisie aimed to anchor and stabilize itself through the potential chaos of the transition from a decaying aristocratic past to a fully-fledged capitalist future. In the oasis of the nuclear family, patriarchal inheritance was preserved, middle-class values reproduced, and the anarchy of money apparently counterbalanced. In all of this, woman's role as linchpin of the family was more crucial than ever – hence Rousseau's obsessive insistence on her 'virtue'.

From the prostitute's point of view, the story was depressingly familiar. On the one hand, the greater the idealization of the wife-mother, the greater the vilification of the whore. On the other hand, the whore remained as essential to society as ever – as the accessory to the family which enabled men to avoid having to practise the sexual abstinence they preached. Middle-class morality was to reach its apotheosis in the 19th century, but for the moment the counterweight of aristocratic immorality ensured that the profession of prostitution still remained relatively stigma-free. Rousseau and his kind were therefore free to act out openly the double standard that men of their class would, a century later, attempt to veil in secrecy.

Typically, they had recourse to high-class whores. In his *Confessions*, Rousseau writes of his encounters with two courtesans in Venice. The first foray apparently left him with an unfounded terror of 'the clap'; although the second seemed – at first glance – somewhat more promising, judging by the fantasies aroused in him by the lady concerned: 'Young virgins in cloisters are not so fresh; the beauties of the seraglio are less animated: the houris of paradise are less engaging. Never was so sweet an enjoyment offered to the heart and senses of a mortal.'[17]

However, on discovering that the whore in question had a withered breast, Rousseau was repelled. He claimed this proved her to be a 'species of monster, the refuse of nature, of men and of love' and charitably told her so; the young woman promptly showed him the door, telling him to leave women alone and study mathematics instead. Unfortunately for women in the 'Age of Reason', Rousseau neglected to follow this sound advice.

Even while the voice of middle-class morality was struggling to make itself heard, and the nuclear family was still restricted to a fairly narrow band of the social spectrum, there was one typical liberal institution which – in Britain, at least – was taking the whole of society by storm: the free market economy.

After the last absolutist, the reactionary James II, had been removed from the throne in 1688 to be replaced by the more pliable William of Orange, the power of the monarchy was further reined in and the economy began to free itself of the last vestiges of medieval constraint:

> The first decades after the removal of King James . . . were in certain senses the most revolutionary in English history. This was the period of bourgeois revolution transcendent, of individualism and capitalism let loose, of the transition from the religion-based ethics of feudalism to the secular ethics of capitalism, of traditional controls removed, of the enclosure movement run rampant . . . Property became King.[18]

For those who already had money – and for those who could beg, borrow or steal enough capital to *make* money – these were extraordinarily successful times. Above all, the free market economy benefited its historical partisans, the bourgeoisie; but this runaway success was not without its problems. For one thing, the market seriously threatened the middle class's image as the 'moral' class, since it had a tendency to dissolve *all* values – including moral ones – in the money economy. Everything had its price – and in the 18th century, when life was cheap and survival often precarious, the price of virtue was at rock-bottom.

Even the much-vaunted family was no haven from the ubiquitous horse-trading; far from it. All the social classes who owned property, from the aristocracy downwards, necessarily made it the basis of their marriages. For men the search for a wife was a quest for more money – potential capital – since, on marrying, a man instantly acquired absolute legal control over his wife's person and possessions. One of literature's whores, the heroine of Daniel Defoe's novel *Roxana* (1724), protests that 'the very Nature of the Marriage-Contract was, in short, nothing but giving up Liberty, Estate, Authority, and everything, to the Man, and the Woman was indeed, a meer Woman ever after, that is to say, a Slave.'

Conmen and sharks were rife – men who, with no money of their own, dressed and acted the gentleman in order to net a wealthy catch. Another of Defoe's novels, *Moll Flanders* (1722), shows the situation from the female angle, as the heroine rides the roller-coaster from marriage to widowhood, through relative comfort as a mistress, via a disastrous marriage to a highwayman, to destitution and a subsequent spell of prostitution and crime.

Marriage was, according to Moll Flanders, a way of entering into 'a settled state of living'; but it could also be a terrible trap if the husband turned out to be dishonest, brutal or feckless. The alternative was, of course, the old profession: prostitution. Even for would-be 'respectable' girls this was the only option at times; whether they were poor girls who held out hopes of contracting a good match eventually, or middle-class girls whose parents had fallen victim to the period's economic uncertainties. Whoring would have been the only means by which a dowry could be raised.

In an age when the morality of absolute monogamy (for women) had not yet been firmly established, the genteel profession of mistress, or kept woman, was quite acceptable. Although the majority of mistresses of this type were from middle-class backgrounds, it was still to some extent a career open to talent and ambition. Often a poor girl who had the wit and tenacity could serve her apprenticeship in a brothel, then move on to become the independent mistress of some favourite regular client – *à la* Fanny Hill. During the mistress phase of her career, Cleland's heroine 'kept house' in Marylebone, which appears to have been an enclave of gentlemen's mistresses. Archenholz noted that:

> In the parish of Mary-le-bone only, which is the largest and best peopled in the capital, thirty thousand Ladies of Pleasure reside, of which seventeen hundred are reckoned to be housekeepers [i.e. homeowners]. These live very well, and without ever being disturbed by the magistrates. They are indeed so much their own mistress, that if a justice of the peace attempted to trouble them in their apartments, they might turn him out of doors; for as they pay the same taxes as the other parishioners, they are consequently entitled to the same privileges.[19]

Far from being morally frowned on, or legally repressed, the profession of mistress was an honourable and recognized one, and, for a brief time in history, the kept woman was once again that rare creature: the 'respectable' whore.

Nevertheless, 'respectability' was by now a commodity and, like all other commodities, it had to be bought and paid for. But for the unfortunate majority of people, the 18th century was far from being a time of triumph and gain; in fact it was a period of squalor and brutalization imaginable today only by comparison with the Third World. The process of tearing the peasantry from the land, which had begun two centuries before, was now reaching its climax, and leaving in its wake a massive class of propertyless poor who were totally excluded from the frenzy of personal enrichment that gripped the middle and upper classes. Indeed, this process itself continually debased the living standards of the poor. The price of labour was held down by unemployment and force; strikes and unions were ruthlessly crushed. Peasants thrown off their land followed the time-honoured pattern of leaving to find work in the cities, but there was simply not enough work to go round. Industrialized production had not yet developed sufficiently to take up the slack; the result was devastating levels of unemployment and poverty. During the period there was an unprecedented decline in working-class housing conditions: 'A broad movement pushed the towns in all directions at once. Appalling districts grew up on the outskirts – shanty towns with filthy huts, unsightly industries . . . pig-raising, accumulations of refuse, and sordid streets.'[20]

For women of the poor, who inhabited the shanty towns which grew up around the cities, the crisis was particularly acute. Their gradual exclusion from the trades, which had begun in the 16th century, meant that if they could not secure a marriage to some respectable tradesman or artisan, they were left with few employment prospects: as servants, seamstresses – or prostitutes. Since they came from the rapidly growing propertyless class, they held no stake in the bourgeois concept of the family and its accompanying morality; nor did they hold out any realistic hopes of finding shelter from the storm in marriage to a man of their own class. In these circumstances, prostitution was inevitable. What were the alternatives?

'For some girls, selling their bodies was a preferable way of earning a living to working 14 to 16 hours a day as a seamstress or mantua-maker.'[21] For others, prostitution was simply a response to unemployment; according to Defoe, huge numbers of maidservants chased a limited number of places; this was 'the reason why our streets are swarming with strumpets . . . Thus many of them roam from place to place, from bawdy-house to service, and from service to bawdy-house again . . . nothing being more common than to find these creatures one week in a good family and the next in a brothel.'[22]

Under such circumstances, respect for morality and property was a luxury urban working-class women could ill afford. And even when they became whores, the struggle to survive was far from over; the lower end of the sex market was so flooded with poor women that it was often impossible to make an adequate living – especially if there were children to feed. Thus the women took to petty crime as well as prostitution.

Degrading and underpaid drudgery, unemployment, devastating poverty, prostitution, and crime: this was the social whirlwind that working-class women found themselves caught up in; it was in this context that they had to make their choices. The neat moral and legal dividing lines we now take for granted were simply inapplicable to their lives; for theirs was a state of existence that most of us in this century would find difficult – if not impossible – to contemplate.

★ ★ ★

London in the 18th century was the most 'advanced' city in the West; it represented the model for all those economies that were developing towards a modern future. All the trades flourished – including prostitution. Here, in the heart of the capital, there was never a dearth of custom; for as well as the traditional clientele – the aristocracy, middle classes, and apprentices – there were plenty of 'eligible' young men from the country, who often came to the city in order to accumulate property and wealth before marrying. The result was that demand for whores soared, and business was conducted quite blatantly in the city – rather too blatantly for some. An anonymous tract, *Satans Harvest Home*, published in 1749, describes, in familiar tones of moral outrage, the scene in Drury Lane, behind the Strand:

> Let a sober Person take a gentle Walk through the antient *Hundreds of Drury*, where ev'ry half a dozen Steps he meets with some odd Figure or another, that looks as if the Devil had robb'd them of all their *natural Beauty* . . . for nothing can be read but *Devilism* in every feature; *Theft, Whoredom, Homicide and Blasphemy* peep out of the very Windows of their Souls . . . Turn your eyes up to the Chambers of Wantonness, and you behold the most Shameful Scene of *Lewdness* in the Windows even at Noon-day, some in the very Act of Vitiation [copulation] visible to all the opposite Neighbours. Others dabbing their *Shifts, Aprons* and *Headcloths*, and exposing themselves just naked to the Passers by . . . *My Dear, will you give me a glass of wine; take me under your Cloak, my Soul, and how does your precious C . . . do?* You hear at the Corner of every Court, Lane and Avenue, the Quarrels and Outcries of Harlots recriminating one another, Soldiers and Bullies intermixing, the most execrable Oaths are heard.

It was a similar story in other parts of London, notably Fleet Street, Charing Cross and the City:

> . . . there being little else but Concubines in all the Lodgings, and nothing but *Lascivious Looks* seen in the Chamber-Windows, from one end of the Verge to the other; nor are very few of these the *Propriety* of *one Man*, but ordain'd for the *Comfort* and *Refreshment* of *Multitudes*, devoting themselves to the service of ALL the loving subjects of *Great Britain*.[23]

The 'Lodgings' referred to were those in which the poorest of London's whores lived. The women picked up trade on the streets and took them back to their rooms. A favourite location was 'that Great Square of VENUS' – the Piazza in Covent Garden, which was handy for the theatres. According to one observer, writing in 1725, there were in the district 'enough lewd Women . . . to people a mighty Colony':

> The front windows of the Piazza [are] filled from seven at Night until four or five o'clock in the Morning with Courtezans of every description . . . who in the most impudent Manner invite the Passengers from the theatres into Houses where they [are] accommodated with Suppers and Lodgings, frequently at the expense of all they possess.[24]

Archenholz describes the street behaviour of these whores:

> At all seasons of the year, they sally out towards dusk, arrayed in the most gaudy colours, and fill the principal streets. They accost the passengers, and offer to accompany them: they even surround them in crowds, stop and overwhelm them with caresses and entreaties. The better kind, however, content themselves with walking about, till they themselves are addressed.[25]

The Scots writer James Boswell, a man who was extremely partial to the 'civil nymph with white-thread stockings who tramps along the Strand and who will resign her engaging person to your honour for a pint of wine and a shilling', has left us some anecdotes of his encounters with these 18th-century ladies of the night:

> 25 March 1763 . . . As I was coming home this night, I felt carnal inclinations raging through my frame. I determined to gratify them. I went to St James Park and picked up a whore. For the first time did I engage in armour [i.e. a condom], which I found but a dull satisfaction. She who submitted to my lusty embraces was a young Shropshire girl, only 17, very well-looked, her name Elizabeth Parker. Poor being, she has a sad time of it!

Boswell's concern for the young whore is touching – but fleeting. A few days later:

31 March . . . At night I strolled into the park and took the first
whore I met, whom I without many words copulated with free
from danger, being safely sheathed. She was ugly and lean and
her breath smelt of spirits. I never asked her name. When it was
done, she slunk off. I had a low opinion of this gross practice and
resolved to do it no more . . .

. . . but . . .

17 May . . . Just at the bottom of Downing Street I picked up a
fresh agreeable girl called Alice Gibbs. We went down a lane to a
snug place, and I took out my armour, but she begged me that I
might not put it on, as the sport was much pleasanter without it,
and as she was quite safe, I was so rash as to trust her, and had a
very agreeable congress.[26]

Boswell even ventured a 'congress' one night with a whore on
Westminster Bridge, 'with the Thames rolling below us'.[27]

In 1710 the young German Baron Zacharias von Uffenbach was
most struck when visiting London 'by the great quantity of Moors
[black people] of both sexes . . . hawking their bottoms round the
Strand and Covent Garden . . . the females in European dress, with
uncovered black bosoms.'[28] The majority of these black prostitutes
had arrived in the country as slaves, and had been either sold or simply
left behind when their white masters went back to the colonies.

Another feature of street life in the 18th century was child
prostitution. This is no real surprise, considering the period's poverty
and the upper-class male obsession with virgin-hunting. As the
century wore on, and conditions for the poor became increasingly
desperate, the forced prostitution of underage girls became common-
place. Prosecutions for this type of sexual abuse were rare, the
protection and welfare of working-class children not being a priority
of the legislators at this time; nevertheless there were occasional court
cases. In 1777 'Mother Sarah Woods' was charged before the
magistrate Sir John Fielding with:

harbouring young girls from eleven to sixteen . . . for the
purpose of sending them nightly to parade the streets . . . after
she had kept them hard at work keeping her house clean all day
. . . some half-naked and drunk . . . The Watch had picked up a

girl of twelve . . . with others of Mrs Wood's servants . . . and a man parading with them to prevent them running away with their Cloaths.[29]

The writer George Alexander Stevens described in 1780 the process by which many of these wretched children became sex slaves:

On Bulks [the wooden outside stalls of shops] and in Alleys we often meet with girls of twelve and thirteen years of age lying in a most despicable condition; poor Objects with a pretty Face. A Pimp will pick them up and take them to a Bawdy-house wherein the poor Wretch is stript, washed and given Cloaths. These are called *Colts*. The Pimp gets paid a Pound or two for his trouble: the girls have thus been bought and must do as the Purchaser pleases . . . I have known a girl pay £11 for the use of a Smock and Petticoate which when new did cost only six Guineas. The girls are obliged to sit up every Morning until Five o'clock to drink with any straggling *Buck* who may reel in the early Morning and bear with whatever behaviour these drunken Visitants are pleased to use – and at the last endure the most Impure connexions.[30]

Girls who had been confined to the workhouses through poverty – and had managed to survive the unbelievably grim conditions within them – would often be sold into forced labour to criminals and put to work on the streets as whores or pickpockets. The story of these children's lives is a terrible one, but it is important to note that their ruthless exploitation was by no means confined to the sex trade. It was a condition of life for all lower-class children, who often – whether they had family or not – found themselves in desperate circumstances, having to provide for themselves whether by begging, stealing, prostitution, or through working in sweatshops and factories in the most appalling conditions. The exploitation and degradation of children was inevitable in a society which valued money and property far more than human life. Nobody knows how many children lived and died in this misery – certainly thousands – but in history's grand scheme of things their tragedy has been largely overlooked, or at least played down. It was not until well into the 19th century that laws which purported to safeguard minors from such savage exploitation were passed.

★ ★ ★

In the more salubrious streets of London, where conspicuous consumption had become a fad of the fashionable, the sex trade quietly boomed. The backrooms of ostensibly respectable establishments (coffee-shops, chocolate-houses, and milliners' shops) were little more than jumped-up brothels, where 'refreshments' – including sex – were sold to clients of both sexes. Another popular sex-haunt for the promenading 18th-century gallant was the tea-garden: Marylebone Gardens, where a variety of entertainments, from restaurants to firework displays, could be found, was prime territory for that parish's ladies of pleasure; so was Belsize House, which stood in its own park near Hampstead, and where the playhouse, racecourse and dance-halls were magnets for whores and their clients. The most popular of the tea-gardens was Vauxhall, on the south bank of the Thames, full of obscure and leafy corners to which couples could retire. And at Ranelagh, another great pleasure-garden, which had been opened in 1742 by the Prince of Wales, there was an added attraction: the masked ball. Here, Londoners of quality could mingle with the *hoi polloi*, thus providing golden opportunities for lower-class whores. These masquerades were immensely popular in 18th-century London; they were also held at 'exclusive' clubs such as Almack's, in St James's, and at the Soho Square mansion of Madame Cornelys – an ex-mistress of Casanova. The non-virtuous poor somehow always managed to dodge the doorman – or pay him a cut of their earnings.

Taverns were, as ever, a major focus of working-class prostitution. The tavern bawdy-house was a longstanding, country-wide institution and in the capital in particular, it offered a remarkably diverse nightlife. The Rose Tavern in Covent Garden was infamous even in its own time; haunt of the most debauched characters in town, it was referred to by the writer Thomas Brown as 'that black School of SODOM . . . [where men] who by proficiency in the Science of Debauchery [are] called *Flogging Cullies . . .* pay an excellent Price for being scourged on their Posteriors by *Posture Molls*.'[31]

The 'Posture Molls' were women who 'stripped naked and mounted upon the table to show their beauties' when they were not flagellating their clients. The Rose, which was a favourite venue of these strippers, was notoriously riotous: bar-room brawls were common, and enjoyed by participants of both sexes. Women would wrestle with each other, stripped to the waist, while customers placed bets on the likely winners. The eclectic clientele included homosexuals, transvestites and lesbians, many of them upper-class slummers. Another Covent Garden tavern – Bob Derry's Cyder Cellar – was popular with both high-life and riff-raff; whilst at the Shakespeare's Head the 'Whores' Club' met in an upstairs room every Sunday, under the aegis of a certain Jack Harris, the 'Pimpmaster-general'.

Also situated in taverns in and around Covent Garden and the Strand were the 'mollies' ' houses and clubs – bawdy-houses staffed by male homosexual and transvestite whores. The most popular pubs were the Bull and Butcher, the Spiller's Head, the Fountain, the Sun and the Bull Head; all were frequented by young male prostitutes and their 'respectable' City magnate clients. In *The London Spy* of 1700, the writer Ned Ward castigates the male whores who operated at the Fountain, a tavern in Russell Square where nightly they would assemble, dressed as women, to play practical jokes on one another and enact little feminine rituals such as mock childbirth. For this particular charade, the boys would use a doll, which was then 'Christen'd and the Holy Sacrament of Baptism impudently Prophan'd'. Other burlesques, such as girls losing their maidenheads and lovers quarrelling, allowed male whores to 'make a *Scoff & Banter* of the little Effeminate Weaknesses of Women gossipping o'er their Cups for all the Purpose to extinguish that natural affection due to the Fair Sex.'[32]

Here, perhaps, lies the origin of the London pub tradition of transvestite female impersonators.

The London coffee-houses, too, were useful pick-up places. Introduced during Puritan rule, when many alehouses had been legally restricted, these were swiftly invaded by whores looking for an alternative base for their profession, and the tradition lingered. The most popular – and colourful – were of course in Covent Garden: Tom and Moll King's coffee-house was located in the wooden shacks which ran the length of one side of the Piazza. Here, people of all ranks and classes would congregate until the early hours; whores could meet their clients and slip away to a nearby lodging-house to consummate their deal; here, too, the artist William Hogarth could be found busily sketching his famous London characters from life.

The Kings' was stamping-ground to London's most fashionable whores, 'all dressed up fine and pritty and elegantly as if going to a box at the Opera'. After midnight these ladies would be joined by '*Bucks, Bloods, Demi-Reps* [actress-whores] and Choyce Spirits of London . . . the All-Night Lads, otherwise the Peep-o-Day Boys'.[33] The whole

crowd communicated in a special underworld slang – 'talking flash' –
to keep police informers off their scent.

Another famous coffee-house was the Bedford Head, which 'was
crowded every Night with Men of Parts . . . Politicos, Scholars &
Wits', who would mingle with the courtesans and theatre stars, still
decked out in their flamboyant costumes; all of them angling for
business and a good time.

Prostitution and the theatre were still seen by many women as
desirable *métiers*, for the simple reason that both represented a means
of climbing the social ladder for low-born women with talent and wit.
The most successful of these became known in society as 'Toasts of the
Town'. One of the first – and most notorious – 'Toasts' was Sally
Salisbury, who was born in 1692, daughter of a bricklayer. Sally
possessed the requisite charms: beauty, intelligence, wit, combined
with a 'trigger-like temper'. At the age of nine she was apprenticed to a
seamstress, but ran away to sell oranges in Covent Garden; at fourteen
she was working as a whore at Mother Wiseborne's house, where she
quickly acquired the manners needed to pull in the gentry. Sally soon
became the star attraction, numbering among her lovers the Duke of
Richmond, the Duke of St Albans (a piquant touch: he was Nell
Gwyn's son), the poet Matthew Prior, and the Prince of Wales (later
George II). After a riot at the house in 1713, Sally was sent to prison,
but did not languish there overlong; Mr Justice Blagney fell in love
with her, had her released, then crowned his infatuation by becoming
her personal slave. When Wiseborne died in 1719, Sally moved on to
Mother Needham's house, and it was here that, in 1722, she stabbed
her lover Lord Finch in a fit of temper. His Lordship expired
romantically in her arms, uttering the words 'I die at pleasure by your
hand.' Sally was arrested and sent to the infamous Newgate prison;
here she developed consumption and died in 1724, at the age of 32.

Other Toasts of humble origins had a happier end. Fanny Murray
was one such: born in Bath in 1729, the daughter of an impoverished
musician, she was an orphan by the age of twelve. Moving to London
in 1743, Fanny prostituted herself to noble and rich middle-class
clients and was soon the most celebrated courtesan in town. Her career
was long and successful – at forty she was still the belle of the ball when
the King of Denmark invited her to a masquerade in his honour at the
Pantheon – and at the end of it she embarked on a happy and fulfilling
marriage with the actor David Ross.

The theatre was still intrinsically linked with prostitution at this time, if for no other reason than that it provided a shop-window in which aspiring whores could advertise their talents and their bodies. Kitty Fisher was one of the most successful 'demi-reps'. According to Archenholz, Kitty was 'indebted to nature for an uncommon portion of beauty, judgement, and wit, joined in a most agreeable and captivating vivacity'. He went on to tell this story of her:

> This lady knew her own merit; she demanded a hundred guineas a night, for the use of her charms, and she was never without votaries, to whom the offering did not seem too exorbitant. Among these was the Duke of York, brother to the King; who one morning left fifty pounds on her toilet [dressing table]. This present so much offended Miss Fisher, that she declared that her doors should ever be shut against him in future; and to show, by the most convincing proofs, how much she despised his present, she clapt the bank-note between two slices of bread and butter, and ate it for breakfast.[34]

Nancy Dawson was another successful demi-rep: born in Covent Garden to a porter/pimp father and greengrocer mother, she too was orphaned at an early age; she was then taken up by a male dancer and introduced to the stage at Sadler's Wells. Nancy used her theatre earnings to set herself up as a professional whore. Dancing a lascivious hornpipe in John Gay's satire *The Beggar's Opera* brought her overnight fame in 1759; she continued to whore, act, sing and dance, finally entering folk memory as the subject of the song 'Here we go round the mulberry bush', which referred to her legendary charms. The working-class actress-whores Harriet Lamb and Liz Farren both succeeded in marrying into the peerage, while others of their ranks became the mistresses of the nobility. Peg Woffington was one of many Irish beauties who managed to overcome class and racial barriers through whoring: the daughter of a Dublin bricklayer, she first became an actress, attracting a string of rich 'patrons', among them the famous actor David Garrick.

Not all of the demi-reps were of working-class origins, however; it was also common to find the illegitimate daughters of the nobility (there was no shortage of these) on the theatrical scene. Anne Bellamy was notable among them. The natural daughter of the Earl of Tyrawly, Anne was born in 1713. As a young woman she became a renowned actress and intellectual, but her life was blighted at the end by anti-whore prejudice. Apart from her brilliant stage career, Anne involved herself in politics, taking a stand for women's independence. Perhaps it was her forthright radicalism which led to the executors of the will of one of her rich lovers peevishly refusing to grant her the annuity he had left her. Deprived of this income, Anne was overwhelmed by debts and thrown into prison in 1786. She died there in poverty two years later.

Although London was the boom city of 18th-century Europe as far as capitalism and trade were concerned, the other great cities of the West had more than their share of poor women who worked as prostitutes. In Paris, headquarters of a massive state bureaucracy, staffed by the nobility, the streets, parks, gardens and public squares swarmed with whores and their clients; the contemporary writer Restif de la Bretonne estimated that there were 20,000 prostitutes in a city of 600,000 inhabitants. One of the most popular haunts was the Palais-Royal (originally built for Cardinal Richelieu), where 1500 whores promenaded daily through the galleries, shops, restaurants and theatres.

This similarity in the street scenes of continental and British cities is striking, given the wide divergence in official attitudes and policies towards prostitution. On the Continent, where absolutist states on the French model were still the rule, the state was often heavy-handed in its tactics of repression. In Austria the authorities fought throughout the entire century to eradicate prostitution once and for all – and met with the usual dismal failure, even though the most brutal methods were used. At the beginning of the century Reformation-style punishments were inflicted on whores: they were pilloried, branded, whipped, banished, and in at least one case, beheaded. Later the authorities experimented with other forms of chastisement: convicted prostitutes had their heads shaved and were made to sweep the streets in very public atonement for their 'shame'; they were left to rot in prison, or put to work in public laundries. The anti-whore regime finally reached its climax in 1751 when the Empress Maria Theresa set up a Chastity Commission, with sweeping powers to purge the empire of 'vice'. An unprecedented moral inquisition ensued: informers were rife; taverns, coffee-houses and billiard-rooms were strictly policed; and the Austrian nation's sex lives were kept under close scrutiny. On the streets, women were summarily arrested on suspicion, interrogated and locked up until they could prove their innocence.

The Austrian campaign shows all too clearly how a literal, rigorous enforcement of the whore-stigma jeopardizes the liberty of *all* women, who can be found guilty at any time on the grounds of their sex alone. At the same time, and like all such attempts before or since, the campaign failed to abolish prostitution; it merely shifted the sex trade underground. At the height of the repression, whores worked with pimps – men who would keep a look-out for police informers. The women also disguised themselves as housemaids or chocolate-sellers. One of the biggest-selling books of the period was a pamphlet by Johann Rautenstrautch; entitled *Housemaids*, it was in reality a guide to the whores of Vienna: a kind of samizdat *Harris's List*.

Prussia was another absolutist power with an iron-fist policy towards prostitution; here, as in Austria, the clamp-downs were eventually succeeded by liberalization when officials wearily realized that they could not enforce the unenforceable. Frederick I had set the ball rolling in 1690 when he shut down the brothels and had their workers publicly flogged. The trade promptly moved into the taverns and coffee-houses, until by the mid-18th century – although prostitution was still officially illegal – there were again more than a thousand bawdy-houses in the capital, Berlin. Here, as in Austria, chocolate-selling was a favourite cover for the trade: Boswell, touring Europe in the 1760s, mentions a rapid 'congress' with a woman who came into his quarters in a tavern 'to sell chocolate'.

Prussia's repressive tactics succeeded only in vastly increasing the incidence of sexually transmitted diseases amongst her people; for criminalization undermined the working conditions of whores so badly that it was impossible for them to protect themselves.

In France, meanwhile, the all-pervasive state was beginning to define prostitution as a 'problem', to be addressed by a programme of measures rather than simply repressed. Thus from the late 17th century onwards, the French authorities began to include whores in a wider shift in their policies towards marginalized groups such as the criminal poor and the mentally ill or handicapped. Dubbed by the philosopher Michel Foucault the *Grand Renfermement*, the new movement entailed dumping people from these groups into so-called *hôpitaux*; institutions which would, supposedly, rehabilitate them into useful members of the social mainstream.

In 1684 the Parisian authorities suddenly declared that convicted prostitutes were to be confined in the Salpêtrière hospital, on the south bank of the Seine. On arrival, the women were compulsorily examined for venereal diseases, and treated with mercury if found to be infected. During their stay they were coerced into repentance, largely by being worked as long and hard as their strength permitted. Religious books were read aloud to them as they laboured, no doubt stressing the Almighty's abhorrence of 'harlotry', along with a few of the perpetual torments in store for them when they fetched up in Hell. Since repentance was rewarded by a lightening of the workload, there were plenty of conversions. The length of the women's imprisonment depended entirely on the whim of one man, the lieutenant-general of police; thus there was plenty of scope for sexual exploitation. One can imagine the newly-converted whore reeling out of the Salpêtrière, her head buzzing with religious exhortations, having just prostituted herself to her jailer in order to obtain her release.

Another institution, founded at around the same time as the Salpêtrière, was the Maison du Bon Pasteur (House of the Good Shepherd), ostensibly a voluntary refuge for repentant whores, but more often than not presented to them as an alternative to imprisonment, fines, and other punishments. Life in this house was regulated down to the number of pleats in the gowns of coarse brown cloth worn by the inmates; waking hours were filled with the usual bleak regime of work and prayers; in short, the house required nothing less than total obedience – 'a complete mortification of the senses, a continual abnegation of the self'.[35]

Whores could thus turn away from their 'sin' and regain female respectability only at the cost of their personal integrity. The institutions of the *renfermement* were specifically designed to crush the morale and autonomy of those they purported to help; and it was no coincidence that the device of female hard labour was one of the major tools used to achieve these ends.

However, there was a big difference between the issuing of policy directives from on high and their application at street-level. The size and extent of the sex trade made both repression and rehabilitation largely unworkable, so the police were effectively given *carte blanche* to deal with it as they saw fit. They eagerly took advantage of the situation. Compromise was the name of the game: the police limited brothels and streetwalkers to certain areas, intervening to close down a house or prosecute individual women only when complaints were lodged by other citizens. They also issued licences to the brothels (the *maisons de tolérance*), on condition that the madams complied with their demands, which included extortion (a cut of the profits), free sex on demand – and detailed information on clients. Operating with these arbitrary powers, often on the borderline of legality, the police thus fulfilled their functions of social control and surveillance, whilst doing very nicely indeed out of the sex trade as both pimps and punters.

Occasionally throughout the century ordinances were issued encouraging the police to take more measures against the sex trade. The 1713 *Déclaration de Marly* empowered officials to banish prostitutes convicted on the signed declarations of neighbours, and to throw their furniture into the street to be sold 'for the benefit of the indigent'. Interestingly, the *Déclaration* segregated whores into two classes, professionals and amateurs. The former were accorded no legal rights whatsoever; the latter were permitted to defend themselves in court, appeal against conviction, and avoid being treated with the usual severity of whippings and imprisonment. Once again, though, the actual enforcement of this ordinance was derisory – the number of prosecutions never rose above eighteen in any one year. In fact the only real significance of the Declaration of 1713 was the *de jure* setting up of a special section of the police to concern itself with public morals offences – an innovation which was to have far-reaching consequences in the following century.

In 1778 another ordinance was passed; this one a curious mixture of prohibition and tolerance. As the writer Hilary Evans put it, *les femmes de débauche* 'were forbidden to exist. If, however, they insisted on existing, they were forbidden to walk in public places or display themselves in windows in such a way as to attract custom; and, if they insisted on doing these forbidden things, they must do them only in certain parts of the city.'[36]

The regulations were as comprehensive as they were contradictory, thus ensuring that, whatever the circumstances, the police retained the power to do as they chose: either turn a blind eye or make an arrest. Meanwhile, the whores continued to trawl the streets and taverns, and pose naked in their windows, as they had always done.

By the eve of the French Revolution, then, the sex trade, officially banned and therefore non-existent, was flourishing in much the same way as its counterpart across the channel. The *filles de joie* were as numerous and blatant as ever.

In Britain the post-1688 monarchy was, in contrast to the continental powers, becoming more liberal. The power of the monarch was based on the consensus of various different groupings within society, with a nascent capitalism increasingly determining policy.

The royal state, therefore, had less and less pretension to absolute rule; it was withdrawing from interference in the affairs of the country in order to leave the field free for the development of trade, commerce and industry. The great legal concern of the 18th century was not morality, but the protection of property; and in this sphere the law was ruthless and bloody – it was an age when a poor person could be hanged for stealing a teaspoon. Prostitution, however, was seen as a trade still, and as such the state made no systematic attempts to legislate for its control or suppression.

However, the middle class was still trying to impose on the rest of a very unwilling society its version of sexual morality. Like the French authorities in the late 17th century, it began to apply itself to dealing with the sex-trade 'problem'; unlike the French, though, the impetus for the new measures came from groups of private, morally-concerned citizens rather than from the government. Thus the notorious Societies for the Reform of Manners came into being.

The societies had their origins in the wave of moral vigilantism which had arisen soon after the Restoration as a response of frustrated Puritans to the vacuum left by the impotence of the Church courts and the indifference of the government to morals offences. At this time, the streets of London and other towns and cities were guarded by corrupt voluntary constables who had more or less arbitrary jurisdiction over prostitution. These parish constables collected 'gin-money' from the street whores in return for not molesting them, while many Justices of the Peace were virtually on the payroll of brothels, using their power to extort protection money from bawds and madams. Indeed, one Wapping magistrate was known to rent space in his own home to prostitutes.

Religious societies had begun to spring up in reaction to this sort of blatant corruption in the late 17th century. The Tower Hamlets Society, formed in 1690 with the aim and intention of 'cleaning up' its area of the city, issued this broadside:

> Here 'tis that Impudent Harlots by their Antick Dresses, Painted faces and Whorish Insinuations allure and tempt our Sons and Servants to Debauchery, and consequently to embezel and steal from us, to maintain their strumpets. Here 'tis that Bodies are Poxt and Pockets are picked of considerable sums, the revenge of which Injuries have frequently occasioned Quarrellings, Fightings, Bloodshed, Clamours of Murther (and that

sometimes at midnight), pulling down of signs and parts of houses, breaking of windows, also other tumultous Routs, Riots and Uproars . . . Here 'tis that many a Housekeeper is infected with a venomous Plague, which he communicates to his Honest and Innocent Wife . . . Here 'tis that Multitudes of Soldiers and Seamen get such bane that effeminates their spirits and soon rots their bodies.[37]

This diatribe clearly illustrates the struggle between respectable citizens and the urban poor: on the side of the former stand the Honest, Innocent and Tempted; while the latter are guilty of everything – Theft, Plague, Bloodshed, Murder, and more.

It was from the ranks of such concerned middle-class citizens that the moral reformers were drawn; and as the societies they formed spread across London and the rest of the country they found powerful friends, not least of whom was Queen Mary (1689–1702) herself. With her support the societies were extended into country-wide networks of citizens, lawyers, MPs and magistrates. In this way they managed to weld together the morally militant elements of the middle classes in an alliance that was dedicated to disciplining the sexual culture of the poor, with whores as their specific targets.

Task forces were organized in order to suppress street debauchery. Scores of agents in society offices throughout London would supply blank warrants to complainants and informers, who could have them filled in with offences of their choice, then signed by sympathetic magistrates and enforced by society constables. The lack of regard for whores' civil liberties was blatant; the legality of the warrants dubious. In the 1720s one society activist, Samuel Cooke, arrested hundreds of prostitutes, many of whom were sent to Bridewell for a month's hard labour; when a complaint was lodged against his activities the authorities were forced to admit that the warrants he was serving were illegal. But there was no shortage of other society members willing to persecute whores and have them sent to the Bridewells – prisons that were specially designed for the 'correction' of convicted prostitutes.

Once inside, whores were savagely whipped or had their noses slit; they were made to walk the treadmill or pick hemp until their fingers bled. The reformers congratulated themselves callously; they were apparently proud of the tortures they inflicted on these women of the poor. In 1699 their annual report claimed that 500 disorderly houses had been suppressed, in the course of which:

Some Thousands of Lewd Persons have been imprisoned, fined and whipt; so that the Tower-end of the Town, and many of our streets, have been much purged of that pestilent Generation of Night Walkers that used to infest them . . . forty or fifty of them having been sent in a Week to Bridewell, where they have of late received such Discipline, that a considerable number of them have chose rather to be Transported to our Plantations, to work there for an honest subsistence.[38]

Unsurprisingly, the victims of these moral pogroms fought back from time to time. One constable, John Dent, was stabbed to death while attempting to arrest a prostitute in 1709; and with soldiers always ready to take the whores' side, there was much violent resistance. Dent was not the only reformer to be killed in action.

Consistent with their concern for decency and decorum, the societies were particularly obsessed with cleaning up public spaces of naughty whores; consequently the largest single category of offences they prosecuted was street soliciting and 'fornication in the open'. In one documented clutch of arrests in 1730, for instance, a whore and her client were arrested for fornicating in a shop window; and a group of women were 'taken at 12 or 1 o'clock, exposing their nakedness in the open street to all passengers and using most abominable filthy expressions.'[39]

Homosexual brothels were also repressed. In one year alone (1726) the societies managed to shut down more than twenty mollies' houses, among them Mother Clap's, a famous gay brothel accommodating up to forty 'Chaps' a night. Mother Clap was found guilty of keeping a 'sodomitical house' and was put in the pillory, fined £13 6s 8¾d, then sent to prison for two years. She got off lightly; three of her whores were hanged. The repression was a severe blow to the homosexual community, making the lives of gay whores extremely precarious. It did not, however, prevent the trade from flourishing.

The reformist campaigns peaked around the beginning of the 18th century; by this time there were societies springing up everywhere: 20 in London, 13 in Edinburgh, and at least another 42 elsewhere in the kingdom. The idea spread right across Protestant Europe, British North America, and even to Jamaica. But by the 1730s the membership itself had grown corrupt, and the societies lost their morale. By the middle of the century they had all but disappeared. In their main aim of eradicating all prostitution, they had met with the usual lack of success; the conditions of the time ensured that the trade kept expanding. One sinister consequence of their victimization of whores had been a series of Ripper-style murders in 1689–90; murders that bore more than a passing resemblance to those which were to occur exactly 200 years later, during a similar period of moral hysteria.

The agitation around street prostitution had, none the less, succeeded in stirring up debate, and the reform societies movement had engendered a 'climate of opinion in which government and administration began to mobilize behind the new values of civility and respectability in sexual behaviour and expression.'[40] Social thinkers began to apply their minds and their pens to the 'problem'. What united all these men – whether they were for or against prostitution *per se* – was the concern for regulation, control, and 'decency'. In 1724 one writer, Bernard de Mandeville, put forward a scheme which recalled the Middle Ages: he recommended that state brothels be set up throughout the country to house, say, 2000 women, all of whom were to be kept 'neat and decent', and who would 'entertain Gentlemen after a civil and obliging Manner'.[41]

All very cosy: but others were not terribly convinced. Among these was Sir John Fielding, a London magistrate and brother of the novelist Henry Fielding; he is famous for having initiated the idea of Britain's first professional police force, the Bow Street Runners. Sir John proposed a public institution to 'preserve the deserted Girls of the Poor of this Metropolis; and also to reform those Prostitutes whom Necessity has drove into the Streets, and who are willing to return to Virtue and obtain an honest livelihood by severe Industry.'[42]

Fielding's 'severe Industry' was to be in the form of a public laundry, where, for a pittance, the women of the poor could sweat the immorality out of their souls by doing the washing of the philanthropic middle classes. The further aims of this ideal institution were to instil the housewifely arts like cooking, knitting and cleaning into the minds and hearts of the formerly rebellious and self-willed prostitutes. The long-term goal was their miraculous conversion into submissive and dutiful wives.

In 1758, Dr William Dodd, 'philanthropist', took up some of these recommendations when he founded the Magdalen Hospital near Goodmans Fields in London. Once again the aim was the conversion of 'the outcast poor into the respectable and disciplined Christian poor';[43] once again the regime was grim and punitive: from 6 a.m. to 10 p.m. in summer and 7 a.m. to 9 p.m. in winter, the inmates were kept hard at work, making clothes or small saleable items; any spare time was devoted to religious instruction. Ironically, these pious activities were designed to prepare the women for domestic service – a way of life which had already furnished the market with countless numbers of whores. There were the usual petty and vindictive house regulations: for example, the women had to ask permission to step outside. Any infringement of these rules was punishable by solitary confinement and loss of meals and wages.

Understandably, in these circumstances, only 2217 ex-whores opted to be rescued by the Magdalen Hospital during the first 40 years of its life. But a precedent had been set, and more homes were opened; many along the lines dreamed up by Fielding, where the women were set to work as laundresses. But the growth of these 'sanctimonious sweat-shops' made little impression on the volume of the sex trade.

In the middle of the 18th century public order once again became the pretext for scapegoating whores, and legislation was introduced to make the closure of brothels easier. From 1752 onwards, two ratepayers presenting evidence could have parish authorities bound over by a JP to prosecute brothels. Fielding took advantage of this tightening of the law to move against the tea-gardens and pleasure-houses, engineering the passage of the *Disorderly Houses Act* of 1752. This decreed that any house, room or garden in London or Westminster which allowed music, dancing or other entertainments without a licence, would be regarded as a disorderly house (that is, a brothel), and punished accordingly. (Westminster Council was still using this Act more than 200 years later: it was levelled at a Soho strip club in 1973). Although the general corruption of the authorities meant that *de facto* licences could always be had in return for cash bribes and sexual favours, Fielding did succeed in closing Belsize House and some of the more celebrated tea-gardens. By making it more difficult for the pleasure-resorts and brothels to operate, he established a legal precedent for the control, regulation and potential suppression of the culture of the urban poor. In doing so, he set the scene for the Victorian era, when moral panic was to reach a climax, and when the triumph – and hypocrisy – of the bourgeoisie would sweep all before it.

CHAPTER ELEVEN

Old World, New World: 19th-Century Prostitution on Two Continents

Why waste your life working for a few shillings a week in a scullery, eighteen hours a day, when a woman could earn a decent wage by selling her body instead?

Emma Goldman, 19th-century activist[1]

Towards the end of the 18th century two epoch-making developments occurred which were to split the old Europe apart at the seams: the Industrial Revolution and the French Revolution. Although the British Industrial Revolution was perhaps, as the historian E. J. Hobsbawm put it, 'the most important event in world history', the political revolution in France exploded with more obvious *éclat*, convincing contemporary observers that their world would never be the same again, despite countless attempts by conservatives to turn back the tide. From the whore's point of view, however, the economic and social transformation that came about as a result of the Industrial Revolution proved more significant.

The processes that brought about the Industrial Revolution in late 18th-century England were by no means new; we have traced some of them in the rise of the bourgeoisie, the creation of a landless working class, and the spread of capitalism from the 16th century onwards. But the late 18th century marked the take-off of a new form of industrial economy, with the creation of a booming manufacturing sector largely based on the production of textiles in factories. The profits that were accumulated out of the labour of the workers (40 per cent of them women and children) in these 'dark, satanic mills' enabled a broad new middle class to emerge from the ranks of the commoners. Factory production was still far from being widespread enough to provide jobs for all the urban propertyless classes, but this did not stem the flow of former peasants who continued to pour into the cities looking for work.

These processes spread further the appalling squalor into which the working classes had sunk in the cities of the 18th century; living conditions deteriorated at an alarming rate. Hideous slums enveloped the poorer quarters – especially the outskirts – of the cities and towns. The resulting degradation that masses of human beings, poverty-stricken and powerless, were subjected to is difficult to imagine today; again and again the intrepid middle-class investigators who began to penetrate 'darkest Britain' during the middle of the 19th century told the same story of working-class living conditions:

> These lodging-houses are the great foci of poverty, vice, and crime, as well as disease. These houses are generally of a very wretched description, in low, unwholesome situations, exceedingly dirty and ill-ventilated, and are frequently crowded to excess, it being no uncommon thing to find 8, 10 and 12 persons in one small apartment, as 9 feet by 8 or 11 by 8. Some of these also have no beds whatever in them, the inmates lying on the bare floor or with a few shavings below them, with their clothes on.[2]

> The Rookery, in St Giles's . . . is one of the most deplorable places in London; the largest number we found occupying one room was 23, composed of six families; there was not what we call a bed in many of the rooms, nor a bedstead, nor a table, nor what might be termed a chair; the only accommodation they had was two planks to lay across two broken chairs, so that they could not slip.[3]

The kind of poverty described in this rather delicately-phrased report was extreme; it was, nevertheless, an extreme in which many thousands of working-class Victorians found themselves, and into which the uncertain economy of the new industrialization could propel them at any time, particularly if they were female.

For the economic revolution had major consequences for working women. While a tiny minority found employment in the factories, the rest found that the economy was not expanding fast enough to provide them with regular jobs. Those who did find work – in sweated garment workshops, as seamstresses or milliners, or in domestic service – were generally paid a below-subsistence wage which forced them either to be partially dependent on the higher wage of a male partner, or to supplement their earnings through prostitution. And even in the factories, women were paid far less than the male workers, which put them at a disadvantage in the desperate struggle for survival: they were the poorest of the poor, underprivileged even among those who had nothing. The social and economic conditions were ripe for the unprecedented boom in prostitution that ensued, firstly in Britain and shortly afterwards in France, the USA and all the other Western countries that saw their own industrialization as the century progressed.

Meanwhile the *ancien régime* of France toppled as the 'people's revolution' exploded in 1789, sending shock waves throughout the whole of French society. Unlike the British, who had reached an accommodation with their monarchy over a century earlier, the French were still languishing under the absolutist state of Louis XVI, which was stifling the whole society, and had even succeeded in turning the aristocracy against it. Exasperated by the situation, in 1789 the middle classes linked up with both peasantry and the urban poor to unleash a revolutionary movement that within a few years had felled the government, unseated the aristocracy, and wiped out the monarchy. For a brief historical moment there must have been a truly egalitarian consensus – or at least the vision of one – but not for long; for after the fall of the leftist Robespierre in 1793, the policies of the revolutionary government swung to the right, with dire consequences for the *menu peuple* – the 'petty people' whose mass mobilizations had enabled a revolution to happen in the first place. The new bourgeois rulers imposed a liberalized economy, in which prices rocketed while wages were held down by force. The disastrous results were described by an observer writing in 1795:

Poverty is at its lowest depths; the streets of Paris present the grievous spectacle of women and children on the point of collapse from lack of nourishment; the hospitals and almshouses will soon be insufficient to house the army of sick and wretched. Poverty and hunger have almost completely silenced their voices; but when, on occasion, their voices are raised, it is in muttered imprecations against the government.[4]

It was this desperate plight of the urban poor which led to the boom in the Parisian sex trade that was such a prominent feature of the revolutionary years. In addition the revolution had swept away all previous legislation, including the laws pertaining to prostitution; as a result the streets of the city openly thronged with whores, who strolled about dressed in the loose, translucent, classical-style fashions of the period. And there was plenty of demand for their services, more than enough to match the supply, since bourgeois men were eager to take advantage of their now unrestricted rule in order to enrich themselves as quickly as possible. Like their revolutionary leader Danton, they alternated between periods of relaxation in the bosom of their families, and frenzied debauches in the brothels of the French capital. French middle-class men had never had it so good.

Of the working-class whores who no doubt took part in the great *journées* (days) of mass revolt and insurrection, nothing remains in the historical record. However, two *demi-mondaines* did manage to leave their traces: Théroigne de Méricourt, a fashionable Parisian courtesan who liked to appear among the revolutionary crowd dressed as an Amazon warrior (and who also attempted to form a women's legion to defend the revolution against the armies of Austria and Prussia); and Olympe de Gouges. The latter's story is better-documented, and more interesting.

Born plain Marie Gouze in 1748, daughter of a butcher and a washerwoman, she decided to profit from her beauty and brains at an early age, and came to Paris to work as a prostitute. By 1780 de Gouges had become a prolific writer, producing among other works an anti-slavery play, *L'Esclavage des noirs*, and a pioneer feminist pamphlet, *The Rights of Woman* (1791), modelled on the Declaration of the Rights of Man and the Citizen which had been adopted by the revolutionaries in 1789.

De Gouges was active in revolutionary politics; as a supporter of the moderate Girondins she hated bloodshed and argued passionately in her writings against the Terror. This brought her into direct conflict with the lovers of the guillotine; her fate was sealed. In July 1793 she was arrested; she was guillotined on 3 November of the same year, abandoned at the end by everyone – including her own son, who publicly disowned her.

In fact the period in which women played a part in the revolution's political activities was extremely short-lived; such is the way with revolutions, it seems. The leaders were men; men of the middle class, moreover, who subscribed to the sexual ideologies of the Enlightenment. The French Revolution inevitably turned into a carnival of the Rousseauist doctrines of Motherhood and Wifely Virtue, as far as women were concerned; and men fought tooth and nail to keep it that way. Two weeks after the execution of Olympe de Gouges, the public prosecutor Chaumette held up her fate as an example – or threat – to ambitious women: 'Remember the impudent Olympe de Gouges,' he thundered, 'who first set up the women's societies and abandoned her household to get involved in the republic, and whose head fell under the law's avenging steel.'[5]

The message to women could not have been clearer; and it was confirmed shortly after Napoleon Bonaparte took power in a coup d'état in 1799. Five years later, in 1804, the new ruler introduced his *Code Napoléon*, which was to become a model for 'enlightened' bourgeois justice throughout Europe in the following century, and in which women virtually ceased to exist under the law. Lumped together with minors and ex-convicts as 'unfit persons', women were deemed incompetent at law and unable, if married, to go to school or take a job without the husband's permission. Husbands were awarded control over their wives' family property, plus any wages they might earn; and while it was acceptable – normal – for a man to have affairs or mistresses outside the marriage, any woman found guilty of adultery could land in jail for up to two years. Along with the urban working classes, women came out of the great revolution empty-handed.

Since whores were both female and, in the main, working-class, it comes as no great surprise to learn that the Revolution was not hospitable to them for very long. Their middle-class sisters, perhaps jealous of the whore's autonomy, petitioned the men in power to set up 'national homes', where whores could be instilled with the virtues of drudgery, as was fitting for women of their class. Here, the prayer readings of the former Magdalene Homes were replaced by 'patriotic talks'. Meanwhile the men began to regard prostitutes as criminals and potential traitors to the revolutionary cause: Chaumette even believed that priests and whores were plotting together to overthrow the revolution. For whores, the underbelly of the Rights of Man soon began to show through the promises of freedom and equality, when a system of police control and regulation – as arbitrary and oppressive as that of the *ancien régime* – sprang up in the early years of the 19th century.

With the two revolutions, then, came the political triumph of the bourgeoisie. In the most advanced countries of the West – France, Britain and the USA, whose War of Independence had liberated the States from British dominion in the 1770s – the middle class was now indisputably the ruling class. This fact inevitably led to the ascendancy of the bourgeois notion of women as either Madonnas or Whores, with separate spheres for each group; spheres that could be bridged only by the double standard which allowed men access to both the sanctity of the home and the 'vice-den' of the brothel.

The 19th-century sex trade in Britain was in essence no different from that of the preceding century: the same locations were centres of the sex market, the same clients catered to, and the same specialities offered. What was different, however, was the sheer scale of the Victorian industry: there were more women working as whores than ever before. There were more clients, too; the sprawling cities thronged with men of all classes who were, as ever, looking for a good time.

The main settings for working-class leisure were still the pubs; and from the early years of the century, brewers took advantage of the booming urban population by building on to their premises saloons and dance halls where the working classes could let their hair down. Some middle-class citizens were of course outraged that the workers – including whores – should have the effrontery to amuse themselves in public; they began to investigate the party rooms of pubs in London's East End, where they found, much as they had suspected, people 'drinking, half-naked, and both men and women sitting in indecent and improper postures, and using very dreadful language.' In these 'rooms continually filled with prostitutes and sailors' and other naughty proletarians, couples could be seen dancing 'in the most libidinous manner'; and when not dancing, they 'indecently exposed' themselves, sat together 'with their hands in improper situations',[6] and bargained together in full and unconcerned view of the company, before retiring along back alleys which connected the saloons with nearby brothels. At this early stage – the year is 1817 – the dismayed observers could do little to put a stop to the heinous activities they witnessed – which must have been terribly frustrating for them.

By the mid-century the makeshift saloons had developed into big complexes known as casinos, and the dancing was augmented by programmes that included music-hall, varieties and even opera. The Eagle Tavern, in City Road, Whitechapel, boasted a fine theatre; also a 'garden with fountains, alcoves and boxes . . . where open-air shows and firework displays were held'.[7]

One police constable, witness to a report (dated 1854) on the evils of working-class drinking habits, called it 'The most detrimental place I know, as far as females are concerned' and noted that he 'had not sat down about five minutes when I was solicited twice and told there were houses outside for me to go.'[8]

Like all Victorian institutions, the dance halls and casinos reflected the strict hierarchies of social class. Slightly higher up the social ladder than the solidly working-class establishments were 'pleasure resorts' such as the Holborn Casino, a huge hall 'glittering with a myriad prisms', where dancers whirled to the tunes of polkas and quadrilles. Here, young middle-class men could mingle with and pick up working-class whores who dressed up 'flash'. The clientele were 'medical students, apprentice lawyers, young ships' officers, clerks, well-off young tradesmen'.[9] A smarter set could be seen at the Argyll Rooms in London's Haymarket, where 'sporting ladies' (a popular Victorian euphemism for whores) could gallivant with sporting aristocrats the like of Lord Hastings, a well known rake-about-town and prankster who once emptied a sack of rats on to the dance floor. But the jewel in the diadem of the London dance halls was the luxurious Portland Rooms, where the priciest courtesans plied their trade between midnight and four or five in the morning: 'The Cancan was danced there, in every unrestrained form, the women behaving in a more bacchantic fashion than in other places, but the police did not interfere.'[10] In such distinguished company, the police were naturally more tolerant.

The theatre kept up its old tradition as sexual market-place; actresses were still associated with the demi-monde, while whores openly worked the auditoria, especially the private boxes and the plush theatre bars, 'these dreadful hotbeds of vice and immorality', as one righteous Victorian describes the scene. A shade wistfully, he goes on: 'When a young man meets there with handsome fine-looking girls, well-dressed with genteel manners, he forgets the indecency of their appearance and the looseness and impropriety of their language and behaviour, if these do not attract him the more;' (here obviously speaks one who knows) 'and he gets interested and entangled with them, and is led astray; and this the more readily as he sees around him much older men of respectable appearance, without scruple talking, and romping with them.'[11]

After an evening's dancing or a visit to the theatre, whores and their clients would drift towards the cafés, divans and supper-houses, which served meals and refreshments through the night. The cafés tended to be more down-market, catering for night workers as well as 'women of the town'; and in some areas – notably St Giles –becoming almost exclusively haunts of the criminal underworld. The divans were more thoroughly masculine environments, where men gathered late at night to buy cigars, smoke, drink and pick up whores. Well-off revellers could retire to supper-rooms, where they could enjoy champagne suppers or breakfasts; alternatively, they could relax in an exclusive night-house like Kate Hamilton's famed Café Royal, in Leicester Square. Here the customer could put away an outrageously overpriced supper before getting down to the real business: negotiating with one of the scantily-clad whores who were permanently in attendance. Most evenings the magnificently overweight Kate herself presided over the company; enthroned on a rostrum, she sipped champagne and watched her bank balance pile up. Held in awe by both her male clients and the high-priced whores who used her premises, Kate was a veritable Queen Victoria of the demi-monde.

A typical London streetwalker of the mid-19th century might visit a variety of establishments in a single night; as one whore recounted to the journalist Bracebridge Hemyng in the 1850s:

> Why, if I have no letters or visits from any of my friends, I get up about four o'clock, dress and dine: after that I may walk about the streets for an hour or two and pick up anyone I am fortunate enough to meet, that is if I want money; afterwards I go to Holborn, dance a little, and if anyone likes me I take him home with me. If not, I go to the Haymarket, and wander from one café to another, from Sally's to the Carlton, from Barns' to Sams', and if I find no one there I go, if I feel inclined, to the divans. I like the Grand Turkish best, but you don't as a rule find good men at any of the divans.[12]

This particular whore's territory was the West End of the city where by night the theatre district of Leicester Square and the Haymarket were crowded with women and their clients. In the East End –

staunchly working-class territory – sailors' whores would parade up and down Ratcliffe Highway, conspicuous in their 'bright, low-cut dresses, lavishly decked out with ribbons and sham flowers . . . short enough to reveal pink or white stockinged calves above coloured morocco boots with glistening brass heels'[13] – a far cry from the drab rags of the 'poor but virtuous' working-class female.

In other areas of the city, working-class whores were obliged to be somewhat more circumspect about their trade, particularly the 'dollymop' or part-time prostitute. One woman, a widow of 32 with two children to feed, was interviewed in the 1880s by the pioneer sexologist Havelock Ellis, who records that:

> She was earning eighteen shillings a week in an umbrella factory in the East End: she occasionally took to the street near one of the big railway stations. A comfortable and matronly person, who looked quite ordinary except that her skirts were shorter than normally worn. If spoken to she would remark that she was 'waiting for a lady friend', talk in an affected way about the weather, and parenthetically introduce her offer. She will either lead a man into one of the silent neighbouring lanes filled with warehouses, or will take him home with her. She will take what she can get . . . sometimes £1, more often only 6d; on an average she earns a few shillings an evening. Though not speaking well of the police, says they don't interfere as much as with the regulars; never gave them money, but sometimes gratified their desires to keep on good terms.[14]

Even the part-time street whore was not immune to police sexual blackmail.

The blatant and raucous nature of the sex trade that had been so evident during the previous century now began to be replaced by a somewhat more restrained version in many parts of Victorian London. Dr William Acton, writing of Cremorne Gardens, Chelsea, in 1857, watched as smartly-dressed prostitutes took over from respectable citizens as soon as night fell: 'As calico and merry respectability tailed off eastward by penny steamers, the setting sun brought westward hansoms freighted with demure immorality in silk and fine linen.' But by Acton's day the 'gay debauchery' of the 18th century had become 'barely vivacity, much less boisterous disorder'.[15]

The more private establishments that had catered to the 18th-century sex trade survived intact, and even flourished, during the Victorian era. Lodging-houses – which were not strictly brothels but houses where whores and other working people could rent apartments or rooms – were used by the majority of whores, both in the capital and in other urban centres. Again, there were various grades of lodging-house – from the appalling rookeries of St Giles, through the marginally less poverty-stricken working-class districts, to the more salubrious areas like St John's Wood. The whores who lived and worked in them catered to different clients accordingly. They worked independently, picking up clients on the streets, in theatres and saloons, music-halls and cafés. While the poorest prostitutes lived in the squalor of areas like St Giles, most whores – especially full-timers – earned well above the best working-class wages of the period, and were therefore able to maintain themselves in relative comfort – even luxury. One writer describes a whores' lodging-house in Liverpool as 'really very clean, and comfortable, and well-furnished',[16] while Bracebridge Hemyng was surprised to find, on visiting sailors' whores in a London street known as 'Tiger Bay', large rooms furnished with old-fashioned four-poster beds and decorated tastefully, with 'crockery ornaments and gilt or rosewood-framed mirrors' over the mantelpiece.

Some independent whores preferred to keep their working and home lives separate, particularly women with young children: the accommodation and introduction houses fitted the bill perfectly. They were ideal for the dollymop, or the woman who lived in the suburbs, for rooms could be hired out for short periods. Accommodation houses were mainly concentrated in the heart of central London, from Bond Street, through the Strand and the Haymarket to beyond Covent Garden. Coffee-houses, restaurants and divans all let their upstairs rooms by the hour, as did certain establishments, mainly de luxe ladies' dress-shops, around the Bond Street/Mayfair areas. Some accommodation-house owners also ran an introduction service, keeping lists of clients and whores, whom they would then advertise in directories (the Victorian version of a contact-magazine) such as *The Man of Pleasure's Pocket Book* of the 1850s. The following are typical entries:

JAN FOWLER. Tall, slender, of graceful form and carriage; light hair, with a surprisingly fair and transparent complexion; a full

blue eye, fringed with beautiful silken lashes, through which her
luscious orbs dart a thousand killing shafts.
MISS MERTON [has] sister hills . . . prominent, firm and elastic.
One guinea.[17]

The madam would circulate her publicity material to affluent men
at their clubs and offices and arrange a rendezvous between the two
parties at her house. It was a good system – discreet, professional, and
safe; quite satisfactory to all concerned.

Given the prevalence of the lodging and introduction houses, the
closed brothel was a relatively rare feature of the sex trade.
Continental-style luxury brothels did exist, but, as Charles Booth of
the Salvation Army noted, 'The men who frequent such houses are
extremely rich'[18] thus by definition a minority. Within these brothels
the specialist trade refined its thrills and tortures, for those who could
afford them: virgins and flagellation being – still – the staple favourites
of the British upper classes.

The more restrictive 'closed-house' brothels, modelled on French
lines, were in the minority, since whores preferred to be free agents.
Brothel-owners had to resort to procurers, who would persuade, lure
or trick inexperienced girls into a house. Once incarcerated, the girl
was often forced to buy or hire, at exorbitant prices, the fine clothes
she needed for whoring, thus falling into the madam's debt and
becoming a virtual captive. Such 'dress houses' were comparatively
few in number in Britain, although their significance was exaggerated
by anti-prostitution campaigners. So was another aspect of the brothel
trade: the sale of virgins.

The sexual exploitation of children and adolescent female virgins is
probably the most notorious aspect of the Victorian sex trade. There is
no denying that these children were badly abused, but again, it must
be pointed out that working-class children were exploited in *all* senses:
this was a time when infants were set to work, in both town and
countryside, under the most appalling conditions. One woman wrote
an account of her childhood as a fieldworker in Lincolnshire in the
1850s:

On the day that I was eight years of age, I left school, and began
to work fourteen hours a day in the fields, with from forty to
fifty other children of whom, even at that early age, I was the
eldest. We were followed all day long by an old man carrying a

long whip in his hand which he did not forget to use. A great
many of the children were only five years of age.[19]

And in Yorkshire during the mid-century, children between the ages
of eight and fourteen worked in the textile trade, many of them dying
before their fourteenth birthday. Records of their death certificates
still exist; they simply state the child's name, age, and cause of death:
'Worn out'.

When seen in this context, the sexual exploitation of Victorian
working-class children is neither more nor less shocking than the facts
of their day-to-day struggle for existence. To sidestep the issue of
poverty that made them so vulnerable to abuses *of all kinds* is to distort
the truth about these children's lives. Yet some modern-day feminists,
sadly, persist in doing so; like their 19th-century predecessors, they
prefer to focus on the lurid sensationalism of child sexual abuse rather
than on the circumstances that enabled it to happen in the first place.

None of which absolves those Victorian gentlemen who clamoured
for under-aged sex. Mass poverty formed a large pool of potential
child whores: some parents, desperately poor, sent their own children
on to the streets to solicit, and there were groups of orphans who lived
and roamed in gangs, struggling to stay alive through begging, petty
crime, and prostitution. Girls as young as twelve worked the West
End streets, and some brothels were staffed entirely by children – boys
and girls. Their clients came from the upright, Christian middle
classes – 'respectable gentlemen', according to one policeman of the
1880s.

The same was true of the trade in virgins. Bourgeois morality, with
its insistence that its women must be sexually 'pure', had focused male
fantasy on defloration; this, combined with the fear of venereal
disease, made the 'virgin whore' the most sought-after commodity on
the sex market. Such was demand that by the late 1880s, the price of a
maidenhead in a top London brothel could be anything from £5 to £25.
With such sums to be made – and bearing in mind the vulnerability of
Victorian children – it was inevitable that young girls would be sold to
individual men or to brothels by their parents, or inveigled, tricked
and coerced by procurers into being raped by rich men.

Nevertheless, the demand was so great that no matter how many
poor young girls were made available, there could never be enough of
them; in any case, the vast majority of working-class girls had already
lost their virginity by their early teens. The Victorian diarist (and

punter) 'Walter', who meticulously recorded his thousands of forays into the night world, was only confirming the findings of other, more objective reporters when he lamented that:

> Few of the tens of thousands of whores in London have given their virginities to gentlemen, or to young men, or to old men, or to men at all: their own low-class lads had them before anyone else . . . that is the truth of the matter, though greatly to be regretted, for street boys cannot appreciate the treasure they destroy. A virginity taken by a street boy of sixteen is like a pearl cast before swine.[20]

The trade in virgins, therefore, was often a figment of the customers' imaginations, aided and abetted by canny young whores who knew lots of ways in which to fake the rupturing of a hymen – for instance the use of strategically-hidden bags of pigeon's blood, combined with the tightening of the vagina (various astringent potions were used for this purpose) – or a young whore would simply have sex during her period. In this game, apparently, you could fool most of the customers all of the time.

Flogging – *le vice anglais* – was the other great stand-by of the specialist trade, to the extent that, by the middle of the century, London was revered by rich masochists the world over as the capital of the flagellation scene. Top of the league was Mrs Theresa Berkley's house at 28 Charlotte Street in London's Fitzrovia. The 1830s anonymous pornographic classic *Venus School Mistress* listed Mrs Berkley's equipment in loving detail:

> Her supply of birch was extensive, and kept in water so that it was always green and pliant; she had shafts with a dozen whip thongs on each of them; a dozen different sizes of thin bending canes; leather straps like coach traces; battledoors, made of thick sole-leather, with inch nails run through to docket and curry-comb tough hides rendered callous by many years' flagellation. Holly brushes, furze brushes; a prickly evergreen called butcher's brush; and during the summer, glass and China vases, filled with a constant supply of green nettles, with which she often restored the dead to life. Thus, at her shop, whoever went with plenty of money, could be birched, whipped, fustigated, scourged, needle-pricked, half-hung, holly-brushed, furze-

brushed, butcher-brushed, stinging-nettled, curry-combed, phlebotomised, and tortured.

Madam Berkley obviously possessed an innovative mind, for in 1828 she unveiled the prototype of an invention which was to make her famous: the Berkley Horse was a device for the flogging of gentlemen. The author of *Venus School Mistress* wrote admiringly:

> It is capable of being opened to a considerable extent, so as to bring the body to any angle that might be desirable. There is a print in Mrs Berkley's memoirs, representing a man upon it quite naked. A woman is sitting in a chair exactly under it; with her bosom, belly and bush exposed she is manualizing his embolon [sic], whilst Mrs Berkley is birching his posteriors.[21]

(An invention rivalled in its ingenuity only by the curious cushioned throne that permitted Queen Victoria's son, later King Edward VII, to enjoy two women at once.)

Another 18th-century tradition still going strong was the male homosexual brothel. In spite of the fact that the single-sex public schools were hotbeds of homosexual activity, gay sex was the greatest of Victorian taboo subjects. Everyone simply pretended that it did not exist. This resulted in a 'secret' but extremely widespread homosexual sex trade, which was frequented almost exclusively by members of the ruling classes, from the royal family downwards. In the gay brothels of the West End, mock marriages were celebrated with orgies: 'men of rank, and respectable situations in life, might be seen wallowing either in or on the beds with wretches of the lowest description'.[22]

Women of the leisured classes were also catered to, albeit on a much smaller scale. One of the most successful sexual entrepreneurs of the period was Mary Wilson, who opened a 'temple' at which she displayed 'the finest men of their species I can procure'. The client would pass her eye over these prize specimens and, 'Having fixed upon one she would like to enjoy . . . ring for the chambermaid, point out the object, and he is immediately brought to the boudoir. She can enjoy him in the dark, or have a light, and keep on her mask. She can stay an hour or a night, and have one or a dozen men as she pleases, without being known to any of them.'[23] All the lady needed was money – and plenty of it.

Literature of the period gives occasional glimpses into the submerged world of marginal sexuality which flourished in the brothels and streets of Victorian Britain. One luxury brothel in Soho Square was known to have a 'Skeleton Room', where 'a skeleton was made by a mechanical contrivance to issue from a cupboard!'[24]

In the late 19th century a young whore who worked the Strand area told Havelock Ellis of some of her wealthier clients' quirks: one young man had orgasms when she and a friend obliged him by undressing and, when naked, wringing pigeons' necks in front of him; another 'chap' paid her a guinea for the privilege of licking her boots (she kept a special pair covered in mud for the purpose); yet another liked to be urinated on. While in straight society, admitted sexual norms became more repressive as the century wore on, in the sex ghettos, bourgeois men were indulging in a range of increasingly bizarre sexual practices. But no matter how outlandish his request, one thing was certain: the Victorian gentleman had no trouble finding a whore who would cater to his desires; for in this era of extreme prudishness there were more prostitute women than at any other time in Western history, before or since.

In France, meanwhile, the great revolutionary ideals of *liberté*, *égalité* and *fraternité* had swiftly been translated into liberty for the bourgeoisie to exploit the poor, equality for those who were already considerably more equal than the rest, and a brotherhood that by definition excluded the female half of the population. Now, as industrialization began to encroach upon the country during the early part of the century, the authorities became increasingly alarmed at the vast numbers of street whores who suddenly began to appear, particularly in the capital. Public morals and social control became major topics of debate amongst the new ruling classes, who could not tolerate the sight of working-class women flaunting themselves with such apparent disdain for the proprieties. Once again the police were given *carte blanche* to deal with the problem of prostitution; once again they fell back on their earlier solution: regulation, toleration – and extortion.

As early as 1810 the Paris police responded to bourgeois concern by setting up a special morals squad, the *police des mœurs*, whose job it was to supervise the inscription of whores on a central register. Once registered, Parisian whores were required to present themselves for monthly vaginal inspection by a police doctor; this privilege cost them three francs a time. If found to be infected with a venereal disease, the women were forcibly confined to a prison hospital (in Paris, the hellish St Lazare).

Whores' lives were also circumscribed by impossibly stringent regulations that dictated when, where and how they could solicit; failure to comply with these rules could lead to arrest and imprisonment. With a typically French mania for bureaucracy, the morals police spent most of their working lives dreaming up more and more rules; by the 1820s whores could be arrested if they were found in or near the Tuileries, the Louvre, the Palais-Royal, the place Vendôme, the boulevard des Capucines, the place des Victoires, the place Louis XV, in or near the Luxembourg Gardens, in the church or the place Ste Geneviève, on the Champs-Elysées, on the bridges or quais, in public places, in the taverns near the Palais de Justice, 'and finally, when they exercise their métier on the streets'.[25] In fact according to these police regulations, about the only place the prostitutes of Paris could operate in was the River Seine.

By the end of the 1820s the women were further forbidden from 'walking together, standing around the streets, forming groups, taking up the pavements, soliciting passers-by, and provoking scandals by their free discourse and indecent dress.'[26] In 1830 new regulations were passed which barred prostitutes from all streets, boulevards, thoroughfares and public gardens; and three years later a new list forbade them to sit at their windows or stand in their doorways, or frequent 'deserted and obscure streets and areas, as well as cabarets and other public establishments' – taverns, hotels, etc. – 'or private homes which favour prostitution'. Whores must on no account speak to men accompanied by women or children, or address anyone 'in a loud voice with insistence'.[27] Any infringement of these ludicrous regulations would lead to a stretch in the Petite Force prison. Moreover, the women had no right of appeal; there were no laws on prostitution, *ergo* there were no regular legal procedures. The police had given themselves total power in a system of their own invention.

In this way the authorities put into action a kind of underworld police state for sex workers. Their system permitted whores to work only in the regulated brothels – *maisons closes* – licensed and regulated by the morals squad, who had free access to these houses at all times. Not only were the inmates of the houses under surveillance; the madam had to register the names of her clients in a visitors' book. If the madam, or any of the inmates, proved unco-operative, the police could always revoke the brothel licence and prosecute.

Within the brothel, the women were subject to the power of the madam, who owned everything in the house, up to and including the clothes worn by her staff. As usual, in the regulated system, the prostitute woman found herself being fleeced from all quarters.

Following the Parisian example, authorities throughout the rest of the country adopted similar tactics, thus encouraging a flourishing brothel industry. Houses ranged from the cheap dives of the poorer areas, through the bucolic comforts of the mid-range and unpretentious village whore-houses, to the exaggeratedly plush interiors and exotic decor of the *maisons de grande tolérance*, which catered of course to a rich bourgeois and aristocratic clientele. Visiting pro-regulationists from other countries, like the English doctor William Acton, who studied the system during the mid-century, penned glowing accounts of these 'retreats of voluptuous splendour', in which the working women were 'to be seen seated on sofa chairs, elegantly attired in different-coloured silks, with low bodices and having their hair dressed in the extreme of fashion'.[28]

The privileged status of these expensive brothels acted like a hothouse on the growth of the upper-class 'speciality' trade, which, as in London, became increasingly diverse and in some ways spectacular. The top-notch *maisons* were equipped with torture-chambers, surrounded by rooms where the arrangement of strategically-positioned mirrors and spyholes enabled a plethora of voyeurs to satisfy their tastes at any time. Some of these exclusive houses began to stage exquisitely-produced *tableaux vivants*, spectacles in which naked whores would appear frozen like wax dolls in voluptuous poses that left nothing to the imagination. A multitude of highly imaginative sexual proclivities were catered to. Apart from oral and anal sex, clients demanded a weird and wonderful array of services: some paid to have long silver pins stuck into their skin under the testicles, or incisions made there with a knife; others had boiling hot omelettes served up on their naked skin; others still preferred shit to food.[29] By the dawn of the 20th century, the brothels of the rich had become virtual workshops for the production and consumption of a breathtaking range of sexual services.

The French regulation system inevitably made life difficult – not to mention dangerous – for both independent whores and working-class women in general. Since the bourgeois public saw *all* working women as whores or potential whores, the police defined as clandestine prostitutes not only those women who went with 'a mob of men', but also those who 'changed lovers frequently'. Under these terms, any working-class woman who did not conform to the middle-class norm of monogamy was liable to be stigmatized – and registered – as a prostitute. Since a single anonymous denunciation was all that was required for a woman to be investigated by the morals squad, the sexual life of a working woman was effectively curtailed. On the streets, any woman found without a man to vouch for her was a target for the police – to the extent that working-class women soon discovered that their own neighbourhoods were out of bounds, particularly after dark. The hotels and lodging-houses where single working women lived could be raided at any time; indeed any woman who lived alone and received one or more lovers could be towed off to the police station and subsequently designated an official prostitute by an act of bureaucratic fiat. The following contemporary account was by no means unique:

A woman . . . milliner, said the hotel register . . . unemployed and engaging in clandestine prostitution, claimed the inspectors' reports. She made some difficulties about opening. There was a man with her. She affected indignation and so did he. They spoke of abuse of power, of violation of domicile, of outraged honour . . . the *commissaire* [police officer] listened patiently to this torrent of words. Then without answering them, he said curtly:

'Get up and get dressed.'

'Are you going to let him take me away like this?' cried the woman in an explosion of sobs.

'Sir, this woman is my mistress; I answer for her!' said the man with an air of perfect dignity.

'Ah! Very well, sir, that is different. Your name, profession, address?'

'What for?'

'Well! If you are answering for her, we must know with whom we are dealing, also if your moral situation will allow us to take your word . . . when this little investigation is finished, we will only have to apologise to you for the inconvenience we have caused.'

'B-b-but, sir,' he stuttered.

'I thought so! Do you have any papers on you, to prove your
identity? That would simplify matters.'

'It is just that I do not want anyone to know.'

'Well then, be quiet and let us do our job.'

The man got back in bed and the girl had to get dressed and
leave. The same scene, or nearly, was renewed in ten other
rooms . . . It was a strange sight, at the same time seductive and
repulsive, to see these girls, some of whom were magnificent
creatures, get out of bed clad only in nightgowns and get dressed
in the sight of a dozen men, in these miserable slums, by the light
of three candles.[30]

Thus, in the eyes of the French morals squad, all single working-
class women who dared to have a sex life were deemed guilty. The job
of the police was to harass and arrest the women; and no doubt one of
the perks of this job was the 'seductive and repulsive' sight of these
'magnificent creatures' obediently dressing in front of them.

Confident of their power in an age that was obsessed with
'morality', secrecy, and above all hypocrisy, about extramarital sex,
the police could always apply this kind of blackmail when challenged
about their methods. The history of the regulation system in 19th-
century France is littered with abuses of all kinds. One documented
case tells of a young worker, Marie Ligeron, who was arrested on her
own doorstep 'at the very moment she left the embraces of her fiancé';
a short spell in prison wrecked her health and she died soon after her
release. In another incident, a registered prostitute, Amélie Renault,
was arrested when she left her house late one night to buy medicine for
her sick child. The police refused to believe her story and kept Amélie
overnight in the cells; the following morning they escorted her home,
where the child was found dead. Later, the morals police threatened
Amélie with vengeance 'if she dared to speak of this affair'.[31] This,
then, was the 'morality' that lay behind the façade of the morals squad.

The system found its great apologist in Dr Alexandre Parent-
Duchâtelet, who in 1836 published a study of Parisian prostitution
which was to become the model for countless later works in many
countries. Parent was the mouthpiece of a bourgeoisie that regarded
working-class sexuality as inherently subversive, on the grounds that
it was not subject to middle-class morality. By firstly defining all
sexually active single working-class women as prostitutes – whether
or not they were working whores – and then confining them to a

watertight round of policed institutions – prisons, hospitals, brothels and, for a few token objects of charity, 'rescue homes' – the authorities reasoned that they could influence and discipline the entire working class.

Women were once again the scapegoats. They were shifted from one oppressive institution to the next, in closed, windowless vans specially designed for the purpose – forerunners of today's 'meat-wagons'. By thus targeting whores and other independent working-class women for repression, the regulation system could effectively terrorize them into submission to middle-class sexual morality, where they would join their 'good' sisters in the Rousseauist utopia of closeted, powerless females: that was what the men in charge hoped, at any rate.

And it worked, to the extent that many whores and other independent women began to be ostracized in their own communities, where before they had been accepted. Now, sexually autonomous women were vulnerable to being officially labelled and put to work in the degraded conditions of the brothel; this both cut them off from their own neighbourhoods and made it increasingly difficult to get out of the sex trade. Other working-class women began to shun them for fear of guilt by association, another card the 'morals' police could play whenever they chose. For the first time in French history, whores were being made into an outcast group in their own communities.

Yet the reality was still very far from the total control dreamed of by police and propagandists. Being human, whores struggled in their various ways for freedom from the system. Throughout the whole of the 19th century there were always many more women working in prostitution independently: 'les clandestines' – non-registered whores who would rather risk arrest and persecution than submit voluntarily to the humiliations and abuses of regulation. These women continued to work in their time-honoured traditional ways; from lodging-houses and hotels, in cafés, cabarets, or restaurants – even in the streets. They used male accomplices as spies and go-betweens: pimps, as straight society called them. Some whores used the *maisons closes* for their own ends, sheltering in them for the winter, then slipping away with the return of spring. Even the full-time brothel-workers exercised their freedom of choice by continually changing houses; when they wanted to get off the register, they simply disappeared. The police were fighting a losing battle, in spite of all their tactics; as the cities expanded, the sex industry escaped their control. By the 1870s the system was at a dead end, and the moralists started fretting about the 'invasion' of clandestine prostitution. What really affronted them, as always, was the fact that working-class women were selling sex, making money – and getting away with it.

The economic and social growth of the early 19th century soon began to pose similar problems of social control in Germany; and the response of the German authorities was predictable. Like France, Germany had a tradition of official tolerance and regulation that stretched as far back as the Middle Ages; and as early as the end of the 18th century the most powerful German state, Prussia, had pioneered a police-regulated system. In 1792 the Prussian crown issued a pious set of police regulations for the sex trade, insisting that it could not 'without impropriety and consequences injurious to morality'[32] legislate on prostitution because any form of legislation would amount to legalization. Whores were thus placed outside the law; as such, they were subject to arbitrary police rule.

Needless to say, the Berlin morals police – the *Sittenpolizei* – operated a system that was no less corrupt and abusive than, and shared many of the same features as, the Parisian model. Unregistered whores were punished by a three-month spell in prison before being sent to the workhouse; registered whores worked under the dictates of the police, and were permitted to operate only in the registered brothels or in certain designated streets. There were the usual compulsory medical examinations – a once-weekly procedure, supervised by the police surgeon; infection was punishable by three months in jail.

Although Germany was split into different states until the 1860s, each with its own separate laws, the police-regulation system was similar throughout. Every local department had its *Sittenpolizei*, which usually aimed to contain the sex trade by concentrating licensed brothels in tightly-supervised areas near the city centres: 'Characteristically, they were in the *Altstadt*, the oldest part of the town, dark, narrow, winding alleys, set well back from the new main thoroughfares and shopping streets which grew up in the course of the nineteenth century, but close enough to them to be easy of access for customers.'[33] Within the red-light areas, each morals squad division devised and applied its own version of state regulation.

The Italian authorities, by contrast, passed a comprehensive set of laws on prostitution. By the 1860s the Italian cities were witnessing spectacular growth; and at the same time the nation, until then a collection of separate states, was being unified under the leadership of the northern state of Piedmont. Thus, with masses of peasant women migrating to the cities, a prostitution boom coincided with the creation of a national legal code, and the result was the Cavour Law of 1860, in which Piedmont's prime minister, Cavour, set in motion a fully legal regulation scheme.

The new law legalized prostitution for women who registered with the police, were examined twice a week, and went voluntarily into a *sifilicomio* (VD infirmary) if found to be infected. *Case chiuse* (closed brothels) were set up – although these were at all times *case aperte*, as far as the police were concerned. Prices were regulated by the state: whores were allowed to keep *one quarter* of their earnings – and on top of this the brothels were taxed. Although the law did afford some rights to prostitute women (for example, it was illegal to ill-treat a whore or keep a woman in a house against her will), the whores of Cavour's Italy had little reason to be grateful. They were surrounded by prohibitions and petty regulations at all times: they were forbidden to 'loiter' in streets and squares, or to wander around their own neighbourhoods; they could not go out 'without just cause' after 8 p.m. in winter or 10 p.m. in summer. When they did leave the *case chiuse* they were to behave 'decently' and 'soberly', dress modestly, refrain from following passers-by, soliciting men or visiting the theatre. If they wanted to change house, leave the brothel for longer than three days, enter hospital or leave the profession, they had to ask permission from the police. Finally, if a whore succeeded in getting off the register, the police continued their surveillance over her for three months. State brothels, state pimping, and police pass laws: here was the reality of legalized prostitution.

Like all systems devised by men to control female prostitutes – whether or not enshrined in law – the Italian model was a corrupt tyranny. Its more-or-less disguised aim was to fill its own coffers with money extracted from the earnings of prostitute women – nothing new there – but it also had a shadow intent: the control of working-class women's sexuality. Thus it became 'a weapon against the entire mass of migrating, unemployed and homeless women who lived on the edge of subsistence'[34] in the Italian cities. The viciousness and brutality of the system was at its most blatant in its treatment of infected prostitutes (and others) in the so-called infirmaries, which were more like prisons than hospitals. Here, hygiene was non-existent, the diet appalling. Treatment for venereal diseases was barbaric:

> After being rubbed with mercury or inhaling its fumes, patients were purged, sweated and drained of blood by leeches. Since it was thought that the evil humour surfaced mainly in the mouth, patients were urged to salivate at least six litres of liquid each day. As the mouth became poisoned from this process, it 'was transformed into one gangrenous ulcer, out of which, together with saliva, often fell teeth, and even the jaws, the tongue, the lips, and the pharynx, eaten away by the necrotic process.'[35]

By the middle of the 19th century, the regulation experience had been repeated again and again across Europe, largely based on the French or Prussian models: registration, forced vaginal examinations, closed houses and/or controlled districts. Although at all times the majority of whores defied the authorities and continued to work as clandestines, their already difficult lives were not made any easier by their increasing isolation and persecution by the state. Many women chose instead to emigrate, in the hope of finding a better life – or at least, more freedom.

The New World of prostitution, its ever-expanding frontier, lay to the West. Although the sex trade had sprung up in many US cities during the 17th century, its major growth had coincided with the 18th-century expansion of maritime trade, with cities like New York and Boston attracting many European whores. By the 19th century, the US was developing a sex industry which could more than match any of its old world predecessors.

The forms the American sex trade took were sometimes similar to those of Europe, sometimes unique to the New World. Luxury brothels – known in the States as 'parlor houses' – were the same the world over. In his 1858 survey of New York's sex trade, William Sanger describes (with characteristic reproach) the discreet brothels of the city's richer neighbourhoods as being 'furnished with a lavish display of luxury, scarcely in accordance with the dictates of good taste . . .' with 'magnificent furniture', 'large mirrors', 'paintings and engravings in rich frames', 'vases and statuettes', 'carpets of luxurious softness', and an abundance of 'sofas, ottomans, and easy chairs'.[36] An evening's hobnobbing in one of these houses would have set the client back around 60 dollars – for an idea of the modern equivalent, multiply by ten.

In New Orleans – described by the sociologist Fernando Henriques as 'the greatest brothel city of all time'[37] – the plushest parlour houses were to be found on Basin Street. At Number 40, Kate Townsend's (opened in 1866), the owner personally vetted each client's 'credentials' – the capacity of his bank account – before he was 'escorted into the drawing-room and formally presented to the ladies'. Kate herself was 'occasionally available for the entertainment of a particularly distinguished client' – her fee a hefty 50 dollars an hour. Down the road at Number 225, the Arlington (named after its owner Josie) was advertised in *The Blue Book*, New Orleans' brothel guide, as being 'absolutely and unquestionably the most decorative and costly fitted-out sporting palace ever placed before the American public'.[38] Stuffed with expensive statues and paintings, the house featured a hall of mirrors, a Turkish parlour, a Japanese parlour, a Viennese parlour, even – for the patriotic client – an American parlour.

In these up-market brothels under-age prostitution and the selling of 'virginities' were the stock-in-trade much as they were in Europe. Some madams specialized exclusively in the selling of 'maidens': Mary Thompson, for instance, used a cigar store as a front and charged clients between 200 and 500 dollars – a fantastic sum – for each alleged virgin. Another famous procuress, 'Spanish Agnes' Herrick, used an employment agency as a cover for her teenage whore trade; whenever she was prosecuted, Herrick was able to call on powerful clients in City Hall to get her off the hook.

It was, however, the city of Chicago which boasted what was probably the most luxurious and profitable parlour house in the whole of the US: the Everleigh Club. Run by two sisters, Ada and Minna Everleigh, daughters of a Kentucky lawyer who had astutely ploughed their inheritance into the sex trade, the club was actually a mansion, complete with library, art gallery, fourteen parlours, bedrooms for thirty top-class whores, and sumptuous private apartments for the two canny madams. 'In every corner of the house there were always fresh roses, and on nights when the mood possessed her, Minna would release live butterflies to flutter round the premises.' Bedrooms were furnished with marble-inlaid beds surrounded by ceiling and wall-mirrors; several had individual touches such as a wall-to-wall mattressed Persian rug or a mechanical perfume-sprayer

ABOVE: St Mary Magdalene, by Correggio (c. 1489–1534): the original repentant whore.

BELOW: 'The indiscreet and wildest creature that ever was in court': Nell Gwynn, by Sir Peter Lely.

BELOW: 'She comes to thee decked like the Queene, and Goddess of Love': Thomas Coryat and a Venetian courtesan: from *Coryat's Crudities* (1611).

ABOVE: French whores being raided by the law: late 18th-century engraving.

BELOW: *Le Sérail Parisien* by Alphonse Naudet, 1802: another scene of upper-class debauchery.

The Harlot's Progress by William Hogarth: Plates 1 and 2.
The whore is depicted as pathetic victim – a new myth is born.

RIGHT: A 'sporting horsebreaker' in
Rotten Row, Hyde Park, London
(1871): a lady not to be trifled with.

ABOVE: The legendary Cora Pearl,
born Emma Crouch near Plymouth
in 1836 and one of the most famous
grandes horizontales in France.

RIGHT: Streetwalkers bribing the
beadle in the Burlington Arcade,
Piccadilly: 1871. *Plus ça change . . .*

RIGHT: *The Salon in the Rue des Moulins,* by Henri de Toulouse-Lautrec, 1894.

LEFT: A raid on a 19th-century French brothel: from *Le Petit Journal,* 1895. There was constant police pressure on regulated houses in France.

Storyville whores, c. 1900. Storyville, New Orleans, was one of the world's biggest red-light districts, stretching over 38 blocks.

LEFT: *Les marraines de guerre:* soldiers get together with their 'penfriends' in a club in wartime Toulon.

RIGHT: An inmate of a *maison close*, Paris, 1930s. Some right-wing French politicians are still clamouring for a return to the 'good old days' of the regulated brothel.

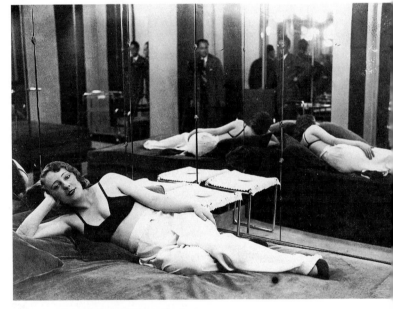

LEFT: The English Collective of Prostitutes celebrate victory in 1982 after occupying a church for twelve days in King's Cross, London, to protest against police illegality and racism.

above the bed which could dispense whatever exquisite scent the customer preferred. Within the inevitable exotic parlours – Japanese, Egyptian, Chinese and Moorish Rooms – ultra-wealthy magnates could frolic in surroundings littered with bibelots made from the metals that had made them their fortunes: the Gold Room, for instance, was kitted out with eighteen-carat gold spittoons, gold-rimmed fish bowls, a gold-plated grand piano, golden draperies, and chairs covered in beautifully-woven gold fabrics.[39] Nothing was considered too excessive for the upper-crust sex trade.

The Everleigh was officially a private club, to which the entrance requirements were a formal letter of introduction and a basic entrance fee of 50 dollars; added to this there were charges for food, drinks, tips, and 'presents' for the ladies; one night's bill could easily amount to anything between 500 and 1000 dollars: a phenomenal sum. In this house a whore could make her fortune – and as for the Everleigh sisters, the shrewd pair cleared up to $10,000 profit per month, after paying off the police and politicians. By the time they retired, after only twelve years in operation, Ada and Minna were millionaires.

For the élite whores who worked the US parlour houses, the wages of sin were excellent. In the houses scrutinized by Sanger, the ladies earned upwards of 50 dollars a week – a tidy recompense when compared with the average mid-century working woman's wage of one dollar a week. The women's skills and accomplishments determined their earning power; Sanger comments: 'Some of them are very well educated; accomplished musicians and artists are sometimes found amongst them, while others aspire to literature. With the greatest number much elegance and refinement of manner . . . is seen.'[40]

The zealous doctor was disappointed to find that many of the whores were capable of saving money: one woman he spoke to had 7000 dollars in her bank account; others told him of their aim to set themselves up in business (legitimate or otherwise) with their savings. Many of the women were single parents; and they all came from the most varied class backgrounds. One New York directory of 1869 lists a few.

'Miss Nellie' is described as 'one of the smartest, shrewdest, most practical women in the metropolis', having saved her money and invested in real estate. 'Being of humble birth and uneducated', Nellie spent her spare time giving herself the thorough education she had missed as a child, specializing in English literature. 'Miss May' is 'very tall, very slender, yet graceful and well-proportioned'; a New Yorker of German immigrant descent, she started her professional life 'connected with a minstrel troupe' in California. From lowly beginnings Miss May raised herself to the top of her profession, acquiring en route fluent French and Spanish (in addition to her native English and German) as well as a passionate devotion to music. She was an accomplished performer, notably 'having a taste for the bizarre', on the banjo, which she played 'comically and creditably'.

At the other end of the social spectrum was the Cuban widow 'Madam C—', known as 'the Cuban sylph'; she was the 'relic of a painter' who, although she had moved to New Orleans and lost property during the Civil War, was still 'worth about one hundred thousand dollars' when she appeared on the New York sex scene – 'to which sum she has added considerably by her own attractions'.[41]

In New Orleans, especially before the Civil War, high-class whoring was the only way in which women with black blood could compete with whites. Quadroon and octoroon ladies – those with one quarter and one eighth black blood – were highly sought-after as mistresses by the white youth of the southern élite. Special 'quadroon balls' were held, where white men and mixed-race prostitutes were the sole guests; the young men negotiated terms with the women's mothers or aunts before setting up their chosen mistresses in the Rampart Street district of the city. 'Mulatto' whores were often as highly educated as the white girls who worked the parlour houses; they were the *hetairae* of the American South. And black whores played an important role in the anti-slavery movement; their money helped finance the struggle that led to the American Civil War.[42] This was not to be the last time that whores in history were the unsung heroines of a resistance movement.

The middle range of American prostitution is sparsely documented by comparison with the upper range; 19th-century investigators preferred to shock and titillate their readers with tales that featured one of the two stereotypes: the voracious high-class whore or the debased low-class slut. One whore did, however, record an account of her days in a Midwest country whorehouse that catered to lower-middle-class clients:

> The prostitutes sat around in their underwear or wrappers . . .
> drank beer, joshed a lot in country talk, felt at home with the

simple horny guests that came to them with dusty shoes and derbys . . . They were Mama and Papa fuckers, doing it mostly the straight and traditional American way, as they had been raised. Frenching was talked and joked about, but rarely asked for or offered. The Italian way, entry through the rear, was a kind of joke carried over from farm boys experimenting on themselves and each other, considered a sign of depraved city sinning. Memories of Bible lessons and sermons on Babylon and hellfire from their country churches was still there in the middle class whorehouse.[43]

In the city, the women who staffed these middling joints would go out on the streets to pick up their 'johns' when trade was slack. As ever, the theatre was a happy hunting-ground: as one disapproving visitor to New York complained: 'There is not a dance hall, a free-and-easy, a concert saloon or a vile drinking-place that presents such a view of the depravity and degradation of New York as the gallery of a Bowery theatre.'[44] A theatre whore would not even bother to take her client home for the 'trick', but considerately did her job on the spot, so that he could then enjoy the rest of the show.

The dance-halls, saloons, and 'vile' drinking-places catered to the working-class trade in every city in the US; although the nature of the work tended to vary. In New Orleans whores danced half- or fully-naked in the dance-halls; the hookers of New York, on the other hand, tended to be more restrained. Sanger thoroughly investigated the New York scene, starting with the German bars and dancing saloons; these establishments were so orderly that the good doctor verged on approving them:

There is a public bar-room opening directly from the street . . . This is the reception-room of the establishment, and a stranger in the city, who might walk in to get a glass of lager beer, without . . . being aware of the signification of the crimson and white curtains festooned over the windows, would find himself followed to the bar by some German girl, who would ask him in broken English if he would 'treat her' . . . [This] room is very clean; a common sofa, one or two settees, and a number of chairs are ranged around the walls; there is a small table with some German newspapers upon it; a piano . . . and a few prints or engravings complete its furniture. Two or three girls are in different parts of the room engaged in knitting or sewing; for German girls, whether virtuous or prostitute, seem to have a horror of idleness, and even in such a place as this are seldom seen without their work . . . [The visitor] is surprised at the entire absence of all those noisy elements generally considered inseparable from a low-class house of prostitution. He can sit there and smoke his cigar in as much peace as at any hotel in the city; and if he once tells a woman he does not wish to have any conversation with her, he will scarcely be annoyed again, unless he makes the first advances. If he thinks it proper to enter into conversation with the proprietor, he will be certain of a courteous reply, and will frequently find him an intelligent and communicative man. Finally, concluding to resist the temptations around him, he leaves the place in the most perfect security, and without the least fear of being insulted. [45]

Here was Sanger's ideal brothel: a whorehouse where no sex was indulged in. Unfortunately, from his point of view, the average visitor knew only too well what was for sale within these understated little bar-rooms. This type of brothel would house several whores in bedrooms in the back basement; renting a room for about ten dollars a week left a woman with at least ten dollars clear – which was still ten times the national weekly average woman's wage. Sanger loved these German establishments, even the dancing saloons, where a piano and violin 'orchestra' played 'national waltzes and polkas' until midnight. Here, too, 'order [was] well-maintained', in spite of the fact that the whores plied their trade at all times.

But Sanger was decidedly less impressed by the behaviour of the Irish sex workers, whose bar-room brothels tended to cater to sailors. He particularly disapproved of the men's traditional pastimes when on leave, which included brawling and/or drinking themselves into a stupor. The in-house prostitutes also came under fire for their drinking habits and general lack of 'neatness'. Presumably these ladies did not spend their off-duty hours knitting. And as for the Irish dancing saloons: 'many scenes there witnessed,' writes a distraught Sanger, 'will not permit description. The women residing in the house are there, dressed in the most tawdry finery they can command, many of them assuming the bloomer costume. The band consists of a violin, a banjo, and a tambourine . . . The bar is very liberally patronised, and before midnight drunkenness is the rule and sobriety the exception.' [46]

New York also had its share of streetwalkers. Known as 'cruisers', these whores filled Broadway and parallel streets – Crosby, Mercer, Hudson and Canal – after dark. They worked from nearby lodging-houses which hung coloured lamps over their doors and displayed fanciful names – 'Sinbad the Sailor', 'The Black Crook', 'Forget-Me-Not' – and which provided the usual facilities – food, booze and music – as well as sex. Whores also circulated in the city's public gardens, picking up clients in Central Park, City Hall Park and around Madison Square. Others still found work in private parks on the outskirts where 'orgies of the most bacchanalian description'[47] were held.

The streets of New Orleans were similarly thronged with whores. The hellfire-and-damnation preacher Philo Tower, after a tour of the Rampart Street district in 1856, fulminated:

> The extent of licentiousness and prostitution here is truly appalling, and doubtless without a parallel in the whole civilised world . . . Three fifths at least of the dwellings and rooms in a large portion of the city are occupied by prostitutes or by one or the other class of kept mistresses . . . The regular prostitutes . . . are composed of a crowd – nay an army of broken-down females so large they can scarcely be numbered . . . I came pat upon whole streets and squares of these localities occupied by these creatures . . . The character of these houses cannot be mis-judged, as the females who occupy them are constantly making voluptuous exhibition of themselves at the doors and windows and very unceremoniously inviting men as they pass to come in. And in some of the principal streets . . . just at evening, it is no unusual sight to see the windows and doors of almost every house as far as the eye can recognise them, filled with these women.[48]

The Californian Gold Rush of 1849, which drew hordes of men to the Far West from all over the world, made that state a magnet for whores. Fortunes could be made there overnight – by both sexes. One French whore was said to have banked 50,000 dollars after a year in the West. The first brothels were tents, erected right on the edges of the gold fields; these soon gave way to wooden bars, saloons and hotels, whose walls were lined with mirrors and 'licentiously seductive pictures'.[49] The first-floor bedrooms were the preserve of the 'sporting girls'. It was a tough, anarchic world for the women in particular; if they did not look out for themselves, the whores were often the victims of male violence and abuse – including gang rape, as the following account relates:

> If one of 'Bull Run' Allen's pretty waiter girls or performers became unconscious from liquor, as frequently happened, she was carried upstairs and laid on a bed, and sexual privileges were sold to all comers while she lay helpless in a drunken stupor. The price ranged from 25c to $1, depending on the age and beauty of the girl. For an additional quarter a man might watch his predecessor . . . It was not unusual for a girl to be abused by as many as thirty or forty men in the course of a single night.[50]

In spite of these and other dangers, women of all nationalities flocked to California to extract gold from the miners. According to one Canadian observer, the somewhat self-opinionated William Perkins, these whores could be judged by their nationality: the French, he wrote, were 'fascinating in conversation but avaricious, vain and shameless', whereas the Spanish girls were 'warm, generous and unartificial'. Lowest of the low were the English and Australian whores, who were 'vulgar, degraded and brutish as they are in their own countries, and a trip to California has not, of course, improved them.'[51]

In fact the Californian sex trade was a remarkably cosmopolitan scene. Women from Chile set up their own fandango houses, where the famous and very explicit dance must have greatly livened up the customers; and the French madams, with typical panache, set up their 'speciality' *maisons*, where the weird and the wonderful were catered to.

But for one nationality of whores the Californian dream did not represent the pot of gold at the end of a rainbow. For the Chinese women who worked the San Francisco waterfront, life was a hell of imprisonment and sexual slavery. Then as now, families in China had little use for daughters, and the poor often sold them to slave traders between the ages of eight and fifteen. The traders brought them across the ocean to California, where some were sold to parlour houses for white customers; but the majority ended up in China town. Here, they were confined to filthy 'cribs' – narrow rooms containing nothing but a bed or mattress. The girls' contracts, agreed between their families and the traders, were officially for a limited number of years, but in fact they were bound to perpetual slavery by 'conditions' that enabled crib-owners to add penalty weeks for every day of illness or menstruation. Chinese entrepreneurs reaped handsome rewards from this trade, since in San Francisco in 1850 there was one Chinese woman to every 1700 Chinese men – and the Chinese would only have sex with their own kind; they regarded other races as 'ghosts'.

Towards the end of the 19th century, when white middle-class reformers and feminists turned their attention to the sex trade and condemned all forms of voluntary prostitution as 'white slavery', the tragedy of these Chinese girl-children – the only real slaves in the sex industry – was completely overlooked.

It would be wrong to leave this survey of 19th-century prostitution without mentioning the *crème-de-la-crème* of the profession: its courtesans. Thanks to the continued expansion of both the bourgeoisie and its finances, the market for high-class whores had never been better, with the result that the Victorian era became another classical age of the courtesan. These ladies referred to themselves as 'great horizontals'; and they were certainly that. In London, where a 'kept woman' could command £25 for a night's casual trade (over and above what she earned from her regular patron), these courtesans could be seen parading through Hyde Park in their horse-drawn carriages. Immaculately dressed in 'ravishing riding habits and intoxicatingly beautiful hats',[52] some of them attracted hordes of fans, like latter-day movie stars. Many of these wealthy whores were of humble origins: Laura Bell, a 'star' of the 1850s, for instance. Originally from Antrim in Ireland, Laura worked as a shopgirl in Dublin; moving to London around the time of the Great Exhibition, she took the town by storm. This Irish prostitute should go down in history for charging – and getting – *one quarter of a million pounds* from a client for a single night's sex work. The client was Jungh Badahur, super-rich prime minister of the Maharajah of Nepal; and he paid up without a qualm.

'Skittles' was another celebrated whore of the period. Born plain Catherine Walters in Liverpool, daughter of an Irish sailor, in 1856, at the age of seventeen, she went to London and set to work in the Haymarket night-houses. Her big break came some five years later, when the Marquis of Hartington fell madly in love with her and installed her in a house in Mayfair with servants, horses, carriages – and an annuity of £2000. Skittles soon became the darling of the

London élite: 'Sir Edwin Landseer painted her portrait and hung it in the Royal Academy; Alfred Austin, Poet-Laureate-to-be, and Wilfred Blunt wrote poems to her . . . even Gladstone himself took tea with her'.[53] The Prince of Wales was perhaps her prize conquest.

Skittles was in many ways the Nell Gwyn of her age, a living contradiction of the class system. Her language was that of the working-class streets and night-houses of her upbringing – it shocked and enthralled her upper-class clients. At the same time, she was intelligent, witty, and well-read; interested in art, music – even religion. This combination of vulgarity and intellect proved irresistible to her Victorian patrons, locked as they were into a rigid pattern of social behaviour. Skittles was doubtless aware of this, and made of her character a prime asset.

The United States also had its share of *grandes cocottes*, most notable and flamboyant of whom was Lola Montez. Another Irish girl, Lola was born in Limerick in 1818, child of an army officer and a part-Spanish mother; after eloping with an army captain at the age of nineteen, she entered the theatre, billing herself as 'Lola Montez, Spanish dancer'. She had little success in London, but her fortunes improved considerably when she moved to the Continent and became a prostitute. After being the mistress of Franz Liszt and Alexandre Dumas *père*, she became the lover of King Louis I of Bavaria, who created her Countess Landsfelt and gave her an income then equivalent to $10,000 a year. Lola was so influential in the state that the king's cabinet was dubbed the 'Lolaministerium'. In 1848, a revolution forced Louis to abdicate, and Lola was deported by the new government. She turned up next in the USA, where she lectured and toured the dance-halls, taking up her old profession. Eventually she married the wealthy proprietor of a San Francisco newspaper, but did not stay with him long. In declining health, she went to New York, where she did rescue work among the poor prostitutes, and died there in 1861.

But it was France that, in the 19th century, boasted the most extravagant courtesans of all. Paradoxically, one of the most famous *grandes horizontales* working in France was an Englishwoman, the legendary Cora Pearl, born Emma Crouch near Plymouth in 1836, to a musician father and songstress mother. According to her memoirs, Cora was seduced by a gentleman at the age of fourteen, after which she became a prostitute, and mistress to another gentleman, William Buckle. When the latter took her to Paris for a holiday, Cora liked the city so much she decided to stay on permanently. Although not startlingly beautiful (some male historians have described her as 'pug-faced', which she most certainly was *not*), Cora had a great deal of vivacity and personality and within no time she had reached the heights of her profession, becoming the mistress of Prince Jérome Bonaparte, cousin of the Emperor Napoleon III. Cora Pearl's personal style was *outré*; one of her favourite little pastimes was to invite her most 'respectable' clients for supper, disappear just before the dessert was served up, then reappear a few moments later, carried in on a silver platter, reclining naked on a bed of Parma violets: 'She had such a wonderful figure,' recalls one of the witnesses of this spectacle, 'that all the guests gasped with admiration.'[54] And, like Skittles, Cora was adored for her *un*ladylike demeanour; as one (unnamed) royal personage observed: 'She is so gloriously vulgar!'[55]

At the pinnacle of her career the Prince gave her a mansion worth £80,000 in the rue de Chaillot. Little Emma Crouch had come a long way, although she did not quite make it to the nobility, unlike her compatriot Elizabeth Howard, who became mistress of Napoleon III himself, and was rewarded with a château, £1,000,000, and the title Countess of Beauregard.

But the woman whose fame eclipsed that of all the other 19th-century courtesans put together was Alphonsine Plessis, who became known to Parisian society as *la Divine Marie Duplessis*, and to posterity as Marguerite Gautier, *La Dame aux camélias*. Her mother, the daughter of a servant and the last remnant of an impoverished noble line, died when Alphonsine was a child of six; she was subsequently brought up by her father, who sold her at the age of fourteen to a band of gypsies. The travellers brought her to Paris, where she became a prostitute, swiftly accumulating a series of distinguished lovers and moving inexorably up the social scale. In 1840 she first caught the public imagination through her affair with Agénor de Guiche, later a minister in Napoleon III's government. This launched her into Parisian high society, and at sixteen, Alphonsine was one of the most fashionable and sought-after *demi-mondaines* of her day. She renamed herself Marie Duplessis and, using the money and security (in the form of an expensive house) she had earned, began to educate herself, learning to read and write, play the piano, and dance.

After de Guiche, Marie took up with the Comte Edouard de Perregaux, a rich army officer who fell deeply in love with her, but whose fortune could not sustain her expensive tastes. Marie's next conquest was the wealthy Comte de Stackelberg, an octogenarian diplomat, who set her up in a house in the boulevard de la Madeleine. Here, Marie entertained (apart from Stackelberg himself) the rich and idle young 'lions' of the Jockey Club and well-known writers – Alfred de Musset, Eugène Sue . . . and Alexandre Dumas *fils*. The last-named was not wealthy – son of the successful author of *The Three Musketeers*, he had yet to make his way in the world, and was still financially dependent on his father when he met Marie. She was to set him on the road to success, however, in a way which he could not have foreseen when the two fell briefly but passionately in love in the autumn of 1844. Alexandre's jealousy put an end to their *affaire* the following summer, after Marie had refused to give up her profession (and with it her independence) for him, and turned back to Stackelberg, Perregaux, and the rest of her illustrious clientele.

Shortly after her break with Dumas, Marie met and fell in love with one of the greatest musicians of the 19th century, Franz Liszt. He too was smitten by *la Divine Marie*: 'She was the most absolute incarnation of Woman who had ever existed,'[56] he later wrote, in typical Romantic style.

For a few months Marie and Liszt were happy together, but she would never allow love to get in the way of her career interests: in February 1846 she contracted a marriage of convenience with Perregaux, at the Kensington Register Office in London. Although the union was not recognized in France (which left her free), it did permit her to style herself 'la comtesse du Plessis'.

Liszt left Paris in the spring of 1846, promising to return; meanwhile Marie was increasingly ill with consumption. She travelled round Europe seeking a cure, but returned to Paris in September, her condition considerably worsened. Liszt did not keep his promise, and slowly, abandoned by all her former lovers and friends except her faithful maid Clothilde – and her creditors – the young woman's health declined. *La Divine Marie*, comtesse du Plessis, died on 3 February 1847, at the age of only twenty-three, with a full and glorious career already behind her.

After her death she was eulogized by the society which had abandoned her. One newspaper wrote that she had been 'the most elegant of women, having the most aristocratic taste and the most exquisite tact: she set the tone for a whole area of society.' The critic Jules Janin remembered Marie's 'young and supple waist . . . the beautiful oval of her face . . .' and 'the grace which she radiated like an indescribable fragrance'. Her ex-lover Dumas recalled her 'long, lustrous, Japanese eyes, very quick and alert, lips as red as cherries and the most beautiful teeth in the world'.[57] In short, they all loved her to death, although not one of these gentlemen saw fit to attend to her when she was desperately ill.

Only a year later, Dumas published his novel *La Dame aux camélias*, loosely based on Marie's life and death; and in 1852 he adapted it for the stage, creating an instant classic. Great actresses from that day since have clamoured to cough their way to the Romantic climax, where Marguerite expires in the arms of her faithful Armand – not to mention great singers, in Verdi's operatic version of 1853, *La Traviata*.

In fact Marie, like many women of her class, died young from a disease of poverty contracted in early childhood; but Dumas' drama exploited the myth of the whore who died early from a life of debauchery. Audiences the world over recognized and applauded this stereotype and, in doing so, made the author a very rich man indeed. But it is the story Dumas left out which is the more telling: the reality of a poor and illiterate orphan who built a brilliant career for herself at the pinnacle of French society, and at the same time gave herself the education denied her by her origins. The real 'dame aux camélias' made of herself and her own life a far greater work of art than anything Alexandre Dumas *fils* could have dreamed up.

CHAPTER TWELVE

Madonnas and Magdalens: the Whore-Stigma in the 19th Century

In the female character, there is no midregion; it must exist in spotless innocence or else in hopeless vice.

Nathaniel W. Chittenden, 1837[1]

The 19th century was the hour of bourgeois triumph in all spheres of activity – economic, political, ideological. After centuries of struggle, the bourgeoisie was now in a position to spread its ideas and customs to the rest of society, and this was to have serious consequences for women.

The role of the female was crucial within the bourgeois family; her faithfulness to her personal lord and master guaranteed patriarchal property succession, and at the same time supposedly anchored the family, thereby enabling it to weather the storms of economic development. To maintain this order, the wife's freedom – particularly her sexual freedom – had to be curbed at all costs. To achieve this end, educated men turned to science and set out to develop a form of psychic castration which they hoped would stifle women's desires for ever. Their strategy was simple enough; it consisted of denying the existence of female sexuality altogether. The Victorian sexologist Dr William Acton summed it up, asserting, with all the bland complacency of the male 'expert' that: 'The majority of women are not very much troubled with sexual feelings of any kind.'[2]

Propagated through the ever-expanding 19th-century media, this lie became a fundamental 'truth' which was used to brainwash middle-class women into unconsciousness and ignorance of their own

bodies and desires. Thus Victorian man created the new Madonna –
the pure, sexless creature of his own fantasy.

With female sexuality banished from existence, the middle-class
male could concentrate on his own, which was of course alive and
kicking: 'It is impossible to exaggerate the force of sexual desire',
boasted Acton, now secure in his assumption that *all* sexual desire was
by definition male. But if the sexual needs of Victorian man were so
overwhelming, they threatened the purity of their guardian-angels in
the home. Therefore another class of women was required in order to
channel away man's unfettered sexual demands from the family: the
whore moved centre-stage once again. According to Acton's French
predecessor, Parent-Duchâtelet: 'Prostitutes are as inevitable in a great
conurbation as sewers, cesspits and refuse dumps. The conduct of the
authorities should be the same with regard to each.'[3]

Once again identified with everything 'filthy' and 'degraded' (the
Christian image of sexuality itself), the whore was seen as both
necessary and disgusting; an ambiguous mixture of sacred defender of
the family and obscene cesspit. Another male writer, William Lecky,
argues:

> That unhappy being whose very name is a shame to speak . . .
> appears in every age as the perpetual symbol of the degradation
> and sinfulness of man. Herself the supreme type of vice, she is
> ultimately the most efficient guardian of virtue. But for her the
> unchallenged purity of countless homes would be polluted . . .
> On that one degraded and ignoble form are concentrated the
> passions which might have filled the world with shame. She
> remains, while creeds and civilisations rise and fall, the eternal
> priestess of humanity, blasted for the sins of the people.[4]

(Note that Lecky writes 'people' when referring to *men.*)

In this tortured passage the whore becomes martyr to a religion of
'shame' – shadow side of the Victorian religion of virtue – just as the
world of the sex trade shadowed that of the family. Sex trade and
family thus became the two pillars of Victorian morality – separate
worlds linked, as always, by the great male double standard. The
duality for Victorian men was firmly established, opposing the all-
pure Madonna to the whore-saint Magdalen. What supported this
division of women was the other great divide in 19th-century society:
class. During its climb to power, the middle class had evolved a deep-

rooted fear and loathing of those upon whose labour they depended –
the working classes. Blind to anything other than bourgeois values,
the middle classes saw only chaos when they looked at lower-class
culture. The absence there of uniform middle-class morality and of
submission to the political hierarchy were particularly horrifying and,
fearing the subversion of their social order from below, the
bourgeoisie fantasized workers as 'the dangerous classes': menacing,
lawless and amoral mobs of *Untermenschen*; the males among them
criminals, the females, whores. This conveniently made working-
class women *by their very nature* immoral; it followed that, as whores,
they could and should take the burden of sexual guilt off the shoulders
of the middle-class men whose demand kept many of them in
business. In other words: if she was a whore, she only had herself to
blame.

Nineteenth-century writing on the subject of prostitution is prolific
indeed; it seems that those gentlemen who were not busy fucking
whores were busier still writing about them. Working through the
acreage of nonsense, much of it unintentionally hilarious, we find the
central theme of the Madonna/Magdalen division cropping up again
and again, leaving a weary trail of unanswerable contradictions in its
wake. For the Victorians could never quite resolve the issue of female
sexuality: if it did not exist in the first place (as they so categorically
stated) how was it that *some* women – whores – *were* sexual creatures?
  The response to this dilemma necessarily involved a form of
doublethink (something the Victorians excelled at) which would
permit some of the facts to filter through, albeit cloaked in a moralistic
haze. This is best seen in action in the explanations of the causes of
prostitution advanced by the new, self-appointed sexperts. For
instance, Parent-Duchâtelet was careful to document the economic
circumstances which drove women into the sex industry – unemployment, low female wages, general poverty and so on. But Parent also
had his moral axe to grind; therefore, according to his study, the
woman who moved into prostitution started out with the sex trade in
her blood: she was a 'certain kind of girl', whose natural inclinations
towards 'idleness and licentiousness' led her into a 'life of disorder'.
This quickly developed in turn into a 'period of debauchery', which
was followed by the girl's entry into fully-fledged prostitution. But
Parent went further; he alleged that it was not simply the girl's natural
disposition that led her off the straight and narrow, but also her family

background. For here she had witnessed the 'disorderly relationships' that predisposed her to a life of prostitution.[5]

So while Parent openly acknowledged the economic conditions that forced many women into prostitution, he did not condemn poverty; he shifted the blame for prostitution on to the prostitutes themselves (and their families) – a classic ploy. And it served the Victorians well; for the first part of Parent's argument pandered to the fallacy of women as passive and asexual creatures who could only be driven into the sex trade through real, economic causes, while the second part of his theory – which carried the most weight – stressed the inherent viciousness of the whore's character and background; and this was taken up eagerly by other 'experts'.

Needless to say, the role of the male customer was not pondered by the likes of Parent; but his study did spawn a legion of enthusiastic disciples who focused exclusively on the prostitute. In 1857 William Acton wrote a study of prostitution which wove the two strands of Parent's argument into a similar tangle. Acton's list of the factors which lead to prostitution stressed personal characteristics such as 'natural desire; natural sinfulness; the preferment of indolent ease to labour; vicious inclinations', before any economic factors. However . . . since 'natural desire' – the first of Acton's 'reasons' – played no part in a woman's life, it could surely be ruled out? In that case, Acton pontificated, many women had obviously fallen into the hands of 'professional seducers', who had manipulated their sexless victims into submission.

In fact, since women were innocent of sexuality, the original list had to be turned on its head, so that the economic reasons came out – reluctantly – on top: 'Many, no doubt, fall through vanity and idleness, love of dress, love of excitement, love of drink, but by far the larger proportion are driven to evil courses by cruel biting poverty.'[6]

To complete the confusion, Acton concluded by attributing prostitution to heredity. This mish-mash of contradictions, directly inherited from Parent-Duchâtelet, was typical of the predigested ideas churned out with strikingly little variation by male sexologists as the century wore on. These ideas in turn fed the imaginations of male novelists of the era, providing them with ammunition for the depiction of the whore as miserable, downtrodden victim. Anthony Trollope lovingly conjured up the spectacle of:

The gaudy dirt, the squalid plenty . . . the flaunting glare of

fictitious revelry, the weary pavement, the horrid slavery to some
horrid tyrant – and then the quick depreciation of that one ware of
beauty, the substituted paint, garments bright without but foul
within like painted sepulchres . . . life without a hope . . . utterly
friendless, disease, starvation, and a quivering fear of that coming
hell which can still hardly be worse than all that is suffered here![7]

The Victorians certainly loved their horror stories. But if this
fictional stereotype of the whore was bad enough, the so-called 'real-
life' version was worse still. For the men of science had begun to turn
their gaze on to the prostitute herself; now her character was to come
under scrutiny. The portrait they came up with was not flattering. It
first of all hinged on the notion that the whore represented the
antithesis of bourgeois values. For it was her laziness and love of
pleasure – the opposite of the work ethic – which led her to refuse all
labour and take up prostitution instead (here, the assumption is that
sex work is not 'real' work). The whore also epitomized 'immaturity'
and 'instability'; she was by turns sullen and wildly frivolous, haughty
and vulgarly familiar; she changed constantly, impulsively – opinions,
outfits, moods, homes, even social classes; she talked constantly
without knowing what she was saying; she lied; she consumed alcohol
and food to excess; she regularly fell into fits of rage; she spent money
like water; she was a lesbian; she had 'the psychology of the child, the
inattention of the young savage, the mobility and emptiness of a
prehistoric brain still bathed in animality'.[8]

In short – a real paragon! The whore was occasionally granted more
endearing qualities, although these were invariably spontaneous
enough to emphasize her childish nature: she was instinctively
religious, thoughtlessly generous, and loved flowers, animals,
children and her pimp. But at all times she was incapable of making
intelligent choices, for the whore had no intelligence – she was only flesh,
wild impulses, animal passions and instincts. Some writers were even
more explicit in their hatred and condemnation, describing whores as
'animated filth' and 'heaps of excrement encased in human skin'.[9] Again,
what was thought of the whore's male customer goes unrecorded.

Inevitably, these stereotypes and prejudices began to find their way
into the fiction of the day. In Zola's novel *Nana* (1880) the heroine, a
top courtesan of working-class origins, encompasses all these paranoid fantasies in one mythical figure. Judging by the notes Zola wrote
before launching into this classic work, he had some strange – though

typical – notions about female sexuality in general, and whores in particular:

> (Nana) ends up regarding man as a material to exploit, becoming a force of Nature, a ferment of destruction, but without meaning to, simply by means of her sex and her strong female odour, destroying everything she approaches, and turning society sour just as women having a period turn milk sour [sic]. The cunt in all its power; the cunt on an altar, with all the men offering up sacrifices to it. The book has to be the poem of the cunt, and the moral will lie in the cunt turning everything sour . . . Nana eats up gold, swallows up every sort of wealth; the most extravagant tastes, the most frightful waste. She instinctively makes a rush for pleasures and possessions. Everything she devours; she eats up what people [sic] are earning around her in industry, on the stock exchange, in high positions, in everything that pays. And she leaves nothing but ashes. *In short, a real whore* . . . she is nothing but flesh [my italics].

The reader could be forgiven for assuming that Nana is some kind of monster – parts of this could just as accurately describe, say, a nuclear weapon: . . . *she leaves nothing but ashes*. Zola, who considered himself something of a scientist, regards Nana as a 'force of Nature' – because she is female. She is destructive to men because of her sex; she eats up men's gold (men are entitled to wealth; women are not). Nana thus becomes the parasite the rich bourgeois male secretly knows himself to be. And, true to Parent-Duchâtelet's picture, Nana is denied any intelligence; elsewhere in his notes Zola writes: 'Don't make her witty, which would be a mistake; she is nothing but flesh.' In fact Nana's fate is sealed at the beginning: 'She has to die at the height of her youth, at the height of her triumph.'[10]

And she does – Zola makes sure of it; Nana's deathbed scene at the end of the book is suitably horrific: 'What lay on the pillow was a charnel-house, a heap of pus and blood, a shovelful of putrid flesh' . . . certainly not a human being. 'It was as if the poison she had picked up in the gutters, from the carcases left there by the roadside, that ferment with which she had poisoned a whole people [sic], had now risen to her face and rotted it.'[11]

This was, according to Zola's 'masterpiece', the reality of the 19th-century whore: a poisoned, diseased but helpless slut who destroyed (male) society. Such views had by now gained wide currency among men of the educated classes: according to George Holden, translator of the Penguin edition of *Nana*, both Zola and Dumas *fils* blamed the collapse of the Second Empire (1870) on prostitution; and it was precisely during this period that the notion of the prostitute as public enemy number one began to filter into the public consciousness as a whole. It has lingered there ever since.

To support the delusions of prostitute-mythology, 19th-century scientists of all kinds began to study prostitutes with increasing fervour. Whores were scrutinized and categorized to ridiculous degrees: according to where they worked, or how 'seductive' (on a scale from one to five) the doctors deemed them – even according to the hoarseness of their voices. On a yet more objectifying – and preposterous – level, Parent-Duchâtelet and his merry followers examined the vaginas of thousands of prostitutes, but sadly failed to find any evidence that corroborated the 'scientific' hypothesis that they were abnormal, with giant lips and clitorises. Not to worry! There was always something – anything – *everything*! – else for the men of science to focus on. In 1848 the German authority on prostitution, H. Lippert, made the following extraordinary statement:

> By the daily practice of their profession for many years [prostitutes'] eyes acquire a piercing, rolling expression; they are somewhat unduly prominent in consequence of the continued tension of the ocular muscles, since the eyes are principally employed to spy out and attract clients. In many the organs of mastication are strongly developed; the mouth, in continuous activity either in eating or in kissing, is conspicuous; the forehead is often flat; the occipital region is at times extremely prominent; the hair of the head is often scanty – in fact, a good many become actually bald. For this, reasons are not lacking: above all, the restless mode of life; the continued running about in all weathers in the open street, sometimes with the head bare . . . the incessant brushing, manipulation, frizzling and pomading of the hair; and, among the lower classes of prostitute, the use of brandy. The rough voice is the physiological characteristic of the woman who has lost her proper functions – those of the mother.[12]

Lippert's response when confronted by those balding, pop-eyed, apelike beings who happened to be mothers as well as working prostitutes is, sadly, unrecorded, but he doubtless had some 'scientific' explanation for this apparent anomaly. In the meantime, however, his views were not received with the derision they merited; on the contrary. By the latter part of the century, this type of imbecilic 'study' had been taken up and added to by an enthusiastic shoal of scientists, headed by Cesare Lombroso in Italy and Pauline Tarnowsky in Russia. Suddenly, it was discovered that the prostitute was a relic of an earlier stage of human evolution: mentally undeveloped, physically deformed, and subhuman. According to Lombroso, *all* prostitutes exhibited the physical characteristics of this retarded development, which included a receding or narrow forehead, abnormal nasal bones, and enormous jaws: while in the much-probed genital region, 2 per cent of whores showed 'exaggerated' growth of the pubic hair, 16 per cent 'hypertrophy' of the vaginal lips, and 13 per cent had 'enormous' clitorises. Tarnowsky – not to be outdone – asserted that whores' craniums were smaller than everybody else's; this of course explained their habitual stupidity, since they must therefore possess smaller brains.[13]

These 'findings' were trotted out again and again to lend support to the growing whore-stigma, which could from then on be based on a firmly 'scientific' foundation of sexism, racism and classism. Indeed, Lombroso's work in particular formed part of a broader study of the 'dangerous classes', which relegated them to the subhuman level of 'primitive' peoples – those who were much lower down the evolutionary tree than the Western bourgeoisie: 'The primitive woman,' he wrote, 'was always a prostitute.'

And by characterizing these subhuman females as 'virile' – biological freaks with masculine sexuality – he could at last solve the Victorian riddle of how a supposedly asexual female could be sexually active:

We have only to remember that virility was one of the special features of the savage woman . . . we have portraits of Red Indian and Negro beauties, whom it is difficult to recognise for women, so huge are their jaws and cheekbones, so hard and coarse their features.[14]

Inevitably, the notion of whores as subhuman beings served to justify experimentation on them by social scientists who 'discovered' that prostitute women were less sensitive to pain than real human beings. For these studies, whores were tortured – electrodes were attached to their hands, tongues, noses, foreheads, thighs, stomachs, breasts, and genitals, and gradated electric shocks were applied to them.

In the psychological realm, Lombroso and his ilk helped popularize the idea that whores were 'feeble-minded', a theory that was eagerly taken up by other social scientists engaged in labelling whores a deviant group. The 'cardinal symptoms' of this 'feeble-mindedness' were spelled out as: 'the general moral insensibility, the boldness, egotism and vanity, the love of notoriety, the lack of shame or remorse . . . the desire for immediate pleasure without regard for consequences, the lack of forethought or anxiety about the future . . .'[15]

In fact the whore, according to these attributes, was about as far from the Victorian ideal of the fragile, egoless, passive female as it was possible to get.

Like the act of prostitution itself, the whore's feeble-mindedness was deemed hereditary: the director of one New York women's reformatory echoed Parent-Duchâtelet by tracing the origin of the whore's condition to 'some actively vicious element or clearly degenerate strain' in her family. She cited, for instance, one prostitute who had apparently inherited her mental incapacity from a tubercular mother and an 'immoral' father who had himself come from 'a degenerate family of worthless alcoholics'. The sage conclusion, then, was that 'the well-known immoral tendencies . . . of the feeble-minded cause them to drift naturally into prostitution. The feeble-minded need only opportunity to express their immoral tendencies.'[16]

In this ideological hall of mirrors each term of abuse was used to define the other: 'feeble-mindedness', 'degeneracy', 'immorality' – 'prostitution'. The net result was to set up a vicious circle of definitions which trapped the whore in an outcast status that was as inevitable – yet nebulous – as fate. From now on she would be Other: for ever set apart from the superior tribe of moral beings who sat in judgement on her.

However, amid the myths and stereotypes of the Victorian social scientists can be found, for the first time, substantial documentation of the real lives of prostitutes. Although the truth is not always easy to decipher, obscured as it is by the prejudices and distortions of the investigators, it is possible to reconstruct a picture of the prostitute's experience.

Firstly, who were whores, and where did they come from? In this respect the 19th century was no different from any other period of history: the overwhelming majority of whores were working-class women – one late-century survey estimates the figure at 90 per cent. Although a minority were the starving, orphan children of the slums, surviving in vagabond bands through various means – begging, stealing, whoring – most young prostitutes came from working families. These families, however, were far from being the havens from the harsh reality of the outside world dreamed of by the bourgeoisie; the economy of the working-class family was extremely precarious – every able-bodied member had to contribute towards its survival. As soon as she was old enough to work, a girl had to earn her keep, and if this entailed becoming a prostitute, so be it: the family would be only too glad of the income. Alternatively, a girl could use the relatively high wages of the sex trade to leave the family and live independently, if she wished.

Many whores came from broken homes, where the early loss of one or both parents deprived them of the support of the family's collective wage-pool. Finally, working girls also used prostitution, then as now, to escape from families in which they faced sexual abuse, violence, parental alcoholism, or other kinds of oppression and distress. One study of juvenile whores found that 'many of the girls had been on the street since they were children, taking care of themselves as best they could, while avoiding the violent tantrums and abuse of drunken parents.'[17]

Significant percentages of prostitutes told of sexual abuse from males in their own families; many also expressed contempt for their parents, and may have been in open revolt against adults' attempts to control or discipline them. Many young women had left home to find 'decent' jobs only to realize that they literally could not survive on the appalling wages on offer. In the 1850s, for instance, when a quarter of working women in the USA were taking home one dollar a week or less, even William Sanger was forced to comment that: 'No economist, however closely he may calculate, will pretend that fourteen cents a day will supply any woman with lodging, food and clothes.'

Indeed the poverty of working-class women at this time is scarcely credible. The pioneering investigative reporter Henry Mayhew,

plumbing the depths of 'darkest London' in 1849 to describe the lives
of poor seamstresses, wrote: 'I had seen much want, but I had no idea
of the intensity of the privations suffered by the needlewomen.' One
seamstress he interviewed sewed shirt-fronts from five in the morning
until midnight and still could not earn enough to keep herself and her
child; she 'dollymopped' – whored – on the side. Another woman
who worked in the 'slop trade' (sewing for cheap tailors) earned
precisely three shillings a week, which was insufficient, after she had
bought her candles, to provide her with food. She told Mayhew of the
other young single women in the slop trade: 'The prices are not
sufficient to keep them, and the consequence is, they fly to the streets
to make their living.'

Mayhew's collaborator Bracebridge Hemyng listed the trades
which 'supplied women to swell the ranks of prostitutes'; they
included servants, slop-workers, milliners, dressmakers, hat-makers,
furriers, silk-winders, embroiderers, shoe-binders, laundresses,
'ballet girls' and shop workers.[18] The story was the same throughout
Western Europe and the USA; in nearly every sector of women's
work, the low value of their labour pushed them inexorably towards
dependence on a man, or prostitution.

But it was not only as a negative choice or as a bolster to inadequate
wages that women turned to prostitution in such huge numbers
during the 19th century. They often did so as a revolt against the
conditions in which they were expected to work. Factories at the
height of the Industrial Revolution are notorious for their twelve- or
fourteen-hour days and squalid working conditions; but even in the
latter part of the century the working day could be as long as ten
hours, while noise, overcrowding, air pollution and lack of ventila-
tion combined to make factory life intolerable for many young
women. The historian Ruth Rosen quotes one young factory hand:
'We only went from bed to work and from work to bed again . . . and
sometimes if we sat up a little while at home we were so tired we could
not speak . . . And still, though there was nothing for us but bed and
machines, we could not earn enough to take care of ourselves through
the slack season.'

Working-class women were also degraded and dehumanized in
domestic service. One whore who had been a servant and a waitress
put it succinctly: 'I'll live fast and die early rather than become
somebody's kitchen slave. Restaurant work is bad enough, but I
won't be a dog in anybody's kitchen.' Another whore used precisely

the same metaphor when she told investigators: 'The ladies when they got money to hire servants imagine they have some form of dog to kick around, and I don't want to be kicked around.'[19]

A prostitute known as 'Swindling Sal' defiantly told Bracebridge Hemyng of her decision to work in the sex trade:

I was a servant gal away down in Birmingham. I got tired of workin' and slavin' to make a living, and getting a —— bad one at that; what o' five pun' a year and yer grub, I'd sooner starve, I would. After a bit I went to Coventry . . . and took up with soldiers as was quartered there. I soon got tired of them. Soldiers is good . . . to walk with and that, but they don't pay; cos why they ain't got no money; so I says to myself, I'll go to Lunnon and I did. I soon found my level there.[20]

Whores were generally unequivocal about their reasons for turning to 'vice'. Even the brothel-workers preferred the tightly-restricted working conditions of a house to the straight scene; for as one brothel-worker testified: 'If I am in a house, I can get my rest, and I am not out late at night . . . I can rest, and I don't have to get up early in the morning. I am provided with good board and with a good room, and I am able to look after my health.'[21]

All the women interviewed by investigators affirmed that prostitution was infinitely preferable to 'respectable' (a misnomer if ever there was one) women's work; indeed the disparity between the two sectors was so great in terms of pay and conditions that, for many working-class women, 'Why don't you do it?' would have been a more appropriate question than the continual 'Why do you do it?' heard from investigators.

Prostitution could also represent a more deliberate revolt against the social oppression of the *status quo*. Denied upward mobility by their class and gender, many women used the sex trade to launch themselves out of dead-end jobs and hopeless situations. A prostitute survey in New York showed that it was often the *highest*-paid workers – 'theatrical workers, office workers, telephone operators, typists, and stenographers'[22] who went on the game. These were ambitious and relatively well-qualified women who saw prostitution as a means of augmenting their meagre pay. In early 20th-century Chicago, whores told Vice Commission interviewers that they wanted money not because of 'abject poverty', but because they liked buying new

fashionable clothes, perfumes, and other luxuries. They refused to
dress in the dowdy rags they were expected, as working-class women,
to wear; instead, the whores told their interviewers, they wanted to
look 'like ladies'.

Middle-class observers pounced on this attitude, condemning the
prostitutes' 'love of dress', 'excessive pride', and so on. Clearly, these
low-class creatures did not know their place. In fact, for many whores
dressing 'up' was a way of attracting a husband from a higher social
class. As one woman put it: 'Men don't hunt in laundries for wives.'[23]

When a working girl or woman did decide to join the sex trade, her
own culture put few obstacles in her way. The living conditions of the
19th-century working classes, with entire families sleeping together in
the same room, often in the same bed, left little to the imagination
when it came to sexuality. Working-class girls were familiar from an
early age both with sex itself and with the selling of it, since all
working-class areas had their whores – often the girls' own mothers.
The concept of 'virtue' was an alien one, as this letter to *The Times*,
written by an anonymous prostitute in 1858, demonstrates:

> I was a fine robust healthy girl of thirteen years of age. I had
> larked with boys of my own age . . . I had seen much and heard
> abundantly of the mysteries of sex . . . For some time I had
> coquetted on the verge of a strong curiosity and a natural desire,
> and without a particle of affection I lost – what? – not my virtue,
> for I never had any . . . I repeat that *I never lost what I never had –*
> my virtue.[24]

Unhampered by the middle-class rigmarole of moralism, or any
other controls on their sexuality, British working girls gave up their
virginity in their mid-teens, usually to boys of their own age and class.
The pattern was similar in the USA, where, at the turn of the 20th
century, young single working women shared a leisure culture from
which middle-class notions of sexual morality were entirely absent.
For many, the arduousness of legitimate work created powerful
incentives for recreation; and sexuality formed both a means of
enjoying their spare time and paying for it. In New York, young
workers mixed at movie houses, cheap theatres, amusement parks,
bars and dance halls, with an ease and familiarity that shocked the
middle classes: 'Most of the younger couples were hugging and
kissing,' complained one prude, who observed the workers at play in a

dance-hall bar-room. 'There was a general mingling of men and women at the different tables . . . they were all singing and carrying on, they kept running around the room and acted like a mob of lunatics.'[25]

The popular dances of the time were unashamedly sexy: *pivoting* was a 'wild, spinning dance that promoted a charged atmosphere of physical excitement'; and *tough dances* 'ranged from a slow shimmy, or shaking of the hips and shoulders, to boisterous animal imitations', particularly distinguished by 'the motion of the pelvic portions of the body'. The young women wore flamboyant clothes in the style of whores: 'If you want to get any notion took of you, you gotta have some style about you,' being the motto here. Male partners would 'treat' their companions, paying for the enjoyments a woman's wage could not stretch to, in return for sexual favours which ranged from mild flirtation to full sex. For factory and sweatshop girls, it was a system that worked well, as an antidote to their harsh working lives; there was thus no coyness on their part about this casual sexual barter which was so close to prostitution that middle-class observers inevitably categorized it as such.[26]

This aspect of working-class culture was the same throughout the industrializing world: in bars, pubs, cafés, saloons, music-halls and dance halls of the teeming new cities, working-class girls who had grown up on intimate terms with their families' and friends' sexual lives and embarked upon their own at a fairly early age, went on to trade their sexual favours in return for 'treats' – or in fully-fledged prostitution. They were free from the reflexes of shame and guilt that the middle classes were busily inculcating into their own young women; the moral inhibitions which might have prevented working-class girls from trading in sex were simply absent, for the most part, from their culture.

The overall picture of prostitution which begins to emerge, then, is very different from that put forward by the doctors, scientists and writers of the period. The average whore in the 19th century was a working-class woman who, after sexual initiation around puberty, and casual relationships with partners of her own age and class, chose the sex trade in her late teens because it offered better pay, easier conditions, and greater autonomy than other forms of female work. When seen in its proper context, it becomes obvious that prostitution for many women was a conscious and positive decision in the face of grinding poverty and lack of opportunity. Far from being 'feeble-

minded' victims of degradation, the majority of whores used their
wits to enter a trade through which they could at least hope to better
themselves, dragging themselves out of living conditions which their
middle-class judges would never have to experience. In this they were
helped by their own sexual culture – much to the disgust of those who
castigated them so.

The careers of most women who entered prostitution were quite
short-lived: after having started at some point during the late teens,
whores usually worked through to their early- to mid-twenties; after
which point they tended to merge back into communities from which
they had never really been distinct. Both Parent-Duchâtelet and
William Acton noted this reintegration of ex-whores into their
communities; and – to give him his due – Acton in particular was at
pains to deny the myth that prostitutes died early from 'debauchery'
or disease. In fact, according to his own studies, prostitutes' relative
affluence meant that they consistently enjoyed better health than other
working women, and were no more likely to fall victim to alcoholism, insanity, suicide or 'complaints incidental to an irregular
course of life'.[27]

Against the trade's major health hazard – venereal disease – whores
were especially vigilant and responsible. In French brothels the
madam or her *sous-maîtresse* examined the client before he got as far as
the bedroom; elsewhere whores themselves performed the inspection.
Customers often resented this: 'She approached,' wrote one peevish
client of a New Orleans brothel, 'and seized my genital organ in such a
way as to determine whether or not I had the gonorrhea. She did this
particular operation with more knowledge and skill than she did
anything else before or after.'[28] The result of whores' 'knowledge and
skill' in this area was a relatively low rate of sexually transmitted
diseases: not that this helped dispel the public's paranoia about
'diseased sluts'.

The other aspect of the sex trade that particularly excited and
outraged the middle classes was, as ever, its economics. In general a
whore could earn in a day, often in a single 'trick', as much as other
working-class women made in a week. The veteran London punter
'Walter', writing in the mid-century, recorded the prices he paid
prostitutes for their services, ranging from a sovereign, which 'would
buy any woman on the streets', through to five or ten shillings for
'quite nice' girls. Even the lowest-paid whore could net a slop-
worker's weekly wage in one transaction. Her overheads were not

necessarily very large: clothes would be the major outlay, with 'a handsome dress' costing £5–£10, while for no more than a pound a week she could rent 'two good furnished rooms near Pall Mall', right in the heart of London.[29] A whore could thus raise her standard of living not only above the poverty line, but into comparative prosperity. One woman told Bracebridge Hemyng: 'I get enough money to live on comfortably, but then I am extravagant, and spend a great deal of money on eating and drinking . . . I have the most expensive things sometimes, and when I can, I live in a sumptuous manner.'[30] For a woman born into the working class, this affluence amounted to nothing less than a personal revolution.

Street whores and brothel-workers generally earned similar wages, but whereas the former kept her money, the latter had her 'cuts' to shell out to the madam. Brothel whores were often in debt to the house from the outset, since they had to pay outrageously inflated prices for clothes, make-up, hairdressing and other facilities. Even so, the women who worked in houses enjoyed a better standard of living than their sisters in 'honest' work.

One unique feature of prostitution at this time, marking it out from all other trades and industries, was that it was essentially women-controlled. Brothels, lodging-houses and accommodation houses were mostly run by women, and whores themselves had control in their own sphere, with large numbers of them living and working independently from their own rooms and apartments. This woman-centred nature of the trade gave a distinctive character to its culture – it was communal, raucous, anti-patriarchal and contemptuous of bourgeois morality. At the same time, it was firmly embedded in – not distinct from – the culture of the urban working classes. A fine example of this whore-centred society is the special atmosphere of the lodging-houses: one English middle-class 'explorer of the social abyss', Mary Higgs, affords us a glimpse of it. At the heart of her disapprobation can be detected a lingering trace of admiration:

> Round the fire was a group of girls far gone in dissipation, good-looking girls most of them, but shameless; smoking cigarettes, boasting of drinks or drinkers, using foul language, singing music-hall songs, or talking vileness. The room grew full and breakfasts were about . . . a girl called 'Dot' danced the 'cake-walk' in the middle of the room.[31]

But perhaps the most visible manifestation of prostitutes' defiant culture was their dress: 'flaunting it first-rate' in the streets, they imitated and to some extent satirized the conspicuous display of well-heeled ladies. At the same time, however, the whores flaunted something else: a freedom of sexual and social behaviour which appalled middle-class commentators, who deplored their 'revolting language and manners' and above all, feared their influence on 'the servants'.[32] For these naughty working-class females were not cowed and exhausted factory-workers, or 'dogs' in upper-class kitchens; they were raucous, they had money to spend, and they knew how to have a good time spending it. Acton, visiting an East End music-hall in 1868, was much disturbed by this freedom:

> My first interest lay in considering the effect produced upon married women by becoming accustomed at these *réunions* to witness the vicious and profligate sisterhood flaunting it gaily, or 'first-rate', in their language . . . accepting all the attention of men, freely plied with liquor, sitting in the best places, dressed far above their station, with plenty of money to spend and denying themselves no amusement or enjoyment, encumbered with no domestic ties and burdened with no children.[33]

Victorian women, having a whale of a time? This was clearly beyond the pale!

Another distinctive feature of the whores' culture that observers reluctantly noticed was the solidarity they displayed towards each other. British reformers commented on the 'kindness and sympathy of these poor girls towards each other and their anxiety to aid and assist each other when in distress of any kind'.[34] In France when a whore died, other prostitutes would appear in a crowd, dressed in mourning, and accompany the funeral cortège to the cemetery.[35] And the autobiography of an American whore recalled many small but telling acts of kindness: 'When a woman could not pay for her child's care at a baby farm, the other women chipped in to help her out. When one prostitute became pregnant and lost her baby, the women surrounded her with all the nurturance "of her own sisters and mother".'[36]

Consistent with a culture which valued solidarity in this way, whores often formed close relationships among themselves, inevitably labelled with horror by outsiders as 'tribadism' – lesbianism –

whether or not they were primarily sexual. Parent-Duchâtelet was very concerned about this 'problem', and recommended that brothels should give each woman a separate bed in order to avoid it! However, the relative freedom enjoyed by women in the sex industry – not to mention the bizarre array of services demanded by the male clientele (most of whom were outwardly respectable) – made a mockery of the institutionalized norms of sexual behaviour. Parent's injunctions were doomed to go unheeded, not only because it was impossible to control whores' relationships, but also because brothel madams exploited them by staging lesbian shows and thus actively promoting a substantial lesbian trade. By the end of the century, Paris had a flourishing lesbian culture whose sexual outlaws necessarily gravitated towards each other by means of the sex trade. Within the Parisian sex industry itself, as Havelock Ellis recorded: 'Lesbianism [was] extremely prevalent, indeed, one might say almost normal.'[37]

One aspect of prostitutes' relationships about which outsiders have always had plenty to say is that with the pimp. The word is misleading, since it can be and is used to define any man who has a relationship with a whore, particularly if he too works in the sex industry or is unemployed. In the 19th century professional pimping was in its infancy; it was largely absent from Britain, and present only in small numbers elsewhere. In France the system encouraged procuring, but even so, a majority of women continued to work independently of both men and the state. However, commentators as always saw what they wanted to see and, particularly towards the end of the century, the reformers and anti-prostitution movement began to make a meal out of the pimping issue. This conveniently allowed society to divert its attention from the profiteers within its own ranks, which included the police, politicians, landlords, doctors, and other apparently respectable men – all of whom took their share of the sex trade's profits.

    This is not to deny the existence of small-time pimps; far from it – but perhaps it helps put these men in context. They generally came from the same social background as their whores, and therefore faced similar problems of poverty and lack of prospects; they could, however, play on what little power patriarchy afforded them by exploiting the sexual labour of their women. Pimping was one of the few ways in which a man from a poor background could achieve upward mobility, or at least a higher standard of living. This from the whore's point of view made entering a relationship with a man potentially dangerous, since there was always the possibility of her being used in this way. For some whores it was an acceptable price to pay for a love-relationship; after all, if nothing else, life in the sex business taught that all forms of love had their price. But the need to survive which turned love into money could eat away at affection until there was nothing left; and pimps were often negligent, exploitative and violent. A prostitute could pay emotionally and physically – as well as financially – for the relationship.

However, it should be remembered that any husband could be just as brutal and manipulative as any pimp; wife-battering was legal and widespread in all sectors of society. The violence towards whores from their pimps should thus be seen in the context of a patriarchal society which did not view marital violence against women as a particular problem.

A violent pimp was often the least of the whore's worries; every prostitute was, on the other hand, afraid of the possibility of being attacked – even murdered – by a client. The whore-stigma ensured that the protection and safety of prostitutes was low on the police agenda, and few prostitute-killers were actually caught; but the words of one man who was arrested, after murdering a prostitute known as 'La Belle Normande' in 1821, provide us with a chilling insight into the parallel dangers of then and now:

> She kissed me and said goodnight. I did not want to sleep, and yet I was tired. But my head was full of my idea, and I roused myself, and seeing that she was sleeping deeply, I got up, and was going to pick up my pruning hook to strike the blow. I do not know if she was awakened by my movement, but at the moment when I was going to strike, she turned and reached for me. I barely had time to throw myself on the bed, my head on the bolster. A few seconds later I slit her throat. She moved, and wanted to cry out. I struck her again. Then, seizing both her hands, I climbed back on the bed and tied them up with a handkerchief. During this operation, I pushed her knees on her stomach, and it was in this position that she died. After her last breath, I got up. I searched her room. And when everything was finished, since there was some water left in her basin, I used it to wash the blood from my hands and shirt. Then, without waiting for daybreak, I left. That morning, I sold a few of the objects I

had taken. After that, I returned to Vaugirard and sharpened my pruning hook. The rest of the day, you know, was Sunday, and I spent it in drinking and dancing. Monday, I did the same.[38]

Seeing male sexuality in all its glory every night, risking life and limb in both work and love with men, small wonder that many whores discovered the homosexual side of their nature, which their own culture allowed to flourish in peace – and safety.

Their knowledge and experience of society's sex life showed prostitutes what a sham the prevailing morality was; consequently they had nothing but contempt for it. American whores saw the 'snide, smug, respectable' men 'out there' as hypocrites who used 'bribery, dishonesty, lies, corruption in high places, and swindled taxpayers'.[39] This view of society was essentially correct; whores saw, for instance, that the much-vaunted respectability of politicians and businessmen was really a front, behind which lay the reality of pay-offs and the double standard. This made whores particularly contemptuous of the pious: 'I'll be hanged,' one woman told Bracebridge Hemyng, 'if I think that priest or moralist is to come down on me with the sledge-hammer of their denunciation.'[40]

And the anonymous whore who wrote to *The Times* in 1858 finished her letter angrily:

We come from the dregs of society, as our so-called betters call it. What business has society to have dregs – such dregs as we? You railers of the Society for the Suppression of Vice, you the pious, the moral, the respectable, as you call yourselves, who stand on your smooth and pleasant side of the great gulf you have dug, and keep between yourself and the dregs, why don't you bridge it over or fill it up . . . Why stand you there mouthing with sleek face about morality? What is morality?[41]

Whores' relationships within their own working-class environment were somewhat more cordial: this was their own milieu, for the sex industry (except where state regulation made it so) was not distinct from the rest of working-class life and culture. Whores lived and worked in working-class areas, catered to working-class as well as middle-class clients, and thus had both neighbourly and commercial relationships with the people who surrounded them. During the campaigns against attempts at regulation in Britain from the 1860s onwards, many working-class women who were not prostitutes mobilized in support of those who were, and many acts of individual kindness between the two groups of women demonstrated that the solidarity among sex workers was an extension of a much broader tradition of moral support among the working class as a whole. While there was a minority of working people – particularly church-going women – who *were* hostile to prostitutes, in the end it was possible to segregate whores from their own class only by state-orchestrated acts of intervention, such as regulation or repression.

In essence, prostitutes were no different from other working-class women; if they were exceptional in any way, it was only in that they were more likely to be young, single, and above all, independently-minded. Judith Walkowitz, historian of the Victorian sex trade, characterizes 19th-century prostitutes as: 'Young women, impatient with the subordination and fatalistic acquiescence expected of their class', and adds that whores were 'Noted for their independent and aggressive behaviour . . . (which) suggests that they were a special group more inclined to self-assertion than most of their working-class contemporaries.'[42]

The concept of the whore as female working-class rebel represented a very real threat to middle-class society, which is of course why all the doctors, commentators, investigators and reformers – whatever their individual differences – were so adamant in their denunciation of prostitution and their denial of the human rights (even human status, in some cases) of prostitutes. Then, as now, the reality of the whore made the moralists uncomfortable – they preferred their theories and fantasies.

What became of prostitutes after they had left the sex trade? Strangely, the men who were so busy delving into the lifestyles of working whores appear to have lost interest in them as soon as they stopped working. They preferred to leave unchallenged the lurid stereotypes of the whore dying early of some horrible, disfiguring disease (*à la* Zola). From the records that are available, it seems clear that the careers of prostitutes were usually brief, and, by the time they reached their early twenties – the age at which other working women were settling down with men – they started to leave the sex industry, often to marry or live with a lover. William Acton noted that whores married men 'from the peerage to the stable',[43] and it is certainly true that many whores made good matches through their careers –

sometimes with ex-clients, sometimes through making enough money to be an attractive catch for a tradesman or businessman. As one whore told Bracebridge Hemyng: 'We often do marry, and well too; why shouldn't we, we are pretty, we dress well, we can talk and insinuate ourselves into the hearts of men by appealing to their passion and their senses.'[44]

The Victorian diarist A. J. Munby recounts the fascinating story of Sarah Tanner, a servant girl turned whore. Munby first encountered Sarah in 1855 on Regent Street, in London's fashionable West End: 'She had got tired of service,' he records,

> and wanted to see life and be independent; and so she had become a prostitute, of her own accord and without being seduced. She saw no harm in it: enjoyed it very much, thought it might raise her and perhaps be profitable. She had taken it up as a profession . . . she had read books, and was taking lessons in writing and other accomplishments, in order to fit herself to be a companion of gentlemen.

Munby lost track of her until their paths crossed again by chance on 30 July 1859. He recorded the meeting in his diary; asking Sarah if she were still on the streets, she replied: 'Oh no. But I'd been on the streets three years, and saved up . . . and so I thought I'd leave, and I've taken a coffee-house with my earnings – the Hampshire Coffee House, over Waterloo Bridge.'

Munby was surprised and impressed by Sarah's new state of 'homely usefulness and virtuous comfort';[45] indeed, her enterprise and self-sufficiency were so close to the Victorian ideal of self-help, he could not help but admire the young woman.

Sarah Tanner was the type of prostitute who consciously used the profession as a means of moving up in the world, profiting by the resources it gave her to educate herself and build up capital. Many other women would have done the same, either through entering small business, or by marrying middle-class men. Not all whores harboured such ambitions: for many working-class girls, the sex trade was a means to survive economically and be independent, but they did not particularly wish to move out of their class of origin. Like other working-class women, many married and settled down during their mid-twenties. Others continued in the trade as madams; and a minority carried on working as whores into their later years, losing in earning power as they grew older. There were no doubt those among them who did die from disease, or male violence, but they were in the minority. For the most part, prostitutes lived reasonably well, especially by comparison with their 'honest' working-class sisters. Meanwhile, their so-called 'betters' showed no sign of renouncing their hypocrisy, or attempting to bridge the 'great gulf' of social inequality between themselves and society's 'dregs'.

CHAPTER THIRTEEN

'Shame, Shame, Horror!': Abolitionism and the Struggle for Social Purity

It is the old, the inveterate, the deeply rooted evil of prostitution itself against which we are destined to make war.

Josephine Butler

During the latter part of the 19th century a second great wave of industrialization began in the West, accompanied by the phenomenal growth of cities. The old certainties of the Victorian middle classes were shaken by these developments: old-fashioned moralists were especially alarmed by the huge new cities, in which familial and neighbourly moral surveillance was swamped by an anonymous tide of humanity, much of it working class and immigrant. Mass trade unionism, revolutionary ideologies, the sexually liberal culture of the urban poor, and the entry *en masse* of young single women into the labour force, all combined to throw elements of the bourgeoisie into a panic: the very fabric of the middle-class social order was apparently under threat.

In response to this 'threat' the middle class turned to its own tradition of social discipline, the puritanical control of sexuality and worship of the work ethic inculcated in the patriarchal nuclear family. If this model of the family could be extended to the 'masses', reforming their most active elements in the mould of the bourgeoisie itself – so the reasoning went – then workers would reproduce middle-class norms in their own behavioural patterns, and civilization would be safe.

This programme was not without sacrifice for middle-class men, however. The campaigns to implant morality in the hearts and minds of the working classes were led by the most moralistic elements of society – notably militant Christians and women who had been galvanized by the first wave of feminism – and the new consensus which emerged from this alliance for 'social purity' deprived middle-class men of the double standard, erecting in its place a single standard of chastity for both sexes. In this new utopia of purity, needless to say, the whore had no place. Not only did she call the double standard painfully to mind, she also represented the obstacles to the spread of the nuclear family model to the 'masses'. For the whore was the autonomous working woman, free of moralistic sexual control and thus beyond the control of patriarchy: as the living embodiment of the immorality with which all workers were supposedly tainted, she became the symbol on to which all the middle-class fears of moral subversion were projected. In the moral crusades of the late 19th and early 20th centuries, then, the whore became the scapegoat for a new wave of anti-sexual hysteria. The result, on the eve of the First World War, was an international climate of anti-prostitute repression.

To Victorian doctors, police and military men, regulation was the favoured solution to the evil of prostitution. By the 1860s and 1870s it seemed to have gained legitimacy throughout the Western world; even in Britain, with its historical antipathy towards state intervention. Repressive measures had already hit prostitutes hard, notably the Metropolitan Police Act in the 1850s, which made loitering an offence. From 1858 any lodging-house which 'harboured' more than one whore was deemed a 'disorderly house' and the landlady could be prosecuted. Publicans were banned from permitting whores to 'assemble and continue' on their premises. Then in 1864 the first Contagious Diseases Act was slipped through Parliament; intended to root out sexually transmitted diseases among enlisted men in the army and navy (and introduced *against* the recommendations of a Royal Commission on enlisted men's health), it provided for the compulsory examination of prostitute women in British naval ports and garrison towns. The Act was named after a previous law dealing with the health of cattle – which neatly summed up official attitudes towards whores. As one mid-Victorian writer commented: 'Prostitutes should be treated as foul sewers are treated, as physical facts and not as moral agents.'[1]

A rationale for this type of attitude was to be found in the metaphor of contagion, which itself centred upon the terror of syphilis. Venereal diseases were widespread at all levels of 19th-century society, and as a 'deviant' group engaged in the commerce of sex, whores were blamed for their spread. Nevertheless, the fear of STDs was exaggerated, and confusion about them rife: the mortality rates from syphilis were relatively small when compared with diseases of poverty such as tuberculosis – and Victorian women generally had much more to fear from the dangers of childbirth than those of venereal disease. Furthermore, doctors were incapable of accurately diagnosing STDs, let alone treating them – as we have seen, the application of mercury was often deadlier than the illness itself. In fact whores, being in the front line of possible infection, were the real experts on the problem, and their preventive measures included examining clients and refusing to have sex with infected men. If a whore found herself to be infected, she would often resort to herbal remedies and simple cleansing treatments that even some doctors had to admit were more effective than mercury poisoning.[2]

In fact the significance of syphilis was, like so many Victorian ideas about sex and prostitution, largely symbolic. For a start, it encapsulated the 'corruption' that the Christian imagination located in all sexuality, thus demonstrating the dire consequence of moral deviance. Men of God loved to terrorize their congregations with the mythical figure of the diseased whore, as in the following extract from one American preacher's sermon:

> Every year, in every town, die wretches scalded and scorched with agony. Were the sum of all the pain that comes with the last stages of vice collected, it would rend the very heavens with its outcry . . . Ye that are listening in the garden of this strange woman [the whore] . . . come hither, look upon her fourth ward [the last stages of syphilis – or mercury poisoning] . . . its vomited blood, its sores and fiery blotches, its prurient sweat, its dissolving ichor [pus] and rotten bones! Stop, young man![3]

Within the storyline of this Victorian horror story, disease and death were the righteous punishments for a life of sin; and so well-circulated were these Christian fantasies that, when faced with the evidence that most whores ended their careers during their twenties, then merged back into society, many authorities on prostitution simply denied the facts: 'The average duration of life amongst these

women does not exceed four years from the beginning of their career!'
William Sanger insisted.

Syphilis also symbolized the bourgeoisie's fear of being polluted by
the working class – the 'great unwashed', as the Victorians so
charmingly put it. If sex itself was dangerous, sex with a working-
class woman was more so; for she could serve as a channel through
which the dirt, disease and immorality of the working classes could
reach into the sanctity and purity of the middle-class home. Syphilis,
the disease of immorality, summed up this fear of contagion by
marking the whore as society's true *enemy within*. The Contagious
Diseases Acts could be rationalized as a means of dealing with this
enemy.

Under the first CD Act, a police morals squad was set up, with the
power to stop any woman and define her as a 'common prostitute'.
The woman would then be summonsed by a magistrate to undergo a
medical inspection; if she refused, she could be confined to a Lock
Hospital, where she was forcibly examined and, if found to be
infected, detained for up to three months. The Lock Hospitals were
pseudo-medical prisons for whores; here, the women were subjected
to a regime of mindless discipline and arbitrary regulation. 'Treatment' consisted of mercury poisoning. Many women were found on
arrival to be free of disease; others were infected by doctors'
unsterilized equipment. If a woman was menstruating, she was kept
until the end of her period. On her return to the outside world, a
woman often found that her children had been taken to the workhouse, her rooms let to others, and her goods sold off to pay rent
arrears.

The system was nothing less than barbaric; it seemed to suit the
authorities, however, since a second Act was passed a mere two years
later in 1866, extending the police powers and introducing two key
elements of the French system: registration and fortnightly inspec-
tions. After the appearance of a third Act, in 1869 (increasing the
number of towns and cities where the Acts were in force), a civilian
association sprang up with the aim of securing the application of the
CD Acts throughout the whole country.

By this time the drift of the legislation from primarily military
measures towards a systematic moral surveillance of the entire
working class had become apparent. The authorities' control was, as
always, to be exercised through the policing of working women. In
the Acts-regulated towns, the morals squads were regularly briefed to

maintain 'a tight surveillance over places where "public women" might congregate, principally the centres of working-class leisure activity and residential quarters . . . pubs, beer-shops, music-halls, fairs, private lodgings and . . . common lodging-houses.'[4]

In fact any woman the police deemed a prostitute could be arrested and registered, and from that point on she was officially labelled a *common prostitute*. A police briefing blandly declared that: 'In all military centres nearly every woman of the lower . . . classes who may happen to possess personal attractions is of a loose character.'[5] And Inspector William Harris, Assistant Commissioner of the Metropolitan Police, opined that: 'any woman who goes to places of public resort, and is known to go with different men, although not a common streetwalker, should be served with notice to register.'[6]

These and other remarks indicate just how arbitrary were the police morals squad's powers. They were quite open about who their targets were: any and all working women who had not confined their relationships with men to long-term monogamy. Under the threat of registration – authorized stigma – it now became dangerous for any woman to spend an evening out at a pub or music-hall, to flirt with her boyfriend on the street at night, or to entertain a male friend in her own home.

The CD Acts institutionalized whores' and other working women's lack of basic human and civil rights. All methods were considered acceptable by the authorities in the drive for registration: police, tipped off by anonymous letters, sought out and harassed women in their homes, or tailed them when they left their factories; they even disguised themselves as clients in order to entrap them. Arrested women were dragged through the open streets to the examining-rooms, a procedure that was clearly designed to emphasize their outcast status; meanwhile, the examination itself was less a medical procedure than an abusive and often sadistic acting-out of the state's power of access to whores' bodies, regardless of their consent. And all this in the context of hypocrisy and double-dealing: 'It did seem hard,' said one imprisoned woman, 'that the Magistrate of the bench . . . had paid me several shillings a day or two before, in the street, to go with him.'[7]

Amongst working women there was confusion over who was and who was not a prostitute. One woman, Harriet Hicks, who was tried under the Acts in Plymouth in 1870, had worked as a whore, settled with one man, left him and settled with another; when asked if she was still a prostitute she replied, 'No, only to the one man.'[8] Indeed, many women who were put on the register did not know what they were signing and were unfamiliar with both the word and the concept 'prostitute' as used by the bourgeoisie. Working-class sexual relationships were fluid and easy-going; young women were 'promiscuous', and even when they did settle down with a regular partner, they seldom bothered to pay the registry office fee to set an official seal on the relationship. Thus since nearly all young working women lived out of wedlock, they were all potentially definable by law as 'common prostitutes'.

As the Acts started to hit working-class communities with their full force, the whores within them became increasingly isolated and ostracized. The 'glaring publicity'[9] that accompanied police activities intimidated working people; consequently, the threat of registration which could be levelled at all working-class women discouraged them from associating with known prostitutes and many lodging-house landladies stopped renting rooms to whores. Clandestine prostitution became increasingly furtive and risky; and it became ever more difficult for women to move into and out of the sex trade – for once on the register, they were publicly identified as professional whores. Through the CD Acts the concept of the whore-stigma finally entered working-class consciousness, and the notion of respectability on the middle-class model was successfully imposed in its wake.

The momentum of regulation peaked in the 1870s and the tide began to turn with the emergence of a broad movement for the repeal of the CD Acts. The first opponents of regulation – or abolitionists, as they were known – were outraged middle-class feminists, one of whom, Josephine Butler, was the prime mover behind the repeal movement: 'Beautiful and histrionic . . . [Butler] was adored by men and women alike. A charismatic leader and a gifted speaker, she was able to capture the popular imagination and inspire a personal loyalty that bordered on idolatry.'[10]

Butler was not only a feminist, she was also a committed Christian. It was the shared moral idealism of the women and men who gathered around her which was to determine the tone and tactics of the repeal movement. The heady mixture of feminism and Christianity ensured that the abolitionists' attitudes towards whores were profoundly ambivalent. On the one hand, abolitionist ladies acknowledged and deplored the economic factors that led women into the sex trade; they also identified with whores as women deprived of civil rights, even daring to speak out openly against 'instrumental rape' of the forced examination with the doctor's speculum. But all these issues were contained within a framework of Victorian Christian ideology that left uncriticized the doctrine of separate spheres for men and women (which Butler and her feminist comrades wholeheartedly approved of), and the obsession with prostitution as the 'Great Social Evil'. Butler was unequivocal about this: 'It is,' she declared in a speech given in 1871, 'the old, the inveterate, the deeply rooted evil of prostitution itself against which we are destined to make war.'

Like the Reformation Protestants, the abolitionists wanted to expunge prostitution from the face of the earth; it was therefore no coincidence that Butler's notion of what was to result from this great purge would be nothing less than the Protestant utopia: 'The original principle of evil itself will be expelled from the earth,' she prophesied; 'and the reign of righteousness will be established.'[11]

Fine Christian rhetoric, but not much was said about what would happen to prostitutes once their work had been wiped out. In spite of the liberal abolitionists' apparent sympathy, the repeal campaign did not augur well for them. The sympathy ran out whenever whores refused to play the duly repentant role expected of them, for the abolitionists could not help but project their basic feelings of repugnance at the act of prostitution on to the whores themselves. Worse, the basic tenor of the Victorian middle-class mind was deeply anti-whore, and as the repeal campaign gathered support it began to slip from the grasp of its original leaders and take on a more thoroughly repressive character.

This ambivalence was reflected in the tactics of the movement right from the outset. On the plus side, women from Butler's Ladies National Association (LNA) plucked up the courage to go into the working-class areas of those towns where the CD Acts were in operation; once there, the ladies incited whores to rebel against forced registration and examination – and they responded enthusiastically to this encouragement and support. Repealers also worked to mobilize public sympathy against the Acts; their propaganda, however, reinforced rather than challenged prevailing Victorian sexual stereotypes. By concentrating on horror stories of innocent girls forced into the sex-trade by the morals squads, of entrapment by police and 'instrumental rape' by doctors, repealers avoided all discussion of voluntary prostitution, let alone women's right to work undisturbed in the sex trade. The whores in these accounts were pitched to appeal to the charitable reflexes of middle-class Christians; once depicted as solely the victims of lustful men and state tyranny, they could not be seen to be actively and unrepentantly engaging in prostitution for fear of undermining the conservative moral consensus upon which the campaign's by now popular appeal was based.

This type of whore-as-victim propaganda also flattered the vanity of the organized male working classes, who saw prostitution as an aspect of class oppression from which they could patriarchally 'protect' their wives and daughters. The depiction of whores and working women as victims encouraged working men to mould their families around the image of the male bread-winner, and to exclude women from many forms of industrial work – a kind of shadowy replica of the bourgeois norm which had in the first place reduced all working women's alternatives to marriage and prostitution. This cross-class alliance for patriarchal morality was successful for the repealers, however; and through the combination of popular mobilization, publicity, and behind-the-scenes lobbying, the Butlerites eventually carried the day, forcing Parliament to suspend the Acts in 1883 and finally to repeal them three years later.

The movement for social purity which was to eclipse the repeal campaign in the 1880s was initiated by, among others, Josephine Butler herself; it was the natural successor to the abolitionist position which had throughout its campaign been explicit in its aim to eradicate all prostitution by imposing a single standard of chastity for both sexes. In 1873, Butler founded the Social Purity Alliance, a young men's league of chastity clubs, to promote the pure life; thereafter the call for chastity was eagerly taken up by religious factions of the middle classes. Churches of all descriptions formed purity organizations, and in 1880, Alfred Dyer and William Coote, two 'working class radical puritans',[12] helped inaugurate the National Vigilance Association (NVA), whose express aims were to guard the nation's morals. A couple of years later Ellice Hopkins, an energetic Christian who admitted she could only overcome her repugnance of prostitution 'with God's help', began to organize other Christian women into associations for the 'rescue' of 'fallen women'. Hopkins also formed the White Cross Army, whose members – mostly adolescent males – pledged:

1. To treat all women with respect, and to endeavour to protect them from wrong and degradation.

2. To use every possible means to fulfil the commandment 'keep THYSELF pure'.

3. To endeavour to put down all indecent language and coarse jests.

4. To maintain the law of purity as equally binding upon men and women.

5. To endeavour to spread these principles among my companions, and to try and help my younger brothers.[13]

Much more than the abolitionists, the social purity campaign looked to the lurid to create its agenda, its two abiding themes being 'white slavery' and child prostitution. The 'white slave trade', supposedly an organized international traffic in women, was a Victorian fantasy which formed part of the stock repertoire of melodrama in fiction and theatre at this time. The typical story involved innocent white adolescent girls who were drugged and abducted by sinister immigrant procurers, waking up to find themselves captive in some infernal foreign brothel, where they were subject to the pornographic whims of sadistic, non-white pimps and brothel-masters. Middle-class moralists were convinced that a 'traffic in women', operated by well-established underworld networks, was going on under their very noses, and they had little difficulty in whipping up a public panic about this non-existent outrage.

In fact the reformers based their evidence for the 'white slave trade' on the actual international migration of whores, which had begun to be a sizeable phenomenon during the latter part of the century. With the internationalization of capitalism and the opening of trade routes to the far outposts of Empire, millions of people were on the move, migrating from Europe to hoped-for better lives in the Americas and the colonies. Whores were no exception; taking the migratory option to escape poverty and oppression in their home countries, they travelled thousands of miles to live and work in the cities of the USA, Latin America, Egypt, South Africa and Asia. Men often moved with them, acting as chaperones and intermediaries who would on arrival in foreign cities introduce whores to sex-trade contacts.

Among other documented cases, the story of Fanny Epstein reveals the realities of the 'white slave trade'. A Jewish immigrant in London's Whitechapel, Fanny met a man named Alexander Kahn in 1891, when she was eighteen, and left home with him and two friends to travel to India. Her father, a tailor, traced her with the help of the NVA and the

Foreign Office to Kamathipura, the red-light district of Bombay. When the Bombay police approached her with an offer to help her home, Fanny refused, saying that she had come to India of her own free will, had no regrets or embarrassment about her work there, and no desire whatsoever to return to her father. She impressed the Bombay police commissioner, H. G. Gell, as 'singularly calm and self-possessed . . . a somewhat determined young woman and well able to look after herself.'[14]

Kahn, meanwhile, had been arrested; the NVA brought charges against him, but when Fanny testified that she had left home of her own accord and that Kahn had provided her with money to set herself up in Bombay, the case against him collapsed.

Like many outward-bound whores, Fanny Epstein was a resourceful, independent and ambitious young woman, who had used Kahn's services as a companion in an age when women travelling alone were conspicuous and vulnerable, and to advance her money when she arrived at her destination. Clearly the opposite of the drugged, helpless victim of stereotype, Fanny obviously knew what she was doing and had chosen emigration as a positive alternative to her former life in Whitechapel.

For the most part, British reformers concentrated their fire on the 'traffic in women' between British cities and continental brothels. In 1880, Alfred Dyer had published a pamphlet, *The European Slave Trade in English Girls*, which purported to prove that British girls were being abducted by the score, and forced to work in the licensed brothels of Brussels. A Parliamentary Committee was set up to investigate and 'uncovered' a small amount of migration between Britain and the Continent: a 'traffic' which was already well known to the British Embassy staff in Brussels, who had helped about 200 women return home during the 1870s. In fact the overwhelming majority of young women who were recruited for the *maisons closes* of Brussels and Antwerp had already been prostitutes in Britain and had migrated voluntarily. It was the regulated brothel system they objected to – not the lurid melodrama of being drugged and kidnapped, which remained a figment of their would-be rescuers' imagination. Those who returned home had found coercion, deceit and blackmail within the Belgian brothels, but this was due to the corruption of police and officialdom – not to white slave traders.

The Committee also looked into the incidence of child prostitution, another preoccupation of the social purity movement. Child prostitution and the sale of virgins did exist, but as we have seen, constituted a very minor part of the sex trade; the reformers, however, blew their obsessions up out of all proportion, with the result that *all* prostitution came to be wholly identified with child prostitution and 'white slavery'. The emphasis on adolescent sexuality – the stereotypical 'white slave' was a girl in her early teens – was not accidental; it formed a crucial part of the social purists' programme for attacking the mores of the urban working classes.

For the middle classes had reacted with panic to the growth of organized labour, retreating into atavistic fantasies of the 'dangerous classes'. Social purity turned this panic into a frantic drive to tame the workforce by injecting its culture with puritanism. Various strategies were put forward by social purists to 'root out the traditional social and sexual habits of the poor'[15] – the Salvation Army's Charles Booth had, for example, suggested forced labour camps for the nonrespectable poor – but in the end it was clear that the key to reconditioning the entire class lay in reaching its rising generations. Purity activists therefore addressed themselves to the young. Thousands of working-class adolescents were recruited into church chastity clubs and organizations such as the White Cross Army, while reformers toured the country lecturing working-class mothers on how to avoid incest in their families and how to curb their children's sexual curiosity. Issues of poverty, overcrowding, and ill-health – the root conditions that blighted working-class lives – were not addressed.

The Puritans began to come out in their true colours, showing themselves to be obsessed with instilling all levels of society with a repressive, coercive morality in which there was no place for any real human sympathy, sexuality, or solidarity. In 1880, Ellice Hopkins promoted the Industrial Schools Amendment Act, which linked the purity emphasis on childhood to their preoccupation with prostitution: it gave the police the authority to remove children from houses where prostitutes lived, and place them in Industrial Schools, thus depriving the children of their own mothers, and vice versa. The entire purity movement, from Butlerite feminists to right-wing Christians, applauded her efforts. Although Josephine Butler later vehemently opposed Hopkins and her social purity colleagues, by then it was too late; indeed the movement had swallowed up many former Butlerites.

The spark which was to turn social purity into a national conflagration ignited in the mid-1880s. By 1883 the CD Acts had been suspended, though not repealed, taking much of the wind out of the repeal movement's sails. To keep up the momentum, abolitionists turned their attention to the pseudo-issues of white slavery and the sale of virgins, campaigning for the raising of the age of consent to thirteen and for laws against 'traffickers in vice', but making little impression on Parliament. Finally, Butler – by now allied with the Booth family, whose Salvation Army was crusading against prostitution in working-class areas – turned for help to W. T. Stead, editor of the *Pall Mall Gazette*.

As an enthusiastic Christian who was sympathetic to the purity cause, Stead leaped at the opportunity to get involved in the issues; and in 1885 he set out on his own investigation of the sex-trade underworld. The result was 'The Maiden Tribute of Modern Babylon', a series of articles which constituted a first in the now all-too-familiar school of muckraking sensationalism. Where previous journalists such as Mayhew and Hemyng had confined themselves to witnessing *and recording* the voices of the labouring poor, whores among them, Stead created his own scoop. Posing as a client, he bought a virgin, a girl named Eliza, from her parents. The girl

> was taken to an underworld midwife who certified her *virgo intacta* . . . and then to a low boarding house where Stead was lurking in grotesque make-up that made him appear like an old rake. He was enjoying himself, and insisted on entering Eliza's bedroom to carry the charade as far as possible. Eliza was terrified and Stead retreated. After being subjected to another examination, this time so that a proper physician could certify her unharmed for their ultimate protection, Bramwell Booth sent the miserable girl off to the Salvation Army in France.[16]

Leaving aside Stead's perverse playacting, the fact remains that both he and Booth had used the girl much as any 'old rake' would have done – for their own ends and without her consent. Stead sold a lot of papers and became famous overnight while Eliza lost her home and family, and finished up an exile in the hands of an extremist religious group. Never mind – her all-important hymen was intact. It was perhaps poetic justice that as a result of this incident, Stead was prosecuted (on a technicality) for the very offences he had sought to expose, and jailed for three months.

With this story, and other similarly lurid accounts of the sale of virgins, Stead played to the Victorian appetite for white slavery stories; consequently, 'The Maiden Tribute' hit the nation like a bombshell. Mobs rioted outside the offices of the *Pall Mall Gazette* in the battle to get their hands on copies of the paper, which was banned by W. H. Smith. Copies changed hands at twelve times the cover price, and the articles were syndicated in the USA and published across Europe in book form, from France to Russia.

In the wake of the scandal created by Stead's articles a massive demonstration (estimated at 250,000 strong) was held in Hyde Park, demanding the raising of the age of consent to sixteen. Feminists, socialists and Christians came together to express their horror at the skeletons Stead had dragged from the Victorian closet:

> With white roses for purity; with banners proclaiming 'Protection of Young Girls'; 'Men, protect the Girls of England'; 'Women of London to the Struggle'; 'War on Vice'; 'Sire, Pity Us'; 'Shame, Shame, Horror'; with tambourines, drums, and fifes, ten columns set out for the park . . . There were wagonloads of young virgins in white flying the pathetic oriflamme, 'The Innocents, Will They Be Slaughtered?' . . . Then there was the hero, described by a bemused French observer 'perched on a wagon, proceeding as a conqueror' to shouts of 'Long live Stead!'[17]

And street vendors shifted record numbers of the pornographic magazine *The Devil*.

This unprecedented display of public sentiment launched social purity as a mass movement, organized around the late Victorian consensus of 'respectability'. From the Butlerites on the left to the Christians on the right, middle-class opinion was united in its aversion to the easy-going social and sexual habits of working-class youth and in its singling out of prostitution as the 'Social Evil' which, once wiped out, would take with it all the nasty habits they so disapproved of.

Parliament swallowed the purity agenda whole, and in 1885 passed the Criminal Law Amendment Act, which raised the age of consent to sixteen, gave the police extensive powers against procurers and brothel-keepers and, incidentally, outlawed male homosexuality. A new wave of repression followed. In the wake of the Act nearly every major city in Britain swung into action, closing down lodging-houses and brothels, and prosecuting whores when they subsequently took to the streets. By the early 1890s, Manchester had reduced its brothels from four hundred to just ten, and Sheffield from three hundred to seven. A Purity Party swept to power in Liverpool in 1890; it swiftly cracked down not only on brothels and lodging-houses, but also on any pubs which dared to serve prostitutes. In London, Glasgow, Cardiff, Belfast and Dublin, purity vigilantes besieged whorehouses and intimidated staff and clients. In 1887, brewery heir turned purity fanatic Frederick Charrington rampaged through the East End of London with his supporters, closing down brothels and assaulting sex-industry workers – in one incident, Charrington was sued for kicking a brothel attendant in the stomach. Seven hundred brothels closed in South London between the years 1894 and 1912, and five hundred in central London during the same period. When the women who had been bounced out of their workplaces flooded on to the streets, the police quickly moved in to 'clean them up'. So many whores were arrested that open soliciting was replaced by 'stealthy glance or mumbled word'.[18]

Not content with the persecution of prostitutes, the purity organizations poured out propaganda about the dire consequences of VD and masturbation; they also campaigned against contraception and 'pornography' – sexual information and education, nude paintings, 'immoral' plays and novels. A special target of their hatred was the music-hall, where working-class audiences enjoyed variety shows that included sexually explicit jokes and sketches and burlesque-type dances. Sadly, the moralists were successful in their repression of the raucous culture of the lower classes. In its place they promoted a stifling atmosphere of inquisition, censorship and hypocrisy.

For whores the results of the social purity movement were catastrophic. Although the CD Acts were finally repealed in 1886, in many places their regime was continued under a different name – with purity activists now patrolling the streets instead of the police. After the demise of the lodging-houses and brothels, whores were forced to take furnished rooms, which often meant posing as a couple with a pimp; the only other alternative was to solicit in the streets. But these were now inhospitable; whores had to work furtively and in fear of the police. Life became dangerous. In 1888, at the height of the anti–whore drive, the Jack the Ripper murders underlined just how vulnerable and isolated whores had become. As one of a plethora of male experts on the savage deaths of the five Whitechapel prostitutes observed: 'the Criminal Law Amendment Act . . . [made] all forms of organised whoring illegal . . . [and] forced the girls on to the streets. Jack the Ripper must have been grateful.'[19] (So must those writers – all men – who have since transformed the Ripper into a legend, styling themselves 'Ripperologists'. They are admirably dealt with in Jane Caputi's book *The Age of Sex Crime*, listed in the Bibliography.)

Segregated from their own communities' support networks, whores had to rely increasingly on pimps for their protection. Outcast, their culture under constant attack, ever more dependent on men, whores became terribly vulnerable to abuse from all quarters of society. Against the combined might of the social purity movement and the state, they had little way of fighting back, and their profession began inexorably to shift from female to male control. This was the tragedy of the abolition movement: that its activities had turned its delusions about whores and the sex trade into harsh realities.

In the United States by the beginning of the 1870s the police authorities and medical profession were arguing for and enacting regulation in response to the prostitution boom. Using the danger of venereal disease as their pretext, and drawing their data from William Sanger's pro-regulationist *History of Prostitution* (1858), the American authorities attempted to push through regulation measures, citing the example set by continental Europe as a brilliant solution to the problem of prostitution. Their efforts were doomed to fail, in a society in which the merest hint of state control of the sex industry was anathema; but where the police and the doctors did succeed was in catalysing the growth of an abolitionist movement that very swiftly overtook the regulationist position. In retrospect, this was inevitable, for from the outset, the American abolitionist movement incorporated a hard-line social purity character that was virtually indistinguishable from the British version; indeed, its aim was identical: to eliminate all 'social evils' (definable as deviations from the moral norms of middle-class society). The chief culprit was once again prostitution.

The US purity campaigns thus had the same double focus as their British counterparts: while they spread wide the net of 'social evils' – the Chicago Society for the Promotion of Social Purity, for instance, envisaged a 'Holy War' against any and all 'habits of sensuality' which could lead to 'vice' – prostitution was still the major enemy, encapsulating as it did the anti-sexual instincts and class prejudices of Middle America in one almighty symbol.

Women, again, were particularly prominent among purity crusaders. Like their European counterparts, they believed that it was the female's special mission to elevate the lustful masculine character to a higher stage of civilization; their aim was to impose the single standard of chastity on both sexes. Good Christian women – especially mothers – would thus rid the nation of 'the Social Evil', and this in turn would lead to the perfection of man on earth. Meanwhile, little or no thought was given to the practical fate of whores once the sex industry, and with it their livelihoods, had been eradicated. In fact the social purity agenda, with its narrow focus on prostitution and sexual morality, actively diverted public attention from the pressing economic and social problems of rapid growth and urbanization. The whore was to be held responsible for all the ills of modern American society, and punished accordingly.

As usual, one of the prime motivations behind the fruitless attempts to regulate the sex trade had simply been the desire of local male élites to make money out of whores. For with the growth of cities, and the parallel growth of prostitution towards the end of the century, male entrepreneurs realized that there were huge profits to be made, and began to invest in 'vice' much as they did in straight business. Regulation, by bringing the sex industry under state control, legitimizing and structuring it, would have made the extraction of profits easier and more efficient. Now, frustrated by their failure to achieve regulation, many city authorities turned to the solution of segregation. Local politicians were instrumental in pushing the trade into red-light districts where it was tolerated without being legalized, thus attracting less attention from genteel society, but still facilitating the making of money by interested parties. Within the red-light districts prostitution began to succumb to a more or less clandestine form of regulation as, increasingly, male profiteers moved in to pimp off the whores' earnings.

Between the last part of the 19th century and the First World War, these segregated districts flourished, usually in the black, immigrant or poorer areas of the cities – well out of range of delicate middle-class sensibilities. The novelist Michael Gold describes the poor Jewish area of New York's East Side during his childhood at the turn of the century:

> There were hundreds of prostitutes on my street. They occupied vacant stores, they crowded in flats and apartments in all the

tenements . . . On sunshiney days the whores sat on chairs along the sidewalks. They sprawled indolently, their legs taking up half the pavements . . . The girls winked and jeered, made lascivious gestures at passing males. They pulled at coat-tails and cajoled men with fake honeyed words. They called their wares like pushcart peddlars . . . [They] were naked under flowery kimonos. Chunks of breast and belly occasionally flashed. Slippers hung from their feet; they were already ready for 'business'.[20]

One low-life investigator, James Marchant, plumbed the depths of Chicago's Levee district in 1912, and was shocked by what he saw:

On every hand the brilliantly lighted dens, with the jangle of their ragtime songs and revelry, and the hoarse laughter of patrons and prostitutes, lined the squalid streets. Outside the resorts, hangers-on bid for custom. Through the blocks and constantly opened doors, groups of men, mostly youths, passed and repassed as at some conventional country fair. Policemen strolled, casual and carefree, through the throng.[21]

During a similar tour of San Francisco's Barbary Coast, Marchant found cheap joints full of 'boys' and 'music, singing and general hilarity', nude shows, cribs, and 'well-dressed, middle-aged men' leaving high-class houses in their chauffeur-driven cars. As well as the brothels and cribs, and the tenements where working-class clients queued for a five-minute fuck, the districts were full of saloons which plied men with liquor, and ran vaudeville shows with burlesque dancers and live sex acts. Upstairs rooms were available in some establishments, while others provided curtained booths.

Storyville, New Orleans, had the biggest, boldest and brashest reputation of all the red-light districts. Created in 1897 and named after Alderman Sidney Story, who had proposed segregation when the usual attempts to regulate had failed, Storyville stretched over 38 blocks that entirely consisted of brothels, assignation houses, cribs, saloons, dance-halls and cabarets, providing work not only for whores but also for scores of jazz musicians. Jelly Roll Morton, the legendary blues pianist, remembered the scene which had nurtured his talent:

This tenderloin district was like something nobody has ever seen
before or since. Hundreds of men were passing through the
streets day and night. The chippies in their little-girl dresses were
standing in the crib doors singing the blues. Some were real
ladies in spite of their downfall, and some were habitual
drunkards, and some were dope fiends . . . They had everything
in the District, from the highest class to the lowest. Creep joints
where they'd put the feelers on a guy's clothes, cribs that rented
for about $5 a day and had just about enough room for a bed,
small-time houses where the price was from 50c to $1, and they
put on naked dances, circuses and jive. Then, of course, we had
the mansions where everything was of the highest class. These
houses were filled with the most expensive furniture and
paintings. It was in these mansions that the best of the piano
players worked.[22]

It was also these mansions – no-expense-spared brothels like Lulu
White's New Mahogany Hall, built in marble at the cost of $40,000 –
which attracted the big noises of the bourgeoisie, the politicians,
lawyers, businessmen who made the most money out of the district.

Business interests were, naturally enough, very keen to invest in the
segregated districts. In the early 20th century, for instance, a small city
such as Kansas could boast 400,000 dollars'-worth of investment in
its red-light area; while in larger cities the figures ran into millions:
Chicago's Levee was estimated to turn over $15 million a year, and in
Storyville: 'Well over ten million dollars a year, probably closer to
fifteen million, found its way into the stockings of the prostitutes, the
cassocks of the clergymen who owned the whorehouse property, the
pockets of the politicians, and the swelling accounts of the landlords.'[23]

There was big money to be made – and police and politicians were
right in there among the other profiteers. Thanks to the quasi-legal
status of prostitution, they were able to extort huge amounts of
protection money from the brothels: they received a cut of the income
and privileged access to the women, in return for which they
guaranteed immunity from prosecution. If anything went wrong, and
somebody was arrested, there were always specialist lawyers on hand
to protect sex-trade interests – at a price. And prostitution became so
interwoven with the political scene that whores were free to operate
within the Capitol at Washington DC. One reporter at a close-of-

Congress junket there in 1895 saw 'an aged senator pass into the private dining-room with hilarious "peaches" on his arms, where a bottle of champagne finished the business possibly begun in a committee-room . . . [and] two women whose calling was plainly indicated in their faces . . . sipping beer in the corner and soliciting trade on the sly.'[24]

Police corruption, too, extended from the rookie on the beat to the highest officials. In Kansas the annual 'fines' extorted from the brothels often amounted to $40,000; while the street cops reaped their own, small-time benefits: 'If you are a good fellow,' one saloon-keeper recounted, 'set up drinks and cigars, and throw in a little business on the side, there will be no trouble with the policeman on the beat.'[25]

The saloon-keepers' biggest earnings came from the sex-trade customers, and breweries and liquor manufacturers linked up with political élites in order to protect this aspect of their business. For landlords, the sex industry represented two or three times the normal return on their investment. George Kneeland, in his 1913 study *Commercialized Prostitution*, gives the example of one landlord who made $6454 a month from a single brothel housing fifteen whores.

The legion of straight profiteers aside, the culture of prostitution also generated its own economic infrastructure. Beauty parlours, pharmacists who dispensed morphine and cocaine, hotel owners, doctors who sold medical certificates, barmen, waiters and cab drivers who tipped off potential clients and conducted them to whores, and ordinary shops and businesses in the red-light areas – all benefited from the money brought in by the sex industry.[26] Then there were of course those who had never disguised their exploitation of prostitutes: the madams, pimps and procurers – or 'cadets' as they were known in the American sex trade.

As on the Continent, the setting-apart of the sex industry from ordinary life created a demand for procurers who could ensure a constant flow of women into the brothels. Cadets sought out unemployed working girls, teenage runaways, young immigrant women looking for work and other vulnerable females, and steered them into the sex industry. Often they befriended the young woman, successfully holding out the tempting promise of a life of relative ease and high pay – but sometimes their methods were coercive, and some young women were forced into brothels and kept there against their will. Others, too, were kidnapped to serve labourers in all-male lumber camps. This type of coercion should not be overlooked; at the same time it should be kept in perspective, and not used as it was by reformers as a weapon against voluntary prostitution. For the relatively rare crimes involved here were not prostitution *per se*, but kidnapping and forced sex – organized rape.

In the main, procurers acted as they did elsewhere in the world: as paid agents who introduced prospective whores into the sex industry and at the same time provided madams with fresh flesh to exploit. Whores on the move from city to city used the services of the cadets as an entry into their new workplace; and procurers were also active in finding work for the thousands of migrating prostitutes who were pouring into the US at major ports like Boston, New York and San Francisco.

It was this whole complex of commercialized sex trading, stretching from Congress to the cadet on the street, which gave rise to the American version of the 'white slavery' panic. The hysteria first broke around 1885, the year of Stead's 'Maiden Tribute', but it was to reach its pinnacle in the early years of the 20th century. Having observed the large-scale commercialization of the trade, American reformers, like their British counterparts, convinced themselves of the existence of underground cartels of 'white slavers', invariably depicted as immigrant men, who drugged and then abducted innocent young virgins and held them captive in a life of vice. Hard evidence for this phenomenon was lacking, however: one contemporary survey found that only 7.5 per cent of prostitutes had been recruited against their will, and modern research puts the figure at well under 10 per cent. The simple facts did not deter the abolitionists, though: 'Remember, ladies,' one feminist told her anti-prostitution colleagues, 'it is more important to be aroused than to be accurate. Apathy is more of a crime than exaggeration in dealing with this subject.'[27]

By their continued harping on the theme of forced prostitution, the abolitionists succeeded in establishing the image of the whore as 'white slave' in the American imagination. By the turn of the century, the hysteria had reached the establishment, and in 1910 a Grand Jury was convened, chaired by the legendary oil millionaire John D. Rockefeller, to investigate the white slave traffic. Failing to uncover evidence of an organized traffic in women, it noted instead the informal links between procurers, cadets, madams, and other sex-trade entrepreneurs across the country. For the anti-whore movement, this was all the ammunition that was needed.

The 'white slave' hysteria fed into the whole gamut of social purity agitation in the USA during the so-called Progressive Era of 1900–1918. By the last decade of the 19th century, social purity had become a mass movement, extending itself through organizations like the male White Cross Army and the female White Shield – bands of chastity militants modelled on the original British versions. As in Britain, the social purists hit the late Victorian consensus on the nerve, shaping the moral and political agenda and repressing any hint of immorality it detected within popular culture, savaging the press, art and literature. Also as in Britain, working-class culture was a favoured target with mothers' meetings called to educate working women in how to suppress their children's sensuality. When in 1887 the New York Saturday Half-Holiday Act was passed, enabling the workers to enjoy a little more leisure time, social purists conjured up the spectre of working people indulging in 'dancing, carousing, low behaviour, rioting, shooting, and murder',[28] and quickly mobilized against all forms of popular entertainment, from dance-halls to boxing and gambling. The American masses did not prove particularly receptive to the purity message, however, and reformers had to change tactics, putting pressure on the state to enact the kind of social control they wanted to exercise. The consequences were various, but uniformly destructive of the sexual culture of the poor. After 1887 the age of consent climbed from an average across the states of ten to sixteen, which no doubt protected some children from sexual abuse; but by 1899 it had reached twenty-one, thus criminalizing the sexual habits and sex work of working women below this age. And in 1910 the Mann Act – supposedly passed to deal with white slavery by outlawing the passage of women across state lines 'for immoral purposes' – made it increasingly difficult for whores to move around the country.

But the biggest blow to prostitutes was undoubtedly the wave of sex industry repression that took off in the second decade of the 20th century. Following the Rockefeller enquiry, 40 US cities and states held their own investigations and denounced the policy of segregation with one voice. The police, aided and abetted by purity activists, followed up with closures and evictions. However, there were still no realistic alternative proposals for working prostitutes once they had been deprived of work; nobody addressed this issue, except as a contemptuous afterthought. One Barbary Coast prostitute wrote to purity women who had, once again, presented the out-of-work dance-hall girls with the enticing option of domestic work:

Possibly you have failed to realise that the majority of these girls are young, fair-looking, well-educated, well-groomed . . . They have had or are now maintaining a home for themselves or other relatives . . . most of them are using that means of livelihood as a quicker road to a home of their own. Some of them have professions or trades, quite a few are musical; if it wasn't for the fear of ridicule or curiosity, they would return to their legitimate labour. I don't believe any one of them would accept the position of kitchen mechanic. If a living wage was offered where the girls could work, meet their instalments, I doubt if they wouldn't gladly accept.[29]

And in Washington, where the authorities closed down the red-light area in 1914, a group of whores addressed the following letter to the public:

Knowing that public opinion is against us, and that the passing of the . . . 'Red Light Bill' is certain, we, the inmates of the underworld, want to know how the public expects to provide for us in the future?

We do not want 'homes'. All we ask is that positions be provided for us. The majority will accept them. We must live somehow. We are human. With all the resorts in nearly all the large cities closed, it is useless for us to leave Washington.

How many citizens will give employment to women of our class? Very few would be so liberal-minded . . . In years past, it has been tried and as soon as previous reputations were discovered, our positions were made unbearable. Then, through necessity, we had to return to the old life.[30]

These letters show the dilemma of prostitutes as laws were enacted and enforced across the USA. Every aspect of their existence was criminalized; it became increasingly difficult for them to work as whores and, because the social purity fanatics had intensified the whore-stigma, it was even more difficult for them to find straight jobs. Thus they were condemned to become both professionals and criminals: forced out of the red-light districts, they moved into clandestine and undercover forms of prostitution in flats, hotels, massage parlours and as callgirls – a situation which inevitably led to their increased dependence on male pimps. But for the majority of whores, their only refuge was the streets, and here, too, they were harassed and arrested: this in turn ensured a constant supply of women for the special courts, prisons and reformatories that were springing up in cities all over the country.

In this chaotic and crazy form, prostitution was integrated and institutionalized in the state and social fabric of early 20th-century America. The separate judicial and penal system that was created to process whores in turn gave birth to a layer of state employees – vice-squad cops, lawyers and judges, social workers and prison warders – all of whom were destined to pimp off the Catch-22 which locked whores into an illegal profession. At the same time, a compromise was finally reached between regulationists and reformers. The state-employed professionals, successors of the policemen and doctors who had wanted to regulate prostitution a few decades earlier, carved out a comfy niche for themselves in this state-organized traffic in women; only they did so under the aegis not of toleration and legality but of intolerance and criminalization. Meanwhile, the social purity reformers – who had failed dismally to eradicate prostitution – saw their cherished doctrine of moral 'deviance' engraved on the hearts and minds of those who ran the new system.

Drawing their ideologies from Lombroso *et al.*, the state-employed pimps now turned the purist obsession with the moral health of the nation into a new whiter-than-white doctrine: 'social hygiene', which in turn became the expert knowledge they dealt in. Instead of regulated prostitution, the social hygienists now advocated chastity as the answer to venereal disease; 'with its scientific [*sic*] approach to the moral and medical issues of eugenics, venereal disease and birth control, [social hygiene] united the medical profession and social-purity forces at last.'[31]

In this way all the contradictions within the middle classes on their approach to sexuality – particularly that of the lower orders – were smoothed over, and finally, after the prolonged struggles of the 19th century, a solution to the 'problem' of prostitution was reached – at the expense of the prostitute. For now she was increasingly vulnerable to abuse from both clients and police, and it was as a direct result of this vulnerability that the pimp became a permanent feature of the landscape, providing protection, emotional support, and legal assistance. At the same time, the spread of prohibition ensured that the sex trade went underground: the illegalization of prostitution naturally enough created a whole new class of criminalized women;

this in turn ensured that the ruthless organized crime syndicates got in on the act. After the First World War these syndicates dominated the sex market in US cities, securing their positions in alliances with local élites – the police and politicians who had earlier made fortunes out of the segregated red-light districts. Once again the moralistic social purity fanatics had succeeded in transforming their delusions into fact: the sinister nationwide network of criminal involvement in the sex industry that they had fantasized had become a reality.

In all of this there was only one major victim: the whore. The determination of middle-class reformers that prostitutes should be both victims and deviant social outcasts was realized, as whores were first victimized by the new legislation, then systematically stigmatized as an outcast group. By the first decades of our own century, American whores found themselves trapped in a nightmare system which in many ways prefigured the totalitarian regimes that were soon to spring up across the Atlantic.

Josephine Butler's European tour of 1874–5 stimulated the growth of a fervent abolitionist campaign across the Continent in much the same form as it had taken in Britain and the US. However, the European movement had its work cut out, for there the regulated sex industry was much more firmly entrenched than the more loosely-structured Anglo-Saxon model.

Like Anglo-Saxon abolitionists, the Europeans emphasized the economic causes of prostitution, but they too had no responses to working women's poverty other than the usual moral panaceas. Fundamentally, they wanted to abolish prostitution altogether, using the magic wand of chastity to make it vanish. This anti-prostitution mentality, coupled with the reformers' moralistic tunnel-vision, led them to be more concerned, in the end, with the morals of the working class as a whole than with the civil liberties of prostitutes – French abolitionists, for example, were preoccupied with the incidence of lesbianism in the *maisons closes* – and, as in the Anglo-Saxon countries, they were soon outflanked by social-purity advocates as the turn of the century approached.

The authorities' reactions to abolitionist demands were various. In France the existing system was already out-moded, and the anti-regulationist campaign simply sounded its death-knell. The *maisons closes* had been in decline since the 1850s; whores so disliked them that they changed houses as often as once a month – or simply left to work independently. This caused chaos for madams, brothel-owners, and police alike. The brasseries, cafés and cabarets had all opened their doors to prostitutes and their clients, and a good time was being had by all. A few years later the *maisons de rendezvous* began to encroach on the brothels' own territory; they were open to all whores and their clients, but enabled the women to solicit on the streets, and come and go as they pleased. Both the whores and their clients preferred this arrangement – and, eventually, so did the vice squad.

For the reform campaigners had succeeded in creating an anti-regulationist consensus in France, and by shifting the emphasis from official regulation of the *maisons closes* to informal surveillance of the *maisons de rendezvous*, the police were able to hoodwink the public into believing that the system was being dismantled. But from the 1880s onwards, the police pressurized *rendezvous* owners into keeping files on the women who used their houses and receiving medical examiners on a weekly basis. When a parliamentary commission of 1903–7 finally abolished the old system, the new police strategy went unnoticed, and, in the guise of dismantling the regulation system, the authorities replaced it with a new, clandestine version, later dubbed 'neoregulation' by historians. The morals squads were officially decommissioned, but their officers still carried out their old duties; inscription was ended, but whores now had to declare their intent to ply the trade, and in place of the old *carte* they were issued with a *certificat de santé* – after an obligatory examination, of course. Infected prostitutes were no longer imprisoned in St-Lazare, but confined to a new 'sanatorium'. Everyone was happy, except the whores them-selves: the public believed that regulation had been discarded, while the police found that surveillance of the inhabitants of the *rendezvous* gave them even better access to the sexual lives of the working poor.

Similar compromises were reached in Italy between the latter part of the 19th century and the First World War. In 1888 the Italian prime minister Crispi introduced a law which partly met the demands of the abolitionists; this dispensed with the *case chiuse*, but allowed the police to continue their registering and surveillance tactics; and by 1891 they had won back their original powers to register all prostitute women, including the clandestines. Once again the police response to the decline of the closed brothel system was to switch their attention to the more open aspects of the sex industry and thus continue their regulationist policies in a covert form. The arrival of a 'white slavery' panic in Italy in the early 20th century allowed them further to extend their surveillance of working-class sexual culture: they began to harass all foreign prostitutes and deter them from entering the country's ports; they spied on hotels, employment agencies, theatres, dance companies – any establishment, in fact, which might attract young unemployed women.

Some gains were made on the health front, however. The Crispi law had closed the coercive prison-hospitals for whores and replaced them with open dispensaries that offered free treatment for sexually transmitted diseases to all. This to some extent helped counter the whore-stigma – even if the actual medical treatments were still far from efficacious. Italy was to follow this strange hybrid of police neoregulation and apparent medical liberalism until the 1920s, when Mussolini reintroduced strict regulation policies.

The situation in Germany was, if anything, even more confusing. With the unification of Germany between 1866 and 1871, an Imperial Criminal Code came into force across the whole country. It contained several contradictory clauses which allowed police to register whores but also provided for the prosecution of brothel-keepers and procurers – thus implying the end of the systems of toleration run by German city authorities for so long. State-run brothels were subsequently closed in Hanover (1866), Frankfurt am Main (1867), Dortmund (1873) and Cologne (1880). But in many cities the police clung tenaciously to their old, powerful system: in Kiel, for instance, the red-light streets were closed in 1876, then surreptitiously reopened only three years later, when the heat was off. Meanwhile in Bremen, Altona and Hamburg, where brothels were directly supervised by the police, it was business as usual, in spite of a ruling in the imperial legislature of 1876 which demanded closures.

The result was a bureaucrat's nightmare: a patchwork affair in which tolerated brothels and red-light districts were closed down in some cities, and left in operation in others. Regulation, however, was little more than irrelevant at a time when the German sex industry was in a state of boom which the authorities could not even pretend to control. By the 1880s, as in other countries, the brothels were in decline, with whores constantly changing address or disappearing from the registers – while the growth of the entertainments industry during the Naughty Nineties provided them with new territories to conquer. Cheap concert halls, *Wiener Cafés, Cafés Chantants* and *Bierkeller* attracted hordes of prostitutes and their clients, and a thriving sub-culture developed, in which bourgeois sexual norms were overthrown. Sexual experimentation – hetero- and homosexual – was the vogue, especially in Berlin; its vice squad was notoriously lax and the city gained a reputation as world centre of homosexual prostitution. Abraham Flexner, writing in the early 20th century, reported that in the main streets of the city:

> Bars exist to which only women resort, as well as bars to which no woman gets access; and at intervals, large homosexual balls are given, attended only by persons of a single sex. I witnessed one such affair, at which some 150 couples, all men, appeared. It is estimated that between 1000 and 2000 male prostitutes live in Berlin; forty homosexual resorts are tolerated by the Berlin police; and it is reported that some 30,000 persons of marked homosexual inclination reside in the German capital.[32]

By the time Flexner was writing, the regulation system was dead; as one whore remarked to him: 'Only the stupid are inscribed.'[33]

In fact the German experience was similar to that of other Western countries: rapid economic development and urbanization led to widespread prostitution and noisy public debates around the issue; but here, the political left and right never managed to unite and form a unified social purity movement. On the right, the male Morality Associations and the female Association for the Protection of Young Persons (who, incidentally, regarded all whores as 'instruments of the devil')[34] pressed for total repression of the sex industry; on the left, Butlerite-tendency feminists opposed prostitution as 'female sexual slavery', and campaigned against regulation. Also to the left, the Marxist Social Democratic Party held up prostitution to symbolize all that was rotten in capitalist society, proclaiming that the evil would disappear with the triumph of the socialist revolution. In short, all who had a hand in the debate manipulated prostitution as a symbol to serve their own ideological interests – and the realities of whores' lives were, as usual, simply bypassed.

In Germany, then, up until the First World War, a stalemate persisted in which remnants of the regulation system survived as islands in a sea of uncontrolled prostitution. The government policy of brothel closures followed a Continent-wide trend towards deregulation from the 1890s onwards: between 1890 and 1914 Norway, Denmark, Finland, Spain, Bulgaria and Holland all put down brothels; none of these countries made any provision for the women they had thrown on to the streets. Throughout the Western world, the whore was scapegoated by decent society: vilified, victimized, and ostracized even in her own working-class culture. This, then, was the moralists' victory: the creation of a sub-class of outcast females. In 1912 a bemused Sylvia Pankhurst, the pioneer suffragist, remarked: 'It is a strange thing that the latest Criminal Amendment Act, which was passed ostensibly to protect women, is being used almost exclusively to punish women.'[35] But her concern came too late in the day for the thousands of women whose lives had been devastated by the reform movements.

CHAPTER FOURTEEN

Prostitution in a Free Society: the 20th Century

Ultimately I have come to understand the legal treatment of prostitution is only a farce . . . Since no one
takes it seriously the entire legal aspect of prostitution is
just bullshit, based on nothing but some kind of
out-of-nowhere sense that they just must get this show
into production over and over again, not because it
matters or because it'll change anything or because
anyone believes there is anything wrong with it at all –
but because it is essential to keep up appearances.

'L', an American legal counsel[1]

In the years between 1900 and 1950 the story of the sex trade is mostly
a reprise of themes thrown up during the previous century; although
some new developments arose around the time of the Second World
War. Luckily for whores – bearing in mind the intense agitation
against the 'Social Evil' of prostitution at the turn of the century – once
the First World War was ended, the spotlight of public concern moved
elsewhere, mainly because the issue was simply exhausted. After
more than half a century of campaigns and counter-campaigns, there
appeared to be little more that could be said or done, and straight
society was weary of the topic.

The social-purist stereotypes of the sex industry and its workers had
been firmly anchored within the public consciousness, but the previous
level of activism could not be sustained. Moreover, there were many
more pressing issues to attend to: prostitution was to take a back seat to
the First World War, the Russian Revolution, the Great Depression, the
rise of fascism, the Spanish Civil War, and finally the arrival of a second,
even more devastating global conflict. Amid all this, the public had little
time to devote to the rights and wrongs of the sex industry.

The moral landscape also changed quite considerably after 1918. The barbarity of the war severely undermined the moral legitimacy of bourgeois ideology, and in the wake of the conflict, young people were less prepared to follow the rules laid down by preceding generations. In the 'Roaring Twenties', sexual experimentation became high fashion among the affluent classes – with the proviso that the young would settle into proper married couples after having had their fling. The newly popularized Freudianism legitimized the existence of sexuality (albeit disturbed) for the female half of the population, and as a result, the prevailing moral attitudes relaxed a little. Nevertheless, the whore-stigma and the division of women into good girls/bad girls remained unchallenged – indeed Freudianism provided yet another 'scientific' means of rationalizing whores' 'deviance'. And the repressive laws and systems which had grown out of social purity were left intact, in spite of the veneer of liberalism.

There were also major changes in the world of women's work during the inter-war years. The mechanization of agriculture up-rooted thousands of women from the land – they made the classic exodus to the cities to find work – and old industries such as the textile trade gave way to the mind-numbing unskilled work of the assembly line. Consumer production and mass distribution expanded, provid-ing jobs for women in shops and bottom-of-the-scale clerical work: hundreds and thousands of women left the dead end of domestic service for these new opportunities. At the same time there were timid signs of the beginnings of a welfare state, as Western governments, terrified by the spectre of Bolshevism, began to grant their workers minimal benefits and social services which in turn created a range of 'helping professions'. Middle-class women were prominent in the social service sector; thus in some ways the period was a success for them – they finally managed to throw off the shackles of housebound labour that had been their lot up to the Great War. However, for the vast majority of working women, nothing much had changed: they still suffered from low pay and terrible conditions – the perennial reasons which led to prostitution.

The Depression hit women particularly hard – although the usual image we are given of those years is that of men queuing or hanging dejectedly around the streets. Many thousands more women were forced into the sex industry: and conditions were grim. They were worse still for whores who worked under the totalitarian regimes of the thirties – Hitler's Germany and Stalin's Russia being the most obvious examples – for these were uniformly reactionary in their sexual politics, and singled out prostitutes for particular victimization. Finally, with the militarization of society in the Second World War, the authorities in Allied countries became sternly repressive of the sex trade. For whores this was truly, in Victor Serge's phrase, 'midnight in the century'.

During the First World War, the power of the military gave authoritarians of all nations *carte blanche* to impose their pet solutions on the prostitution 'problem'. In France and Germany, regulated brothels sprang up overnight, to cater to the 'rest and recreation' needs of the troops. The English poet Robert Graves saw 150 men queuing for the services of just three resident whores at the house in Béthune, northern France. These regulation brothels appear to have been run along similar lines to the slave-brothels of ancient Rome – except that the whores who worked in France were technically free, and could retire on their earnings after three weeks' duty, 'pale, but proud', as one officer told Graves.

Meanwhile, women flocked to Paris to capitalize on the thousands of men on leave there; arrests for 'clandé' prostitution soared by 40 per cent at this time. In England, feminist social purists were allowed by the authorities to set up special women's patrols, just to make sure there was no hanky-panky going on. The duties of these uniformed women police were to 'influence, and, if need be, restrain the behaviour of women and girls who congregate in the neighbourhood of [army] camps . . . to safeguard our girls from the result of unnatural excitement produced by the abnormal conditions now prevailing,' and to reprimand girls who had been 'speaking to men on duty or behaving unsuitably.'[2]

The social-purist police also enforced curfews *for women*, and had powers to search women's houses to flush out enlisted men and put a stop to private drinks parties.

In the USA, militarization allowed the authorities to set the seal on the anti-prostitution efforts of the 'Progressive Era': by 1917, every important red-light district had been closed down, including the hitherto untouchable Storyville, which was closed in 1917 by order of the nearby naval base. By the following year the repression was complete, with prostitution itself now illegal in nearly every state in the union.

As could be expected, one of the most devastating effects of this repression was the takeover of the sex trade by the criminal underworld, both big and small-time. By the mid-1920s prostitution had fallen under the control of the syndicates in most American cities. The prohibition of alcohol in 1919 had vastly expanded the power of these men at a single stroke; gang-run speakeasies where illegal liquor was sold – many with rooms for whores to work from – flourished in New York, Boston, Philadelphia, Pittsburgh, Los Angeles and San Francisco. Those brothels which had been lucky enough to survive the Progressive Era – mostly high-class houses with high-class connections – now had to face the depredations of the protection racket.

'If the take was a thousand dollars for a particular night,' recalled the wealthy Detroit madam Helen McGowan, 'five hundred went to the rackets boys, four hundred to the girls and one hundred to me . . . The great bulk of our funds went to hoodlums and lawyers, thanks to our righteous laws that "protect" the public against the oldest profession.'[3]

The gangsters also ran their own brothels: 'Motzie' Di Nicola was making around $2,500,000 a year from his ring of Connecticut 'vice resorts', while Al Capone raked in millions of dollars from a chain of 'hotels' that stretched from Chicago to Seattle. One of his Chicago houses – the largest brothel in the entire US at the time – was the aptly-named Speedway Inn:

> After passing a bar and a cigar franchise, the customer came to a turnstile where, having paid from $2 to $5, he was handed a towel and soap. Upstairs, he was assigned to one of the fifty prostitutes who each had a small room. Having had his pleasure, he left by a second staircase so as not to hold up the traffic. Each girl's output was periodically evaluated, and those who didn't achieve a satisfactory turnover were replaced.[4]

Whores had rarely known so little power in their work sphere; and everywhere in the US they risked being 'slashed' or murdered if they refused to hand over the biggest part of their earnings to the mobsters. It was mainly due to the courage of one prostitute, Renée Gallo, that the Mafia stranglehold on the New York sex industry was finally broken. The young woman testified against Mafia boss 'Lucky' Luciano, telling the court that out of a gross weekly average of $260 she took home precisely $13. Her story was backed up by those of other whores called by the prosecution, landing Luciano a 30–50-year sentence for compulsory prostitution.

The inter-war years in the States also saw innovations that were designed to get round the illegality of the trade, some of which were to become permanent fixtures on the scene. Whores began to operate in cars – usually taxis at this stage, although a few women did cruise for trade in their own automobiles. In the thirties the mobs opened 'juke joints' – roadhouses with jukeboxes, pinball machines and whores, operating outside the city limits on the southeastern highways. The waitresses doubled as prostitutes, working from cabins near the main buildings. Some cities featured 'cigar stores' as fronts for syndicate-run brothels, and in 'private dance studios', female 'instructors' performed naked for their 'students' before offering sexual services. Massage parlours became a popular means of evading the law, and in California and New York, the first escort and callgirl agencies were set up.

But regardless of the ploys it invented to circumvent the law, the American sex industry could not have survived without the connivance of the authorities; and, just as in pre-prohibition days the police and politicians had colluded with other profiteers to exploit the trade, they now milked it alongside the underworld gangs. In Chicago, Mayor William Hal Thompson represented the combined interests of both the establishment and the syndicates – indeed the latter had so much to gain from his re-election in 1927 that they contributed five million dollars to his campaign fund. The following year, with Thompson safely back in office, the 2000 sex industry outlets in the city were paying between $100 and $750 a week in protection fees – to the police. Any that failed to pay up were raided and closed down, in the name of law and order. In effect the authorities and the syndicates were running parallel protection rackets; to the extent that the former quickly became a greater problem than the latter. When Judge Seabury conducted his investigation into the New York sex trade in 1929, it was the law that came under attack. Polly Adler, celebrated proprietor of one of the city's most luxurious brothels at the time, wrote:

Personally, I had nothing to fear from Judge Seabury. This time the heat was on the law givers and the law enforcers. Investigators knew I had entertained many members of the magistrates' court and vice squad and numerous other city officials and . . . I had paid thousands of dollars in bribes to keep my house running smoothly and my girls and me out of jail.[5]

Seabury's investigation subsequently uncovered 'a blackmailing ring of stool-pigeons, corrupt policemen, crooked judges, bondsmen and lawyers [who] were extorting money from women accused of prostitution.'[6]

The odd high-level clean-up notwithstanding, by 1933, when the prohibition of alcohol was repealed, the dual exploitation by criminals both legal and illegal was a firmly entrenched feature of the sex trade, and a typical up-market brothel would still be paying more than $600 a week to the city police out of weekly takings of $5000.

The thirties are famous as the decade of the slump; and in the gang-run brothels of the United States, whores found themselves put on short time, just like so many other workers – they were permitted to work only three days a week by their bosses. At the same time, the worsening poverty of the lower classes was pushing more and more women into the sex market, both in America and in Britain. In 1933 the British working-class writer Walter Greenwood published *Love on the Dole*, a novel in which the young daughter of a Manchester mill-working family, Sally Hardcastle, prostitutes herself to a wealthy and influential bookie who in return pulls a few strings at the town hall to get her father and brother jobs. Another British 'proletarian' novel of the time, Simon Blumenfeld's *Jew Boy* (1935) features a young woman who gives up work as a servant to become a whore in London's West End:

> 'It's not so terrible,' she said. 'Really, I'm lots better off than I was before. When I was in service, the master would always be after me, or if it wasn't the master, there was sure to be a son . . . And they expected all that thrown in buckshee, with scrubbing the house, and clearing out the slops. And I couldn't say anything, or I'd lose my job. Now if I have to do that, I get paid for it, and at least I get SOME time for myself.'[7]

Sally's words have more than a ring of truth to them, 'all that' being a euphemism for the sexual harassment many working women had to put up with – and still have to – in straight jobs. Leaving that aside, it is striking that, in focusing on prostitution as a viable – if last-ditch – option for working-class women in the thirties, these working-class male writers take a pragmatic and sympathetic view of their prostitute characters, unlike the middle-class male writers of the previous century, who invariably condemned their prostitute heroines to a grisly death – on moral grounds.

The Depression also produced a new peak in the migration of whores fleeing poverty and oppression in their home countries; many were Jews escaping from the pogroms of Eastern Europe. After the disruption of international travel caused by the First World War, the routes and networks used by migrating prostitutes were re-established during the twenties. It was no coincidence, then, that around this time, the new international watchdog the League of Nations, created in 1919, began to express interest in the sex trade, carrying out investigations and passing interminable resolutions which echoed 19th-century positions on the issue. The League in fact continued the tradition of Josephine Butler's International Abolitionist Federation, in its condemnation of both 'white slavery' and government regulation of prostitution. But the issue no longer had the power to stir up the populace or the authorities: in the thirties, with the slump, the rise of Nazism, and the world on the brink of a new world war, the minds of both governments and peoples were elsewhere. The 'white slave' myth remained a minor theme of popular melodrama, surfacing in many lurid films, for instance; but it had already done its worst in the hearts and minds of the people. No new legislation was passed and there were no new anti-prostitution campaigns: social purity had had its day.

Which brings us to the ostensibly new approaches to prostitution put into effect in the totalitarian states that emerged in Europe during the 1930s, the two most prominent and powerful of which were Soviet Russia and Nazi Germany. The young USSR had abolished the old tolerated brothels of the Tsarist regime, but in the chaos of the years immediately following the 1917 revolution, prostitution was not a major concern. The 1920s, however, saw a sexual revolution in Russia, and when the New Economic Policy of the early twenties allowed the partial re-emergence of the market economy, prostitution once again became visible.

The Party magazine *Izvestiya* showed its solidarity with the moral tradition of the European middle classes when it reported in 1922 that: 'The tide of prostitution, which disintegrates social life, is rising.'[8]

The response of the Soviet authorities was predictable: they set up *prophylactoria*, in which whores were forcibly detained, put to sweated labour, and 're-educated in a proletarian spirit'[9] after which the young women were sent into factories, 'to introduce them into working life'. Thus Soviet Russia caught up with 18th-century England, creating rehabilitation institutions which might have been modelled on Sir

John Fielding's moral sweatshops – with proletarian piety to replace the Christian version.

Worse was to come. When Stalin tightened his grip on the USSR from the late twenties onwards, bringing into being the totalitarian dinosaur-state which was to endure for nearly sixty years, the sexual-political agenda shifted from libertarianism to the reconstruction of the family. Prostitution – a vice of degenerate capitalist societies which could never exist in the socialist utopia – was abolished overnight: the great leader decreed that it had vanished along with the bad old days of capitalism.

In reality, of course, the sex trade was alive and kicking, in a clandestine environment; men continued to require sex, poor women continued to sell it – and there were always private brothels for the privileged members of the Soviet bureaucracy. But, as in post-revolutionary France, legislation on prostitution disappeared, leaving whores once again subject to the arbitrary rule of the police. In practice this meant that they could be picked up for conveniently vague crimes such as 'parasitism' – and packed off to the labour camps of the gulag, where many of them died alongside other victims of the self-styled 'most democratic nation in the world'.

In the fascist states the approach was more conservative: Mussolini issued legislation confirming the regulated brothels in 1923, 1931 and 1940, and the Nazi Party reintroduced them in Germany as soon as it came to power in 1933. Needless to say, this did not make the life of a whore any easier under Hitler than under Stalin. Nazi sexual politics were hysterically patriarchal, based on the fetish of motherhood and the whore-stigma; clandestine prostitutes were branded with black stars on their clothes and sent to the concentration camps. Whores were among the first female inmates of Auschwitz: 'These women were issued evening gowns in which they were forced to help build Auschwitz in rain or snow. Of the hundreds, only a handful survived.'[10]

In fact Nazism and totalitarianism were as much a tragedy for sex workers as for all the other stigmatized and minority groups; but history has, as usual, overlooked them. Little is known about the lives of whores during the Second World War; nothing has been written about them. There are a few hints, here and there, that many of the best safe-houses for European Resistance fighters were brothels, and that many of the most daring Resistance members were themselves prostitutes. In her biography of the legendary French singer Edith

Piaf, Simone Berteaut, who was close to her during the years of occupied Paris, recounts how she and Edith lived at one stage in a brothel where whores entertained senior Gestapo officers – and 'clients' from the French Resistance. In fact Piaf's friend and secretary Andrée Bigeard started working ostensibly as a prostitute in the brothel:

> At first Edith was amused, 'Good lord, the place has gone to Andrée's head. She has an awful lot of men, I'd never have thought it of her.'
> Later we learned that she was using her place in the heart of enemy territory to do Resistance work, and that the 'clients' who came to see her were 'terrorists', as the Germans called them.[11]

Better documented than this type of anecdotal incident is the process by which the US authorities once again used war as a pretext for clamping down on the sex industry, closing the brothels that had spread across the States in the inter-war years. As men went away to fight, and women entered the industrial labour force, earning relatively good money and raising the ominous spectre of working-class women's liberation from the low pay/no pay ghetto, the men in power succumbed to an attack of moral panic. Whores were scapegoated, punished with the traditional state-sponsored sexual repression: the authorities empowered health and police officials to arrest any woman they defined as a 'sexual delinquent', and subject her to VD examinations. In the period 1940–44 there was a 95 per cent increase in the number of women charged with morals offences, mostly whores but often so-called promiscuous women. Thousands of women – very few of whom actually had VD – spent four or five days in jail waiting for the results of their examinations; during which time they were 'counselled' by social workers in an attempt to make them give up their evil ways.

By the middle of the 20th century, then, the life of a whore was as difficult and dangerous as it had ever been, whether she lived in Hitler's Germany, Stalin's Russia – or the 'Land of the Free'. But the Western world was on the brink of another revolution: the 'sexual revolution' of the 1960s.

The shocks and crises which shook the world during the inter-war years were the birth pangs of a new mass society, the prospect of which had so disturbed the Victorian middle classes. From 1917 on, various political and economic models, from mass democracy to fascism and authoritarian socialism, competed fiercely and bloodily for leadership of this emerging modern world; until by the end of the Second World War a stalemate had been reached. The threat of fascism had been defeated, and while in the West the Americanization of society got under way in earnest, the Cold War froze central and eastern Europe in the grip of totalitarian Communism: the map of contemporary society was fixed for the next 45 years.

West of the Iron Curtain, the post-war period saw the triumphant expansion of the consumer economy, with the mass production of consumer items from cars and washing machines to Levi jeans and pop records. Consumerism spread the benefits of technology to the masses, but – paradoxically – the members of those masses now had to work as hard as ever in order to afford these one-time luxuries. Thus larger numbers of married women now joined their single sisters in the workforce, both in production and in new forms of distribution (such as supermarkets), until by the 1980s working women in the USA and western Europe made up around 40 per cent of the total labour force.

The post-war economy offered work for women, then; but for the great majority it remained unskilled, low-paid, and often part-time work which did little to raise women's self-esteem – or their standards of living, for that matter. The availability of jobs, especially in the boom years of the sixties, reduced the numbers of women entering the sex industry to some extent – although prostitution still remained the only occupation in which women could earn more than a man's wage and at the same time have some measure of control over their working hours and conditions. Particularly for working-class women bringing up children on their own, prostitution was the only kind of work through which they could raise themselves out of the poverty trap, and give their children the kind of living standards that the brave new world of television advertising presented as the norm.

Culturally, consumerism introduced an interesting new contradiction. The process had already begun in the 1920s, with the moral relaxation of that experimental decade; now, after a grey period of reconstruction during the fifties, traditional bourgeois morality again found itself under attack. To maintain the dynamic of the consumer society it was everyone's duty to consume as well as to produce; hedonism therefore became *de rigueur*, co-existing uneasily with the old work ethic. In part this was what created the generation gap – the clash between the old values of work and thrift, and the new ones that emphasized pleasure and spending: more importantly, these new values were incorporated into the sexual revolution of the swinging sixties.

For while the work ethic – the favoured doctrine of the bourgeoisie from the 16th century onwards – depended on the tight reining-in of sexuality, the consumer ethic revolved around putting sexuality on display, actively promoting it – in other words, selling it as the archetypal form of enjoyment with which the glamour of consumer goods was (and is) associated. The contradiction can best be seen in the advertising media, where the idolatry of motherhood and the family rubs shoulders with the commercialization (another euphemism for selling) of women's bodies. Sex became a product – especially after the advent of the contraceptive pill, which allowed more of it to happen. Businessmen and admen cashed in, and continue to do so to this day.

With advertising showing women soliciting sexual attention, and with millions of young women discovering their sexual independence – both activities hitherto reserved for prostitutes and film stars – the whore/virgin dichotomy was seriously undermined, and the whore-stigma came out of the closet, to become visible and subject to debate and criticism.

It might seem logical that our society, passing through its most radical period of moral relaxation for centuries, would become more tolerant of the prostitute – but in many ways the opposite has happened. Whores have always been under the jurisdiction of the most repressive and reactionary sections of society (police, politicians, and the legal system), and in recent decades it has been precisely these people who have been the most panicked by the disintegration of the traditional middle-class moral universe. Thus, threatened by the new sexual freedoms and with a militant moral backlash behind them, the authorities have kept up a running battle against the liberalization of the sex industry. The hypocrisy this has involved was probably best epitomized by the Keeler/Profumo scandal, which rocked the British political establishment in the early sixties.

In 1963, rumours began to circulate about a liaison between John Profumo, Tory minister for war, and a London 'show-girl', Christine Keeler. This was bad enough in itself; however, the security services were alarmed at further stories which suggested that Christine was also sleeping with an attaché from the Soviet embassy, rumoured (as were most Russians at the time) to be a KGB agent. In mid-1963 Profumo resigned, writing to the Prime Minister Harold Macmillan: 'I said there had been no impropriety in this association. To my very deep regret I have to admit that this was not true, and that I misled you.'[12]

Far from being abated, the rumours grew wilder still, with allegations of sex orgies in various country houses and at smart London addresses:

> To these were added other stories about a party in Bayswater, attended by Keeler, [Mandy] Rice-Davies and [Stephen] Ward, at which a cabinet minister had served a dinner of roast peacock while wearing nothing except a mask and a bow tie . . . the man also had a card round his neck . . . 'If my services don't please you, whip me.' Still more rumours mentioned an orgy involving eight high court judges. 'One perhaps,' groaned Harold Macmillan to a colleague, 'two, just conceivably. But eight – I just can't believe it.'[13]

Unfortunately, the British public did.

Later that year Lord Denning issued a report on the Profumo affair; it was an overnight bestseller, with hundreds of men queuing outside HM Stationery Office at midnight to get hold of an early copy. Meanwhile, the establishment had its scapegoat, in the form of Dr Stephen Ward, who was charged with 'living off immoral earnings' – pimping. 'The public furore became even greater when Stephen Ward was convicted . . . Other than a few vague insinuations from the prosecution, no evidence had been produced to show that Ward was a pimp. He committed suicide after the verdict was announced.'[14]

In fact Stephen Ward, who had introduced Keeler to Profumo, was probably providing a go-between service, but since all who were involved were consenting adults there was absolutely no justification for hounding and criminalizing the man to the point where he took his own life. If anything, this was the most sordid aspect of the Profumo affair – the crude and hypocritical behaviour of a political establishment which was squirming to get off the hook. In any case, it failed dismally: by the following year, Harold Wilson and the Labour Party were in power.

The immediate post-war atmosphere was far removed from the moral detente of the 1960s, however. Women had been prominent in the war effort, both in taking men's places in industry and in fighting in Resistance movements; they emerged strengthened from the war – and this to Western governments was a threat that had to be contained at all costs. Women in industry suddenly found themselves being prised out of their jobs, expected to revert to full-time domesticity, and the sentimental cult of bourgeois sex roles was re-established. This did not, of course, augur well for whores; and sure enough, the late forties and fifties saw new legislation being passed which would make life as difficult as possible for them.

Ironically it was a woman, the French war heroine Marthe Richard, who in 1946 made the first move in the anti-prostitute cold war. Between the wars France, home of the *maisons closes*, had clung to the neoregulationist policies which had allowed various kinds of houses to be unofficially tolerated by the police; the Richard law ostensibly aimed to put an end to this system once and for all, and thus rid French society of the scourge of the regulated brothel. Unfortunately it did not stop there: it also outlawed street prostitution (notably soliciting) and the advertising of sexual services. This made it impossible for a whore to work without running into trouble – even though the law hypocritically made prostitution itself legal. To demonstrate the absurdity of Richard's law, we need only apply it to, say, a shopkeeper. He could legitimately be in the retail trade, and neither he nor his customers would be committing any crime by engaging in commerce; but if he tried to open a shop, or peddled his goods to passers-by, or simply advertised them, he would be prosecuted. In fact the real thrust of the new law lay in the criminalization of prostitutes' visibility; for in the post-war context of pushing women back into the home, it became once again 'obscene' (a Greek word meaning something which should occur off-stage) for whores to be seen or heard.

Indeed, the 1946 law did not even go so far as to abolish police registration of prostitutes: and this is still the situation to this day. French prostitutes remain subject to the same kind of arbitrary police rule that has always existed in France, and the police still require them to register and carry health cards. Worse, the quasi-legal safeguard of the protected house no longer exists, and French whores cannot practise their trade without risking legal penalties. In sum, the French post-war system combines the disadvantages of illegality with those of registration, in that it tends to fix the prostitute permanently in that role, even if she herself wants to get out of the life. As one woman who had been forcibly registered told the French journalist Claude Jaget in 1975: 'For me, that was it. I was booked, registered as a whore. I was a whore and that was that. I really think that it's because I was put on file that I became a prostitute . . . I'd decided to go back to my parents; I didn't think I was cut out for that job . . . Once I'd been booked, all that was over.'[15]

Once registered on police files, not only is it difficult to get off, it is also next to impossible to find another job; word soon gets round to prospective employers that the applicant is a 'known prostitute', in the legal phrase. In this way, whores are put in precisely the position the French establishment wants them in: prone – to control and exploitation. For once the *maisons closes* were finally shut down, a lucrative source of income was lost to the state; it is for this reason that the practice of clawing back the lost revenues in the form of fines has become a major part of the sex industry. By the mid-1970s, whores in the second largest French city, Lyons, were being fined as often as four times *a day*, often by just a wave of a cop's hand from a passing car. The only way for the women to pay off their fines and avoid imprisonment was by going straight back on to the streets to earn the money – thereby risking further fines.

Not satisfied with this, the French political class periodically renews the call for the *maisons closes* to be reopened – in 1990 Michèle Barzach, Conservative ex-minister of health in the Chirac government, resurrected 19th-century ideas by proposing the *maisons* as a solution to the AIDS crisis.

In Italy, a similar law was sponsored – again by a female politician, the socialist senator Lina Merlin – in 1958. Taking the same kind of abolitionist stance as Marthe Richard, Merlin closed the brothels and criminalized soliciting and advertising; she also introduced severe penalties for procurers or 'anyone who in any way favours or profits from the prostitution of another'. As ever slightly more enlightened than their French counterparts, the Italian authorities banned all forms of registration and even went so far as to legislate in favour of special reformatories for women who wanted to get out of the life, and a special female police squad to work with whores – although neither of these two schemes had been put into operation by 1990, a mere 32 years later.

As could be expected, the Merlin law has had effects similar to the French version. The criminalization of soliciting means that the police have the power to stop prostitutes on the street or in their cars at any time; the women can have their driving licences confiscated, are frequently banned from public places, and even in some cases sent back to their city of birth. Since 1958 the police have also made liberal use of the clause concerning those who 'favour' prostitution to arrest landlords, husbands and boyfriends of prostitutes, not to mention whores who share the same apartment (they are defined as 'favouring' each other's prostitution). Again as in France, every aspect of the women's trade is criminalized whilst the act of prostitution itself is hypocritically defined in law as being perfectly legitimate. And, needless to say, in neither country are the 'procuring' or 'favouring' laws applied to the greatest profiteers from prostitution of all – the states of France and Italy.

The same drive to turn back the gains made by women during the war inspired the British government's legislation in the 1950s. By this time the British economy was beginning to pick up again, and prostitution once more became highly conspicuous on the streets. Although the police could fine whores for 'disorderly, riotous or indecent behaviour'[16], neither prostitution nor soliciting was illegal – a situation the government decided it could not tolerate. A comprehensive schedule of legal action was set in motion: in 1954 the Wolfenden Committee was appointed, its brief being to report on the sex trade; in 1956 the Sexual Offences Act was passed, and in 1959, following the recommendations of Wolfenden, the notorious Street Offences Act became law.

Under this Act a woman could now be convicted of soliciting on the 'uncorroborated word of a single policeman';[17] the term 'soliciting' covering 'not only spoken words but also various movements of the face, body and limbs such as a smile, a wink, making a gesture and beckoning or wriggling the body in a way that indicates an invitation to prostitution.'[18]

This definition – broad enough to include any manifestation of public sexual behaviour on the part of women – capped the long struggle of the state (dating at least as far back as the 18th century) to control women's freedom of sexual expression. Since 1959 the unspoken but all-pervasive threat has hung over all women who venture into the streets of Britain at night – that if they don't watch their appearance and behaviour carefully, they can be arrested on a charge of soliciting simply on the word of the police. As the English Collective of Prostitutes have observed:

Prostitution laws are not only about prostitutes. They keep all women under control. At any time, any woman can be called a whore and treated like one. Each woman has to watch in her own life whether what she's doing is 'good' or 'bad', to censor her movements, behaviour and appearance.[19]

The Street Offences Act effectively introduced an underhand form of police registration, since after two cautions for soliciting, a woman could now be labelled 'common prostitute'. The woman is thereby branded for life and, if she appears in court, the term is read out as the first item of 'evidence' against her before the trial even begins, whether or not the woman is still working in the sex trade and *even if she has no previous convictions for prostitution*. This is a startling anomaly in the legal system: even convicted rapists and murderers do not have previous records read out in court before being tried. In rape and child custody cases, too, this offensive and infantile legal smear is read out and is obviously prejudicial to the outcome of a woman's case.

Like the French and Italian legislation, the English Act decreed that prostitution itself remained legal while surrounding it with conditions of illegality. Where the Street Offences Act criminalized street prostitution, the Sexual Offences Act of 1956 dealt with 'brothel-keeping' and 'living off immoral earnings'. This Act defined a brothel as 'a house resorted to or used by more than one woman for the purposes of fornication' – a nice, biblical turn of phrase; also a conveniently vague and broad definition that has since allowed the state to prosecute whores who work from shared flats, or even non-prostitute women who live together and admit more than the regulation number of boyfriends to their beds. The Sexual Offences Act also makes all men who associate with whores, be they boyfriends, husbands, sons, friends or family, liable to prosecution for 'knowingly living on the earnings of prostitution'. The law states that 'a man who lives with or is habitually in the company of a prostitute, or who exercises control, direction or influence over a prostitute's movements in a way which shows he is aiding, abetting or compelling her prostitution with others, shall be presumed to be knowingly living on the earnings of prostitution, unless he proves the contrary.'

Thus whores are prevented from plying their trade, living together, and associating with any other human beings apart from their clients – even women friends can be charged with controlling prostitutes: 'A

72-year-old woman was imprisoned for six months in 1979 because she was frequently visited by a friend who was a prostitute.'[20]

In 1985 the Thatcher government brought in new legislation against kerb-crawling, a move that was given a great deal of support by anti-pornography and anti-prostitution feminists in Britain. This law was supposed to represent 'equality' between the whore and the client; now he too could be arrested. As Nina Lopez-Jones of the English Collective of Prostitutes commented at the time: 'That's like lowering men's wages to make them equal to women's.'

In fact the kerb-crawling law, widely promoted as a measure to increase the safety of women on the streets, did no such thing:

> . . . [it] further increased police powers against prostitute women and black and other working-class women and men. Prostitute women are always the first to be arrested, and now any man police choose can be arrested and convicted for kerb-crawling on police evidence alone.[21]

And as prostitutes' campaigner and writer Eileen McLeod notes:

> Any behaviour which causes public nuisance can be dealt with by section 5 of the Public Order Act (1936). This makes it an offence to use 'threatening, abusive or insulting words or behaviour whereby a breach of the peace is likely to be occasioned.'[22]

The fact is that women's safety on the street – or anywhere else for that matter – has hardly been seen to be of great priority to the forces of law and order, as any glance at the rape statistics will show. The kerb-crawling law, then, is another blatant attack on the prostitute's right to work, and should be acknowledged as such.

In the USA, meanwhile, prostitution is still entirely illegal, as is anything connected with it. This does not of course mean that the sex trade no longer exists; far from it. The immediate post-Second World War period had seen a boom in prostitution as the country was demilitarized, but – again – from the 1950s onwards legislation was tightened across the States, with the police under orders to crack down on whores. However, any action taken by the police has tended to be largely cosmetic, due to their fear of losing the huge profits they have reaped from prostitution over the years – especially since the war, after the gangs had progressively deserted the sex trade for more lucrative rackets such as narcotics and property speculation. Since the 1950s the sex trade has been allowed to exist in 'tenderloin' districts – usually inner-city areas of the transient poor – which are only occasionally 'cleaned up' during an election campaign or when a change of bosses at city hall necessitates a face-lift. Predictably, the trade soon re-establishes itself in another neighbourhood, and the various players of this futile and costly game return to square one.

When taking advantage of the illegality of prostitution to enhance their arrest statistics and earn money for the state in fines, the US police indulge in some distinctly squalid practices. One favoured method of bringing in a hooker is 'entrapment' – and it is not unknown for a cop to have sex with his potential victim before showing her his badge:

> He seemed all right but I guess I should have known better. He was kind of nervous. He looked around a lot and never looked me in the eye. Afterwards, before he even dressed, he took out his ID and told me I was under arrest. The bastard. He knows he doesn't have to screw me to have a case. When I took his money, that was enough. I hate that son-of-a-bitch. [23]

Sometimes the police go to extreme and outrageous lengths in order to persecute women, as this account by American whores' activist Priscilla Alexander makes clear:

> The police in . . . Washington set up a phony escort service . . . they placed ads in the paper recruiting employees and customers. The ads to recruit prostitutes merely offered a high-paying job. Women who answered the ads – many of whom had never worked as prostitutes before – were asked if they would be willing to engage in prostitution. When they agreed, they were arrested.

The case was subsequently thrown out of court:

> however, all of the women now have permanent records of a prostitution arrest and are, in fact, described as 'known prosti-tutes'. One officer . . . had sex with one of the women, justifying it in court by saying he didn't 'come'. [24]

America's finest also make free use of informers and – another popular ploy – sit around in their cars spying on streetwalkers, moving in after a hooker gets into a client's car. The ease with which officers can arrest whores means that they spend disproportionate amounts of time patrolling tenderloin districts, leaving other districts unprotected and open to real crime. Payoffs, too, are rife, in cash or kind. The sociologist Bernard Cohen, in his 1980 study of street prostitution in New York, found that the city's vice squad had selected (procured) prostitutes to service judges and politicians. One woman, who had had sex with the state legislator, remarked: 'I didn't charge; that was public relations.'[25]

The US in fact originated the fines-and-convictions treadmill which has become so popular elsewhere, with its inception early this century of the 'revolving door' policy of legal treatment, in which an arrested whore comes to court to collect her fine and goes straight back on to the street to earn the money to pay it. Long years of usage have instilled a hard core of cynicism at the heart of this system, a powerful form of corruption in itself. A woman who worked as counsel in New York's prostitute courts gives an insight into the absurdity of this assembly-line of legal rake-offs:

The actual situation in this city is that prostitution is accepted by everyone – police, judges, clerks, and lawyers. Arrest and prosecution are purely gestures that have to be made to keep up the façade of public morality. The method of dealing with it is simply a form of harassment . . . there is no conviction at any level that prostitution is a crime on anyone's part, only a total and satisfied acceptance of the double standard . . .

Ultimately I have come to understand the legal treatment of prostitution is only a farce. The court is merely a machine, processing an average of thirty women a day on loitering and prostitution charges, spitting out people like paper wads . . .

Since no one takes it seriously the entire legal aspect of prostitution is just bullshit, based on nothing but some kind of out-of-nowhere sense that they just must get this show into production over and over again, not because it matters or because it'll change anything or because anyone believes there is anything wrong with it at all – but because it is essential to keep up appearances . . . What happens to [prostitutes] matters to no one. They're no threat, but the law keeps on picking them up

. . . the whole system bleeds them sexually and economically.
They put out and they pay their fines. Public decorum is satisfied
because whores are arrested. This is the justice men bestow on
women.[26]

There is, however, one state in the Union where prostitution is
allowed to exist on a more or less legal footing, in rural counties with
fewer than 250,000 inhabitants: Nevada. Here, so-called 'sex ranches'
are permitted; these are in reality little more than functional, styleless
brothels, licensed by the county. For whores, they are akin to the
19th-century regulated brothel system; here, the 'civil servants of sex'
are photographed and fingerprinted by police before being allowed to
work; once installed, they are barred from all gambling casinos and
bars and not allowed to be seen with a man in the streets or in a
restaurant during their time off. Small wonder, then, that the vast
majority of Nevada's whores prefer to work illegally: Las Vegas, the
state's biggest city, where all prostitution is illegal, is one of America's
great centres of the trade, with thousands more women working there
than in all the 'sex ranches' put together.

Only in Northern Europe have governments developed approaches
which vary from the abolitionist-prohibitionist policies prevalent in
the West. In West Germany, a patchwork of systems not unlike those
of the 19th and early 20th centuries has been allowed to grow up; these
range from 'a tightly-controlled, single-zone brothel system in
Hamburg, to a laissez-faire, open-zone system in West Berlin'.[27]
In the late sixties the regulated brothel made a comeback in the
modernized form of the Eros Centres. These private ventures, built
with government blessing, are multi-storey, concrete, barracks-like
sex supermarkets, where management and state pimping is open for
all to see. The first opened in Hamburg in 1967; other cities soon
followed with their own – Dusseldorf, Bonn, Cologne, Stuttgart and
Munich. A French prostitute who worked in one Eros Centre
describes it from the inside:

There are about forty or fifty rooms, and every girl has her own
room. There are always about four or five girls on each landing,
and the girls just stand outside their doors, inside the building.
The clients come up and look around. So when people talk about
looking at us as though we were animals, well there they do, they

look at us like animals. Because in Eros Centres you work in a bra and panties . . . Girls who want to wear clothes, who want to wear more than little panties and a bra, can't work there. It's the boss who hires and fires the girls, so he makes the rules. Now that's real high-powered pimping, industrialized pimping.[28]

The Eros Centre worker has to hire her room from the boss at a daily rate (around £60 per day in Dusseldorf at the time of writing), so she must service several clients before even clearing her rent. The larger centres (such as Hamburg's) have accommodation for 136 women, and the management's profits are obviously considerable – not to mention the state's rake-off in taxes from the workforce. This 'enlightened' approach is not popular with the whores, however. Although in various German cities they are also allowed to work in saunas and in special streets like Herbertstrasse in the St Pauli district of Hamburg (a walled-off street devoted to the sex trade as in the Middle Ages), most German prostitutes reject the industrial regimentation these systems impose on them. As one woman comments: 'It's worse than science fiction, a society completely organised around the men who've got enough cash, and their pleasure.'[29]

The vast majority of whores continue to work outside the legal system: in the early 1970s Dusseldorf had 3200 'clandestine' to 450 'controlled' prostitutes, Bremen 1000 to 500, and West Berlin 18,000 to 4920. The Eros Centres always have plenty of vacancies.

Although the most relaxed regime in Europe is probably that of Denmark, where most of the laws restricting whores' rights to work have been repealed and new ones passed to help women who want to leave the sex trade, it is the Netherlands which has the reputation for being Europe's liberal haven for prostitutes. The laws there are now semi-abolitionist – prostitution and brothels are legal, third-party involvement is not – but the sex trade is tolerated within fairly wide limits. Dutch whores can work from their rooms, often ground-floor apartments with shop-style windows in which they are permitted to sit and entice clients; an arrangement which appeals aesthetically to male writers like Hilary Evans, who refers to Amsterdam's famous brothel quarter as 'surely the most picturesque red-light district in Europe', with its girls 'sitting in the windows of neat little rooms'.[30]

Amsterdam's brothel district has enhanced its acceptability by attracting tourists and their money from all over the world; even so, as the Dutch prostitutes' campaigning group Red Thread notes: 'Prostitution in Holland is not as accepted as is commonly believed.'[31] The toleration and 'respectabilization' of brothels serves to isolate street-walkers, for whom soliciting is still illegal; they become more vulnerable to abuse as a result; and whores of all kinds often face pressure from straight citizens to get out of their neighbourhoods, whether or not they are operating legally. Thus prostitution in the Netherlands is a regulated trade that conforms to bourgeois notions of public decency – and the whore-stigma is still enforced, both by law and by public prejudice.

Finally, since *glasnost* has opened the USSR to Western influence, it has looked increasingly likely that Soviet prostitution laws may well evolve in the Western mould. Prostitution is now officially acknowledged to exist in the USSR, although there are as yet no laws to deal with it; a situation which has prompted a lively debate on possible forms of future legislation, with lobbying for both US-style prohibition and more liberal approaches. Attitudes to the sex trade are depressingly familiar, with men in particular coming down hard on whores for failing to live down to the wife-mother roles expected of Soviet women; and the police are already using AIDS as a pretext for the idea of control through registration, supplemented by the practice of 'health monitoring'. Natasha Averina, a Soviet police captain interviewed recently in a BBC programme about prostitution in the USSR, opposed calls for the definitive criminalization of prostitution in favour of health registration and laws against pimping, procuring and brothel-keeping. Thus it seems that the most liberal position in the Soviet establishment favours the kind of legislation we have in the West; although given the state's Big Brother tradition, it seems likely that some form of regulation will be involved.

Meanwhile, Soviet prostitutes are still on the receiving end of repression, like any other group of dissidents. Although the days of the gulag are over, the women can still be prosecuted for 'parasitism', along with other offences designed specifically to punish those marginalized in Soviet society. If their trade is with foreigners, and they change their foreign-currency earnings into roubles on the black market, they can be jailed for currency speculation. The television documentary mentioned above featured a Moscow prostitute called Ella, who serviced foreign clients until she was arrested for 'speculating', and sent to prison for four years. Other whores, particularly teenagers, can find themselves incarcerated in so-called 'rehabilitation centres', which are as grim as the euphemism suggests.

Once out again, these women face exactly the same problems that pushed them into the life in the first place. For in the USSR, as in the West, women's wages are low and their options limited, despite the apparent success of the Soviet system in absorbing women into the middle reaches of the professions – 73 per cent of Soviet doctors are women, for example. In general, women are still concentrated in the lower and worst-paid sectors of all kinds of work; added to this is the curse of the double-shift: it is women who do all the housework, child-care, queuing at the shops, and so on. One Soviet prostitute told the BBC: 'It's very hard to live on your wages in this country. I realized that [prostitution] was the only possible way for me to make a normal sort of life for myself.'[32]

The problems of women in the USSR are the problems of women the world over; the Soviet male hierarchy does not even begin to address them and, *glasnost* notwithstanding, it seems unlikely that they ever will.

The panoply of legal approaches developed in the West in the course of this century may appear at first glance diverse, but in fact the *effects* of legislation have been and are similar everywhere, making the daily reality of whores one of harassment, persecution and constant fear of arrest. The laws prevent whores from working freely, penalizing the most vulnerable – streetwalkers – with particular severity, and, through provisions against 'pimps', 'brothel-keepers' and so on, criminalizing their relationships, both professional and personal. At the same time, the policing of the sex trade diverts huge amounts of resources away from areas of real, serious crime. Worst of all, the legal institutionalization of the whore-stigma promotes violent crime against prostitutes and, by extension, all women.

The ones who bear the brunt of this legal oppression are the streetwalkers. On the one hand they are the most visible of all sex workers, and a major priority of the law has always been to 'protect' people by policing public spaces where – according to the bourgeois public code – a submissive decency should prevail. On the other hand, streetwalkers are simply the easiest targets; it is a much more complex operation to raid a massage parlour or bust a callgirl network than it is to drive round the block and net a few whores walking the beat. Thus in the USA, although only 10–20 per cent of whores work on the street, those who do make up 85–90 per cent of women arrested for prostitution offences. These figures also perpetuate the classist and racist biases of Western legal institutions, since streetwalkers are the most likely of all whores to be working class and women of colour. American arrest statistics give a vivid indication of police racism at work. Sociologists Charles Winick and Paul M. Kinsie, in their 1970s survey of the US sex trade, estimate that black women are ten times more likely to be arrested for prostitution than their white sisters. On the street, Bernard Cohen found that 50 per cent of New York streetwalkers were white, 45 per cent black, and 5 per cent hispanic; nevertheless, the arrest rates for these groups ran at 58 per cent black women, 11 per cent hispanic and 31 per cent white. (The New York Police Department, incidentally, is 90 per cent white.)

Ratios of imprisonment are even more blatantly skewed against women of colour, who represent 85 per cent of prostitutes sent to jail in the USA. This criminalization of black women does not only affect the women involved, since a high proportion of them are working as prostitutes in order to support families, especially in the welfare-starved USA. This means that families of non-white whores are particularly vulnerable to being broken up and the children taken into care while the mothers go to prison.

The current systems of law and policing whores are exploitative, oppressive, classist and racist; they are also extremely expensive. Individual cities spend millions of dollars annually to combat a trade which has always existed. The situation in the UK is little different: in 1983 30% of the Wandsworth police force was tied up in dealing with prostitution, and therefore unavailable for real crime.[33] Claims that prostitution is inevitably associated with serious crime, and that the repression of whores somehow counters these criminal activities are at best dubious. Bernard Cohen found that in areas of New York where street prostitution has a high profile, real crimes such as mugging, burglaries, robbery and murder actually decreased. He comments:

> Female street prostitution is a stable, money-making enterprise. It involves a covert economy that not only nourishes itself but also feeds into the legitimate economy. Street deviance may even contribute to the economic stability of a community . . . Prostitutes, johns, and other street actors [sociologese for those involved in the sex trade] patronise hotels, parking lots, bars, pizza parlours, coffee shops and luncheonettes. The survival of an enterprise may depend on business generated by street actors. Therefore, it is in the interests of prostitutes, patrons, pimps,

passersby, proprietors and police to assure neighbourhood stability. In other words, there is a vested interest for street actors who share a common purpose to cooperate in order to exclude from an area unrelated forms of deviance and crime, especially those that might undermine the covert economy and the community's sense of security. Street crime, for instance, often results in highly visible victims and citizen complaints. These lead to police action aimed at eliminating or containing the area's illegitimate behaviour, including female street prostitution.[34]

What this passage makes clear is that the presence of women selling sex on the city streets is incompatible with serious and dangerous crime, so that neighbourhoods associated with the trade are actually safer for residents and other users. Even the police are only one factor amongst many coming together to protect the stability of the trade – and trade in general – in these areas; and even without the police all interests would still tend to combine to exclude the disruptive influence of serious crime. None of which, of course, prevents whores from being scapegoated when crime does occur.

CHAPTER FIFTEEN

Women in Danger:
Prostitution Now

Everyone's discussing what should be done for the
prostitute, what kind of laws should be made for her
. . . Are they going to do the same thing with
shopkeepers or journalists? What right have they got to
always want to make decisions for us? To protect us
from pimps! That's the excuse. From the beginning of
time, they've always made a song and dance about
pimping to avoid listening to our problems, to muffle
our voices. On the left, on the right, among feminists,
among Christians, everybody wants to protect us.

'D', a French prostitute[1]

One of the most contentious of the legal restrictions of whores' private
and public relationships is the prohibition of 'pimps' which figures in
all legislation on the sex trade. Yet, as we have seen, it is the
criminalization of the trade itself that creates conditions that are ripe
for exploitation – if the sex trade were not illegal or quasi-illegal
everywhere, prostitutes would be able to organize against their
exploitation both by small-time pimps and the big-time bosses such as
the men who run the Eros Centres. In any case, the whole question of
'pimps' is a loaded one, carrying with it a host of false assumptions.

To read media accounts and feminist publications on the sex
industry one could be forgiven for thinking that all prostitution is
controlled by organized crime and pimps. In fact in the West,
organized crime has very little hand in the trade and, while estimates
vary, the majority of prostitutes work independently of men. Even in
the USA, where myth has it that all street whores are run by pimps,
investigators have found this not to be the case. In New York,
Bernard Cohen reports that less than half of streetwalkers – those
whores most vulnerable to exploitation by third parties – work with

'deviant agents' (men), and that in many cases it is the women who control these 'agents', not, as is supposed, vice versa. Even the women who do work with pimps have much more autonomy than is generally assumed, often changing or simply ditching their man if they don't like him or if he does nothing for them. An English estimate of women who work in saunas puts the number of women with 'heavy ponces' (men who control them through violence) at less than 10 per cent.[2] One English prostitute, Anita, who has worked at all levels of the trade, from streetwalking to agency work, confirms the fact that only a minority of English whores have pimps: 'I can honestly swear over the years I've been hustling, the majority have been independent, like me. I've never, ever held a ponce. Just through principles, anyway – *never*.'[3]

From the whores' point of view the use of the word 'pimp' – as understood by straight society – to describe their men is questionable in the first place. 'E', a French prostitute, estimating the number of French whores forced to work at less than 5 per cent of the total, explains that the subject cannot be separated from women's relationships with men right across the spectrum:

People say that it's hard to tell the difference between a pimp and a boyfriend. Well it's true. You can never know for sure what the girl's real interest in the guy might be, or the guy's interest in her. In fact, it's exactly the same as in straight life, in a 'normal' couple. Between a husband and his wife, a lover and his mistress, a girl and her guy, it's exactly the same thing, but set in a different context. The difference is not that the guy's a pimp, but that the girl's a prostitute – that's all. The guys with pros aren't any worse bastards to them than husbands generally are to their wives. The girls are often freer, more independent, richer. They're not forced to stay at home . . .

. . . There's no such thing as girls going on the game for a guy without getting something from him in return. Pros can't be ruled by a rod of iron any more; what pros respond to is feelings, tenderness, presents, just like any other woman. Yet all the guys who make their wives slave away while they're off treating themselves to a good time aren't arrested for pimping . . .

What you do find are girls with men, who live with them, even if these guys have sexual relationships with several girls. These men might more often be crooks than doctors or shopkeepers, because there aren't many professional people or shopkeepers who want to live with a pro, but that's got nothing to do with what people call being a pimp. You can argue about whether the guys are decent in sometimes agreeing to live off a prostitute's earnings, you can argue about whether pros are really free, or whether there are 'pressures' other than physical ones – more refined ones, subtle ones, feelings for instance – but none of this is illegal. The girl has the right to do what she wants with her cash, and she does do what she wants with her cash – what little the State lets her keep for herself.[4]

Two women from the English Collective of Prostitutes also make it clear that they reject outsiders' definitions of 'the pimp':

If every other excuse to persecute us fails, there is always the excuse of pimps. Claiming they want to protect us from pimps, the forces of law and order make criminal any man who associates with us by calling him a pimp. He may be your son, your husband or a friend, men who are in no way pimps as far as we are concerned. And yet the law gets at us through them. The police harass entire communities and circles of friends under the pretext of catching pimps.

Some of us, if we have the money, prefer and are proud to support friends or lovers, men or women, rather than send them out to a factory or a hospital job and get them back destroyed after a day's work. We consider this *our* business. It is our right, or rather it should be, to decide how to spend our money, and not the business of the law.[5]

In fact the song-and-dance about pimping is the old story of the state intervening in sex-industry culture, ignoring the reality of sex workers' lives in order to define their people with reference only to its own priorities of control and repression. While the law can define a boyfriend, husband, friend or any man associating with a prostitute as a pimp – and prosecute him accordingly – the real pimps are allowed to get away with their exploitation:

Some police and pimps work very closely together in order to control us and have a cut of our money . . . In Britain, and other countries, charges that individual policemen, some of them high up, are pimping on an organized basis can never be proved or disproved until we are not gagged by illegality.

The biggest pimps, the people who make money directly or indirectly from prostitutes, operate with the blessing of the law – owners of chains of nightclubs, massage parlours, the champagne industry, hotel owners, the government through fines and taxes . . . the State [is] the biggest pimp.[6]

Even when whores do face violence from their men, they argue against treating this as a special case labelled 'pimping'. Eileen McLeod, author of *Women Working: Prostitution Now*, comments: 'Prostitutes' experience of violence from ponces and their reactions to it echo much of women's experience generally of domestic violence',[7] and Carol, one of the prostitutes she interviews, concurs:

People think because a girl's been beaten up by her boyfriend it's because she's not earning enough money. There are other reasons. My boyfriend's threatened to kill me if I go off with another man, so if I get a beating it's not because he wants money off me, it's because I'm going out with another man. Every man does it really.[8]

To mark out domestic violence against whores as being somehow different from (worse than) that against other women only reinforces the whore-stigma, since an artificial category of men is thereby stigmatized with the label 'pimp' (stigma being apparently contagious). Carol's casual 'Every man does it really' speaks volumes about women's experience of male violence and shows that whores, like all women, need proper legal protection from this violence – not an embargo which totally isolates them and prevents them relating to men in safety and security, *and on their own terms*. The 'pimp' issue is a variation on the 19th-century preoccupation with white slavery, a red herring which deflects attention from the real issues that concern prostitutes: poverty, isolation, scapegoating, and so on.

In fact, far from preventing violence against prostitutes, the laws as they now stand actually promote it; for the stigma and social isolation imposed on sex workers ensure that these women are the prime targets of rapists and murderers. American whores' activist Priscilla Alexander writes: 'Those countries with the most restrictive (anti-whore) legal systems, including the United States . . . have the most problems with violence against prostitutes (and women perceived to be *like* prostitutes).'[9] Since the mid-1970s, with increased police pressure on the sex industry, an epidemic of prostitute killings has swept the West. Prostitute campaigner Margo St James noted in 1985 that: 'every American city that has proclaimed the loitering law to be valid and ordered street sweeps has seen a serial killer emerge from the woodwork within a couple of years . . . Seattle, Portland, Oakland, Los Angeles.'[10]

In France during the mid-seventies a series of brutal whore-killings sparked off a protest movement; and Peter Sutcliffe, the so-called 'Yorkshire Ripper', terrorized the female population of northern England for six years, killing thirteen streetwalkers and other women, and maiming seven, before he was finally captured in 1981. A story relating to Sutcliffe's capture shows how directly law enforcement is implicated in violent crime against prostitutes. His last intended victim, a Sheffield streetwalker, Ava, got into his car to do business with him *because she had spotted the police nearby*: she 'had a lot of fines off the courts, thousands, so she wanted to get off the square, so she got in his car. Denise tried to warn her not to go as he was too pushy, but she jumped straight in the car . . . She just wanted to get off the square, away from the police.'[11]

Ava was lucky, in the event; the car was stopped by police before Sutcliffe could do her any damage – but how many other women had jumped into Sutcliffe's car 'to get away from the police'?

Virtually all prostitutes, especially streetwalkers, have stories of rape to tell; and the threat of murder is present immediately an ostensible client turns violent. Chloe, a former prostitute who worked on London's plush Park Lane, had an experience all street prostitutes dread when she and a colleague were picked up by three men posing as clients. The girls were held at knifepoint and driven out to the motorway where the second girl, Jody, was raped on the grass verge; finally they were taken to a flat in south London where this time both were raped and physically abused.

While working for an escort agency, Anita was repeatedly raped and tortured by a wealthy customer who kept her prisoner in his hotel room at the prestigious London Intercontinental; she was only able to escape after the man drank himself senseless.

Prostitutes who escape from ordeals like these have no recourse to the law, since the response the police give them is inevitably indifference. Former prostitute Yasmin was raped by a respectable-looking client: 'I didn't go to the police because . . . I wouldn't have stood a chance . . . I wouldn't have been able to say I were a prostitute because immediately *I* would have been the one on trial . . . it would have been *my* fault.'[12]

And Chloe finishes her account of the gang-rape she and Jody suffered by corroborating Yasmin's distrust of the law: 'Well we didn't go to the law . . . if we *had* gone to the cops it would've been, "Well you're a loose sort of girl . . . what do you expect? Forget it." They would take down the particulars as a formality, then push the file into a rack and that's the last you see or hear about it.'[13]

This culpable indifference extends also to the murder of prostitutes. In Los Angeles during the mid-1980s, the South Side Slayer murdered at least seventeen women in a period of three years: 'All but three of the victims were black . . . The police waited until ten women were already dead before notifying the public that a serial murderer was operating, and fourteen women were murdered before they even formed a task force to investigate the murders.'[14]

The LAPD tried to explain away their lack of concern by claiming that the murdered women were all prostitutes, so presumably they didn't count as human beings. But as the whores' campaigner Margo St James pointed out: 'Murderers can't tell who's a prostitute and who's not any more than a customer can. It's their assumption. That kind of violence is generated when any single woman on the street is under suspicion and can be stopped and asked for an explaining of herself.'[15]

Peter Sutcliffe was questioned by the police *seven times* before he finally confessed. The investigating officers had had at least one perfect description of Sutcliffe but had ignored it because it was given to them by a black prostitute, whom they dismissed as 'stupid'.

Indifference to prostitutes' legal right to protection, however, is hardly the worst aspect of the police's attitude towards women who work in the sex industry. One of the most sickening exposures about the recent wave of murders of prostitutes (and straight women) has been the actual complicity of both police and legal establishment with the aggressors. The woman-hunters' game becomes easy when pillars of the establishment like the British Attorney-General Sir Michael Havers can say, of Sutcliffe's victims, 'some were prostitutes, but perhaps the saddest part of this case is that some were not', implying that, in the eyes of the law, the torture and murder of prostitute women is acceptable. The link between the state's repression of sex

workers and Sutcliffe's lethal hatred of prostitutes is also clarified by
the words of Jim Hobson, Acting Assistant Police Chief Constable of
West Yorkshire during the Ripper hunt. In his 'anniversary plea' to the
murderer, Hobson said: 'He has made it clear that he hates prostitutes.
Many people do. We, as a police force, will continue to arrest
prostitutes.'[16]

This breathtakingly offhand and gratuitous statement makes an
explicit identification between the 'work' of the 'Streetcleaner', as
Sutcliffe called himself, and the police work of 'cleaning up' the
streets; it also makes Sutcliffe a part of that fictitious public consensus
of hatred ('many people' – including no doubt Hobson and his force)
which purportedly justifies police action against whores. When
Sutcliffe himself says that: 'The women I killed were filth, bastard
prostitutes who were just standing round littering the streets. I was
just cleaning the place up a bit,'[17] he is only openly expressing the
same kind of murderous contempt that lies behind the more veiled
statements of both Havers and Hobson.

Hobson's message went on to spell out further how, in this case, the
whore-stigma was operating: 'But the Ripper is now killing innocent
girls. That indicates your mental state and that you are in urgent need
of medical attention. You have made your point. Give yourself up
before another innocent woman dies.'[18]

Here, a senior police officer is actually saying quite openly that
some women – whores – are guilty, and deserve to die. Guilty of what
crime? Of a 'crime' that is actually legal in nearly every Western
country – prostitution. What Hobson has to say amply demonstrates
that, behind the apparently civilized façade of the law, its spirit still
decrees that whores – and any woman who can be fitted into this
category – are 'guilty' of their stigma, and that a hideous and barbaric
death is a fitting punishment for their guilt.

These Old Testament attitudes have no place in a civilized society.
But even more chilling is Hobson's tone of intimate understanding,
his avuncular concern for the murderer's health: 'You are in urgent
need of medical attention'. Where is the concern for Sutcliffe's
victims? Did eighteen-year-old Helen Rytka, an orphan who spent
most of her brief life in care and who wanted to save money for a better
life, deserve to die? What about the 23 children who were orphaned by
Peter Sutcliffe – where is the compassion for them?

In fact – and as could have been predicted – the media circus turned
Sutcliffe into a heroic descendant of the original 'Jack the Ripper'. A

spate of books about Sutcliffe – written by the latest generation of male 'Ripperologists' – quickly came out; a new legend was born. But what none of these men has so far said about Peter Sutcliffe is this: that he was a cowardly, opportunistic sadist who preyed on the most vulnerable women of all.

Perhaps the most explicit demonstration of police solidarity with whore-killers comes from Brooklyn, New York. A 28-year-old Puerto Rican streetwalker, Carmen Velez, was beaten to death by a client in August 1983.

> The police had a suspect immediately. A number of prostitutes in the . . . district reported that they had been assaulted by a john who fit his description . . . he was 'middle class, with a job, and married' . . . had a long police record . . . although local police were convinced of his guilt, no charges were brought . . . due to lack of physical evidence at the scene of the crime . . . Carmen's murderer is still out there.[19]

Chief of Homicide, Brooklyn, Dale Campbell, was interviewed about the murder for *New York Newsday* magazine:

> Campbell's description of police attitudes toward prostitute murders was more revealing than his denial of their low priority among law enforcement officials. He described sexual homicides involving prostitutes as titillating, both to himself and the officers investigating the case. 'I think there's something juicy about a prostitute getting killed,' he said. 'Some of them are young and attractive, and I've seen how some cops act around them . . . They act differently. It's maybe a little more exciting to investigate that type of case.'[20]

Here we see the patriarchy in its extreme form: serial killers, police chiefs and Attorney Generals who share their outlook, public apathy – all combining to enforce the whore-stigma, even to eroticize it. And men in positions of power are not slow to capitalize on this situation. While the Ripper was at large, two officers of the local vice squad arrested a Yorkshire streetwalker, then raped her, threatening to kill her if she resisted, and 'make it look like a Yorkshire Ripper job'.[21] Such attitudes, it must be stressed, endanger all women, not just prostitutes. We are all by now only too familiar with the way women

are put on trial in rape cases, their dress, behaviour and sexual histories
dredged up to justify the crime by tainting them with the whore-
stigma – as if every woman, especially when young, single and/or
independent, carried around with her the shadowy label 'common
prostitute', transforming the victim of violent crime into the
criminal. And in reality no woman is free from the imputation, since
the police, the legal establishment and men in general make up
definitions of who is and who is not a whore to suit themselves. Any
woman can at any time be branded 'whore', and subjected to male
violence. As Margo St James observes:

> As far as violence is concerned, I feel that the stigmatising, the
> whore stigma, is what legitimises violence, even in the home,
> because when the husband slugs his wife, he precedes the abuse
> with 'You slut!' 'You whore!' So I think it's very clear that this
> official condemnation feeds the violence against women in
> general, and that we have to stop it at the root.[22]

Partly as a result of repressive legislation, partly in response to the
relaxation of morality and the rise in living standards, new forms of
the sex industry emerged in the West after the Second World War. As
the most advanced Western economy – not to mention the country
most hostile to prostitutes – the USA was the trail-blazer of these new
styles of work and organization; for as we have seen, it was the
prohibition of the sex industry there which led to the creation of
covers such as the massage parlour and escort agency during the
inter-war years. Since the Americanization of the Western world and
the wave of repression after 1945, these new ways of plying the old
trade have become almost universal.

With the demise of the brothel, the massage parlour and sauna set-
ups have – especially since the mid-sixties – displaced all rivals to
become the dominant form of indoor prostitution. These latterday
revivals of classical and medieval settings are as diverse in decor and
atmosphere as the old brothels, ranging from the cheap and cheerless
to the plush and expensively furnished. Advertising claims tend to be
extravagant:

'Beautiful Models for Private Sensitivity Sessions' . . . 'the
incredible Pleasure Island that begins where all others leave off, where
your most erotic daydreams become a reality, the most beautiful, the
most sensuous, most provocative girls completely and privately at

your service'. What they actually provide is generally on a more mundane level; it usually consists of a quick rub-down followed by whatever 'extras' – masturbation, oral sex, full coitus, or 'half-and-half' – the client requires. The extent to which the client can indulge his 'most erotic daydreams' is somewhat circumscribed by the set-up, in which – as in most sex-trade transactions – the woman is firmly in control, setting her own limits. A former sauna worker, Yasmin, explains:

> It's entirely up to you, from the minute they enter the room. It's your shrewdness that decides how long they're going to be. I give them forty minutes at the most, from the massage through to whatever, and if by that time they haven't achieved anything, it's just a case of me picking the money up and saying 'I'm sorry' . . . They're at your mercy, regardless of whether they actually make it or not . . . It's normally about twenty minutes, from the beginning of the massage right through.[23]

The prostitute's self-confidence – which is vital – and her methods of taking control of the situation from the start are nicely illustrated in an anecdote from an Australian parlour, quoted in Roberta Perkins' and Garry Bennett's excellent book *Being a Prostitute*:

> Anyone doubting the amount of control the women have over a situation involving a client should sit alongside the workers . . . and listen to the way they handle clients as they enter. The men show obvious signs of nervousness as they face the line of women staring at them. As they attempt to negotiate a contract, many will try a show of bravado and an air of authority. The women greet these men coolly and then proceed to cut them down to size.

The authors then go on to give an example of an incident where a client tried to get more for his money during negotiations:

> First woman: 'Come on love, tell us what you want for the price then.'
> Second woman: 'That much, eh? Think you can handle it? D'ya reckon you can last the distance?'
> Third woman: 'Tell you what, show us what you've got and

we'll decide whether you're capable of doing all that for the price.'

The client quickly lowers his demands, while the price remains unaltered.

First woman: 'Well, that's better. You were being a greedy boy, weren't you?'

Thus an initially overbearing client was led to a room very much subdued. The mixture of humour and condescension in the women's tone is very noticeable.[24]

The parlours have a number of advantages over other forms of prostitution, not least of which is that the nudity (or near-nudity) and physical contact necessary provide an alibi which is not easy for the police to dismantle. This, since the efforts of the police tend to follow the line of least resistance, can act as a disincentive to enquiry; and massage-parlour workers are therefore relatively free from the harassment their street sisters have to contend with virtually every day. However, it is not unknown for police to raid the parlours from time to time, as the English prostitute Yasmin relates:

They came from every exit . . . they just charged in like the Sweeney. It was as if we were armed robbers or something. They sectioned everything off and officers came to each of the girls and made sure they were hovering over us and all that rubbish. They went running around, looking upstairs in the bathroom for proof . . . My handbag was searched, and we had to put up with the policewomen with the medical gloves on, fishing for used rubbers.[25]

The police are nothing if not thorough in their search for evidence; they have to be, in Britain, since the fact that prostitution itself is legal in this country puts the onus on them to prove that a parlour is a brothel, that commercial sex is taking place on the premises with the connivance of the owner. And since incriminating their bosses for pimping would mean the closure of the parlour, the women who work there are not likely to co-operate with the police – in which case there is little the law can do except admit that the whole exercise has been a waste of time, energy and taxpayers' money, as happened in the above incident.

From the whores' point of view another major factor in favour of the parlour and sauna is the protection from violence these places offer. The enclosed setting, and the presence of other women, management and sometimes bouncers, act as a powerful deterrent to any would-be aggressor (although this does not rule out the isolated maniac). Also, in this relatively sheltered environment prostitutes can often exercise a wide degree of autonomy, working to their own rules and requirements.

'We girls pretty much ran the parlour,' notes one American whore. 'The owner didn't know too much about the business. He'd stop by in the morning to pick up his take, before any of us came to work. We rarely saw him. Most of the decisions were made on a seniority basis by the girls who operated the place.'[26]

The owners themselves are nearly always men, since it is men who invariably control the kind of capital necessary to start up any business. Many parlour-owners are in fact ordinary businessmen with interests in the straight sector as well as the sex trade. The American sociologist Lewis Diana gives one instance of a used-car dealer whose massage parlour effectively financed his 'legitimate' business ventures.[27]

A final advantage of the parlours and saunas is their discretion, as far as the general public is concerned. As the New York Times reported in 1974: 'They appear to be widely tolerated by the public. Massage parlours that advertise sex blatantly but provide it discreetly seem to generate little of the community outrage that is often aroused by a few streetwalkers on a downtown corner.'[28]

Another way in which whores shelter from police harassment and public disapprobation is by working in hotels and motels. Hotel work can be more difficult than streetwalking, and (for black women in particular) it is often well-nigh impossible to avoid the attentions of hotel security staff. Sometimes the answer is to pay off sympathetic members of staff, as an English prostitute, Michelle, describes:

Hotel hustling is a messabout. You've got to look right to fit into the scene. You've got to dress right. You've got to know how to chat your clients up and you've got to know your hotels, how to get into them and which part to use. Like you got to sit in the coffee bar and from there you get into the lifts and go up to the floors. Or you go into the bar and get a drink. The men will come and chat you up, you don't have to go and chat them. You've just got to look out for the hotel detectives . . .

You give the waiters a fiver each time they give you a client. If you're in with them you're made. You can walk in hotels and sit there until about half past ten. After that you've either got to be in with someone who's a resident . . . or if you're in with the waiter, they can come across and say, 'There's a guy over there' – when you come out of the hotel, you always tip the guy on the door.[29]

In the US, the hotel trade has declined with the rise of the motel, where a whore can easily rent a room with her client. American prostitutes can also find work at establishments in the tradition of the 1930s juke joints. Truck-stops – located on the main highways – look from the outside like ordinary diners, but with sex on the menu they are popular haunts for long-distance truck drivers and travelling businessmen. Roadside lounges are a similar set-up – sex is for sale from rooms at the back or on the second floor – but these tend to be five to ten miles from the nearest city and attract a regular local clientele, usually businessmen and professionals at lunch-times, working-class men in the evenings. Both truck-stops and roadside lounges are easy-going workplaces, where conditions are unpretentious – homely, even – and the pace of work low-key: 'The money's good. The work isn't hard. You meet a lot of interesting people, and the place I work in is nice . . . it's been good to me.'[30]

Again, the lounges tend to be owned by local entrepreneurs, who protect themselves in the grand old tradition, through payoffs to police, politicians and government officials – in cash and kind.

Undoubtedly the best way to avoid the law is by working as a callgirl. Callgirls are the élite of the contemporary sex industry and its highest-paid workers, catering to the wealthiest clientele. Some women work from their own homes, advertising through contact magazines; others register with agencies which do the initial work of bringing in the client in return for a cut of the fee. Often this merely entails a whore being in touch by telephone with a woman who co-ordinates the dating services of several callgirls, although sometimes the agency also has a place where the girls can relax together between 'dates'. Yet in spite of the glamorous image, the callgirl is not immune to male violence – witness Anita's experience at the London Intercontinental – nor to legal repression; the agency Anita worked for was raided and closed down, forcing her back on to the streets. Apart from the drawbacks and dangers, however, and 'whether or not they work through an escort service, or completely on their own, the prostitutes who work in this way are the most independent, and the most in control of their lives on and off the job.'[31]

A novel form of today's sex trade is the provision by some firms of prostitutes to their own clients; the whores are often on the payroll as 'public relations' staff. As one New York businessman explained: 'This is the fastest way I know to have an intimate relationship established with a buyer . . . It sort of gives me a slight edge; well, we will not call it blackmail, but it is a subconscious edge over the buyer. It is a weapon I hold, and I could discreetly drop it at any time when the [buyer's] wife is present.'[32] All's fair in love – and business.

In spite of all the social and legislative changes in this century, the more traditional forms of the sex industry continue to exist, albeit precariously. In France, Marthe Richard's law failed to close all brothels; now, as ever, the authorities allow certain discreet and well-connected houses to carry on their trade, provided they keep up protection payments. From whores' own accounts, French brothels still seem to be characterized by collusion between management, clients and powers-that-be to produce a repressive regime for their workers – now more than ever, since the brothel-worker has far fewer houses to choose from than in previous centuries. One former brothel-worker told the journalist Claude Jaget: 'You aren't free in brothels. The only thing you can do is not go into them or else leave them for good . . . from the moment you're in one, you're like a prisoner. You can't do anything without the madam's consent.'[33]

The practice of displaying women like cattle in the brothel salon is still a feature of the French scene:

[It is] . . . the worst thing about all the brothels in France. That's when you feel like an animal. It's terrible. I never wanted to go in. What's more, the clients who go to the salons are 'respectable' people, there were even cops and men very high up the ladder . . . They'd make us file in and then we'd stand there, planted in front of the client, or clients . . . it was horrible, they'd look you up and down. That moment, when you felt them looking at you, sizing you up, judging you . . . and those men, those fat pigs who weren't worth half as much as the worst of us, they'd joke, make comments.

'This one has beautiful breasts, her arse is too this, her legs too

that, this one must be good at it, look at that mouth! . . .' etc
. . . They made you turn and face in all directions, because of
course a front view wasn't enough for them. It used to make me
furious . . . I felt really put down. It was the man who'd chosen
me, who'd had me, I was the thing he came and literally bought.
He had judged me like he judged cattle at a fairground, and that's
revolting, it's sickening . . . You can't imagine it if you've never
been through it yourself.[34]

This ritual humiliation plays out the powerlessness of the prostitute
in the brothel – particularly the modern brothel, where illegality and
hypocrisy combine to keep whores in dehumanized, degraded
conditions, and turn them into things, without rights or freedoms or
any vestige of human dignity. It is for this reason, as the same ex-
brothel whore says, that in France 'all the girls are dead against the
brothels.'[35]

In Britain, with its more liberal tradition in which the numbers of
closed houses were always insignificant, and in which the state failed
in its one attempt to regulate the trade, the brothel takes a more easy-
going form. Some women, often ex-whores themselves, rent rooms
in their homes to prostitute friends, or combine brothel-keeping with
childminding. Sometimes a former whore will take up brothel-
keeping as a fully-fledged commercial venture, as was the case with
the famous 'luncheon-voucher madam' Cynthia Payne who, having
worked in the trade for some years herself, used the money she had
saved to set up a brothel in a detached house in a leafy London suburb.
Cynthia's house proved highly successful, becoming a home-from-
home for various isolated 'perverts' (including a transvestite ex-army
officer) until it was raided by police. As usual, Cynthia was
scapegoated while her clientele (some of whom were pillars of the
establishment) were let off the hook; but although she was convicted
for brothel-keeping and sent to prison for a short stretch, she later
followed in the footsteps of other great madams, cashing in on her
experiences by writing her memoirs, which were sympathetically
filmed under the title *Personal Services*.

There are also some less benign versions of the brothel to be found
in Britain: 'the flats' are direct descendants of the tenement-houses and
cribs of the 19th century, and illicit counterparts to Germany's Eros
Centres. Anita went to work in these in the early 1980s after being told
that she could earn £400 a day there. Housed in a run-down Soho

block, the flats were organized in assembly-line style by the same kind of management that dreamed up the Speedway Inn:

> It was ten pounds a time, straight sex, eight minutes. Then the maid would knock on the door and if he wanted to stay longer it was extra money; plus if he wanted you to take your top off it was an extra five pounds, oral was an extra five pounds, everything was always extra . . . You always had six or seven waiting to come in, the door never stopped, and it was a twelve-hours shift. The insides of my thighs used to *kill*.[36]

Although the pace and volume of work was crushing, and the flats were obviously run by criminal interests, Anita was nevertheless not under the kind of constraints often found in regulated French brothels. Entering the work freely, she was also free to leave whenever she wanted.

In the States the illegal brothel – as opposed to the legalized sex ranches of Nevada – still exists, and there the situation appears to be similar to that of the French brothels. As 'M', an ex-brothel whore, told the feminist writer Kate Millett:

> My first experience with prostitution was in a whorehouse, and you're in a cage no matter which way you look at it . . . That was a real dragged-out horror; I'll never forget that as long as I live . . . This place was too much to believe. The police, the detectives used to come every day for their payoff. They used to talk to the madam of the house; they'd pick up their money and leave. Only white men came into this place . . . The girls were all black, with a few exceptions . . . A guy would come in; he'd look everybody over and he'd pick you and you'd go off to the room. You could never see your money. The madam would demand the money, and when you got ready to leave she would give you your half. I decided after three days it wasn't for me. I didn't like it, and I wanted to leave. And she didn't have my money. She'd gambled it away.[37]

Xaviera Hollander, whose book *The Happy Hooker* describes in glowing terms the high-class houses she ran in the States, kept up a war of attrition with the law in spite of her powerful connections and police payoffs amounting to over $1000 a month. The vice squad raided her on average once a year – but still, she says: 'my best clients represent the highest echelon of government and business circles and keep me in business no matter how often I am harassed by the police and have to change addresses.'[38]

The wealthy and powerful men who formed Hollander's clientele will always, whatever the legal situation, have access to some kind of brothel to cater to their sexual demands, in high-priced comfort and privacy. A new form of service is the 'key club', membership of which affords each client his own key to the brothel; here, ' "Private" membership offers these upper-class men the kind of police protection provided to gentlemen of an earlier era.'[39]

The days when there were houses to cater for all income brackets, however, are long gone. Men without wealth and influence must nowadays resort to the newer forms of prostitution offered by massage parlours and the like. Alternatively, they can turn to one of the oldest varieties of all: the streetwalker.

In the West, streetwalking has declined markedly since its all-time peak in the 19th century. The trade's fraught relationship with the law has led to many whores being forced into other areas of the sex industry. In her 1982 study, *Women Working: Prostitution Now*, Eileen McLeod estimates that in England's second largest city, Birmingham, three times as many women work indoors than out on the streets; in all, she estimates a total of only 200 women working the streets of the city – a far cry from the throngs of streetwalkers of the Victorian heyday. And in the USA, according to Winick and Kinsie, writing in the 1970s, streetwalking at that time was on the decline – although the slump of the late 1970s and 1980s has indisputably contributed to a steady growth in lower-class prostitution and especially street-walking, always resorted to by the women with least resources. In France the Richard law made streetwalking more hazardous in terms of brushes with the law, but – as in other countries – the trade continues. The rue St Denis in Paris has become the beat of many whores, particularly women migrating from French-speaking Third World countries in the hopes of a better life – or at least a life – in the West; and the Bois de Boulogne is nightly crowded with transvestite and transsexual hookers of all nationalities. A stalemate between the police and street whores seems to exist in most Western countries; however, the streetwalker remains the principal target of both the law and public disapproval.

A major change in the street scene followed the increase in car ownership. Some streetworkers still take clients to short-stay hotels or their own apartments, but many contemporary prostitutes will do business in the client's car:

> You just stroll around and a car will pull up. If he stops, you know that if he's passed you once he's looking for business . . . You talk about a price and tell him he must wear a Durex and if he agrees, you go somewhere . . . if you haven't got a place to take them, or if you live too far out, you have to find somewhere where you don't think you're going to get disturbed and manage the best you can. Generally it's in the car – on a bit of waste ground or behind old houses. I never like going too far out with them because you never know what's going to happen.[40]

Kathy's comments underline one of the disadvantages of using the client's car – it gives him more power than if the transaction were taking place in the woman's own home or even in a hotel room. Often the women working an area will keep an eye on each other for safety, sharing experiences – and warnings – about regular clients: 'He's a time-waster', 'He's no trouble', and so on. As Chloe explains:

> I did (street) hustling for one year, all of us lasses together. We survived. We lived comfortably. There's always men out there that want it . . . We girls stick by each other and respect each other . . . What we've got amongst ourselves is a lot of love and affection . . . I've met some lovely people, made some good friends on the game, amongst the girls . . . We stuck by each other through thick and thin, and if you ever needed anything you could guarantee one of them'd be there. It is lovely.[41]

Many tabooed aspects of the sex trade are still going strong, male prostitution being perhaps the most notable. Male whores can be seen hustling on the streets of most big cities, and found alongside all-male massage parlours in the advertising columns of contact and gay publications. In New York, male prostitutes, mostly in their late teens and early twenties, work the streets and gay bars, tending to cluster in up-market locations and charging slightly more than their female counterparts. They are easy targets for entrapment by policemen posing as clients. In France, male hookers use coded messages on the computerized Minitel information system (linked into the telephone network) to make contact with their clients, who are largely executives and professional married middle-class men – the same client bracket using female whores. Whores' campaigner Marie Arrington explains:

> The boys get into it for the same reason [as the girls]: many of them running away from home need the money. Sometimes the boys are not accepted for their homosexuality and are kicked out of home . . . There are many boys hustling on the street that have girlfriends – not all . . . are homosexuals. But they do have a saleability until they are a certain age, and once they hit that certain age and they're not cute enough or they don't have enough of a tight ass for the males that are driving around, then that's when they start cross-dressing. The whole myth is that the males are homosexuals and for homosexuals. Not true. It is the same men that are buying the girls that are buying the boys.[42]

A facet of the male prostitution scene which has existed since time immemorial is the transvestite trade, but it now has acquired a new twist, with the invention of surgical and hormone techniques which can physically transform men into women (and, more rarely, vice versa). One study[43] estimates that as many as half of all male transsexuals have at some point in their lives passed through prostitution as a means by which to raise the substantial sums necessary to pay medical expenses. These transsexual hookers are often only distinguishable from their female counterparts by their more flamboyant styles of dress and soliciting; Bernard Cohen describes the 'drag queens' of New York as being more outrageous in both dress and behaviour, and more aggressive in their approach to potential customers than the women. Some transsexuals walked the beat with their hormonally-induced breasts fully exposed, while others reached through car windows and fondled the drivers' genitals.

It seems that the provision of male whores for female clients is the latest growth area of the sex trade market, although it has a long way to go before it catches up with the usual trade. Canadian whore-activists Valerie Scott and Peggy Miller remark that:

> As women get more financial power, more and more women are calling up escort services. There are now a couple of escort

services in the Yellow Pages that advertise for women. It's the money, because they don't have the money. Not only that, [women] have not yet learned to give themselves permission to need that. They don't know how to say it's okay that they just have someone over for their own lustful purposes.[44]

It will be interesting to see if and how this new sector of the trade develops over the next few years.

Another aspect of the sex industry which goes back a long way but which has become more widespread and visible in the last twenty years or so is juvenile prostitution. The catastrophically impoverished inner cities of the United States, in particular, produce large numbers of runaway children trying to escape from abusive and/or disintegrating families. In New York alone, around 50,000 girls are estimated to arrive annually, with nowhere to go but the streets. Their options for survival are little different now than in the last century: stealing, begging, or prostitution – with the added modern opportunity of drug-dealing.

The stereotypical scenario has the young runaway arriving alone in a strange city and being picked up by a pimp at the bus station; the pimp shelters her for a short time and then, by force or deceit, turns her out as a hooker. While this does happen, it is also the case that: '[some] young girls deliberately go to big cities to find pimps to turn them out. These young women are also likely to leave pimps they don't like, either for another pimp, or to be independent, or sometimes to return to their families.'[45]

Many young prostitutes also work independently of pimps, ganging together in groups, sharing their money, and working as whores only when funds are low. One thing is certain: these children find no shortage of customers, as a young Chicago whore testifies: 'I've been in the racket since I was twelve years old. There are lots of guys who are kinky for young girls. Most of the baby pros I know are about 13 or 14 or 15. Some are so busy they travel a lot, especially to resort towns.'[46]

While some young prostitutes can make a lot of money working conferences, expensive hotels and holiday resorts, the reality for most juvenile whores is somewhat grimmer. Prostitution is just a means of day-to-day survival on the streets, with all the dangers that involves. Many former runaways grow up in the trade, given the lack of opportunities for other work. As one 23-year-old prostitute, in the life from the age of twelve, explains: 'I never tried to get a job because if you are black you can't get much of a job beyond cleaning a shit-house and I can make a lot more pushing my ass.'[47]

Although child prostitution has always been found wherever there is mass poverty and social dislocation, as in the chaotic slums of the 18th and 19th centuries, the scale of the problem has increased alarmingly in the resource-starved ghettos of our own times. According to Canadian prostitutes' campaigner Marie Arrington, when she was a young runaway thirty years ago the street women helped her to survive and thus prevented her from having to sell sex; but nowadays there are simply too many kids running for the adult whores to help them. The problem, in fact, has little to do with the sex trade itself and more to do with the almost total lack of support facilities for runaway children. In the short term, as Arrington points out: 'They need money to survive, they need a good ear, they need a safe place to run to.'[48]

Unfortunately, none of these basic facilities exist. Runaways, often desperately abused children, are treated as criminals by the law; in the US both police and voluntary shelters are obliged to inform the parents when a juvenile falls into their hands, making it unsafe for children fleeing abuse to use the shelters or seek assistance. In Britain it is illegal to harbour a runaway minor; thus the law makes it impossible to provide them with shelters.

In the longer term, the problem of juvenile prostitution goes back to what the children are running from. It is a problem of child abuse, of the poverty which splits families and blights young people's lives and prospects; it is also a problem of the indifference of society in general and the state in particular to these 'disposable children', as Marie Arrington so poignantly – and accurately – describes them. Too often the child prostitution issue is turned into yet another stick with which to beat the adult women who work in the sex industry. Too often the children themselves are burdened with stigma; their plight is sensationalized and the focus shifted on to their prostitution rather than the circumstances which drove them on to the streets in the first place.

In an article in the British newspaper the *Guardian*, a 13-year-old runaway was described as being 'self-sufficient, a seasoned prostitute with her own bank account and capable of earning £150 a night'. The article went on to characterize Katie – and all juvenile prostitutes – as 'sick children'. A young King's Cross prostitute, Marrianne Stevens, wrote a succinct letter in response to the article:

Katie herself had walked out of a 'sick' situation in a children's home and at home where she was being raped by her father. Her refusal of rape and violence by running away and going on the game is not 'an act of extreme self-abasement' [as the article had claimed] . . . but an act of extreme courage. Why is she being reduced to a 'sick' victim?

True to its Victorian Values, the government is trying to starve young people back into their families regardless of whether rape or violence is happening there. If we had money of our own and safe houses where we could be anonymous to protect us from being picked up by the police and sent back 'home' we wouldn't need to go on the game to escape from violence.

But what about all those children who haven't run away and who are still being beaten and raped by their father or other adults? Aren't they worthy of support? Like the government [the author of the article] finds the fact that some young people have used prostitution to get out of rape more criminal than the rape itself. That is really sick.[49]

While plenty of middle-class men still patronize the sex industry, the large working-class clientele of previous centuries has diminished considerably, according to recent studies. Contemporary whores now report that working-class clients are in the minority, and that 70 per cent or more of their customers are middle-class, middle-aged, white, married professionals. This is true of every sector of the trade: Chloe, an English former prostitute, asserts that: 'It is the middle-class men who are keeping the girls on the street, because they are the majority that use prostitutes';[50] and in US massage parlours, Lewis Diana encountered mainly middle-class men, including (in one up-market parlour) 'a prominent attorney, a state legislator, two local judges, and a president of a state university'.[51]

This narrowing of the customers' class base is partly due to the rise in living standards in this century, especially since the last war, which has drastically reduced the numbers of women entering the sex trade. Gone are the days when there were so many whores on the streets of Western cities that their company could be bought for a few shillings and a glass of wine. Fewer whores has meant higher prices, and most working men cannot now afford to use the services of prostitutes to the extent that they did in former times. Changes in the moral climate have also affected the flow of business according to class. On the face of it, the 20th-century moral thaw has reduced the numbers of men going to whores by destroying the sex industry's monopoly of extra-marital sex; however, the truth is rather more complex.

In the 19th century, the working class was not affected by bourgeois standards of moral decency; extra-marital sex, paid or unpaid, was accepted as normal, and there was always a large pool of unattached men who would pay for a night with a good-time girl. After the social-purity hysteria, however, the working classes in the developed countries began to accept the bourgeois model of monogamous marriage and the middle-class disapproval of whores which was to result in the legal repression of the sex trade. This in turn made prostitutes less visible as a sexual option for the young, unmarried male, forcing the trade to become more discreet – and again, raising prices.

Finally, the relaxation of sexual mores during the sixties meant that premarital sex once again became acceptable while prostitution – and prostitutes – remained stigmatized; this again cut into the trade with young working-class men in particular. As for those clients who have been more or less unaffected by all these changes – the middle-class, middle-aged, married men – they have, as ever, the money, time and hypocrisy necessary for them to patronize whores.

For all that good manners are supposed to be the preserve of the middle classes, these well-heeled customers are generally disliked by whores: 'One thing I've noticed is that the ones who give us the least shit and treat us decently are the workers . . . On the other hand, the ones highest up are all the biggest bastards, the biggest shits. They're the ones who treat you like shit.'[52]

The nature of clients' demands has also evolved – if you can call it that – in recent years; the blossoming of the 'specialist' trade being one of the effects of the post-war change in the social background of whores' clients. Once, the demand was overwhelmingly for conventional intercourse, with perhaps 10 per cent asking for fellatio or some other speciality; now, those wanting straight sex are often in the minority. In part this is because the liberalization of sexuality since the 'sexual revolution' has made peccadilloes like oral sex and masturbation more acceptable. It also, however, stems from the narrowing of the clientele, since the wealthier types who have always gone for the more outlandish practices now take up a larger proportion of a reduced trade. The concentration of masochists and other assorted 'perverts' in the upper income brackets is amply confirmed by whores' experiences: 'It's never the working class guys that want all the crazy stuff,' says Chloe. 'It's always the posh ones, the really posh ones who want all the plastic macs, leather, whips, laying in coffins.'[53]

And one French whore explained to Claude Jaget about her masochistic clientele:

> They want us to hit them, stub out cigarettes on their chest, stick pins through their penis, drag them round the room by a string tied round the tip of their tongue, defecate in their mouth, insult them. They reply, 'Yes, mistress, fine, mistress.' It's a clientele of regulars, they've often got a whole ritual. For example, they'll come by in the morning and give me a laxative. They calculate their hours scientifically, and tell me what time they'll come back . . .
>
> There are some men you have to tie up very tight with chains, and some stay chained up like that for a very, very long time. A friend of mine had several rooms so that she could deal with several guys at a time; one time she forgot about a guy she tied up. In the evening when she came home, the guy had turned blue, but he was really happy . . . They pay well . . .
>
> . . . When they want you to stick pins in their penises, the blood really gushes out because when they come all the blood rises and when you take the pins out there's a flood. For this operation, you have to pull everything tight with elastic so there's no loose skin, really stretch it, and then dig the pins in. They don't scream while it's going on, they tremble, they get their kicks from it.[54]

Catering to the specialist trade is clearly a skilled occupation; apart from necessitating a firm but careful hand, it requires imaginative expertise also. For the dominatrix's work is essentially about fantasy; she is constantly required to wear costumes, act out roles, insult and castigate her clients in the appropriate terms. A perennial favourite is the scene in which the client is punished by an irate (and interestingly matriarchal) schoolteacher, nurse, 'Mummy' or Nanny. One German dominatrix whore working in France found that she could double her money by insulting her clients in German. Naturally, this made her work a lot easier: not only could she speak her native tongue, but since the clients could not understand it, she could give her imagination a rest and reel off anything that came into her head – shopping lists, recipes . . .

San Francisco B&D (Bondage and Discipline) Queen Mistress
Lilith Lash first got into the scene at the age of nineteen:

> I was . . . broke, my girlfriend . . . turned me on to a guy who
> paid me to tie him with his neckties and throw oranges at his balls
> from across the room at ten bucks a hit. Even nearsighted it was
> an easy and well paying gig. He was lucky I had been such a bad
> pitcher in high school, or I probably would have liberated his life
> savings.

Mistress Lash later went on to make a career out of being cruel to be
kind, becoming increasingly sophisticated – and scientific – in her
technique:

> The spankings are like specific and advanced massage. They can
> be deliciously built up to what seems like hard corporal
> punishment, if that was their purpose rather than erotic stimula-
> tion. Beginning lightly and briskly to bring the blood to the
> surface of the skin, which helps prevent later bruising, using furs
> and feathers to tease when the pain seems to outweigh the
> pleasure, and eventually wailing away to a crescendo that often
> produces spontaneous orgasm . . .
>   The reason pain and pleasure can be merged by an experienced
> hand is because both reactions come from the same place in the
> brain. When excited . . . endorphins are released. This is a
> natural opiate the body provides. The trick with s/m is to apply
> enough pain and/or fear to bring out the endorphins without
> inflicting unnecessary damage.[55]

Apart from the regular masochist clientele, men sometimes go to
whores to act out the most strange and, frankly, uncategorizable
fantasies: 'One guy,' says Australian B&D specialist Mistress Kelly,
'used to come in once a week and we would undress him and sit him
on a mantelpiece, which we had built especially to take his weight. He
used to crouch up there for hours on end. He put a lot of guys off
sitting up there like a bookend, but he was paying good money.'[56]
    One of English prostitute's Chloe's clients wanted her to talk about
flowers; another gained relief by showing her a video of his own
mother's funeral. The male hooker 'Sequinned' Sid tells the story of an
upper-class man who wanted to put him naked into a harness and

gallop him round the grounds of his country estate. Sid refused: 'I would've caught my death of cold!'

Weird as these fantasies are, many whores have an astute understanding of the reasons behind their clients' strange demands. The English prostitute Rosa:

> I'd say 90% of men who come to me are in control of other men all the time and they come to me to get that burden of responsibility off them and put themselves in my hands and reverse the role. The most common thing they're after is the feeling of being completely under someone else's control and being helpless.[57]

Which brings us back to the men who go in for these specialist services. According to Mistress Kelly: 'the more bizarre requests come from men of higher class, like businessmen, company directors, and things like that.'[58] 'C', a French SM specialist, agrees: 'The masochist clientele is something of a special breed. Generally, they're men who are "cultured", who've got money and who've got some pretty incredible vices . . . When you see an intellectual type coming, smartly dressed, there's a nine in ten chance that he's a masochist.'[59]

Typically, these men always have plenty of money with which to employ prostitutes to stage their wild fantasies; that said, there is a politics of identity involved here. In a working-class man's personal life, his masculinity is one of his few sources of power – to deviate from the straight and narrow path of conventional sexuality, playing games with powerlessness, would be too threatening; he would fear losing what little power he has. On the other hand, the social power of middle-class men is assured, and this can free their personal life from the constraints of straight masculinity, allowing them to indulge in a more richly varied fantasy life.

Generally, most whores who provide the bizarre range of sado-masochistic services required by these men do not sit in judgement on them. It is their hypocrisy which comes under fire. Pointing out that the middle-class clients who use prostitutes most are also the ones who come down on them hardest in public, Chloe indulges in a little fantasy of her own:

> What I would like to do would be to go on television at peak viewing time, with a lie-detector strapped on my arm, and look

straight into the camera; and I'd say 'Hello, it's Chloe. You out
there, you know who I mean, don't you? You're the barrister
that pays my friend to piss on your face. And you know who I'm
talking about – you know who you are . . . The *top* barrister in
this city.' – And he'd be shaking in his shoes![60]

CHAPTER SIXTEEN

Coming Out of Stigma:
Contemporary Whores and the Creation of a Movement

From the moment I decided to sell, or rather, rent my body, I figured it's my own business and nobody else's. No one's got the right to come and make me explain myself. I'm not interested in criticisms of any kind, whether it's the most contemptuous of them coming and telling me I'm a slut, or whether it's people who come and tell me that I'm lacking in affection, or people who come and tell me I should try and get out of it . . . What right do they have to put us down, what right do they have to come and tell us we shouldn't do this job? My body belongs to me, and I'll do what I like with it. I might well have wanted to do something else, I might well dream of another life; but in the meantime I'm a woman, a woman as respectable as any other, a grown woman, and I can't stand people who want to make decisions for me.

'D', a French prostitute[1]

The contemporary prostitute has much in common with her sisters from previous centuries: she is just as likely to be working class, unskilled and relatively uneducated, and to be in the life for the money. Contemporary sociological surveys show that the overwhelming majority of whores in all sectors of the sex trade are from working-class backgrounds. Even in the more expensive spheres, they are in the majority; according to Lewis Diana, only a quarter of massage parlour workers and a third of callgirls are of middle-class origin, although it must be said that a middle-class girl can set up as a callgirl more easily than a working-class girl.

One new datum for prostitution in Western society is race. The 20th century has seen black people in the US migrate from the south throughout the rest of the country, as well as the immigration of other groups, notably hispanics from Central and South America; in Europe, too, there have been large influxes of people from former colonies into the metropolitan centres. In the field of prostitution, as in other areas of Western life, these people are doubly oppressed, since Western society ghettoizes 'immigrants' (that is, non-whites) in the poorest-paid sectors of the economy, so that the burden of class oppression is added to that of race. Within the prostitute population, non-white women are concentrated on the streets and in the massage parlours; the further up-market you go, the fewer non-white whores you find; although white working-class women are in the majority throughout.

Black women are therefore particularly visible as prostitutes, since they are disproportionately represented on the streets, and they suffer greater stigma accordingly, as women, as non-whites, as workers, as whores – and as the most stigmatized of all prostitutes: streetwalkers. The impression given by their visibility that black women are overrepresented in the prostitute population is false, however; in the US, for instance, 94 per cent of prostitutes are white, although black people form 11 per cent of the total population.[2]

The motivations for women entering the sex industry are the same as ever, major considerations being money and working conditions. The perennial pattern – that whores can earn as much or more in a day as they can in a week's straight work – persists; as does the fact that women's wages in all sectors are still less than two-thirds those of men. Lewis Diana's study includes whores who have worked in professions such as teaching, as well as the usual poorly-qualified working-class jobs; nevertheless, he concludes that: 'What is clear . . . is that in the entire sample there is not a single woman who could not but have improved her income as a prostitute.'[3]

Other studies bear this out: the fact is that for the vast majority of women, whatever their class, education and career prospects, prostitution still represents the most lucrative option. Not every woman can become a prime minister.

Nowadays it need not always be absolute destitution that drives women into the sex industry, at least in the West. Many whores tend to look around at their options before making their choices. Diana questioned one American truck-stop whore about her decision to work in the sex trade:

Q: Were you having money problems when you decided [to become a prostitute]?

A: Not any more than usual. But I was tired of working and not having money to pay for things you didn't expect . . . life's a struggle. There's always somebody's hand in your pocket.

Q: Did your girlfriend [already a truck-stop whore] keep on urging you to go to work?

A: Sure. And I could see what it was doing for her. She could work a week then have a week off and more money than she'd ever had. She bought herself new clothes and a car. It looked easy.

Q: Was it easy?

A: It really was.[4]

Another prostitute, quoted by Winick and Kinsie, clearly rejects the low pay and servitude of working-class women's labour:

When I found out I was sitting on a goldmine, I decided to use it instead of being pushed around in some crummy job where you don't get any kind of decent money. By the time I was eighteen, if I still had a cherry it would have been punched so far back I could use it for a tail light. And I had nothing to show for it. I can make some *real* money hustling . . . I buy nice clothes, I live well, and I take good care of myself.[5]

And the English former prostitute Yasmin asserts her right to the kind of lifestyle middle-class people take for granted:

If you want money and you want the finer things in life . . . Why shouldn't we have the finer things in life? I want them. And I've not got an education, I've no career, so what is there left? Work in a factory? I'm not gonna do that . . . We don't do what we're meant to do, toe the line as working class women, but why the hell should we? We're not just brought into this life for – what? – reproduction and to cater for men? Why? Why can't we go our own way as well, and be independent? And earn money, and make a better life for ourselves, and our children.[6]

As Yasmin's statement makes clear, whores do not think only of themselves when they work in the sex industry – the majority of them are also mothers. Making enough money to bring up children independently of men is a theme which crops up continually in prostitutes' motivations. Bernard Cohen was surprised by the 'unusually positive attitudes about their work' of the Puerto Rican prostitutes he interviewed in New York: the women, aged between 18 and 23, were all in the sex trade 'as the single way available to them of making enough money to support their children'.[7]

Another whore, quoted by Winick and Kinsie, expands this theme: 'I take all I can get. I have one big reason for doing this – my little girl, who means everything to me. I need the money to raise her. I want her to have the best of everything. I'm divorced from my husband and he doesn't contribute a cent towards her support.'[8]

Yasmin echoes this attitude: 'My daughter is the number one in my life . . . And, as much as *I* want nice things, I also want the best for her. I like coming home from work and coming to my daughter, being her mother, playing with her, cooking for her, and keeping a lovely home.'[9]

In 1980 the English Collective of Prostitutes found in a survey of working prostitutes that over 70 per cent were single mothers. This clearly shows up the patriarchal division of women into either whores or good mothers as one of the biggest lies about prostitution. It also shows the laws that are used against whores – declaring them unfit mothers and putting their children into care – in their most callous light.

A good concrete example of the process of choice single prostitute mothers engage in is Anita's experience working the Soho flats. After her first two-day session, she had a difficult decision to make, knowing that the work was brutally hard, but having to weigh this against the fact that, as a single mother trying to live on inadequate state benefits, she desperately needed the money: 'I came back home after two days. I'd got £600. And then I had to sit in my house and weigh it up, because there is *no* way I could've got that money any other way.'[10]

Anita's decision to continue working the flats is a prime example of the unsung heroism of prostitutes: forced by the low pay/no pay/no childcare facilities trap into a choice between poverty and prostitution – in this case in dreadful conditions – Anita stuck it out for four weeks. Although the work was, in her own words: 'Horrible, horrible, horrible . . . the lowest form of prostitution,' her decision was to some extent compensated: 'But then again, I had that money; I stuck it in the bank, and I felt great.'[11]

If for working-class women the high pay and flexibility of sex work still provide the only opportunity of attaining an adequate standard of living independently of men, even middle-class women appear to be tempted these days; recent studies such as Diana's show a steadily increasing number of them entering the sex trade, often as part-timers. They are usually students working their way through school or university, white-collar workers supplementing their regular income (always much less than men's), or academically qualified single parents. Middle-class, educated whores cluster in massage parlour and callgirl work; they tend to spend fewer years in the trade than their working-class sisters, avoiding becoming professionalized hookers and instead moving on to more prestigious kinds of work (which often involves a substantial drop in pay).

It seems that, having discarded some of the Victorian and post-Victorian sexual shame, these middle-class women are now prepared to use prostitution as a stepping-stone towards their own goals. Nevertheless, the whore-stigma is still strong enough to dissuade many of them from 'coming out' about their part-time dabbling in the old profession.

Working as a callgirl is one of the few ways in which even highly-qualified women can get near to the kind of earnings many professional men make. An American former whore, 'J', gives us an insight into these economic incentives (at 1973 rates):

> With most uptown call girls, the choice is not between starvation and life, but it is a choice between $5000 and $25,000, or between $10,000 and $50,000. That's a pretty big choice: a pretty big difference. You can say that they're in this business because of the difference of $40,000 a year . . . But you can't say, even of the call girl, that she has so many other ways to earn an adequate living. Even with an undergraduate degree, chances are that she couldn't do better than earn $5000 or $6000 a year, outside of prostitution. Because it's very *hard* for women to earn an adequate living and so we do not have much economic choice – even the call girl.[12]

Apart from putting themselves through higher education or setting themselves up in business, the desire to give their children 'the best of everything' looms as large with middle-class as with working-class women. Tracy Leah Landis, an ex-massage parlour worker, writes of her friend and colleague Colleen:

She had two sons. The eldest came from her husband's previous marriage, but she always referred to him as her son. Colleen had provided her family with a big suburban home in one of the outlying districts of the city. It had all the nice things, a big freezer and a double garage, and a big boat on a trailer and a couple of cars in front. The living-room was a huge family gathering spot, with a great big fish tank by the door and a nice color television next to the fireplace.[13]

Another American woman, Sunny Carter, tells the moving story of her decision to work as a callgirl in order to give her small son Brennan, who suffered from cystic fibrosis, the kind of life that most children can only dream of. In 1976, when Sunny learned that her baby had the disease, she found that it would cost her $10,000 a year simply to keep him alive. At that time she was earning only $9000 annually. She decided to become a prostitute, and, through a friend of a friend, got connected into a callgirl network, using her own apartment as a work-base. Sunny's feelings after her first client had left reflect the positive reactions many callgirls have to their work:

> I sat on the bed, holding the hundred-dollar bill. He had actually *tipped* me. It was that easy. He had literally come and gone, and I was one hundred dollars richer in just twenty minutes.
> I went into the bathroom and looked at my reflection. I didn't look different, just happier. And I felt . . . well . . . just *fine*. No pangs of guilt, no remorse, no shame. What I felt was smug, joyous elation. By God, I was on to something here, *and I knew it*.

When Sunny's mother subsequently found out that her daughter had accumulated $4000 in a couple of months through whoring, she commented: 'My God, I wish I had thought of doing this when *I* was your age.'

Sunny goes on to complete the story of her son's short but full life:

> My earnings enabled us to travel, gave him an opportunity to see more than would otherwise have been possible. By the time my son was seven, he had flown in an airplane more than many people in a lifetime. We lived in New York for a year, where he saw dinosaurs and whales at the Natural History Museum. We

lived on an island in the US Virgin Islands for several years, where he learned to snorkel the incredible coral reef, seeing the splendour of the underwater world. He collected hundreds of hermit crabs and built them an intricate home in an aquarium which he called Crab Condo. He learned to strip the outer edge of coconut fronds away, leaving only the long, fibrous centre which he tied into a slipknot, the perfect way to sneak up on a fat lizard, slip the noose knot round its neck and with a flick of the wrist, capture it. Together we caught whole jars full of lizards, picked a favourite, then let them go from the centre of a huge chalk-drawn circle, cheering for our favourite as the lizards raced away.

I provided as full a life for my son as I could, and money was the key. Prostitution provided the money, and, even more importantly, it gave me the spare time I wouldn't have had with any nine-to-five 'real' job. It provided the best private schooling, the chance to travel, the best medical care.

On October the first, 1985, my son died. He would have been ten years old that December.[14]

Sunny's was a special case, but it is still a supreme example of prostitute mothers' love and concern for their children: 'No Vice Squad or Special Branch can stop mothers loving and caring for their children and wanting a better life for them . . . Until governments provide women with decent financial alternatives, no amount of police harassment and brutality can prevent us from feeding our families.'[15]

The kind of lifestyle Sunny was able to give her child would have been impossible in any 'straight' women's work; but it is important to add that the good life is not only available to the well-educated and well-connected whore; Yasmin, who spent part of her career servicing a wealthy and exclusive clientele, enumerates the benefits she would never have had, as a working-class woman, in any other line of work: 'I certainly wouldn't have gone halfway round the world if I hadn't been a prostitute. I wouldn't have been to Barbados, I wouldn't have stayed at the Ritz in Paris, all the best hotels everywhere I went, like Monte Carlo . . . and be bought the finest clothes, and eaten the finest food.'[16]

From any point of view, in a society which worships money and material achievements to the extent that ours does, becoming a prostitute is a rational decision for a woman to make. Living standards may have risen since the 19th century, but so have expectations; and women are still in the business of refusing poverty when they take up sex work – particularly those disadvantaged women who form the majority of prostitutes. How else are they supposed to give themselves and their families the kind of lifestyle promoted by the Western media as the norm – a life of security, comfort and consumerism? Faced with the choice between drudging for a pittance – with no guarantee that they can keep their heads above water – and making real money through prostitution, these women are making a responsible decision when they turn to the sex trade. It is not an easy decision to make, nor an easy life to lead, for the work – especially on the streets – is hard and wearing, with the law and public prejudice combining to make life extremely difficult and dangerous. But given the paucity of options women still face today, sex work is often the most assertive choice they can make. To condemn women for becoming prostitutes, or continually to divert attention from their demands to the small minority who are forced into the life, is to ignore whores' courage and add to their burden.

None the less, the rationality that lies behind women's choices has continued to evade the male 'experts' who, in the eternal quest for female pathological deviance, are constantly updating the 19th-century tradition of stereotyping whores with new-fangled psychoanalytical mystification. Modern explanations of why some women become prostitutes revolve around their supposed sexuality in relation to their early family life, a typical psychoanalytical myth being that whores are 'frigid' and that they enter the sex industry to take revenge on their fathers. As Winick and Kinsie summarize it:

> Psychoanalytic studies stress prostitutes' frigidity, immature psycho-sexual development [immaturity, we recall, was a staple of 19th-century stereotyping], and severely deficient object-relationships . . . the prostitute may be revenging herself on every man for the love she expected to get but did not receive from her father. Her frigidity can be regarded as involving a humiliation of all her clients and therefore a mass castration on an unconscious level.[17]

This gobbledegook shows male paranoia at its most tortuous; it also resurrects the old Victorian dilemma: are women sexual or asexual? – the patriarch's recurring nightmare.

Two main elements are involved in this theory: firstly, frigidity, and secondly, mass castration. In the first case, the fact that whores do not respond with ecstasy to their many sexual contacts with men is a blow to the collective male ego, since the penis in all its glory is supposed to be irresistible (as William Acton claimed in the 19th century among many others); prostitutes, who are daily exposed to its charms, should therefore swoon with pleasure at every trick. The fact that sex work is just that for prostitutes – work, not play – seems to have escaped these eggheads. In reality, whores place strict barriers between their work and their pleasure, reserving their sexual responsiveness for the men or women they choose to see in their private lives. The psychoanalysts, however, continue to explain away whores' unresponsiveness to their clients as frigidity.

Also behind the frigidity claim looms the spectre of women's sexuality, always seen as threatening to the male, or 'castrating', in the Freudian jargon. Patriarchal men, as we know, fear the liberated sexuality of women; therefore the prostitute, whose only-too-visible sexual independence from men threatens male power, is projected as the primary symbol of this dangerous sexuality. So what the analysts have to say is very interesting in some respects; it provides us with some fascinating insights into *male* pathology. For while these men are reassuring themselves that there is really nothing to fear from whores because they are all 'frigid', at the same time their 'mass castration' fantasy gives the game away, showing what they really fear: that women are indeed sexual beings, and that their sexuality is in the process of evolving towards liberty.

Back in the real world, of course, whores cannot be lumped together into all-embracing stereotypes any more than any other group of people; their personalities – and sexualities – are as diverse as all women's. In spite of their giving credence to psychoanalytical views, Winick and Kinsie themselves admit that 'there are no data to confirm that prostitutes of today have more disturbed personalities or backgrounds than non-prostitutes',[18] and Lewis Diana concludes from his studies that 'there cannot be said to be a personality type or profile of the prostitute.'[19] In other words, whores' backgrounds and personalities are not noticeably different from other women's. One study in the 1970s found that 'the only measurable difference between prostitutes and controls, who were matched for education and economic background, was that the prostitutes earned more money.'[20] The stereotyping is in fact an integral part of the whore-stigma, and has the same aim now as it had in the 19th century – to reinforce and justify the oppression of prostitutes by branding them abnormal or deviant.

One new feature of prostitute-stereotyping in the 20th century has been the image of the 'junkie-whore' – the drug dependent woman, ultimate victim, who trades sex to support her habit. Undoubtedly there are addicts working in the sex industry, just as there are addicts working in every industry, but they are not as rife as is generally supposed. As Priscilla Alexander comments: 'Prostitution is hard work, both in physical and emotional terms. Therefore, it is not surprising that a significant number of prostitutes use drugs of one kind or another to make the work easier.'[21]

Nevertheless, to leap to the conclusion that the 'typical' hooker is a heroin addict would be an error: 'Given how widespread the use of drugs in society is, we doubt there is much difference in the percentage of prostitute women on drugs and the percentage of others on drugs.'[22]

Lewis Diana's survey tends to support this statement. He found (in 1985) that the most popular drug used by prostitutes was marijuana, followed by alcohol, amphetamines and tranquillizers, in that order; this roughly duplicates the pattern of drugs most popular in mainstream US society. Only 4 per cent of his sample used heroin, and 2 per cent cocaine. Although recent years have seen a visible increase of addicted women (particularly juveniles) taking to prostitution, they are still a small minority, inflated by popular media horror stories. In general, they work on the streets, where turnover is quickest and sex the most basic; and they gravitate towards whoring because it is quite simply the only way they can earn the large amounts of money necessary to support a habit.

Prostitution itself is neither a cause nor an effect of drug addiction – in fact addiction causes problems for the sex industry just as it does in straight society, since addicts, to increase their turnover, will undercut prices and offer the kinds of sex other whores refuse to undertake. The 'junkie-whore' image is just another way in which society attempts to obscure the basic truths about prostitution – which are, as always, economic – by blaming prostitutes for its own evils.

Another way in which the stereotyping of whores has been used to scapegoat them in the last decade has been evident in the debate around AIDS. Syphilis is no longer the bogey it used to be, but the sudden appearance of AIDS and its spread to the heterosexual population has given the moral right-wingers a field day, reviving the old fantasies in which the 'dirty whore' is held solely responsible for the transmission of sexual disease.

Prostitutes, however, being in the frontline of infection from all sexually transmitted diseases, were practising 'safe sex' long before AIDS was identified; and since then they have only increased their vigilance. This includes streetworkers, incidentally, in spite of the criminally irresponsible behaviour of the police, who routinely confiscate condoms from the whores they arrest, to use as evidence in court. The American former prostitute and campaigner Gloria Lockett describes the police's actions towards her after they stopped and searched her car:

> They found the condoms. They said, 'Oh, what have we here?' They took each condom out of its package, and using their penknives, cut holes in each one. They laughed, and one officer said, 'Now go use these.'
>
> Another time . . . I had just purchased twelve dozen condoms. I was stopped by the police and they did something very similar. After they had made holes in every condom and gave them back to me, useless, they said 'Happy hunting!'[23]

Whores know that it is not themselves who are the problem, but the men who use their services, many of whom will offer from two to five times the going rate for unprotected sex. One London streetwalker told *Time Out* journalist Sarah Baxter in 1989 that one in three men wanted sex without a condom. A Soho prostitute called Mandy described her prophylactic method: 'Usually I just shove it on them. It's too late then to complain. If a man doesn't want to use a rubber, I say "There's plenty of AIDS about" and show him the door.'[24]

As a result of this safe-sex awareness, whores are not a high-risk category for AIDS or for any other sexually transmitted diseases, contrary to the claims of some governments. Dr Helen Ward and anthropologist Sophie Day, who monitored the health of 150 prostitutes at London's St Mary's Hospital, found that only three were HIV positive; two had been infected by shared needles and the third had contracted the virus from her boyfriend. In addition, the women were found to have extremely low levels of other STDs, such as herpes and gonorrhea. Dr Ward concludes that all of this 'points to just how safely these women have sex'.[25]

The statistics are little different in the US, where as the prostitute activist Margo St James notes (speaking of STDs generally):

The VD rate among prostitutes has always been lower than among the general public of their own age group – quite a bit lower, in fact, considering that most female prostitutes are between eighteen and twenty-five, particularly on the street. Their rate is 5 per cent for VD, but if you go into the college campuses, you find the rate is around 25 per cent.[26]

In an excellent essay on the subject of prostitution and the transmission of AIDS, Priscilla Alexander clarifies the situation, astutely observing that: 'If prostitutes were effectively transmitting the AIDS virus to their customers, there would be far more cases of white, heterosexual males diagnosed with AIDS than is reflected in the current statistics'. Since the average street whore services 1500 clients annually, and given an estimated rate of female-to-male transmission of 20 per cent, if only 5 per cent of New York's 20,000 prostitutes were infected the result would be 300,000 cases of AIDS among their clients. 'However, only approximately seventy men have been diagnosed with AIDS who claim contact with prostitutes as their only risk factor . . . In terms of contact tracing, there has not been a single documented case of a man getting AIDS from contact with a prostitute.'[27]

Even before the AIDS virus appeared on the scene, prostitutes were using condoms, not simply as a measure against STDs but also as a physical barrier between themselves and their clients. As Margo St James observes: 'Condoms are used for privacy . . . that's the way prostitutes separate their work from their play.'[28]

In fact it is the client who is in need of health education, not the whore. Men persist in demanding, bribing, cajoling hookers to provide unprotected sex; as one of my prostitute friends remarked: 'It never ceases to amaze me, these are *educated* men, they have families, they have wives and kids; there's AIDS about and *still* they're coming it: "I'll pay you so-and-so if you don't use the rubber", and they're still moaning about it being "like eating a sweet with the wrapper on". These men are imbeciles.'

The inevitable calls for a return to regulation of prostitutes which have accompanied the resurrection of the 19th-century prejudice that stereotypes whores as carriers of disease are as redundant now as they were a century ago. Measures against AIDS would be better directed towards raising the awareness (not to mention responsibility) of white, heterosexual, middle-class men – the bulk of prostitutes' customers.

The scapegoating involved in the 'junkie-whore' and 'diseased-whore' stereotypes only adds to the real health problems of women who work in the sex trade. One such problem is a hazard shared by millions of workers throughout the contemporary world: stress. Prostitution is hard, stressful work; its effective illegality means that whores are always looking over their shoulder for the law; they live in constant fear of arrest and imprisonment, and are frontline targets for any passing psychopath. In addition, 19th- and early 20th-century anti-whore attitudes have so successfully filtered into the public consciousness that prostitutes also have to deal with a constant assault on their self-esteem in the form of society's image of them as pariahs, sub-human and unnatural women – the scapegoats of a sexuality constructed around fear, ignorance and disgust.

Finally, sex work, like other kinds of specialized work in our highly specialized society, carries its own intrinsic problems for the workers: the daily contact with men's demands, the alienation of dealing with a constant stream of impersonal sex, the pressures of facing alone the fall-out from society's sexual hang-ups. These combined stresses, most of which are entirely unnecessary, can make a whore's life a misery – truly *une vie de putain*, as the French put it – but unlike other workers, prostitutes cannot seek professional help to deal with their work problems. Hounded and oppressed, criminalized and isolated, they have only each other to turn to. Companionship – what feminists would call sisterhood, in any other context – is the rule among whores; although the majority of outside observers have rarely bothered to notice this solidarity. As Yasmin says: 'We prostitutes might all be different in our own ways, but I think the main thing is that we all give each other love and kindness. Little things like kindness, generosity, consideration, respect – we give each other all those things.'[29]

These 'things' clearly make up in some part for the contempt and indifference of the straight world. Chloe enlarges on the theme: 'To other people we might be . . . all prostitutes, but this is where the real respect lies – feelings, loving. We carry a community in our hearts, really.'[30]

In spite of the fact that society does its utmost to make their work difficult and degrading, many whores feel positive about and proud of their work. Lewis Diana found that 60 per cent of the prostitutes he interviewed were happy about their work, despite all the drawbacks. One woman had this to say in response to society's attempt to moralize:

> Q: What about the morality of prostitution?
> A: I don't believe it's immoral . . . Look, I'm doing what I want to do. It's my choice. I can stop anytime I want to. I have something they want and I give it to them for a price. It's a mutual thing, an agreement.
> Q: So you don't feel exploited?
> A: No . . . Can I say something about morals? What about all the girlfriends and wives who put out when they don't want to? Are they exploited? And if they aren't usually turned on, still they are expected to have sex.[31]

Many whores find that their ability to earn real money, as opposed to a pittance, for their work can be a source of self-esteem. Like an American prostitute, Debra:

> I've had a lot of different jobs. I've worked in canning factories, which is horrendous work. That's why prostitution was so nice for me. Because you got a lot of money. You didn't take harassment. You didn't allow it. You were in control of the situation. You know? If someone patted my bottom, I got money for it. They didn't expect it to be part of the job. Which is very basically what I was going through with a lot of the other jobs. Being told that I should be thankful for the job. You know? . . . Please kiss my ass and thank me for giving you this shit job. And I was getting totally fed up with it. So I started prostitution and took to it immediately . . . Face it, the people who ran the factories and the jobs were mostly men. I got sick of men doing that to me. [In prostitution] I made between three and five hundred dollars a night and sometimes more. I lived better than I did in my life.[32]

Debra's pride stems from the contrast between sex work and other forms of women's work – in which she was systematically degraded, her self-esteem under constant attack through low pay, bad conditions and sexual harassment – in other words, 'normal' working life for many straight women. Another American prostitute, Phyllis Luman Metal, started hooking at the age of 57, and has some interesting things to say about the comparison between the life of a whore and the life of a 'respectable' straight woman:

When I first charged for it, I had much more self-respect and self worth than I ever had before. I felt appreciated. When I was a wife I was expected to do a lot of shit work and service my husbands and their desire, not mine. I felt used and abused. No trick ever broke my ribs like my husband did. No trick ever took all my money and left me when it was all gone – another husband did that. No trick ever urged me to neglect my children to accommodate him. No trick ever threw a bunch of in-laws who made my life miserable at me. No trick ever came home drunk every night . . . And I always had money, which I did not when I was married. And I never got a venereal disease. And something else. I got to know people of all nationalities in a way I never could have otherwise. My customers in Paris were from all nations. They were Swiss, British, German, Norwegian, Italian, Spanish, French, Syrian, Berber, Algerian, Senegalese, Saudi, Iranian, Japanese. I felt like a citizen of the world. Prostitution made me feel that all of us on the planet were one family.[33]

(At the age of 69, Phyllis was at graduate school completing a master's degree.)

Finally, callgirl and writer Carol Leigh (alias 'Scarlot Harlot') expresses her pride in the work she does as a prostitute: 'I'm proud. Sex work is nurturing, healing work. It could be considered a high calling. Prostitutes are great women, veritable priestesses.'[34]

We are beginning to come full circle here, with whores rediscovering the glories and achievements of their ancient past; and becoming actively aware that there is a great deal more to their profession than the mess modern society has made of it.

The inevitable outcome of this reclamation of their old dignity has been the growth within the last two decades of a worldwide prostitutes' movement. Now, the real experts are beginning to speak up for themselves.

★ ★ ★

The radicalism of the 1960s spawned a whole generation of new-style struggles based on the organized activism of minorities in Western society. The Civil Rights movements of black people in the USA and South Africa, and Catholics in Northern Ireland; student rebellions; gay and lesbian pride campaigns; all these fuelled the awareness that people could make a difference in their own lives, on their own terms, outside the tired old political institutions; and all of these movements contributed to the climate of popular confidence which encouraged the growth of prostitutes' own campaigning groups. But un-doubtedly the most influential and visible of these developments – the most important catalyst of the whores' struggle – was the rebirth in the late sixties of the Western feminist movement.

Only a few years later, with women's issues firmly on the agenda, prostitutes began to organize and put forward their own agenda, using a set of references that was undeniably feminist. Nevertheless, relations between the politicized whores' movement and their feminist sisters have been strained from the start. For while feminism may have provided a major impetus to prostitutes, it has been a largely middle-class movement reflecting middle-class concerns – and, to some extent, middle-class prejudices. It is no coincidence that many feminists remain ambivalent towards the whores' movement, and that the anti-pornography/prostitution faction of contemporary Western feminism has tended to reproduce the attitudes of their predecessors, the 'First Wave' feminists of the 19th century. These women tend to regard all prostitution as female sexual slavery and all sex work as degrading to women in general; they also take care to ignore any manifestations of whores' pride.

This refusal of feminists to listen to prostitutes can be traced to the early years of the Second Wave. What was probably the first modern feminist conference on prostitution was held in the US in 1971; Kate Millett, one of the founding mothers of the movement, was in attendance. According to her account, the first day of the conference made a promising start, with 'excellent papers on theory, definitions, statistics, history, and convolutions of the law, its arbitrary enforce-ment . . . and with proposals for reform.'[35]

Amid all the theorizing, defining, and proposing, however, one small detail had been omitted: whores, the real experts on the sex industry, were missing, excluded both by the academic set-up of the conference itself and by the blatant lack of consultation on the part of its organizers. But on the second day – 'Against all likelihood,' notes

Millett, with bland surprise – several prostitutes turned up. Perhaps they believed they might be consulted about their viewpoints and wishes; if so, they were rudely disappointed. For when the whores expressed their anger at the conference's assumption that their work should be 'eliminated', the feminists, seeing their control of both agenda and debate challenged, became hostile and insulting towards their 'sisters'. The meeting ended in uproar, blows were exchanged – a 'shambles', Millett calls it – and feminists lost a unique opportunity to listen to what whores had to say.

Kate Millett herself is a prime example of the feminists' inability to see past their own prejudices. She refers to prostitution as 'slavery';[36] she then goes on to follow the time-honoured tradition of stereotyping when she characterizes the whores at the conference as acting 'with the unerring instinct of the unconscious'[37] . . . well, we know that whores have no conscious awareness: the 19th-century male pundits told us often enough! But the gloves don't come off till Millett is dealing with one of the dissenting whores in person. Suddenly, her writing disintegrates into a purple passage of character assassination worthy of the most misogynistic 19th-century male scientist, describing a prostitute 'whose grandiose neuroticism, however paradigmatic of the personal disorientation of an Uptown call girl, rendered her completely impervious to logic of any kind'.[38] Sound familiar? Nowhere in the account of this conference are the prostitutes allowed to speak for themselves. With 'feminists' like these . . .

The obsession with eliminating prostitution crops up again and again in feminist writings, gaining particular currency with the rise of the anti-pornography movement in the late seventies. This movement has sprung from an extremist radical/revolutionary tendency whose gurus are largely middle-class Americans who were student radicals during the sixties. It comes as no surprise, then, to find that much of their rhetoric is filled with references to revolution, war, the enemy, and so on; and that their discourse is littered with demands for the 'elimination' of this that and the other.

In one 'paradigmatic' paper, delivered to a 1980 Women Against Violence Against Women conference in Leeds, Sheila Jeffreys gives the radical feminist's view of the sex industry. Jeffreys opens her paper with a quote from the English Collective of Prostitutes (ECP) on women's motives for entering the sex industry:

. . . we are forced into prostitution by poverty, we are also fighting poverty through prostitution. Getting money for sex is one of the few ways open for women to make some money of our own and be financially independent from men. It's a way to have better control over our lives and dictate what kinds of relationships we want and on what terms.[39]

Jeffreys brusquely dismisses this blazingly rational statement with the comment that it 'will not help us to explain why prostitution exists'.[40] In other words, what organized whores have to say, speaking from their own experience, means nothing to this radical feminist. Jeffreys continues by making the same careless mistake as most other outside observers of the sex industry: she equates prostitutes with prostitution, asserting that 'payment reduces the woman to a bought object'.[41] In fact, what is being bought is not the woman, but the sexual services she offers.

Having thus silenced prostitutes and reduced them to objects, Jeffreys goes on to offer us the fruits of her own meditations. Men, she reveals, use whores for practice in honing 'the valuable weapon of sexual aggression', which they use in their social control of women; thus she concludes that: 'Prostitution . . . serves as a *guerilla training camp and rehabilitation centre for sexual terrorists.*'[42] (Her emphasis.)

It is important to recognize that this kind of 'theory' has helped fuel the anti-sex industry/pro-censorship movement of recent years; and that this in turn has had a negative impact on the way in which women who work in the sex industry are viewed by the rest of society. From the perspective of this severely paranoid fantasy of revolutionary war, there can obviously be no quarter given to the sex trade. Since it serves such a dangerously counter-revolutionary purpose it must clearly be eliminated. The reader's expectations are not disappointed, as Jeffreys goes on to reproduce with uncanny accuracy the feminist position of a century ago, paying lip-service to whores' needs, but leaving us in no doubt as to the fate of their profession: 'The main question seems to be how we can both support women who work as prostitutes whilst working to *eliminate the institution of prostitution.*'[43] (My emphasis.)

The evangelical rhetoric of the Butlerites has given way to the secular rhetoric of contemporary radicalism – but the message is still the same: the sex industry is evil and must be stamped out. Thus Sheila Jeffreys and feminists like her play into the hands of the moral reactionaries who are always waiting in the wings, ready and eager to jump out at any time and blame prostitutes for all of society's ills.

When put into action by the state – as with the case of kerb-crawling laws, which were supported by many feminists – the concrete effects of this kind of theorizing are wearily predictable, costing many whores their livelihoods and, all too often, their lives, as the whore-stigma is translated into violence on the streets.

With feminists at best ambivalent towards prostitutes, and with the extremely vociferous anti-sex industry faction silencing support for sex workers within the movement, it became clear that to make their demands heard, whores would have to organize themselves independently. The pioneer in this field was an American former prostitute, Margo St James, who had felt the force of the whore-stigma – and its practical applicability to all women – before she had even turned a trick.

In the early sixties St James had been 'a latterday beatnik and goodtime girl' in North Beach, San Francisco, keeping an open apartment which was 'a hangout for many young people to smoke pot and dance to recorded music'. The police, naturally, became suspicious of the number of people seen coming and going at her place and sent a member of the vice squad to see her, incognito. He offered her money to sleep with him, and when shown the door, suddenly 'flashed his badge, said he was a cop, and told me I was under arrest for *soliciting him!*'

Convicted as a prostitute in court (on the grounds that she knew what the word 'trick' meant – the judge had told her: 'Anyone who speaks the language is obviously a professional'), Margo fought and won an appeal; but the damage was done; she was tainted with the whore-stigma:

> I found that, as soon as I was officially labelled, all cocktail waitress jobs were out the window. I ended up working for the bailbonds office for free for a year to pay my bail . . . To this date, I have never been able to secure any but the most menial and insecure of jobs. Even though my record is supposedly expunged, San Francisco is a small town where everybody knows. But I'll be damned if I am going to be run out of town . . .
>
> Once I won my appeal I lost interest in law school and the hypocrisy it supported. Eventually, I said 'Yes' to the lawyers and judges who constantly solicited me . . . I worked very little, just enough to pay the bills, and since I was not into the 'business' to make a fortune, I drifted out of it after a few years.[44]

Margo had experienced the injustice of the prostitute laws at first hand. In the early 1970s her knowledge of the sex trade and the law coalesced with the formation of the whores' organization COYOTE (Call Off Your Old Tired Ethics). By 1973 there were many groups working in San Francisco for women's rights in general, but none addressing the issues of prostitution, particularly from whores' own point of view. With the founding of COYOTE, Margo St James became the first spokeswomen of what she calls 'an invisible constituency'[45] in reference to the illegality which prevents whores from coming out in public.

The moment was well-timed; within months similar organizations sprang up in other parts of the country. These included: New York PONY, Massachusetts PUMA, Hawaii DOLPHIN, Detroit CUPIDS, Michigan PEP, Florida COYOTE, Kansas City KITTY, Los Angeles KAT, New Orleans PASSION, Sacramento COYOTE, San Diego OCELOT, Seattle ASP, and others.[46]

Because of the difficulties of coming out as whores and of getting funding for their struggles, many of these groups were short-lived, but at least the ball was rolling and the original organization, COYOTE, has maintained a consistently high profile in San Francisco and other American cities. To get round the funding problem, the San Francisco chapter initiated an annual Hookers' Ball – 'a Hallowe'en costume bash' – at which whores and the public could mingle with all the anonymity of a Restoration masked ball; this event, which has since become a major tourist attraction, raised COYOTE enough cash to publish its own newsletter, make a film (*Hard Work*) about the sex trade, and establish the National Task Force on Prostitution.

The second flashpoint of the world whores' movement was the city of Lyons in France. In 1974, two horrific prostitute murders sparked off a protest meeting at which about fifty hookers, lawyers, community activists and journalists took part in drawing up a statement of the prostitutes' demands. On the level of security, the women pointed out that the law and police repression were making it impossible for them to work in the relative safety of hotels, furnished apartments, or their own shared flats; at the same time the police were failing to protect streetwalkers. There had been a series of gruesome murders of young prostitutes during the preceding years, but the police had done little to try to capture the perpetrators. The Lyons prostitutes demanded an end to police repression and brutality, the system of fining (some women, remember, were being fined three or four times daily), and the harassment and raiding of bars which served prostitutes.

A short time after the first event, another young prostitute was found tortured to death and mutilated; a second protest meeting was held. In the meantime, the police stepped up their repression, openly fuelling the climate of anti-whore violence. A pattern evolved: the women organized meetings; the police upped the number of fines: 'They were playing cowboys and Indians. "We have to collect at least thirty fines a day," a young inspector admitted to some prostitutes who were questioning him.'

Many women faced prison sentences because they could not keep up with the payments of fines that were raining down on them daily. Finally: 'the height of irony – the girls would find in their mail, along with fines to pay, reminders of taxes going back several years, calculated from hasty enquiries and justified with the description "liberal profession, lady companion or kept woman".'[47]

The crunch came when, soon after the whores' spokeswoman, Ulla, had appeared on television to state their demands, the first prison sentences were handed down by the courts. The prostitutes decided that some dramatic action was called for, something that would get them maximum publicity: they would occupy a church. At 10 a.m. on Monday 3 June 1975, 'after two hours of hide-and-seek with the police, 100 to 150 prostitutes enter[ed] one of the main churches in the centre of Lyons – the church of St Nizier.'

The women hung a banner over the façade of the church: NOS ENFANTS NE VEULENT PAS LEUR MÈRE EN PRISON (Our children don't want their mothers in prison), and appealed to the public in an open letter: 'We are mothers talking to you. Women trying to bring up their children alone as best they can, and who today are scared of losing them.' They went on to condemn the police for attacking them, and the state for making money out of them, and threw down a direct challenge to the authorities: 'None of us will go to prison. Or if we do, the police will have to massacre us to drag us there.'[48]

It was a powerful message, and one which made a sensational impact in the media. Public sympathy was evident from the start: people brought food to the church, the women of Lyons came to show their solidarity and find out just who these prostitutes were – and whores arrived from all over France to support their sisters. Soon the movement spread, with churches occupied in Marseilles, Grenoble,

Montpellier (birthplace of medieval regulation), followed by prostitutes' strikes in Toulouse, St Etienne and Cannes. Finally, the whores
of Paris threw down the gauntlet in front of the national government:
they occupied the St Bernard Chapel in Montparnasse.

By this time, the whores' movement was drawing the attention of
the world's press, as well as stirring up a hornet's nest of debate in
France. It had become an acute embarrassment to the French
government. Thrown into a panic by a week of historically unprecedented prostitutes' rebellion, the authorities' response was predictably
brutal. At 5.30 a.m. on Tuesday 11 June, vice squad police tricked the
priest (who had been sympathetic to the whores' action) into opening
the doors of St Nizier and swarmed into the building. Barbara, one of
the whores' spokeswomen, describes the ensuing scene:

> Everyone was asleep except for the girls on the door. Suddenly
> we heard them shouting 'Police! Police!' They'd arrived. First
> some plain clothes guys, the whole vice squad, about forty of
> them. Then others in uniforms with helmets on, in the gear they
> wear for demonstrations. They invaded the church and shouted,
> 'You're surrounded, everybody out immediately'. I got up, I had
> just enough time to slip on my dress. As soon as they came in,
> they said quite openly that they had to take care of Ulla and
> Barbara first. Meanwhile, both of us were trying to calm the girls
> down. We were all sitting on the floor. Then they laid into us,
> they dragged us along the ground by our hair. I clung on tight to
> a door. We all tried to resist the best we could. But there were at
> least ten of them to every two of us. Punching and kicking, they
> dragged us all the way to the vans. They threw me in literally
> head first. They threw my head against the driver's seat.
> Outside, Ulla had grabbed on to me, and the cops had pulled her
> off by the hair. They beat her brutally round the head. She
> fainted and fell flat on the floor, out cold.[49]

Similar operations took place simultaneously at the other occupied
churches in France, likewise carried out with all the Gallic charm for
which the French police force is so justly renowned.

Nevertheless, the whores' movement did not, as the authorities
hoped, meekly disband; French prostitutes began holding regular
General Assembly meetings in the Lyons Trade Union Hall. A few
days before the summer holidays, in the same year, they convened an

Assembly on the lawn of President Giscard d'Estaing's château at Channonat, near Clermont-Ferrand, hanging their banners and posters from its gates and trees: 'We've come from all over France to visit the château that Giscard d'Estaing's been able to buy for himself with the money from our fines and taxes,' they informed the astonished media.

The actions of the Lyons prostitutes provided the catalyst for the formation of the French Collective of Prostitutes, a political union which in turn inspired similar organizations throughout the world. The idea of the church occupation also spread beyond the borders of France. The English Collective of Prostitutes (modelled on the French Collective) took it up. The ECP had been formed as an autonomous organization within the International Wages for Housework Campaign in 1975; in order to get round the problem of coming out publicly, they appointed Selma James, an experienced non-prostitute activist and founder of Wages for Housework as their first spokeswoman. From its very inception, the ECP campaigned at grassroots level on behalf of whores, and in 1982 it opened a Women's Centre in King's Cross, an inner-city area of London with a high number of streetwalkers.

The centre offered a meeting-place for all women, as well as a free professional legal service, LAW (Legal Action for Women). Local prostitutes immediately started seeking the service's help in their many problems with the police; and in June 1982, the organization supported a woman in pleading 'Not guilty' to a charge of soliciting which would have branded her a common prostitute. The woman was acquitted and, after this initial victory, 'encouraged by the Centre, by LAW and by the "not guilty" verdict, prostitute women began to construct a minor volcano.'[50]

The King's Cross Centre became crowded with prostitutes holding civil rights meetings and arranging their 'not guilty' pleas, after having been arrested while out shopping or collecting their children from school. In October a second 'not guilty' verdict was returned; this was too much for the local police, who had already started harassing the women who were using the Centre. They began a counter-attack in earnest.

The police opened hostilities by accusing a woman who had sought police help after being raped of being a prostitute; they also accused her boyfriend of being a pimp. They followed this up by arresting other women who used the Centre, and terrorizing their friends and families. Selma James:

Monday morning, I was to go to court with a woman pleading not guilty. A single mother with a disabled child, she had dropped into the Centre on her way home . . . as she left the Centre she was arrested. At the court, I found she was in a panic because the witness who had seen the arrest (and who could testify to its illegality) was herself appearing in court at the other end of London on a trumped-up probation charge. Her closest friend who was in court with her was a woman from the north of England. She had just heard that her mother with whom her six-year-old son lived had been visited first by the police and told that her daughter was a prostitute (which freaked the old woman out completely). Then the Social Services came and said in front of her grandson that she was too old to be taking care of him, and that he would be taken from her and put into care. The boy begged his granny not to let them take him away. He had an attack of asthma and was hospitalized.

The defendant herself had her hands full. The police were watching her house to get her boyfriend, who lived with her, for pimping, and they eventually did get him.[51]

From their outrageous behaviour, it was clear that the police were prepared to use any means – including blackmail and intimidation – to break the ECP's challenge. Feeling themselves to be cornered, the Collective, like their French sisters, decided to raise the stakes and occupy a local church.

From the outset the two occupations had almost identical themes, focusing on whores' resistance to police repression. The slogans hung from the spire in King's Cross read: MOTHERS NEED MONEY. END POLICE ILLEGALITY AND RACISM IN KING'S CROSS; the demands put out by the prostitutes and their supporters inside the church echoed the Lyons 'open letter':

1. An end to illegal arrests of prostitutes.
2. An end to police threats, blackmail, harassment and racism.
3. Hands off our children – we don't want our kids in care.
4. An end to arrests of boyfriends, husbands and sons.
5. Arrest rapists and pimps instead.
6. Immediate protection, welfare, housing for women who want to get off the game.[52]

Once again the world's press turned up in droves to report on the whores' occupation, and television coverage ensured that it made nationwide impact. Members of the public were sympathetic: they brought food and drinks; and prostitutes from other red-light districts came – at one point, prostitutes all over London wore masks (as did the women inside the church) in order to demonstrate their solidarity with the occupation. Support from the feminist community was noticeably absent, although some women from Greenham Common joined the prostitutes during the occupation.

With widespread public sympathy generated by the media attention, the women were able to play on their position of strength and put pressure on the authorities to fulfil their immediate demands: meetings with the police and MPs, an independent monitor to scrutinize police activities in King's Cross, and the appointment of officials in the local council's housing and social services departments to help women who wanted to get out of prostitution. By 29 October, twelve days into the action, Camden Council had agreed to employ a monitor, and delivered firm promises that the ECP's further demands would be met. These concessions were a vital new precedent for the organized prostitutes' movement; they proved that victory in the long term was – and is – an inevitable outcome.

COYOTE, the French Collective of Prostitutes, and the ECP are only three among the many prostitutes' organizations that have sprung up all over the world since the 1970s. Back in the States, the New York Prostitutes Collective (NYP), a group of black sex workers and other black women activists, was formed in 1979 as a sister organization of the ECP; one year later they had become multi-racial and grown into the nationwide network USPROS. Along with COYOTE and PONY (Prostitutes of New York), USPROS have worked hard for whores' rights, organizing police watch teams, setting up a grassroots legal service based on LAW, combating anti-prostitute vigilantes in a number of US cities, and taking their protest against serial killers right up to international level.

North of the border, Canada has its own Association for the Safety of Prostitutes (ASP), recently redubbed POWER and especially active in Vancouver, where it held the first Hooker Pride march in 1982. In 1984, after an injunction banning whores from the west end of Vancouver had dramatically increased the level of violence against prostitutes, ASP occupied a church in protest.

Canada also has its nationwide organization, the Canadian Organization for the Rights of Prostitutes, which, like COYOTE, has been particularly concerned to promote dialogue with the rest of the community. To this end CORP recently collaborated with feminists to set up a conference on the Politics of Pornography and Prostitution; exchanges between the two groups of women – sex workers and feminists – were often heated, but the conference should be seen as a success, if only because it was a concrete sign that a real dialogue between the two sisterhoods is in process. In 1987 the Citizens' Organization to Repeal Prostitution-Related Laws was formed, to campaign for the decriminalization of the sex trade in Canada – the way ahead . . .

In Australia, prostitutes (inspired by their sisters in France, the UK and the USA) formed the Australian Collective of Prostitutes in 1983. Their actions have since included taking Sydney City Council to court for restricting prostitutes' trade, speaking out on police corruption, taking legal action against residents' groups that harassed sex workers, pleading 'not guilty' after illegal arrests, and, last but by no means least – the boycotting of political clients because of their support for the police in governmental enquiries into the sex industry.

Meanwhile, the European whores' organizations have taken root and spread fast. In 1982, Italian prostitutes formed a Committee for the Civil Rights of Prostitutes 'in response to continued violence at the hands of American soldiers at the NATO base at Aviano and the failure of the Italian police to protect them from it'.[53]

In 1983 the CCRP organized a national convention on prostitution and began publishing its own newspaper, *Lucciola*. Italian whores are especially concerned to throw off the centuries of marginalization imposed on them by the law, saying: 'Today we rebel against this status of marginalization and the role which has been imposed on us [and] we vindicate the right to control our bodies and to carry on our work without . . . being "ghettoized" by the law.'[54]

While the CCRP has won the support of several parties on the Italian left, notably the Socialist and Radical Parties, Italian feminists have remained ambivalent towards the whores' organization, despite ostensibly agreeing with its aims.

At the time of writing, Dutch prostitutes are still alone in having secured government funding for their organization. The Netherlands has two related groups: the Red Thread, initiated in 1984 as a self-help group of whores and ex-whores, and the Pink Thread, which is composed of sympathetic non-prostitute women. The latter was formed in 1985 to bridge the gap between the feminist and the prostitute movements – an excellent (and necessary) idea. Red Thread works specifically for 'Improvements in legislation, working conditions, social work and public opinion';[55] the organization runs a unique library and documentation centre on prostitution and in 1987 it received a government grant which enabled it to hire three full-time workers. The Pink Thread is active in supporting the whores' group, through promotion of discussion of the sex trade within the women's movement and 'developing ideas about the relationship between prostitution, sexuality and women's subordination'.[56]

On the international scene, the ECP and its sister groups have come together to form the International Collective of Prostitutes; and Margo St James of COYOTE has also been active in establishing international links between the various organizations. St James was one of the prime movers behind the International Committee for Prostitutes' Rights, which held international whores' conferences from 1985 onwards. In 1986, as a result of the ICPR's lobbying, the European Parliament took significant steps towards decriminalization, including the following clauses in its resolution on violence against women:

> In view of the existence of prostitution the European Parliament calls on the national authorities in the Member States to take the necessary legal steps:
> a) to decriminalize the exercise of this profession.
> b) to guarantee prostitutes the rights enjoyed by other citizens.
> c) to protect the independence, health and safety of those exercising this profession . . .
> d) to reinforce measures which may be taken against those responsible for duress or violence towards prostitutes . . .
> e) to support prostitutes' self-help groups and to require police and judicial authorities to provide better protection for prostitutes who wish to lodge complaints.[57]

Unfortunately, most of the EC's member-state governments have yet to act on the recommendations of this resolution.

Today the prostitutes' movement – like any other political movement – has its internal dissent and disagreements; nevertheless its presence on the international scene is undeniable and growing. It represents a new departure in the history of the sex industry; a precedent which cannot now be turned back: for it not only marks the beginning of the struggle to reinstate whores as full human beings, it also means the reclamation of the ancient dignity and sexual autonomy of the prostitute-priestess, stolen in the centuries-long process of repression. This in turn has implications for women the world over; it is a vital clue to the reclamation and celebration of the female principle.

To move forward, we have to know our past, and nurture it as a source of pride and power. By recognizing and accepting the untamed 'arrogant and rebellious' spirit of the whore, we can begin to rid ourselves of the patriarchal division of all women into 'good' and 'evil', and put an end to the burden of shame and guilt that so many women have been forced to endure for so long.

Afterword:
Abolition – the Way Forward

'The United Nations' figure, that women do two-thirds of the world's work and receive ten percent of the world's income and own one percent of the world's assets, spells out the basic truth about prostitution. Women, who work at least twice as much as men, get much less income; therefore we are the sellers to men who are the buyers.'[1]

The historical record of Western society shows the impossibility of eradicating prostitution. Every attempt to do so, whether by absolutist monarchies, moral vigilantes or police states, has met with failure; there are simply too many positive factors motivating women to sell sex: compelling reasons of economic survival and personal independence above all, as the above quote testifies. In the light of this, to debate the morality of prostitution is meaningless when the fundamental issue of women's poverty is not addressed; and yet this is what has happened over the years. Commentators and moralists of all persuasions have simply by-passed economics and chosen instead to focus on women's supposed sexual immorality as an underlying factor which disposes them towards prostitution. But in a society which is dominated by the marketplace, and in which the vast majority of people have to sell their labour in order to survive, it is *inevitable* that some women – and men – will continue to provide sexual services.

Equally, it is far from certain that prostitution would not exist in any other form of society. The so-called 'socialist' states of the now defunct Eastern bloc, for example, have always had their particular forms of sex trade. In the USSR – as with other kinds of trade – it took an illicit, black-market form. Looking farther afield, there is no idyll of noble savagery free from the potential of sex trading. When Captain Cook's ships 'discovered' Tahiti, a trade in sexual favours was soon flourishing between his sailors and the island women. Theirs not being a money or a market economy, the wages of sin took the form of nails, much prized amongst the Tahitians – and a currency available to even the lowest-ranking seaman. The economically innocent, sexually uninhibited Tahitian women had no qualms about exchanging sexual favours, which rather indicates that sex can become an object of trade in any society, once women become aware that it can be exchanged against something they want or need.

The historical record also shows that, even if it were possible, the eradication of prostitution would not necessarily be a good thing. In the West, campaigns to rid society of 'the scourge of whoredom' have sprung from an unholy alliance of moral and political forces which aimed at the thorough repression and control of people's sexuality. Christianity and the state have seen it as being in their interests to police our bodies in order to render us more docile and manageable; and there can be no doubt that from their point of view this has worked – at a cost to us all. Nowadays, more than ever, this kind of surveillance is redundant, or should be, since we supposedly live in secularized, free and democratic societies. We should be extremely wary of reinforcing the hand of moral conservatives who want to turn back the clock.

Legislation against the sex trade historically goes hand in hand with intolerance of sexual freedom in general, and women's sexual freedom in particular. Whores have always been primary targets of this repression. The whore is seen as dangerously free: her financial and sexual autonomy strikes at the root of patriarchy, threatening the interests of male moralists and legislators – some of whom are among her best customers. And the whore *is* free in the sense that she does not bind her sexuality to any one man; on the contrary, she openly challenges the notion of female monogamy. Many women recognize this and identify their active sexuality as 'whorish' in their fantasies; but the fact that straight women dare not identify with prostitutes publicly shows the extent to which this last, unexplored aspect of sexuality has yet to come out of the closet.

A glance at other times and places shows that repression of the sex trade is the exception and not the rule in world history. In medieval India, religious prostitution was a central institution in the temples, and secular whores were accepted by both state and society. Indian culture celebrated sensual pleasure and sexuality in highly developed erotic arts; although, as in ancient Greece, its patriarchy had set up a caste of subservient wives, it had not destroyed the sexually uninhibited culture, rooted in matriarchy, of the common people. Indeed the tradition of the *devadasi*, or temple dancer/whore, continued well into our own century – until Western mores became the norm amongst the rulers of Indian society. Ancient China – source of the Taoist doctrine of sexual enlightenment – and the Japan of the *geishas* present a similar picture: one in which patriarchy is dominant and women subservient to men, but prostitution is an accepted facet of social life, preserving something of the earlier matriarchal ways in the arts of pleasure. In the main, this was also true in the West until the time of the Reformation. It is only in modern Western societies that the sex trade has been thoroughly vilified and repressed.

The 'sexual revolution' of the 1960s, however, challenged both this modern regime and, more deeply, 2000 years of Christian anti-pleasure doctrines. However limited – particularly for women – the gains made since then have proved, the liberalization of traditional mores is in everyone's interests. The feminist and gay movements especially have made important steps towards opening up freedom of sexual choice for everyone, whatever their orientation. Uncomfortable as it may be for some feminists, though, it is implicit in the demand that women have control over their own bodies that they also have the right to sell their sexual services, if they wish to. There is no way that this can continue to be left off the feminist agenda; for what feminists and gays have been saying for twenty years now is that *no one should have the right to legislate over the consensual sexual choices of others.* Legal restrictions on consensual adult sexual behaviour are incompatible with civil liberty and with the self-determination the minority movements campaign for; and from women's point of view, there can be no real freedom while we are still subject to the whore-stigma.

The evidence in this book makes it clear that the whore-stigma is above all a means of policing the sexuality of all women, and is constantly being used as such. It is *the* original tool of patriarchal oppression, fettering women's sexuality, splitting them from each other, and subordinating them to men. There can be no getting rid of it while the laws that enforce it remain on the statute books; therefore the abolition of all laws concerning adult prostitution has to be the first step in this direction.

Obviously the whore-stigma will not simply vanish overnight when the laws are scrapped; some people will continue to harass whores and to seek to ostracize them from the community; thus, in the wake of the abolition of prostitution laws, it would be good to see the women's movement organizing to support prostitutes, as they should already be doing. *All* feminists should be aware of the gains to be made from the destruction of the whore-stigma, and should be actively engaged in bringing this about. The more support whores have in the wider community, the more difficult it will be for moral reactionaries to harass them once the laws have been consigned to history's dustbin.

From the health point of view, it is surely self-evident that an open and above-board sex industry, in which workers are not stigmatized and outlawed, would be to the benefit of all concerned, whores and clients alike. It is often argued that prostitution should be legalized with state regulation for health reasons; but research has always shown that sex workers are already among the most health-conscious in the community: *they have to be.* This is particularly striking when one considers the level of repression they suffer. It is the client-class – heterosexual males – who consistently present the greatest danger; their irresponsibility has to be acknowledged and addressed. The state could and should provide health facilities for sex workers – as indeed it should for the rest of society – but coercive measures are not the solution; they merely discriminate against whores and as such are a basic violation of their human rights. Prostitutes are perfectly capable of looking after themselves – and may indeed have a vital role to play in educating others in safe-sex awareness.

Many problems that are currently associated with the sex trade would start to diminish once whores were no longer criminal outcasts. Since they would be able to work from their own homes, this should reduce the numbers operating on the streets, with the attendant risks of male violence. Violence against women in general would also be reduced once the rape and murder of one particularly vulnerable group of women is no longer socially sanctioned. There may be problems of integration; neighbours, for instance, may object to prostitutes working from their own homes. In the past, any dispute arising between a whore and her neighbour would invariably be 'solved' by the intervention of the vice squad – with predictable results for the whore. When this kind of violation is no longer feasible, people will have to work things out between themselves instead of relying on the heavy hand of the state. Neighbours will have to confront prostitutes in person, learn who they are, relate to them as human beings – and accept that they have the same rights as others. Problems will have to be solved by agreement and consensus, which is surely appropriate in a democratic society. But will this sort of problem be widespread? Research suggests not. Writer Eileen McLeod cites a BBC programme in 1979 which presented the case for and against the liberalization of the prostitution laws; viewers, invited to phone in their responses, came down overwhelmingly on the prostitutes' side.[2] There is already a silent majority which is sympathetic to whores' demands; only the remnants of Victorian public morality stand in the way of the reintegration of the sex trade.

The 'public decency' to which some people remain attached is actually the public face of this old sexual oppression. As we've seen, since the 18th century the bourgeoisie has laboured mightily to 'clean up' the public environment of any kind of display which shows women to be sexual beings. Women's bodies were policed very tightly from the consolidation of the anti-whore campaigns in the late 19th century until the 1960s, and we are still dealing with this legacy. It is now acceptable for women's bodies to be displayed as sexual in advertising posters, but not in the flesh – and this anomaly has led many women, particularly some feminists, to fall back on old reflexes, rejecting the public expression of female sexuality and instead clamouring for censorship and repression – a disastrous strategy. The right of public sexual expression is one which women must fight for and win, and whores are in the forefront of this battle merely by existing. At the same time, 'public decency' could well be redefined from women's point of view as a regime which allows them to be sexual when and however they choose without fearing the retribution of male violence – for it is violence, not sex, which is truly obscene.

Finally, it may well be difficult for some people to tolerate those who are sexually different from them. It may be difficult for some to admit to the reality of our society, in which sex – like everything else – has become a commodity. In this sense, too, the experience of sex workers has a great deal to teach the society which has ostracized them. Women in particular could certainly benefit from a cold shower of disillusionment as regards the ideology of romantic love, since it is that which keeps so many of them dependent on oppressive men. One thing is certain: no woman can ever be free in a society which perpetuates the division of all women into whores and madonnas. When whores have the same rights and liberties as other citizens, then we will know that our society has taken a decisive step towards greater democracy for us all. When any woman can walk the streets at night, on her own, dressed as she pleases, without running the risk of being branded a whore, arrested for streetwalking, or raped and *then* branded a whore, we will know that the theory of women's liberation from male violence has been translated into fact. Only then can women claim to be truly free, in a free society.

Notes

Names of the authors in the notes refer to their books listed in the select bibliography.

H I, II & III Henriques, *Prostitution and Society* Vols 1, 2 & 3 respectively.
Bullough 1 Bullough, *The History of Prostitution*.
Bullough 2 Bullough, *Sin, Sickness and Sanity*.
H. Evans Evans, *Harlots, Whores and Hookers*.
R. Evans Evans, 'Prostitution, State and Society in Imperial Germany'.
L. Stone Stone, *The Family, Sex and Marriage*.
M. Stone Stone, *The Paradise Papers*.
Del & Al Delacoste and Alexander, *Sex Work*.

CHAPTER 1 Origins: the Goddess and the Whore

1. Interested readers are referred to works by Fisher, Reed, Sjöö and Mor, and Stone, listed in the bibliography.
2. Reed 105.
3. Sjöö, *The Great Cosmic Mother* 13.
4. Lerner 132.
5. Walker 820.
6. Lerner 126.
7. Walker 501.
8. Tannahill 50.
9. Fisher 307.
10. *Ibid.* 308.
11. Bullough 1, 27–8.
12. Sanger 38.
13. M. Stone 198–9.

CHAPTER 2 Classical Attitudes: Wives, Slaves and Whores

1. Quoted H. Evans 34.
2. Atkins 2, 123.
3. H I 83.
4. Wells 6.
5. O'Faolain 27.
6. H. Evans 37.
7. H I 48.
8. *Ibid.* 54.
9. *Ibid.* 58.
10. Quoted Friedrich 199.
11. Grigson 113.
12. O'Faolain 27.
13. Wells 7.
14. Licht 406.
15. H I 68.
16. Atkins 2, 123.
17. Friedrich 137.
18. Sanger 60.
19. Quoted Pomeroy 90.
20. Wells 7–8.
21. Friedrich 143.
22. H I 50–1.
23. Bullough 1 212.
24. H I 79–80.
25. *Ibid.* 77.
26. *Ibid.* 61.
27. *Ibid.* 62.
28. *Ibid.*
29. Sanger 50.

CHAPTER 3 The Roman Circus: the Imperial Sex Trade

1. Kiefer 8.
2. Sanger 82.
3. *Ibid.*
4. Kiefer 300.
5. Sanger 82.
6. *Ibid.*
7. *Ibid.*
8. *Ibid.*
9. *Ibid.*
10. *Ibid.*
11. H I 133.
12. Kiefer 307.
13. Quoted Burford, *Bawds* 18.
14. H I 117.
15. Quoted H I 130.
16. Sanger 75.
17. Sanger 72.
18. H I 132.
19. Walker 1043.
20. H I 108.
21. H. Evans 41.
22. H I 116.
23. Burford, *Bawds* 16.
24. Pomeroy 222.
25. Quoted H. Evans 46.
26. Bullough 1 108.
27. *Ibid.*
28. Kiefer 168–9.
29. *Ibid.* 212.
30. *Ibid.*
31. *Ibid.* 212–3.
32. *Ibid.* 214.
33. *Ibid.* 91.
34. *Ibid.* 181.

CHAPTER 4 The Dark Ages: the Martyrdom of Sexuality

1. Fisher 379.
2. I Timothy 2, 11–12.
3. I Corinthians 6, 15–16.
4. Bullough 2 23.
5. Proverbs 5, 3–4.
6. Sjöö 69.
7. Bullough 1 65.
8. Sanger 89.
9. Taylor 35.

CHAPTER 5 The Roaring Trade: Prostitution in Medieval Europe

1. Quoted Burford, *Bawds* 108.
2. Cleugh 141.
3. H. Evans 53.
4. Gabrieli 204–6.
5. Quoted Burford, *Bawds* 32.
6. Quoted H II 57.
7. Fisher 380.
8. Wade Labarge 37.
9. *Ibid.* 38.
10. Quoted H II 45.
11. Geremek 240.
12. Bullough 1 112.
13. Otis 19.
14. H II 42.
15. Otis 17.
16. Quoted Burford, *Bawds* 73.
17. Wade Labarge 201.
18. Quoted Orme 38.
19. Wade Labarge 198.

CHAPTER 6 An Unholy Trinity: Organized Prostitution, the Crown and the Church

1. Quoted McCall 190.
2. Quoted H II 37.
3. Quoted H. Evans 58.
4. Quoted Bullough 1 114–5.
5. Villon 164.
6. Sanger 95.
7. Taylor 37.
8. Quoted Sanger 158.
9. Quoted McCall 197.
10. Quoted H. Evans 60–1.
11. Geremek 221.
12. H II 50.
13. Sanger 160.
14. Quoted H II 46.
15. Otis 61.
16. Orme 38.

CHAPTER 7 Splendours and Miseries: Prostitution in the Renaissance and Reformation

1. Quoted Murphy 100.
2. Bullough 1 121.
3. H II 75.
4. Quoted in Dian Dincin Buchman, *Feed Your Face* 96.
5. Murphy 92–3.
6. Quoted H II 77–82; H. Evans 66–8.
7. H II 89.
8. Murphy 101.
9. Murphy 101.
10. Quoted Dobb 255.
11. L. Stone 411.
12. Kitch 6–7.
13. Quoted H II 38.
14. *Ibid.*
15. Otis 42.
16. Quoted Orme 40.
17. Quoted Otis 43.
18. Orme 41.
19. Otis 96.
20. Quoted H II 63.
21. *Ibid.* 60–1.
22. Quoted Burford, *Bawds* 124.
23. Quoted Orme 40.
24. Orme 39–40.

CHAPTER 8 Feign'd Tears and Forg'd Smiles: Prostitutes' Lives in the 16th and 17th Centuries

1. Quoted H. Evans 63.
2. Quoted Burford, *Bawds* 137.
3. *Ibid.*
4. Quoted Salgado 62.
5. Ben Jonson, *Bartholomew Fair*, Act IV sc III.
6. Quoted Salgado 59.
7. Quoted Burford, *Bawds* 170.
8. Quoted L. Stone 137.
9. Tannahill 309.
10. H II 65.
11. Thomas Dekker, *The Honest Whore Pt I*, Act II sc I.
12. Quoted Quaife 84–6.
13. Quoted Salgado 56–7.
14. Quoted Tannahill 313.
15. Quoted L. Stone 109.
16. Quoted Quaife 179.
17. Quoted " 146–7.
18. *Ibid.* 147.
19. *Ibid.* 147–8.
20. *Ibid.* 149.
21. *Ibid.* 150–1.
22. *Ibid.* 152.
23. Quoted Fraser 467.
24. Quoted Burford, *Wits* 13.
25. Quoted Fraser 220.
26. *Ibid.* 221.
27. *Ibid.* 220.
28. Quoted Burford, *Wits* 13–14.
29. Quoted Burford, *Synne* 224.

CHAPTER 9 Almighty Curtezan: the Triumph of the Aristocracy

1. Quoted Adlard 73–4.
2. Quoted H II 98.
3. Fraser 460.
4. Quoted H. Evans 71.
5. Quoted H II 99.
6. Quoted Latham 69–70.
7. Quoted Greene 95–6.
8. *Ibid.* 121.
9. Quoted Fraser 466.
10. Quoted Greene 39.
11. Quoted H II 107–8.
12. *Ibid.* 106.
13. Quoted Fraser 471.
14. *Ibid.* 472.
15. *Ibid.* 481.
16. *Ibid.* 491.
17. *Ibid.* 495.
18. *Ibid.* 493.
19. *Ibid.* 496.
20. Quoted Wilson 47.
21. *Ibid.* 55.
22. Quoted Latham 187.
23. Quoted H II 110.
24. Quoted Wilson 149.
25. *Ibid.* 232.
26. Wilson 235.
27. Tancock 14.
28. Quoted Rattray Taylor 187.
29. *Ibid.* 190.
30. H II 118.
31. Castelot 300, 307.
32. Quoted H II 129–30.

CHAPTER 10 The Age of Debauchery: 18th-Century Europe

1. *The Whore* (1782), quoted Burford, *Wits* 221.
2. Quoted Fraser 470–1.
3. Quoted H II 149.
4. *Ibid.* 147.
5. Quoted Burford, *Wits* 228.
6. *Ibid.* 44.
7. *Ibid.* 45.
8. *Ibid.* 71.
9. Rattray Taylor 188.
10. Quoted H II 151.
11. Quoted H. Evans 90.
12. Quoted Burford, *Wits* 228.
13. L. Stone 336.
14. Quoted Burford, *Wits* 106.
15. Quoted L. Stone 336.
16. Quoted Abby R. Kleinbaum, 'Women in the Age of Light', Bridenthal 227–8.
17. H II 133–4.
18. Mitchell 10.
19. Quoted H II 144.
20. Braudel I 434.
21. L. Stone 392.
22. Quoted L. Stone 392.
23. Quoted H II 155–6.
24. Quoted Burford, *Wits* 92, 37.
25. Quoted H II 145.
26. Quoted H. Evans 89.
27. Quoted Bristow 51.
28. Quoted Burford, *Wits* 36.
29. *Ibid.* 231.
30. *Ibid.* 232.
31. *Ibid.* 91.
32. *Ibid.* 32.
33. *Ibid.* 58.
34. Quoted H II 167.
35. Harsin 62.
36. H. Evans 99.
37. Quoted Bristow 16.
38. *Ibid.* 24.
39. *Ibid.* 26.
40. *Ibid.* 31.
41. Quoted H. Evans 94.
42. Quoted Bullough 1 165.
43. Bristow 64.

CHAPTER 11 Old World, New World: 19th-Century Prostitution on Two Continents

1. Quoted Rosen 66.
2. Quoted H III 135.
3. *Ibid*. 171.
4. Quoted Rudé 176.
5. Gouges iii.
6. Quoted H III 15–16.
7. Chesney 404.
8. Quoted H III 166.
9. Chesney 366.
10. Quoted H III 167.
11. *Ibid*. 53–4.
12. Quoted Chesney 364.
13. *Ibid*. 380.
14. Quoted H. Evans 115–6.
15. Quoted Chesney 404.
16. *Ibid*. 383.
17. Wells 57.
18. Quoted H. Evans 113.
19. Mrs Burrows, 'A Childhood in the Fens', Quoted *Spare Rib Diary 1985*.
20. Quoted Harrison 240.
21. Quoted H III 62–3.
22. *Ibid*. 66.
23. *Ibid*. 60.
24. *Ibid*. 59.
25. Quoted Harsin 52.
26. *Ibid*. 43.
27. *Ibid*. 53.
28. Quoted H. Evans 144.
29. Adler 74, 129–30.
30. Quoted Harsin 35.
31. *Ibid*. 329.
32. Quoted Bullough 1 168.
33. R. Evans 109.
34. Gibson 164.
35. *Ibid*. 181.
36. Sanger 550.
37. H II 254.
38. H. Evans 168–9.
39. Murphy 208.
40. Sanger 550–1.
41. Quoted H II 276–7.
42. Brown 27.
43. Quoted Rosen 92–3.
44. Quoted H. Evans 154.
45. Sanger 560.
46. *Ibid*. 563–4.
47. Quoted H II 290.
48. *Ibid*. 254–5.
49. Rugoff 338.
50. Quoted H. Evans 163.
51. Quoted Murphy 192.
52. H. Evans 111.
53. Harrison 247.
54. Quoted Bullough 1 205.
55. Henriques III 184.
56. Quoted Dumas xi.
57. *Ibid*. x.

CHAPTER 12 Madonnas and Magdalens: the Whore-Stigma in the 19th Century

1. Quoted Rosen 6.
2. *Ibid*. 5.
3. Quoted Adler 15, our translation.
4. Quoted Harrison 244.
5. Quoted Corbin 19–20, our translation.
6. Quoted Harrison 228.
7. *Ibid*. 246.
8. French author of 1892, quoted Adler 100, Harsin 304.
9. Quoted Harsin 304.
10. Zola 12–13.
11. *Ibid*. 470.
12. Quoted H III 185–6.
13. Adler 101–2, our translation.
14. Quoted Gibson 138–9.
15. Quoted Rosen 22–3.
16. *Ibid*.
17. *Ibid*. 162.
18. Quoted Harrison 229–30.
19. Quoted Rosen 154, 156.
20. Quoted Walkowitz 13.
21. Quoted Rosen 157.
22. *Ibid*. 155.
23. *Ibid*. 158–9.
24. Quoted Harrison 241.
25. Quoted Peiss, in Snitow 129.
26. *Ibid*. 122–30.
27. Quoted Harrison 246.
28. Quoted Rosen 95.
29. Quoted Harrison 231.
30. *Ibid*. 235.
31. Quoted Walkowitz 27.
32. *Ibid*. 26.
33. *Ibid*. 30.
34. *Ibid*. 201.
35. Adler 107.
36. Rosen 105.
37. Quoted H III 189.
38. Quoted Harsin 166–7.
39. Quoted Rosen 107.
40. Quoted Harrison 235.
41. *Ibid*. 242.
42. Walkowitz 194.
43. Quoted Harrison 246.
44. *Ibid*. 247.
45. *Ibid*. 248–9.

CHAPTER 13 'Shame, Shame, Horror!': Abolitionism and the Struggle for Social Purity

1. Quoted Wells 65.
2. Gibson 189.
3. Quoted Rugoff 57.
4. Quoted Pearsall 345.
5. Quoted Wells 69.
6. Quoted Walkowitz 80.
7. *Ibid*. 109.
8. *Ibid*. 203.
9. *Ibid*. 207.
10. *Ibid*. 114.
11. Quoted Bristow 75–6.
12. *Ibid*. 87.
13. *Ibid*. 103.
14. Quoted Ballhatchet 127.
15. Walkowitz 251.

16. Bristow 109.
17. *Ibid.* 113.
18. *Ibid.* 165.
19. Daniel 188.
20. Quoted Rosen 83.
21. Quoted H II 310.
22. Quoted Evans 171.

23. Quoted Rosen 72.
24. Quoted H III 227.
25. Quoted Rosen 74.
26. *Ibid.* 75.
27. *Ibid.* 114.
28. Quoted Pivar 233.
29. Quoted Rosen 63.

30. *Ibid.* 31.
31. Walkowitz 255.
32. Flexner 31–2.
33. *Ibid.* 157.
34. R. Evans 121.
35. Quoted Walkowitz 256.

CHAPTER 14 Prostitution in a Free Society: the 20th Century

1. Quoted Millett 85, 93, 94.
2. Quoted Bland, in Cartledge 16.
3. Quoted Murphy 228.
4. H. Evans 201.
5. Quoted Murphy 218.
6. Bullough 1 198.
7. Blumenfeld 187.
8. Quoted H III 278.
9. *Ibid.* 279.
10. Quoted Nestle, in Del & Al 244.
11. Simone Berteaut, *Piaf* Harmondsworth, 1984, 193.

12. Quoted Francis Wheen, *The Sixties*, London, 1982, 93.
13. *Ibid.*
14. *Ibid.*
15. Quoted Jaget 122.
16. Evans 213.
17. ECP.
18. Sion 83.
19. ECP in Jaget 21.
20. *Ibid.* 24.
21. Lopez-Jones in Del & Al 274.
22. McLeod 101.
23. Quoted Diana 87.

24. Alexander in Del & Al 202.
25. Quoted Cohen 174.
26. Quoted Millett 85, 93, 94.
27. Alexander in Del & Al 195.
28. Quoted Jaget 172.
29. *Ibid.* 173.
30. H. Evans, 218.
31. Del & Al 298.
32. Quoted *The Listener*, 26 April 1990.
33. ECP *Network*, June 1984.
34. Cohen 147–8.

CHAPTER 15 Women in Danger: Prostitution Now

1. Quoted Jaget 118.
2. McLeod 45.
3. Quoted Roberts 175.
4. Quoted Jaget 156–7.
5. ECP in Jaget 22–3.
6. *Ibid.* 23.
7. McLeod 49.
8. Quoted McLeod 50.
9. Del & Al 195–6.
10. Bell 85.
11. Quoted Roberts 173.
12. *Ibid.* 133.
13. *Ibid.* 214.
14. USPROS in Del & Al 284–5.
15. Bell 85.
16. Quoted Caputi 93.
17. *Ibid.* 33.
18. *Ibid.* 94.
19. Sarah Wynter, in 'Whisper' News no. 3, 11.
20. *Ibid.*

21. Ward Jouve 174.
22. Bell 130.
23. Quoted Roberts 143–4.
24. Perkins 233.
25. Quoted Roberts 145–6.
26. Del & Al 150.
27. Diana 34.
28. Quoted H. Evans 230.
29. Quoted McLeod 8.
30. Quoted Diana 128–9.
31. Alexander in Del & Al 190.
32. Quoted H III 302.
33. Quoted Jaget 66–7.
34. *Ibid.* 75–6.
35. *Ibid.* 66.
36. Quoted Roberts 171.
37. Quoted Millett 75–6.
38. Quoted H. Evans 224.
39. Rosen 171.
40. Quoted McLeod 5–6.
41. Quoted Roberts 226.

42. Bell 126.
43. Perkins and Bennett 12.
44. CORP in Bell 217.
45. Alexander in Del & Al 204.
46. Winick & Kinsie 53.
47. *Ibid.* 72.
48. Bell 124.
49. *The Guardian*, 17 February 1986.
50. Quoted Roberts 220.
51. Diana 34.
52. Quoted Jaget 86.
53. Quoted Roberts 220.
54. Quoted Jaget 105–6.
55. Del & Al 51–2.
56. Quoted Perkins 127–8.
57. Quoted McLeod 71.
58. Quoted Perkins 77–8.
59. Quoted Jaget 105–6.
60. Quoted Roberts 220.

CHAPTER 16 Coming Out of Stigma: Contemporary Whores and the Creation of a Movement

1. Quoted Jaget 117.
2. Diana 43.
3. *Ibid*. 68.
4. Quoted Diana 120.
5. Winick & Kinsie 47–8.
6. Quoted Roberts 129, 148.
7. Cohen 170.
8. Quoted Winick & Kinsie 62.
9. Quoted Roberts 147.
10. *Ibid*. 171.
11. *Ibid*. 171–2.
12. Quoted Millett 35.
13. Leah Landis, in Del & Al 151.
14. Carter in Del & Al 162–5.
15. Jaget 30.
16. Quoted Roberts 136.
17. Winick & Kinsie 58.
18. *Ibid*. 37.
19. Diana 80.
20. Del & Al 333.
21. Alexander in Del & Al 202.
22. USPROS in Del & Al 282.
23. Lockett in Del & Al 158.
24. *Time Out* 8–15 February 1989.
25. *Time Out* 20–27 June 1990.
26. St James in Bell 84.
27. Alexander in Del & Al 249.
28. St James in Bell 84.
29. Quoted Roberts 147–8.
30. *Ibid*. 226.
31. Quoted Diana 128–9.
32. Quoted Del & Al 93–5.
33. Luman Metal in Del & Al 120.
34. Leigh in Del & Al 123.
35. Millett 14.
36. *Ibid*. 17.
37. *Ibid*. 18.
38. *Ibid*. 17.
39. Quoted Jeffreys in Rhodes & McNeill 60.
40. Jeffreys 61.
41. *Ibid*. 66.
42. *Ibid*. 68.
43. *Ibid*. 69.
44. St James in Jaget 197–8.
45. *Ibid*. 199.
46. COYOTE in Del & Al 291.
47. Jaget 41.
48. *Ibid*. 45–6.
49. Quoted Jaget 52–3.
50. James in Holland 187.
51. *Ibid*. 190.
52. *Ibid*. 192.
53. Gibson 280.
54. Quoted Gibson 232.
55. Del & Al 298.
56. *Ibid*. 302.
57. *Ibid*. 317.

Afterword: Abolition – the Way Forward

1. Del & Al 272.
2. MacLeod 103–4.

Select Bibliography

This bibliography lists those works quoted in the text and/or used extensively in the research for this book.

Acton, William: *Prostitution, Considered in its Moral, Social and Sanitary Aspects*, London 1857.

Adlard, John (ed.): *The Debt to Pleasure*, London 1974.

Adler, Laure: *La Vie quotidienne dans les maisons closes 1830–1930*, Paris 1990.

Anderson, Perry: *Passages from Antiquity to Feudalism*, London 1974.

— *Lineages of the Absolutist State*, London 1974.

Aron, J-P.: *Misérable et glorieuse: la femme du XIXᵉ siècle*, Paris 1980.

Atkins, John: *Sex in Literature*, 3 vols, London 1970–78.

Ballhatchet, Kenneth: *Race, Sex and Class under the Raj: Imperial Attitudes and Policies and their Critics 1793–1905*, London 1980.

Balsdon, J. V. P. D.: *Life and Leisure in Ancient Rome*, London 1969.

— *Roman Women, their History and Habits*, London 1974.

Beauvoir, Simone de: *The Second Sex*, Harmondsworth 1972.

Bell, Laurie (ed.): *Good Girls/Bad Girls: Sex Trade Workers and Feminists Face to Face*, Toronto 1987.

Bellocq, E. J.: *Storyville Portraits: Photographs from the New Orleans Red-Light District, circa 1912*, New York 1970.

Bloch, Iwan: *A History of English Sexual Morals*, London 1936.

Blumenfeld, Simon: *Jew Boy*, London 1935.

Brassaï (Gyula Halasz): *The Secret Paris of the 1930s*, New York 1976.

Braudel, Fernand: *Capitalism and Material Life 1400–1800*, 3 vols, London 1973.

Bridenthal, Renate, and Koontz, Claudia (eds): *Becoming Visible: Women in European History*, Boston 1977.

Briffault, Robert: *The Mothers*, 3 vols, London 1927.

Bristow, Edward J.: *Vice and Vigilance: Purity Movements in Britain since 1700*, London 1977.

Brown, Wilmette: *Black Women and the Peace Movement*, London 1983.

Bullough, Vern L. and Bonnie: *The History of Prostitution*, New York 1968.

— *Sin, Sickness and Sanity*, New York 1977.

Buonaventura, Wendy: *Belly Dancing: The Serpent and the Sphinx*, London 1976.

Burford, E. J.: *Bawds and Lodgings: A History of the Bankside Brothels c. 100–1675*, London 1976.

— *The Orrible Synne: A Look at London Lechery from Roman to Cromwellian Times*, London 1973.

— *Wits, Wenchers and Wantons: London's Low-Life: Covent Garden in the 18th Century*, London 1986.

Caputi, Jane: *The Age of Sex Crime*, London 1988.

Cartledge, Sue, and Ryan, Joanna: *Sex and Love*, London 1984.

Castelot, André: *Madame du Barry*, Paris 1989.

Chesney, Kellow: *The Victorian Underworld*, Harmondsworth 1970.

Chester, Lewis, Leitch, David, and Simpson, Colin: *The Cleveland Street Affair*, London 1976.

Cleland, John: *Fanny Hill, Memoirs of a Lady of Pleasure*, London 1784/1989.

Cleugh, James: *Love Locked Out*, London 1970.

Cohen, Bernard: *Deviant Street Networks*, Lexington 1980.

Coontz, Stephanie, and Henderson, Peta (eds): *Women's Work, Men's Property:*

Origins of Gender and Class, London 1986.

Corbin, Alain: *Les Filles de noce: misère sexuelle et prostitution*, Paris 1978.

Cordelier, Jeanne: *The Life*, London 1978.

Daniel, Mark: *Jack the Ripper*, Harmondsworth 1988.

Defoe, Daniel: *Moll Flanders*, London 1722/Harmondsworth 1978, ed. Juliet Mitchell.

— *Roxana*, London 1724/Harmondsworth 1982.

Delacoste, Frédérique, and Alexander, Priscilla (eds): *Sex Work: Writings by Women in the Sex Industry*, San Francisco 1987.

Diana, Lewis: *The Prostitute and her Clients*, Springfield 1985.

Dobb, Maurice: *Studies in the Development of Capitalism*, London 1946.

Dover, K. J.: *Greek Homosexuality*, London 1978.

Dumas (*fils*), Alexandre: *La Dame aux camélias*, Paris 1848/Oxford 1986.

El Saadawi, Nawal: *The Hidden Face of Eve: Women in the Arab World*, London 1980.

Elton, J. R.: *Reformation Europe*, London 1963.

English Collective of Prostitutes: *A–Z for Working Girls – A Guide to the Rules of the Game*, London n.d.

Enloe, Cynthia: *Does Khaki Become You? The Militarisation of Women's Lives*, London 1988.

Evans, Hilary: *Harlots, Whores and Hookers*, New York 1979.

Evans, Richard J.: 'Prostitution, State and Society in Imperial Germany,' *Past and Present* no. 70, 1976.

Feminist Review (ed.): *Sexuality: A Reader*, London 1987.

Finnegan, Frances: *Poverty and Prostitution, A Study of Victorian Prostitutes in York*, Cambridge 1979.

Fisher, Elizabeth: *Woman's Creation: Sexual Evolution and the Shaping of Society*, London 1980.

Flexner, Abraham: *Prostitution in Europe*, New York 1917.

Foucault, Michel: *The History of Sexuality, Vol. 1: An Introduction*, London 1979.

Frankl, Viktor: *The Failure of the Sexual Revolution*, London 1974.

Fraser, Antonia: *The Weaker Vessel*, London 1984.

Friedrich, Paul: *The Meaning of Aphrodite*, Chicago 1978.

Gabrieli, Francesco: *Arab Historians of the Crusades*, London 1984.

Geremek, Bronislaw: *The Margins of Society in Late Medieval Paris*, Cambridge 1987.

Gibson, Ian: *The English Vice: Beating, Sex and Shame in Victorian England and After*, London 1978.

Gibson, Mary: *Prostitution and the State in Italy 1860–1915*, New Brunswick 1986.

Gouges, Olympe de: *The Rights of Woman*, Paris 1791/London 1989.

Graves, Robert: *The Greek Myths*, 2 vols, Harmondsworth 1955.

Greene, Graham: *Lord Rochester's Monkey*, London 1974.

Grigson, Geoffrey: *The Goddess of Love*, London 1976.

Harman, Chris: *The Fire Last Time: 1968 and After*, London 1988.

Harrison, Fraser: *The Dark Angel: Aspects of Victorian Sexuality*, London 1977.

Harsin, Jill: *Policing Prostitution in 19th-Century Paris*, Princeton 1985.

Henriques, Fernando: *Prostitution and Society*, 3 vols, London 1962–8.

Hill, Christopher: *Reformation to Industrial Revolution*, London 1967.

Hobsbawm, E. J.: *The Age of Revolution*, London 1962.

— *The Age of Capital*, London 1975.

— *The Age of Empire*, London 1987.

Holland, Joy (ed.): *Feminist Action no. 1*, London 1984.

Jaget, Claude: *Prostitutes – Our Lives*, Bristol 1980.

Kiefer, Otto: *Sexual Life in Ancient Rome*, London 1934.

Kitch, M. J. (ed.): *Capitalism and the Reformation*, London 1967.

Lannoy, Richard, and Baines, Harry: *The Eye of Love in the Temple Sculpture of India*, London 1976.

Latham, Robert (ed.): *The Illustrated Pepys*, London 1979.

Lerner, Gerder: *The Creation of Patriarchy*, Oxford 1986.

Lewis, Oscar: *La Vida*, London 1967.

Licht, Hans: *Sexual Life in Ancient Greece*, London 1932.

McCall, Andrew: *The Medieval Underworld*, London, 1977.

McLeod, Eileen: *Women Working: Prostitution Now*, London 1982.

Manniche, Lise: *Sexual Life in Ancient Egypt*, London 1987.

Marcus, Steven: *The Other Victorians*, London 1966.

Masson, Georgina: *Courtesans of the Italian Renaissance*, London 1975.

Mayhew, Henry: *London Labour and the London Poor, Vol. 4: Those Who Will Not Work*, London 1862.

Mernissi, Fatima: *Beyond the Veil*, London 1985.

Millett, Kate: *The Prostitution Papers*, St Albans 1975.

Mooers, Colin: *The Making of Bourgeois Europe*, London 1991.

Morewedge, Rosemary T.: *The Role of Women in the Middle Ages*, Albany 1975.

Morgan, Robin: *Sisterhood is Global*, London 1984.

Murphy, Emmett: *Great Bordellos of the World*, London 1983.

Nestle, Joan: *A Restricted Country*, Ithaca 1987.

Neumann, Erich: *The Great Mother: An Analysis of the Archetype*, London 1955.

O'Faolain, Julia, and Martino, Lauro: *Not in God's Image*, London 1973.

Orme, Nicholas: 'The Reformation and the Red Light,' *History Today*, March 1987.

Otis, Leah Lydia: *Prostitution in Medieval Society*, Chicago 1985.

Pearsall, Ronald: *The Worm in the Bud: The World of Victorian Sexuality*, Harmondsworth 1971.

Pearson, Michael: *The Age of Consent: Victorian Prostitution and its Enemies*, Newton Abbott 1972.

Peradotto, John, and Sullivan, J. P. (eds): *Women in the Ancient World*, Albany 1984.

Perkins, Roberta, and Bennett, Garry (eds): *Being a Prostitute*, Sydney 1985.

Pivar, David: *Purity Crusade: Sexual Morality and Social Control, 1869–1900*, Westport 1973.

Pomeroy, Sarah B: *Goddesses, Whores, Wives and Slaves: Women in Classical Antiquity*, New York 1975.

Prévost, l'Abbé: *Manon Lescaut*, Paris 1731/ Harmondsworth 1949, ed. L. W. Tancock.

Quaife, G. R.: *Wanton Wenches and Wayward Wives*, London 1979.

Rattray Taylor, G: *Sex in History*, London 1953.

Reed, Evelyn: *Women's Evolution*, New York 1979.

Rhodes, Dusty, and McNeill, Sandra (eds): *Women Against Violence Against Women*, London 1985.

Roberts, Nickie: *The Front Line: Women in the Sex Industry Speak*, London 1986.

Rosen, Ruth: *The Lost Sisterhood: Prostitution in America 1900–18*, Baltimore 1982.

Rossiaud, Jacques: *Medieval Prostitution*, Oxford 1988.

Rudé, George: *The Crowd in the French Revolution*, Oxford 1959.

— *Revolutionary Europe 1783–1815*, London 1964.

Rugoff, Milton: *Purity and Passion: Sexuality in Victorian America*, London 1972.

Ryan, Michael: *Prostitution in London, with a comparative view of that in Paris, New York, etc*, London 1839.

Salgado, Gamini: *The Elizabethan Underworld*, London, 1984.

Sandford, Jeremy: *Prostitutes: Portraits of People in the Sexploitation Business*, London 1975.

Sanger, William: *A History of Prostitution*, New York 1859.

Shuttle, Penelope, and Redgrove, Peter: *The Wise Wound: Menstruation and Everywoman*, London 1978.

Sion, Abraham A.: *Prostitution and the Law*, London 1978.

Sjöö, Monica, and Mor, Barbara: *The Ancient Religion of the Great Cosmic Mother of All*, Trondheim, Norway 1981.

— *The Great Cosmic Mother: Rediscovering the Religion of the Earth*, San Francisco 1987.

Smart, Carol and Barry (eds): *Women, Sexuality and Social Control*, London 1978.

Smith, Bradley: *The American Way of Sex: An Informal Illustrated History*, New York 1978.

Snitow, Ann, et al. (eds): *Desire: The Politics of Sexuality*, London 1984.

Stafford, Ann: *The Age of Consent*, London 1964.

Stone, Lawrence: *The Family, Sex and Marriage in England 1500–1800*, London 1977.

Stone, Merlin: *The Paradise Papers*, London 1976.

Stuard, Susan Mosker (ed.): *Women in Medieval Society*, Philadelphia 1976.

Tannahill, Reay: *Sex in History*, London 1979.

Thompson, E. P.: *The Making of the English Working Class*, London 1963.

Thomson, George: *Aeschylus and Athens*, London 1941.

Trudgill, Eric: *Madonnas and Magdalens: The Origins and Development of Victorian Sexual Attitudes*, London 1976.

Unwin, J. D.: *Sex and Culture*, Oxford 1934.

Vicinus, Martha (ed.): *A Widening Sphere: The Changing Roles of Victorian Women*, Bloomington 1977.

— *Suffer and Be Still*, Bloomington 1977.

Villon, François: *The Legacy, the Testament and Other Poems*, trans. Peter Dale, London 1973.

Wade Labarge, Margaret: *Women in Medieval Life*, London 1986.

Walker, Barbara G.: *The Women's Encyclopaedia of Myths and Secrets*, San Francisco 1983.

Walkowitz, Judith R.: *Prostitution and Victorian Society: Women, Class and the State*, Cambridge 1980.

— 'Male Vice and Female Virtue: Feminism and the Politics of Prostitution in 19th-Century Britain,' in Snitow.

Ward Jouve, Nicole: *'The Streetcleaner': The Yorkshire Ripper Case on Trial*, London 1986.

Weideger, Paula: *History's Mistress*, Harmondsworth 1986.

Wells, Jess: *A Herstory of Prostitution in Western Europe*, Berkeley 1982.

Williams, E. N.: *The Ancien Régime in Europe*, London 1970.

Wilson, John Harold: *Nell Gwynn, Royal Mistress*, London 1952.

Winick, Charles, and Kinsie, Paul M.: *The Lively Commerce: Prostitution in the US*, Chicago 1971.

Wiskemann, Elizabeth: *Europe of the Dictators*, London 1966.

Zola, Emile: *Nana*, Paris 1880/ Harmondsworth 1972.

Index

Arrangement is word-by-word, thus black women precedes blackmail.